Taxation of Intellectual Property

For Michael, always.

And for Haydn, in memory.

Taxation of Intellectual Property

3rd edition

Anne Fairpo

MA (Oxon), CTA (Fellow), ATT, Barrister

Bloomsbury Professional

Bloomsbury Professional Ltd, Maxwelton House, 41–43 Boltro Road, Haywards Heath, West Sussex, RH16 1BJ

© Bloomsbury Professional Ltd 2012

Bloomsbury Professional, an imprint of Bloomsbury Publishing plc

A CIP Catalogue record for this book is available from the British Library.

ISBN: 978 1 84766 931 5

Printed in the United Kingdom by Hobbs the Printers Ltd, Totton, Hampshire.

Preface

I would particularly like to thank Michael Reed, for his support and patience in the rather drawn-out process of writing this third edition (continuing changes and updates to legislation didn't help). Thanks also to Dave Wright and all at Bloomsbury for their patience!

I'm grateful to Virgin Atlantic for the quiet few hours on flight VS002 from Newark, post-Hurricane Sandy, in which this book was *finally* finished.

The law is as at 31 October 2012 and, as ever, all errors and omissions are the responsibility of the author.

Anne Fairpo
November 2012

Contents

Contents

Contents

Table of Statutes

Table of Statutes

Table of Statutory Instruments

[All references are to paragraph numbers]

Table of Cases

A

General introduction

Chapter 1

Introduction

- What is intellectual property (para **1.1**)
- Business intellectual property (para **1.4**)
- Use of intellectual property in business (para **1.12**)
- Overview of transactions using intellectual property (para **1.17**)
- Overview of tax issues affecting intellectual property (para **1.18**)
- Differences in approach between legal and tax/accountancy (para **1.19**)

1.1 This book is intended to provide a detailed review of the UK tax rules relating to intellectual property (Chapters 3–15) and an overview of international tax considerations (Chapter 16). The book then considers the UK tax implications of typical transactions (Chapter 17) and typical structures and businesses (Chapter 18).

1.2 It should be noted that this book only discusses in detail the tax rules that are specific to intellectual property; where tax rules apply that are not specific to intellectual property, these are discussed in brief, with a focus on the impact on intellectual property, but the book does not discuss general tax rules in detail, both because this is a specialist text and for reasons of space.

1.3 The reader is directed to the *Bloomsbury Tax Annuals*, for example, for information on other tax rules. For example, the general rules on deductibility of expenses in calculating taxable income will affect any business creating intellectual property in the same way that they affect other businesses; the rules are briefly discussed at para **3.46** onwards, with consideration of intellectual property-related cases, but for more detail the reader will need to consult other texts.

WHAT IS INTELLECTUAL PROPERTY?

1.4 The intellectual property of a business is part of the intangible assets of that business: intangible assets are assets which are neither physical nor financial but are 'identifiable and controlled by the business through custody or legal rights' (FRS 10, para 2). 'Intangible assets' therefore cover a wider range of assets than pure intellectual property but, in many businesses, the intellectual property assets are the prime generators of value in the business. In particular, intellectual property is used to generate income and return on investment that exceeds the costs and normal profit margins in business. This is clear from statistics which indicate that, for example, around 75% of the market value of all companies is attributable directly to intangibles (including goodwill). In contrast, tangible assets contribute only around 25% of the market value of such companies (PwC, 'Reporting the value of acquired intangible assets', 2005).

1.5   Intellectual property includes patents, copyright, trademarks, trade secrets, know-how and a variety of other related rights. These are all intangible assets and the principal value to a business derives from the fact that they allow the business to prevent another entity from exploiting the protected information. Intellectual property assets are monopoly rights granted to creators in order that they have a period of time in which they can exploit the product of research, and similar activities, without competition from others using the product of such research and obtaining an advantage. Developing intellectual property can involve some considerable time and expense before producing an income-generating asset and, without such protection, businesses would have less incentive to undertake the research and development and associated costs to create such assets. Although intellectual property has become more important with modern knowledge-based businesses, the history of legal protection of intellectual property dates back more than two thousand years, with the Greeks providing a one-year protection period for 'any new refinement in luxury' (Charles Anthon, *A Classical Dictionary*). The Venetian Republic was probably the first to codify protection for new and inventive devices in the late fifteenth century; England took nearly 150 years to catch up in the early seventeenth century (*Statute of Monopolies*, 1623).

The different types of intellectual property are considered in more detail in Chapter 2.

BUSINESS INTELLECTUAL PROPERTY

1.6   All businesses have intellectual property: the value may vary, but a business is likely to have at least a trademark, even if unregistered. The assets of the business will be both tangible and intangible, with intellectual property included in the intangible assets. Knowledge-based businesses will generally understand the importance of their intellectual property, as this will be the key asset group for the company, but the value of intellectual property to more traditional businesses is much less well understood.

3

1.7   Some businesses will specifically create and exploit intellectual property: for example authors, artists, biotechnology companies, computer software developers. These businesses will have tax issues at all points of the intellectual property lifecycle, from creation through to extinction or disposal. They will benefit from ongoing review and planning of their intellectual property portfolio and strategy for tax reasons as well as for general business reasons.

1.8   Many more businesses, however, create intellectual property through their operational and developmental activities, primarily in areas such as trademarks and know-how. The accumulated experience and knowledge in the business forms the basis of intellectual property that may not be considered— or even recognised—until the business reaches a particular transaction, event, or point in its development. Those assets may give rise to tax issues and opportunities when the business decides to sell some or all of the trade, or expands overseas and so starts to trade with related parties across border.

1.9   In part, the distinction between awareness of intellectual property assets in businesses arises as a result of the way in which intellectual property and other intangible assets are dealt with for accounting purposes: acquired intellectual property is generally reflected in the balance sheet of the company and so will be recognised and at least some understanding of its value to the business will exist. However, the internally-generated copyright, trademarks, and similar intangible assets that arise as a result of doing business do not show up on the balance sheet. As a result, the value contributed by these intellectual property assets may well not be properly recognised.

1.10   This lack of recognition can be the biggest problem in dealing with taxation of intellectual property (particularly if HMRC recognise the existence of the intellectual property before the company does): it is difficult to deal with an asset correctly for tax purposes if the existence of the asset is not acknowledged, and it can be difficult to determine that such assets exist if the business has not recognised the existence of such assets. Therefore, even before we get to the question of disputes with HMRC over intellectual property, businesses should consider the intellectual property that they have—not only for tax purposes, but to ensure the continuing contribution of the intellectual property to the business.

1.11   The value of the contribution of the intellectual property to the business will vary from business to business depending on the nature of the business and the way in which the intellectual property is used. However, almost all businesses—including the smallest—will have a trade name which is capable of being registered as a trademark, for example. They will have other intellectual property including copyright (any document which the business has published, including their website); there may be know-how in the form of confidential business information relating to processes or services which the business supplies; any products made by the business will have some form of intellectual property attached to them, perhaps a patent, otherwise know-how in the production process. Some businesses may directly use intellectual property by licensing the intellectual property of others for their own use (for example most franchise businesses will have licensed the intellectual property of the franchisor).

1.12   For smaller businesses, it is worth looking at one sector as an example: the creative industries (including music, arts and architecture, and which mostly consists of SMEs) are anticipated to shortly account for approximately 5% of the UK economy (Inter-Departmental Business Register, 2011).

1.13   It is perhaps not surprising that HMRC are becoming much more aware of the importance of intellectual property to business and, in some cases, may have a better understanding of the value of intellectual property than the business itself does. This will particularly be the case where the business has not recognised that it has intellectual property—the problem is particularly acute with goodwill, but its application elsewhere should not be underestimated.

USE OF INTELLECTUAL PROPERTY IN BUSINESS

1.14   Intellectual property may be created or acquired. Generally, intellectual property is developed in the early part of the life cycle of a business and then exploited later on. Often, complementary intellectual property is acquired to broaden the scope of a business's offerings. Intellectual property will be exploited to gain market shares and generate or increase income for the business through direct use in the company, in products and services sold by the company. Alternatively, it may be exploited through indirect use through licensing or sale to other businesses that are able to commercialise that intellectual property. In addition, intellectual property rights can enhance the value of the company through intellectual property such as the company trademarks, particularly where regular monitoring is carried out to ensure that possible infringement is quickly identified and dealt with.

1.15   However, businesses will do considerably more than simply create, acquire, exploit and to dispose of intellectual property. Increasingly, businesses are developing active strategies to manage their intellectual property so that it is not simply created or acquired on an ad hoc basis. The use of existing intellectual property may be kept under review to ensure that it is properly protected and provides an appropriate return to the company.

1.16   Where a business actively manages its intellectual property with care, the entitled property assets of the business may be more available for use as security collateral for a loan or—with larger companies—created tradable security. An increasing number of businesses have securitised future revenue streams derived from portfolios of intellectual property assets. Such benefits can only come from well-managed intellectual property.

1.17 Where a business exists to create intellectual property and then effectively disposes of the economic value of the resulting rights (for example, through outright sale, or by exclusive worldwide licence), the intellectual property held by such a business may not be regarded as assets of the business: instead, they are more likely to be classed as 'trading stock'; the company trades in the IP that it has developed or acquired, rather than using it to trade in a physical product.

1.18 Many biotechnology companies, particularly biopharmaceuticals, operate on this principle, preferring to create new intellectual property that may then be licensed to a pharmaceutical ('big pharma') company for late-stage development, and sales and marketing. The big pharma trades in the physical product, the biotech company trades in the intellectual property. The biopharmaceutical industry is sometimes referred to as the 'outsourced R&D department' for big pharma.

OVERVIEW OF TRANSACTIONS INVOLVING INTELLECTUAL PROPERTY

1.19 Broadly, intellectual property assets could be involved in virtually any transaction entered into by a business but, in general, the most common transactions that will involve intellectual property are:

- licensing: permitting a third party to use intellectual property rights owned by the business (see also para **17.1**). There are two main types of licence:

    — exclusive: an exclusive licence prohibits others (including the owner) from using the intellectual property rights within the area of exclusivity. Such exclusivity can be limited to a specific geographical area, and/or to a specific business sector or product type;

    — non-exclusive: these licences allow the use of the intellectual property rights but confer no exclusivity as to area, or business sector. The owner of the intellectual property may continue to use it as well. Non-exclusive licences are very common: most commercial software licences, for example, are non-exclusive.

    In tax, the type of licence does not generally matter, except in the case of the patent box relief, where the relief is only available to a licence-holder where the licence is exclusive (see para **13.16**);

- assignment: this is the outright transfer of intellectual property to another party. This is usually treated as a capital transaction, although the distinction between capital and revenue is generally more important for individuals and other unincorporated entities than for companies (see para **7.8**);

- research and development: this is the activity leading to the creation of certain types of intellectual property; it is important for tax purposes because there are very generous tax incentives for a specific type of research or development activity (see Chapter 10);

- mergers and acquisition: these business transactions generally involve the sale and purchase of shares, rather than trades and assets, but the intellectual property involved can still have a significant contribution to the value of the business and the structure of the transaction to maximise tax planning opportunities for the business after the merger/acquisition.

OVERVIEW OF TAX ISSUES AFFECTING INTELLECTUAL PROPERTY

1.20   The key questions when considering intellectual property are

- When can I get a deduction for expenditure on creating intellectual property?

  — most expenditure on creating intellectual property is immediately deducted from taxable profits (see Chapter 3 and Chapter 9);

  — additional deductions may be available, particularly from the research and development tax reliefs (see Chapter 10).

- When can I get a deduction for the costs of purchasing intellectual property?

  — individuals and other non-corporate entities can, generally only get a deduction for the costs of acquisition when the intellectual property is disposed of or expires (see Chapter 5 and Chapter 14) although some earlier deductions may be available for acquisitions of patents and certain types of know-how (see paras **5.60** and **5.108**);

  — Companies will usually be able to deduct the costs of acquiring intellectual property over the useful economic life of the intellectual property asset (see para **11.25**).

- Are there any tax reliefs against income or gains from intellectual property?

  — companies will soon be able to take advantage of the patent box relief (see Chapter 13);

  — some deferral and spreading reliefs are available when selling intellectual property (see paras **6.45**, **7.41** and **18.267**).

- What do I have to consider when dealing with intellectual property across national borders?

  — withholding taxes: many countries require payers of royalties to withhold an amount of tax from the payment, as the royalty is considered to be local source income. Tax treaties may reduce these withholding taxes, and/or relief from UK tax may be available for the amount of the tax withheld (see para **16.173** onwards);

  — controlled foreign company rules: the UK government, in common with many other governments, is concerned about the prospects of businesses avoiding UK tax liabilities by simply transferring intellectual property to a low tax jurisdiction. These rules mean that a UK company with an overseas intellectual property holding subsidiary may be subject to tax if the (recently revised) rules mean that the intellectual property is regarded as UK-connected (see para **16.139** onwards);

  — transfer pricing: this is, arguably, similar to the controlled foreign company rules. In order to prevent companies from manipulating prices with other group companies to gain a tax advantage, companies are generally required to use market value when calculating profits and losses from connected party transactions for tax purposes (see para **16.94** onwards).

DIFFERENCES IN APPROACH TO INTELLECTUAL PROPERTY BETWEEN LEGAL AND TAX/ACCOUNTACY

1.21 It is important to note that intellectual property law and tax/accounting rules approach intellectual property in very different ways: the mismatch can lead to confusion where the lawyers and tax advisers do not appreciate the difference.

Intellectual property law is principally concerned with the legal ownership of intellectual property, and the novelty and/or exclusivity conferred by intellectual property rights.

In contrast, tax/accounting is concerned almost exclusively with the economic benefit that derives, or may be derived, from intellectual property and who is entitled to that economic benefit.

Chapter 2

Introduction to intellectual property

Summary: To set the scene and provide background information for non-IP specialists, this chapter provides an overview of the most relevant types of intellectual property for tax purposes, and considers where intellectual property assets will be considered to be located for tax purposes.

- Location of intellectual property (para **2.5**)

- Patents (para **2.15**)

- Data exclusivity and supplementary protection certificates (para **2.45**)

- Copyright (see para **2.49**)

- Design rights and registered designs (para **2.61**)

- Trademarks (para **2.71**)

- Know-how and show-how (para **2.87**)

- Other intellectual property rights (para **2.93**)

- Tax definition of intellectual property (para **2.106**)

- Perspectives: tax/accountancy contrasted with legal (para **2.107**)

- Legal characteristics of intellectual property: summary (para **2.112**)

INTRODUCTION

2.1   The distinction between the different types of intellectual property has become much less important for companies, as the corporate tax regime largely ignores the distinction. However, it is still very important for the taxation of unincorporated entities such as individuals, and unincorporated association such as charities, and when considering intellectual property held by a company (or a related party) at midnight on 31 March 2002.

2.2   For companies, the key question is whether the item of intellectual property is recognised as an intangible fixed asset in the company's accounts and, accordingly, a brief overview of the treatment of intellectual property under UK GAAP and IFRS is given below.

2.3   This is necessarily a simplified overview of the principal types of intellectual property that are important from a tax perspective and is not intended to provide an exhaustive list of intellectual property, or a detailed analysis of how such assets are treated from the point of view of intellectual property law.

2.4   Intellectual property rights are generally territorial. Certainly those which are registered will generally only be protected in the country of registration. International conventions may extend protection but, usually, only to a limited extent.

LOCATION OF INTELLECTUAL PROPERTY

2.5   In general terms, intellectual property rights are located in the jurisdiction in which the rights are recognised and protected. In the case of intellectual property which must be registered, this is usually a single jurisdiction. Arguably, an invention which is the subject of a UK patent and a US patent is two separate items of intellectual property, one located in the UK and one located in the US. In other cases where the intellectual property does not require registration, such as copyright, the owner may be entitled to protection for that copyright in more than one country, depending on the laws in each country.

2.6   The EU also widens the scope, as owners of copyright in the UK can sue under UK law for infringements of that copyright in another EU Member State. Ordinarily, a UK owner of intellectual property seeking (and able) to enforce that intellectual property in another country would be required to bring the action in the country in which the infringement took place.

2.7   From a tax law points of view, intellectual property rights which are capable of registration are regarded (for capital gains tax purposes) as situated where the register is located. Patents, trademarks and registered designs are located in the UK if the intellectual property, or any right derived from it, is exercisable in the UK, and similar rules apply to copyright, unregistered design rights and franchise intellectual property (TCGA 1992, s 275(1)(h), (j)).

Location of intellectual property income and gains

2.8   Usually, for tax purposes, the location of revenue or gains related to intellectual property is the location where the owner, or licensor, is tax resident. Where the owner is a UK tax resident, they will generally be liable to UK tax on the worldwide income from that intellectual property (note: this includes any income derived from countries where the intellectual property is not actually enforceable).

WHAT IS INTELLECTUAL PROPERTY?

2.9   Intellectual property rights are effectively monopoly rights. The owner does not have the right to use the intellectual property: instead, the owner has the right to stop someone else using the intellectual property. As with other legal rights, intellectual property rights are generally considered to be assets (they are intangible assets, in contrast to tangible assets such as real estate) which may be owned by a business. This is supported by accounting standards, which treat intellectual property as an intangible asset, in general. Obviously intangible assets cannot be touched or physically moved, but such assets are as important to a business as tangible assets. Indeed, it has been estimated that as much as 75% of the value of companies on a stock exchange is derived from intangible assets such as intellectual property. However, as with other assets, they are capable of being transferred (in full or in part) and may also be mortgaged as security.

2.10   The intellectual property of a business is not simply a single asset, although a number of different types of intellectual property may be aggregated for accounting purposes within goodwill. There are a number of different types of intellectual property that a company may have or use. As noted above, it is important to have an awareness of these different types of intellectual property when dealing with unincorporated entities and pre-April 2002 assets for companies.

2.11   The main types of intellectual property include:

- copyright;
- database rights;
- design rights;
- know-how and show-how;
- patent rights;
- plant breeders' rights;
- registered designs;
- semiconductor topographies; and
- trademarks.

2.12   In addition there are a number of other rights which may also important for tax purposes. Most recently, the latest consultation on the patent box (at the time of writing) includes data exclusivity rights and supplementary protection certificates within the range of intellectual property assets that may be covered by the patent box. Both of these are rights that are primarily granted in the pharmaceutical sector and provide additional protection for products that have a long development cycle.

2.13 There are also other intellectual property rights that, from time to time, can be a focus for tax authorities. For example, HMRC have spent some time investigating the payments made to certain footballers for image rights; this is not something that would be of widespread relevance but is nevertheless related to taxation of intellectual property rights.

2.14 The most important intellectual property assets for a business that uses intellectual property to produce goods or services will usually be the patents, trademarks and/or copyrights underlying those goods or services. The importance of other rights is generally less fundamental to a business model, although those rights will have value in building up the asset base of a business, particularly if those rights could be protected by registration as (for example) a design right. Protection of non-registerable assets such as trade secrets (know-how) is more difficult and their value to the business may be less secure. The value of unregistered rights should not, however, be entirely dismissed: the Coca-Cola formula is not registered as a patent (although such a formula is likely to be capable of registration in the US) but it would be difficult to contend that its value is not secure as a result of not being registered.

PATENTS

2.15 A patent gives the inventor of the subject of the patent a monopoly right to stop others from making, using or selling the invention; if a product or process is not patented, it is harder to protect it from unauthorised use. The protection is for industrial products and processes—functional and/or technical—and most patents are, in fact, given for new developments of existing technology. There is no particular requirement for the product or process to be complex, only that it be *novel*, involves an *inventive step* and is *industrially applicable*.

2.16 Patents are granted by national patent offices (or similar): for example, in the UK they are granted by the Intellectual Property Office (see para **2.25**). The location of registration of a patent has gained importance for tax purposes as the patent box only applies to patents granted by the UK, the European Patent Office and a number of specific jurisdictions (see para **13.12** and para **13.13**).

2.17 Patents are not given in the UK or Europe for business methods, unless they are specifically technological. In contrast, the US does grant patents over business methods even where they are not technological. For example, for a while, it was possible to patent a tax saving strategy in the US; legislation was passed in September 2011 that effectively prohibits the granting of such patents.

Software

2.18 Computer software may be patented in the UK, but only in exceptional cases where the program produces an improvement in technology.

For example, a program that improves the rendering speed for graphics might be patentable, but a dictionary-based program that translates text from one language to another would not be patentable. In practice, it is effectively the underlying methodology which is patented.

2.19   As with business methods, the US has a more liberal approach and often grants patents for methodologies underlying software that would not be patentable in the UK or Europe.

Biological material

2.20   Biotechnology products involving biological material may be patentable, as may processes by which biological material is produced, processed or used. However, plant and animal varieties are not patentable and neither are essentially biological processes for the production of plants and animals. Plant varieties may be separately protected under UK or European plant variety rights. Inventions relating to plants or animals may still be patentable if the technical aspects are not specific to a particular plant or animal variety.

2.21   Gene sequences—full or partial—may be patentable but the simple discovery of the sequence or partial sequence of a gene is not a patentable invention. If it is isolated from the human body or otherwise produced by a technical process, it may be a patentable invention, even if the structure of the final product is identical to that of a natural element.

Ownership

2.22   In general, in the UK, the right to apply for and own a patent belongs to the inventor or inventors. The inventor can sell or give away that right (in addition to being able to license or sell the patented product or process once the patent has been granted) or, in certain circumstances, the law may determine that someone else has that right. For example, this will be the case where a patent results from an invention made by an employee in the UK. Unless the employee and the employer agree otherwise, if the invention is made in the course of an employee's duties then the invention belongs to the employer if either:

- it is reasonable to expect an invention to result from the employee's duties, for example, if they are employed to carry out research and development (R&D); or

- if the employee had a particular obligation to improve the employer's interests, for example, as a company director.

2.23   Where the employee has developed a patent in the course of his employment which has a material impact on his employer's business, the employee may have rights to payment in addition to his regular salary, reflecting the benefits to the employer of the patent (see para **3.66**).

2.24   If the invention is made overseas, the laws of that country may apply instead, and default ownership may be different from that in the UK.

Applying for a patent

2.25   Patent rights are not created automatically, in contrast to copyright (see below). To be able to claim the protection of patent rights, the patent needs to be specifically registered. In the UK, registration is with the UK Patent Office (www.patent.gov.uk/patent/index.htm) or through the European Patent Office (www.european-patent-office.org/).

2.26   The registration process can take a considerable length of time. Whilst registration is pending, the 'patent rights' (the right to be granted the patent) created by the application are also regarded as an intellectual property asset and will often be subject to tax in the same way as a patent.

2.27   A patent granted by the European Patent Office is protected in all countries of the EU, through a single registration. This is important to note for companies which may wish to make use of the patent box tax incentive (see Chapter 13) as it is only UK patents and European Patent Office patents which will qualify for the reduced tax rate. Patents registered in other European countries on a country-by-country basis will not qualify (at the time of writing, although the June 2011 consultation paper did envisage the possibility of patents granted by other countries being eligible subject to HMRC being convinced of the adequate rigour of the local registration process).

Patent strategy: is a patent the most appropriate protection?

2.28   It may not always be appropriate to apply for a patent on a product or process; the application procedure for patents requires the disclosure of a considerable amount of information, which is then published by the Patent Office. This information is available to anyone who cares to look for it, including competitors. Included in the information must be the industrial application of the product/process. Depending on how the application is made, the public information may provide a blueprint to the product or process which can be used to recreate the product/process outside the territorial protection of the patent; in this case, the patent rights provide no protection unless the product/process is resold into the UK (or into other areas where a patent right has been granted).

2.29   The patent box (see Chapter 13) may make applying for a patent seem more attractive or appropriate, but the tax benefits should (as always) be measured against the commercial implications of the application. A patent attorney or specialist IP lawyer should be consulted on these points – their assistance would also be required in making an application for registration.

2.30 Once a patent has expired, the information in the patent application can be used by anyone. Generic pharmaceuticals usually appear shortly after the patent on the original drug has expired; as the information is publicly available, the manufacturers can get ready to produce the drugs whilst the patent is in force so that they can sell immediately it expires. (This is dependent on the generic drug being able to demonstrate bioequivalence—that is, show that it performs in the same manner—with the original patented drug.) Ultimately, a business will need to balance the protection given by a patent application against the requirement to publish potentially sensitive information.

2.31 A patentable product/process can still be protected to some extent by copyright and/or design rights, or—as with Coca-Cola—be protected by confidentiality agreements, even if the patent is not applied for. If it is important that details of the product/process are not disclosed to the extent necessary to apply for a patent, then it may be commercially more effective to rely on those rights instead.

2.32 For example, Coca-Cola has not patented its recipe —and most likely will not. If it were to do so, it would be required to disclose the ingredients. Given the mystique with which Coca-Cola and folk history has endowed the 'secret recipe', this could possibly be a commercial disaster for the company. The original formula was patented in 1893 but, when the formula changed, the company chose not to patent it again in order to avoid the information becoming publicly available. Instead, the formula is protected by limiting the number of people who know it, and using non-disclosure agreements to prevent those with access from disclosing it.

2.33 If a product or process is expected still to have significant value at the end of a patent protection period, it may be more appropriate to rely on treating it as a trade secret and protecting it by confidentiality agreements: these may be more difficult to enforce than patent rights, but the product or process remains secret as long as the confidentiality is unbroken. Using Coca-Cola as the example again, if it had patented its current recipe more than 20 years ago, it would now be unable to prevent a competitor from using that recipe.

Protection

2.34 A patent right does not last as long as, say, a copyright; in the UK, patent rights are granted for 20 years from the date the application is filed. The right is also restricted to the UK; if patent protection is required elsewhere, then patent rights will need to be separately acquired in the relevant countries.

International protection

2.35 European or international patents can be obtained, where appropriate. The Patent Co-operation Treaty (PCT) provides for a single application procedure for an international patent; application in the UK is via the Patent Office and the application must list the Treaty countries for which the patent is to apply. Over 70 countries are currently signed up to the Treaty and an international patent is treated as a series of patents, one for each country, each subject to national law in the country in which it is valid.

2.36 A European patent is valid in most western European countries and application can be made in any country in Europe, or via the European Patent Office. In the UK, application is usually made via the Patent Office. The countries for which the patent is to apply must be listed on the application and a fee paid for each country listed; this is usually a cheaper route than opting to make separate patent applications in each country. The resulting European patent is treated in the same way as an international patent, ie as a series of national patents, each subject to national law in the country in which it is valid.

2.37 A patent granted by the European Patent Office will qualify for the patent box relief to be introduced in 2013 (see Chapter 13).

Renewal

2.38 Although a UK patent right is granted for 20 years, it must be renewed annually after the fifth anniversary of the filing of the application for grant of the patent right. If the patent is not renewed within six months of the renewal date it will expire, although the patent holder can apply for the patent to be restored within 13 months of the expiry date.

2.39 The cost of renewing patents should be considered. If the patent has no active value or anticipated value, it may not be worth the fees involved in the later years. Renewal fees for patents increase each year. The payment on the fifth anniversary is currently £70, whereas the payment on the 20th anniversary is currently £600 (at the time of writing). For a company with a number of patents, the renewal fees can be a significant cost.

Enforcement

2.40 An infringement of patent rights is dealt with by requesting the UK Patent Court, or the High Court, to award:

- an injunction to stop the infringer from using the patent; and
- damages to compensate for any financial losses resulting from the infringing activity (including legal costs).

2.41 Legal action can only be taken in respect of registered patents, not pending patents still in the application process, although some compensation may be available for infringement that occurred while a registered patent was in the process of being registered (after the date of publication of the registration).

In practice, most patent infringement cases settle (a specific mediation process is available) before reaching court.

Basic tax points

2.42 Patents are usually exploited by licence, with royalty payments from licensee to licensor. These may be related to use of the patent, or to milestones achieved in further development (eg passing a clinical trials stage, if the patent is for a pharmaceutical product). Income and gains from patents are always taxed as income.

2.43 The payer may be required to deduct income tax at basic rate from the payment and account for it to the local tax authority. Buyer's tax deductions (if any) will depend on the purpose in holding the patent.

2.44 If purchased outright, deductions may be available to buyer against tax over time to (arguably) reflect diminution in value through use/time. A UK vendor of patent rights will be subject to income tax or corporation tax on any profits of the disposal.

DATA EXCLUSIVITY AND SUPPLEMENTARY PROTECTION CERTIFICATES

2.45 The length of time involved in developing certain types of patent-protected product, particularly in the pharmaceutical sector, means that a patent period of 20 years may only protect a relatively short period of the commercial life of the product. As a result, there are two additional intellectual property rights which relate to patentable products in this sector which can effectively extend the protection period for the product. These are important for tax reasons as they are included in the list of qualifying intellectual property for the patent box (see Chapter 13). To the extent that these rights are capable of exploitation by licence or transfer, the tax treatment will be the same as for the patent to which they are related.

2.46 These two rights are data exclusivity and supplementary protection certificates. 'Data exclusivity' protects the clinical test data which must be submitted to the relevant pharmaceutical regulatory authority which oversees the safety and effectiveness of new drugs. Depending on the circumstances, the data exclusivity period may last beyond the patent protection period. Where this is the case, competing manufacturers cannot rely on the developer's data when the patent expires. The data exclusivity rights mean that the generic manufacturer would need to carry out its own clinical trials to be able to apply to have its generic version of the drug approved. This is an expensive undertaking and so the data exclusivity rights can provide substantial protection. Data exclusivity provides protection for approximately 10 years from approval of the drug, including a period of market exclusivity. Accordingly, it is primarily useful for products which have taken more than 10 years from grant of patent to obtain authorisation from the relevant regulatory authority.

2.47   A 'supplementary protection certificate' effectively extends the protection period of a patented active ingredient in a pharmaceutical product, or plant protection product. The certificate is given to recognise the length of time it can take to get regulatory approval for pharmaceutical and plant protection products in the UK. The certificate normally has a maximum protection period of 5 years.

2.48   Income related to both these rights will generally arise from the sale of products that exploit the original patent to which these rights are related; these rights improve the market position of the owner, and are not typically capable of being exploited in their own right.

COPYRIGHT

2.49   There are two principal types of copyright: artistic (covering visual works, including dramatic works) and literary (covering written works, including music). Literary copyright covers computer software, as the code is a written work, albeit one that is rarely published as such. A copyright work must be original and must be capable of being produced in physical form.

2.50   Copyright is an automatic right, which is created when the work is created and recorded in some way (on paper, electronically, etc). There is no registration required for copyrights in the UK. Copyright covers only the expression of an idea; it does not cover the idea itself. In the UK, copyright protection lasts for the life of the author, plus 70 years (previously 50 years; the limit was extended in 1996 and may be extended again). Where the author is not an individual, the protection period is 70 years from release of the copyright work. There is no need to renew the protection: it automatically extends from one year to the next. Other countries have different protection periods.

2.51   Copyright gives the creator the right to control use of the copyright material in a variety of ways: making copies, issuing copies to the public, performing in public, broadcasting, adaptation (including the conversion of a piece from software from one computer language to another) and use online. Copyright also gives the creator the right to object to distortion or mutilation of the copyright material. There are exceptions to copyright protection, for example, limited use of material for review purposes, or for reporting of current events, is allowed without the permission of the copyright owner.

Ownership

2.52   Copyright belongs to the creator of the work, or to their employer if provided for under the contract of employment. Businesses need to ensure that their contracts of employment and contracts with subcontractors explicitly provide that any IP (not just copyright) created as a result of the contract will be the property of the business.

Protection

2.53   The UK has no registration process for copyright: the work is automatically protected from the point of creation. However, as there is no registration process for acquiring a copyright, it can be difficult to prove when a copyright arose if a legal challenge is made to the use of the copyright material. As far as possible, a date should be fixed for the initial existence of the copyright. This can be done in a number of ways, including depositing a copy of the copyright material in a safety deposit box, or by the creator mailing a copy to themselves by recorded delivery. Provided that the envelope containing the copy is not opened after receipt, this can then be produced as evidence of the creation date to rebut a challenge to the copyright.

International protection

2.54   Copyright protection—and the requirements to achieve protection— vary more widely in respect of copyright law than either patents or trademarks.

2.55   Unlike the UK, some countries do have formal registration requirements in order for a work to be copyright; the US, for example, has a registration procedure. It is not compulsory, but a copyright work must be registered before an infringement action can be brought. The Universal Copyright Convention (UCC) allows some degree of flexibility in establishing international protection for a copyright without the need to follow each country's registration procedures. Essentially, provided that every published copy of the work contains the © symbol, the year of first publication and the name of the author, the work will then be given protection in each member country of the UCC as if it had been generated and protected locally.

2.56   For UK copyright holders, it is generally good practice to ensure that the UCC information is contained on all published copyright work; this ensures protection if the work happens to be taken outside the UK, even where there are no initial plans to export it. In particular, any copyright material published on the internet should contain the UCC information, to ensure that copyright protection is available outside the UK.

Enforcement

2.57 An infringement of copyright is dealt with in a similar way to patent infringement, by requesting the High Court to award:

- an injunction to stop continued use of the copyright; and

- damages for financial losses resulting from the infringement (including legal costs).

As with patents, most cases of infringement are settled by negotiation before the parties reach a court hearing.

2.58 If copyright is intentionally infringed on a commercial scale, the infringer can be prosecuted for a criminal offence; this mostly occurs with music and video pirating. The criminal prosecution can either be pursued privately (usually only an option for copyright holders with substantial financial capacity) or by reporting the infringers to the police.

Basic tax points

2.59 Copyright is usually exploited by licence, with the licensor being paid royalties which are taxable as income. However, any proceeds–whether a single payment or a series of royalties–relating to copyright are generally taxable in the UK as income of the licensor where the licensor carries on a trade or profession, even where the copyright is assigned outright to a purchaser. Receipts from licensing one-off copyrights (ie those not created as part of a trade or profession) are likely to be taxed as miscellaneous income.

2.60 Outright assignment of copyright may be taxed as capital where the copyright was held as an investment (see para **7.16** for more information on the distinction between capital and income).

DESIGN RIGHTS AND REGISTERED DESIGNS

2.61 Designs are increasingly important; the shape or overall appearance of a product can have an appreciable commercial function. Designs may be protected either by registration or by design rights.

Design rights

2.62 Design rights are similar to copyright in that they arise when the design is created and no application is necessary to grant them. They apply to original, non-commonplace designs of the shape or configuration of an article. Only three-dimensional designs are protected; two-dimensional designs (such as textile patterns) are not protected, although they may be protected by copyright.

2.63   A design right is rather shorter than copyright, lasting for 10 years after an article with the design is first marketed (or, if shorter, for 15 years from the creation of the design). Protection is given in the UK for individuals and companies in the EU or nationals from New Zealand or and other countries which give reciprocal protection to the UK.

2.64   As with copyright, a date for the creation/existence of the design right should be established as far as possible by keeping a record of when the design was first recorded in material form and when articles with the form are first sold or rented. A prototype and/or example of the finished product could also be deposited—if feasible—in a safety deposit box.

Licences of right

2.65   Design rights are not as extensive as copyright; only the first five years of existence of the right provide a monopoly on exploitation for the creator. For the remaining five years of the right, it is subject to licences of right: anyone will be entitled to a licence (subject to paying appropriate royalties) to make and sell articles copying the design. The owner is not, however, required to make drawings or other know-how available to the licensee. The exception here is in the design of semiconductor chips; to fit with European law, the design right in semiconductor chips lasts 10 years in full with no licences of right available at any time in 10 years.

Exclusions

2.66   Design rights are not available for objects that are required to fit or match one or more other items, for example, this ensures that competition is not stifled in trade in spare parts for cars. Competitors cannot be prevented from copying features of a protected design that are necessary to allow them to produce something to be fitted to or matched to the design. However, copying features where there is no requirement to do so is not permitted.

Registered designs

2.67   New, aesthetically appealing, designs may be registered to protect them; this gives the owner of the registered design an effective monopoly over the design for the registration period.

2.68   To be registered, a design must:

- have *significant eye appeal* (there must be design freedom: articles whose design is dictated purely by function are not protected; car panels, for example, are not protected);

- be *new* (the design must not previously have been published, other than by exhibition in certain approved exhibitions not more than six months before application, and must not be materially similar to an already registered design); and

- *not be excluded* (certain articles are automatically excluded from registration, including sculpture, medals and printed materials which are primarily literary or artistic. This includes advertisements and dress patterns).

Registration

2.69   Registration is by application to the Patent Office; as with application for other rights, the assistance of a patent or trademark attorney may be worthwhile. Where a set of articles is produced, one application may be made to register the set, rather than making individual applications; this will only be possible if the articles in the set have sufficient commonality of design. Protection for the design overseas is only available by making separate applications to each country; there is no international treaty that permits an application in one country to cover several countries. Registration does not eliminate any copyright or design right existing in the same article. Once registered, the design can be sold or licensed in the same way as other IP.

Renewal

2.70   Registration of a design gives a monopoly on the outward appearance of a manufactured article; it is valid for up to 25 years from the date of registration, but it must be renewed every five years to prevent the registration from expiring. As with patents, the renewal fee increases with the length of time the design has been protected. Currently, the first renewal fee (on the fifth anniversary) is £130; the renewal fee on the 20th anniversary is £450 (as with patent renewal fees, these fees have remained the same for several years and may be due for increase).

Compulsory licence

2.71   If a registered design is not used, an independent party can apply to the Patent Office for a compulsory licence to be granted to them so that they can exploit the design.

Enforcement

2.72   An infringement of design rights or registered designs is dealt with in a similar way to patent and copyright infringement, by requesting the High Court to award:

●   an injunction to stop continued use of the design right or registered trademark; and

●   damages for financial losses resulting from the infringement (including legal costs).

As with patents and copyright, most cases of infringement are settled by negotiation rather than in court.

Basic tax points

2.73   Designs are usually licensed for royalty payments, and the receipt taxed as trading income of the recipient.

2.74   Where the design is sold for a lump sum, the receipt may be taxed as capital where it was held as an investment. Where the design was created to be sold by the creator, the receipt will generally be taxed as income of the creator.

TRADEMARKS

2.75   A trademark is a sign or mark which distinguishes the products of one trader from those of another. The trademark can include words, signs, logos, slogans, and sometime sounds and gestures. It is primarily a marketing tool, and must be capable of being graphically reproduced (in words or in pictures) in order to be registered in the UK. Once registered, the owner of the trademark has the exclusive right to use that trademark. It is not mandatory to register a trademark, but it is easier to protect a registered trademark.

2.76   Unregistered trademarks are considered to be part of the goodwill of the business which owns the mark under intellectual property law. This can be important for tax purposes, particularly where the trademark has been licensed to a third party, as this can give rise to disputes with HMRC as to whether value arising from the use of the trademark should be attributed to the goodwill of the licensor (as owner of the trademark) or the goodwill of the licensee (as operator of the business utilising the trademark).

2.77   The ™ symbol does not denote a registered trademark; it indicates that the word or logo is used as a trademark, but not necessarily that it is registered. The ® symbol, however, does indicate that the word or logo is protected by registration somewhere in the world.

Registration

2.78   In the UK, the Patent Office is responsible for dealing with applications to register trademarks. As with patents, once an application is made a search is done to ensure that the mark is unique. The mark must also not be confusingly similar to existing registered trademarks. A European trademark, giving protection throughout the EU, can be registered at the Office for Harmonization in the Internal Market (http://oami.eu.int/). Trademark or patent attorneys can assist with making the application. The Institute of Trademark Attorneys (http://www.itma.org.uk/) and the Chartered Institute of Patent Agents (http://www.cipa.org.uk/) can both provide directories of appropriate attorneys.

2.79   Trademarks are registered for use in one or more specific classes of goods and services; there is no blanket registration for a trademark across all possible goods and services. Outside the registered class(es), a trademark will be regarded as unregistered. For example, the 2007 dispute between Apple Inc and Apple Corps over iTunes related to Apple Corps' trademark of 'Apple' in respect of music (and related classes); Apple Inc had trademarked 'Apple' in respect of computers (and related classes).

2.80   Registration makes it easier to protect the mark: it provides evidence of ownership of the mark, and provides protection throughout the territory. It is more difficult to defend an unregistered trademark, as there is no proof of ownership and it is much harder to prove that there is a trading reputation related to the mark throughout the UK (or in whichever market it is necessary to defend the mark). Care should be taken in selecting the classes in which the trademark is registered, to make sure that it is sufficiently protected in the key areas to which the business relates.

Renewal

2.81   Trademark rights need not expire, unlike patents and copyrights. However, they need to be renewed every 10 years to maintain the rights. If not renewed, the mark will expire. An application to restore the mark can be made within a year of expiry. Unlike patents, the cost of renewing a trademark remains the same no matter how long the trademark has been protected. At the time of writing, the renewal fee for trademark protection is £200 for the first class and £50 for each subsequent class of registration. These rates have not changed for a number of years, and so may be due for an increase.

Enforcement

2.82   Registered trademarks can be enforced in the same way as copyright and patents, requesting the High Court to issue an injunction to stop continued use of the trademark and damages for financial losses resulting from the infringement.

2.83   However, registered trademarks are very specific and this type of enforcement only works for direct copying of the trademark; it is not so successful where the problem is someone using a similar (but not identical) mark, and is not available at all for unregistered trademarks.

2.84   Where an injunction is not available, the remedy for the trademark owner is to bring an action for 'passing off' (the unauthorised use of a mark that is considered to be similar to another party's registered or unregistered trademarks). This is a common law action rather than a specific statutory remedy.

2.85   A claim for 'passing off' effectively allows the trademark owner to prevent misrepresentation (for example, that the product with the similar mark is made by the owner of the trademark). As it is not a statutory right, the owner of the trademark will need to show that there was some value in the trademark, that the value has been damaged by the similar mark, and that there has been misrepresentation—broadly, that there has been deception or public confusion between the trademark and the similar mark. The test of public confusion requires more than peripheral confusion, leading to the classic judicial comment (first used in *Morning Star Cooperative Society v Express Newspapers Ltd* [1979] FSR 113, and quoted later that year by Lord Denning in *Newsweek Inc v British Broadcasting Corpn* [1979] RPC 441) that the test is not whether a 'moron in a hurry' would be confused.

Basic tax points

2.86   Trademarks are usually licensed for royalty payments, and the receipt taxed as trading income of the recipient. An outright disposal of a trademark may be treated as a capital transaction where the disposing entity cannot continue to trade without the trademark.

KNOW-HOW AND SHOW-HOW

2.87   Trade secrets—also described as 'know-how' or 'show-how'— are not specifically protected but do need to be included in a discussion of intellectual property; whilst copyright and other such assets are valuable, the expertise to use and develop the rights is perhaps more valuable. It is certainly something for which businesses can and do pay significant amounts of money. For example, where a business takes the decision not to patent an invention— to avoid having to publicly disclose information—the process that would otherwise be patented would be know-how.

2.88   Know-how is protected commercially by maintaining security within the business and by the use of confidentiality; there is no statutory protection for know-how or show-how. Payments for know-how need to be distinguished from payments from any associated intellectual property, as the tax treatment will be different.

Confidentiality

2.89   Relying on protecting a product or process as a trade secret—for example, where the commercial risk from disclosure of the details of that product or process via a patent application is unacceptable—requires detailed adherence to confidentiality. A business relying on maintaining confidentiality should ensure that there are procedures in place to protect that confidentiality. In particular, consider the following:

- document confidentiality procedures to be able to enforce them;

- ensure employees are educated about the procedures relating to confidential information, and include restrictive covenants relating to any confidential information in contracts of employment;

- keep confidential information locked in files, and encrypted if held on computer;

- restrict the number of people who know the confidential information; and

- put in place non-disclosure agreements with third parties to whom information is—or may be—disclosed.

Enforcement

2.90   Enforcement of know-how and show-how is only usually possible where non-disclosure agreements or employee restrictive covenants have been put in place; then the remedy is to sue for damages as compensation for financial loss caused by the breach of the agreement or covenant.

Basic tax points

2.91   Fees for the licence of know-how are generally taxed as trading income of the business; the UK tax authority in particular will not generally accept that know-how is capable of being owned as an investment.

2.92   Where the licence for the know-how is effectively a disposal of the rights (because the licensor is prevented by the terms of the licence from using the know-how commercially) then the receipt may be taxed as capital.

OTHER INTELLECTUAL PROPERTY RIGHTS

Plant breeders'/plant variety rights

2.93   These are a particular form of intellectual property, similar to patents, which specifically provide protection for breeders of new varieties of plants;

the right must be registered. Income from these rights is also capable of falling within the patent box (see para **13.12**).

2.94 The holder of a plant breeder's right can prevent others from dealing with the protected variety, including:

● production or reproduction;

● sale; and

● export/import.

2.95 The plant variety must be:

● distinct (clearly distinguishable by one or more characteristics);

● uniform (the distinctive characteristics remain uniform on propagation);

● stable (the distinctive characteristics remain unchanged after repeated propagation); and

● new (not sold within the UK more than one year before the date of application, or outside the UK more than four or six years—depending on the type of plant—before application).

2.96 Plant breeders' rights last for 25 years from the date of grant of the right; that period is extended to 30 years for varieties of trees, vines and potatoes. A renewal fee is required each year for the rights to remain in force.

2.97 International protection for plant breeders' rights is available through the UK's membership of the International Convention for the Protection of New Varieties of Plants.

Copyright-related intellectual property

Semiconductor designs

2.98 Designs of semiconductor chips may be protected by design rights (see above) but, in accordance with EC Directive 87/54/EEC (implemented in the UK by The Design Rights (Semiconductor Topographies) Regulations 1989) relating to such rights, exclusive rights in semiconductor chip designs will last for the full 10 years in the market. In contrast to other design rights, licences to copy the semiconductor design will not be available during the last five years of the term of protection.

Database rights

2.99 These are a form of copyright. A database right provides 15 years' protection, from the creation of the database (or from any later date of publication). The protection is against unauthorised extraction and reuse of the contents of the database, and there must have been substantive investment in the creation of the database contents. The database right protects only the contents of the database, not the results of queries of the database, or selection from the database (although these may be protected by copyright). Database rights are not universally recognised, although most of Europe does recognise some form of database right.

Performing rights and performance rights

2.100   Performing rights are part of copyright; the owner of the copyright in a work may permit someone else to perform that work, and that performance then creates an additional performance right belonging to the performer. The rights will arise regardless of where a performance takes place, whether on stage, in the making of a film or whilst making a recording.

2.101   Performing rights give the copyright owner, and performance rights give the performer, the right to control:

- the communication of a live performance to the public by, for example, broadcast; and

- the making of copies of a recording of the performance.

2.102   Performing rights exist in tandem with the copyright. Performance rights last for 50 years from the date of the performance or, if the performance is recorded and that recording is released, for 50 years from the date of release of the recording.

Enforcement

2.103   These rights are generally enforced in the same way as copyright— they are all (broadly) specialised forms of copyright, albeit with different protection periods—and so the owner of the right can obtain an injunction for infringement and damages for related financial losses.

Goodwill

2.104   Goodwill is not specifically an intellectual property asset; it is, however, classed with intellectual property assets as an intangible asset. It is relevant for intellectual property purposes because certain types of intellectual property may be taxed part of goodwill (particularly unregistered trademarks and similar intellectual property).

2.105   Goodwill is most often relevant to an acquisition. For accounting purposes, it is the difference between the cost of acquisition and the fair value of the purchased assets and liabilities (FRS10) and will, on acquisition, usually be treated as an asset of the business. Internally created goodwill is not, however, recognised as an asset of the business.

TAX DEFINITION OF INTELLECTUAL PROPERTY: CORPORATE TAX

2.106 For corporation tax purposes, Part 8 of the Corporation Tax Act (CTA) 2009 is a specific regime that applies solely to the gains and losses of intangible fixed assets, which includes intellectual property: the definition of intellectual property in this context is covered in detail in para **8.23** onwards.

PERSPECTIVES: TAX/ACCOUNTING VERSUS LEGAL

2.107 It should be noted that the tax/accounting perspective of intellectual property is very different from the legal perspective: from a tax/accounting point of view, the economic benefits derived or to be derived from the intellectual property are almost all that matter. From a legal perspective, the economic benefits are perhaps almost incidental. With any tax and business planning, a failure to accommodate the differing points of view can create difficulties both in implementation and the continued operation of an intellectual property holding structure.

Ownership

2.108 Intellectual property law is concerned with the legal ownership of intellectual property and, in particular, who has the right to enforce the intellectual property. In contrast, tax and accounting rules are not particularly interested in the legal title to the intellectual property but, instead, in who has the right to receive the economic benefit of that intellectual property and who has paid to create or acquire the intellectual property.

Defining characteristics

2.109 In intellectual property law, the principal characteristics of an intellectual property asset are based on its innovation or novelty. For tax/accounting, the main characteristic of an intellectual property asset is that it can be measured in monetary terms.

Value

2.110 The value of an intellectual property asset for legal purposes relates to exclusivity: the ability to prevent competition in a market for a period of time, or to distinguish a company or product from others. Tax and accounting considers value only in terms of the future economic benefits which are likely to arise from the intellectual property.

Life

2.111 Tax and accounting focuses on the useful economic life of an intellectual property asset—the period over which it is expected to continue to generate economic benefits—as opposed to the specific period for which protection lasts in law.

LEGAL CHARACTERISTICS OF INTELLECTUAL PROPERTY

2.112

Intellectual property	Includes	Owner (subject to alternative agreement)	Length of protection	Automatic protection
Copyright	Literary; artistic works; and computer software	Creator or employer	Life of owner plus 70 years	Yes
Database rights	Contents of database	Creator or employer	15 years from creation	Yes
Design rights	Original, non-commonplace three-dimensional designs	Creator or employer (including commissioner)	10 years from first marketing (to a maximum of 15 years from creation). Compulsory licences can be applied for in last five years.	Yes
Goodwill	Difference between acquisition cost and fair value of purchased assets/ liabilities	Acquirer	None	N/A
Know-how & show-how	Trade secrets	Creator	None	N/A

Intellectual property	Includes	Owner (subject to alternative agreement)	Length of protection	Automatic protection
Patents	Novel product/ process capable of being applied in industry	Inventor or employer	20 years from application for patent (but must be renewed annually after fifth anniversary)	No
Plant breeders' rights	Distinctive, uniform, stable and new plant varieties	First applicant	25 or 30 years (depending on variety) from date of grant; must be renewed annually	No
Performance rights	Live and recorded performances	Performer	50 years from performance or later release of recording	Yes
Registered designs	New aesthetically appealing designs	First applicant	25 years from date of registration, but must be renewed every five years	No
Semi-conductor designs	As for design rights	As for design rights	10 years (but no compulsory licences)	Yes
Trademarks	Words/symbols distinguishing the products of a business	First applicant	Indefinite, but must be renewed every 10 years	No

B

Tax law

IP tax: individuals

Chapter 3

Creating intellectual property

Summary: This chapter considers the tax implications for individuals and non-corporate entities creating intellectual property. The following chapter discusses the tax consequences for companies creating intellectual property—the rules are now very different to those which apply for companies, as almost any intellectual property created by a company will now be within the corporate intangibles rules.

As with other areas of tax, the focus is on the capacity of the creator – is the intellectual property being created as part of a trade? At this stage in the intellectual property lifecycle, the concern is generally with expenditure in creating the intellectual property: when are the costs deductible for tax purposes. This will depend on the nature of the expenditure – is it regarded as revenue or capital?

Finally, the chapter considers the tax treatment of casual intellectual property-related income, generally that from assisting with the creation of intellectual property.

- Business: trade, profession or vocation (para **3.10**)

- Capital or revenue (para **3.26**)

- Tax treatment of revenue expenditure (para **3.45**)

- Tax treatment of capital expenditure (para **3.72**)

- Income from assisting with creating intellectual property (para **3.85**)

INTRODUCTION

3.1 The creation of intellectual property is principally a cost issue, from a tax perspective, so that the focus is on getting a deduction against tax for the costs of creation of that intellectual property. At the end of this chapter is a short section covering the tax treatment of income received for assisting in the creation of intellectual property. More usually, income relating to intellectual property is derived from the exploitation or disposal of that intellectual property and so is covered in later chapters dealing with those aspects.

3.2   Creating intellectual property is the beginning of the lifecycle of intellectual property; and more often than not, it can be the end of the lifecycle—each idea that achieves commercial reality represents many thousands that were set aside.

3.3   This is the lifecycle stage that is perhaps the most open; rigorous exploitation of intellectual property is generally the preserve of business, but anyone can create intellectual property. For each research and development laboratory of a multinational pharmaceutical company creating carefully planned and patented products there are many individuals who create intellectual property without necessarily being aware that they are doing so: a doctor who takes photographs as a hobby will create the copyright in those photographs.

3.4   Equally there are businesses creating intellectual property without specific thought to the later exploitation of that intellectual property: a report written and subsequently reused as the basis of another; the copyright in the first report feeds and enables the production of the second report which, in turn, has its own copyright.

3.5   A person creating intellectual property will generally incur expenses in doing so (from staff and substantial equipment costs in developing drugs, to digital camera cards, software, and perhaps travel costs in creating photographs). Whether and how this expenditure can be deducted for tax purposes depends on whether the expenditure is capital or revenue, and the capacity in which the creator incurred the expenditure.

3.6   Intellectual property may be created as part of the business, or for investment purposes, or as a hobby. As with many other areas of tax, deductions are more readily available for intellectual property which is created by and for the use of the trade, rather than intellectual property which is created for investment or as a hobby.

WHO DO THESE RULES APPLY TO?

3.7   This chapter considers the tax treatment of expenditure on creating intellectual property outside the corporate intangibles tax rules; as these have now been in place for over 10 years, all intellectual property created by companies should now be within the corporate intangibles tax rules (see Chapter 9). This chapter, therefore, will be principally of interest in respect of intellectual property created by individuals and other non-corporate entities. However, some intellectual property assets, and some companies, are excluded from the corporate intangibles rules (see para **8.29** onwards). Where that is the case, the rules in this chapter will continue to apply to that expenditure and those companies.

Partnerships

3.8   The rules in this chapter also apply to individual and other non-corporate members of a partnership. Where a partnership has a corporate member, that partnership must calculate its profits twice:

- once under the income tax and capital gains rules for an unincorporated trade (including the rules following this chapter); and

- second under the corporation tax rules (CTA 2009, s 1259). The calculation under the corporation tax rules should include the provisions of the corporate intangibles rules, set out in the next chapter.

3.9   An individual (or other non-corporate partner) is taxed on their share of the profits that are calculated under the income tax and capital gains tax rules; a corporate partner is taxed on their share of the profits that are calculated under the corporation tax rules.

BUSINESS: TRADE, PROFESSION OR VOCATION

3.10   Most of the following rules to allow a tax deduction for expenditure on creating intellectual property require that the taxpayer be carrying on a trade, profession or vocation. These terms are considered below.

3.11   As this book is particularly looking at the taxation of intellectual property rather than the overall UK tax regime, this is, necessarily, a very brief overview of what is meant by a trade, profession or vocation. A person who is non-trading is someone who is not, in the context of the particular item of intellectual property, carrying on a trade, profession or vocation.

Trade

3.12   A trade needs primarily to be distinguished from one-off or casual transactions and investments. Note that the fact that a business has not yet started trading does not mean that it is automatically non-trading for tax purposes (see para **3.18**).

3.13   The key difference between traders and non-traders is the availability of deductions for expenditure. A trader will generally be able to deduct a wider range of expenditure from income when calculating the taxable profits of the trade in the year in which the expenditure is incurred: it is not matched to income arising from that expenditure. In contrast, even if a deduction for expenditure of a non-trader is actually available, such deduction will generally be deferred until income or a gain connected with that expenditure is achieved.

3.14   A trade 'includes every venture in the nature of trade' (ITA 2007, s 989); whether an activity is enough to amount to a trade is a question of fact, and there is substantial case law in this area. The main danger areas for intellectual property are:

- non-commercial activities: if the overall activities of a taxpayer are not commercial, then the taxpayer will not be considered to be trading.

  This is the case even where some of the activities could be regarded as consistent with a trade in another case: for example, in *British Olympic Association v Winter (Inspector of Taxes)* [1995] STC (SCD) 85, the BOA was held not to be trading because its overall purpose was non-commercial (to send a team to the 1992 Olympic Games), even though a substantial amount of its income came from licensing its logo. In contrast, in *Noddy Subsidiary Rights Co Ltd v IRC* (1967) 43 TC 458, the company was held to be carrying on a trade, licensing the rights to Enid Blyton's 'Noddy' character;

- hobbyists: HMRC will generally enquire into tax returns that seek trading reliefs for people that they believe may only be carrying on business as a hobby (see also para **18.292**).

  This can be a problem for people in the early years of an inventor's business, for example, where tax losses can arise as a result of work developing intellectual property for later exploitation: loss relief carried forward to set against future profits is only available to those carrying on a trade, profession or vocation.

  To minimise the risks, the individual should try to maintain as much evidence of business activity as possible (eg business plans to obtain loans, for example; actively seeking future customers or investment). Simply applying for a patent will not be sufficient evidence, as HMRC are well aware that patents can be applied for by, and granted to, non-traders (indeed, there are limited reliefs for such hobbyist inventors).

Profession or vocation

3.15   'Profession' and 'vocation' are not defined by legislation. In the context of intellectual property, an author, musician or other creative professional will generally be carrying out a vocation rather than a trade, but the distinction between these and trade is generally less important for tax purposes than the distinction between someone who is carrying on a trade, profession or vocation and someone who is not carrying on any one of those.

3.16   A profession or vocation is also treated as a trade for most income tax purposes (ITTOIA 2005, s 5), so that artists, musicians, and authors will be treated as if they are carrying on a trade (there are some exceptions, and these will be clearly noted). As with trade, the question of whether a profession or vocation is carried on is a question of fact.

Pre-trading expenditure

3.17   A business may not yet be trading, but that does not mean that it is carrying on non-trading activities. A number of intellectual property businesses will incur pre-trading expenditure when setting themselves up to trade. For example, expenditure may be incurred in developing intellectual property which is to be later exploited; depending on the business model, trading may not start until the development has been substantially completed and the exploitation begins.

3.18   The business may raise substantial amounts of capital on the strength of its ideas and initial intellectual property but if, for example, no decision has been taken as to whether the business will exploit the intellectual property personally, or license others to do so, then the business may not be able to convince HMRC that it has met the criteria for commencing to trade. HMRC generally want some indication that profits will be sought (even if they are never achieved) before accepting that a taxpayer is preparing to trade.

3.19   In general, expenditure is deducted when calculating the profits of the accounting period in which the expenditure occurred; for there to be an accounting period, a trade must be carried on at the time the expenditure is incurred. Without specific legislation, pre-trading expenditure would not be deductible because it is not incurred during an accounting period.

3.20   However, relief is provided for pre-trading expenditure—where the taxpayer has established they are preparing to trade—if it is expenditure that would qualify for deduction if they were actually trading (ie it would be deductible under ITTOIA 2005, Pt 2). Pre-trading expenditure can only be deducted if it is incurred no more than seven years before the commencement of trading (ITTOIA 2005, s 57(1)). This relief is available to all businesses; it is not specific to intellectual property businesses or to creators of intellectual property.

3.21   Care needs to be taken over commencing the trade after incurring pre-trading expenditure; relief is only given for expenditure incurred by the person who commences the trade. If, for example, an individual incurs the expenditure but incorporates the business when trading begins, the company would not be entitled to relief for the expenditure incurred by the individual. In the same way, there is no relief for expenditure incurred by a group company in respect of a trade subsequently commenced by another group member company.

Effective date

3.22   Where an individual or partnership begins to trade the pre-trading revenue expenditure incurred before the trade commences is treated as incurred on the first day of trading and is deducted as trading expenditure in that period (ITTOIA 2005, s 57).

3.23   The first day of trading is generally the first day on which the business can offer goods or services and does so.

Example 3.1

A business doing research into a particular area of biotechnology may be regarded as trading immediately, if it would be prepared to licence its intellectual property from the beginning.

In contrast, a business that is developing intellectual property which it intends to use to manufacture particular products is likely only to begin trading when it has reached the point of being able to manufacture those products and in fact does begin manufacture.

Qualifying expenditure

3.24   Deductible pre-trading expenditure includes expenditure on rent and rates (on property to be used for the purposes of the trade) and employees' costs.

3.25   Certain set-up costs, such as expenditure on the formation of a partnership or other capital expenditure, are not deductible. Similarly, expenditure incurred on items such as feasibility studies and market research may not be deductible; it is likely to be difficult to show that this type of expenditure is wholly and exclusively for the purposes of the trade: it is more likely to be considered to be for the purpose of deciding whether to trade.

IS THE EXPENDITURE ON CREATING THE INTELLECTUAL PROPERTY CLASSED AS CAPITAL OR REVENUE?

3.26   Generally an item of expenditure is deductible in computing the profits of a trade chargeable to tax if the deduction is justified by commercial accounting principles (ITTOIA 2005, s 25). However, legislation or case law may prohibit a deduction even where it is justified by commercial accounting principles. For example, expenditure on entertainment (even of business clients) is not deductible for tax purposes.

3.27   Beyond the prohibited deductions, the key test for the tax deduction of expenditure for unincorporated entities in business is whether the expenditure on creating the intellectual property is considered to be capital or revenue. This may be clear from the accounting treatment of the expenditure, but it is necessary to consider the tax rules and case law in some less clear-cut cases. The distinction is important because revenue expenditure can be deducted in full in the accounting period in which it is incurred, reducing taxable profits, whereas capital expenditure is usually only deductible for tax purposes when the asset to which it relates is sold.

3.28   For non-traders, the distinction is less relevant, as the deductions available for the costs of creating intellectual property are much more limited and are generally specifically given, rather than needing to be considered under general tax rules.

What is revenue expenditure

3.29   Qualifying revenue expenditure can be deducted in the year incurred when calculating tax (see para **3.45**), and so immediately reduces the tax payment for the business for that year. For an individual in business, the deduction effectively saves tax at up to 45% (from April 2013), depending on the overall income of the individual).

3.30   Revenue expenditure relates more closely to production and operating costs—the staff, services and materials, costs of producing, distributing and marketing products, and services for sale—and consumables (items which are used up in a short space of time; for example, clean room filters, blank recordable CDs or paper).

Example 3.2

A photographer above will have to buy printer paper to produce invoices and correspondence, as well as blank CD/DVDs onto which digital negatives can be recorded for clients. These items have no particular enduring value in and of themselves to the business, as they have a one-time use to the photographer (even if scrap printer paper is re-used for notes!).

What is capital expenditure

3.31   Capital expenditure is generally that which is spent on assets that have some enduring benefit to the creator: the asset on which expenditure has been made is capitalised for accounts and tax purposes, and the expenditure is deducted from income over a period of years to reflect the contribution over time of the asset to the creator. In creating intellectual property, this could be anything from sophisticated laboratory equipment to off-the-shelf computers; anything which is not expected to be used up within a year or so of purchase.

3.32 Capital expenditure cannot be immediately deducted in full as a matter of law but may be eligible for a tax deduction which is spread over time and so reduce the tax payment for the business by a smaller amount in the year of expenditure and again in future years. As a result, there is a much smaller tax saving (and possible no saving, if spreading is not available) in the year of expenditure, compared to revenue expenditure, but there are future tax deductions which will be available.

3.33 The accounts of the business will generally include an amortisation deduction relating to capital expenditure, as accounting standards allow most capital expenditure to be deducted over a period of time corresponding to the useful economic life of the asset. This amortisation deduction is *not* tax deductible and so it needs to be added back when calculating the taxable profits of a non-corporate business.

3.34 Instead, tax rules will usually allow a 'capital allowance' for such expenditure. This also allows the expenditure to be deducted over a period of time, but it is usually a much longer period of time than the accounting deduction for amortisation, as the tax deduction is not generally related to the useful economic life of the asset acquired (see para **3.74** onwards).

Example 3.3

A professional photographer buys a professional digital camera, and expects that the useful economic life of the camera is five years (taking into account the development cycle of digital equipment) and will enable the photographer to carry on his business over that time. As the photographer earns income with the cameras during a period of years, the cost of those cameras is also spread over a period of five years so that, for accounts purposes, 20% of the cost of the camera is deducted in the profit and loss account each year.

This accounting deduction has to be added back for tax purposes. The tax deduction, capital allowances for plant and machinery, is not specifically matched to the expected useful economic life of the camera. Instead, the capital allowance deduction is 20% of a declining balance each year (see para **3.74** for more detail) and it will take over 20 years to fully write off the cost of the camera—even if the camera has been replaced in the meantime.

3.35 The distinction between capital and revenue is not always entirely clear; the decision depends on the specific facts in each case, and has been the subject of numerous cases over the years. The outcomes of those cases are not wholly consistent, and the judges' reasoning in the cases could be described as even less consistent.

3.36 Where expenditure would have been capital if the related transaction or project had been successful, it will still be capital: the failure of the project or transaction does not change the original intention behind the expenditure (*ECC Quarries Ltd v Watkis* (1975) 51 TC 153).

3.37   In light of this, neither the legislation nor HMRC guidance sets out any specific criteria that would unequivocally determine expenditure on the creation of an intellectual property asset to be either capital or revenue: the general circumstances need to be taken into account in each case (see HMRC Manual BIM35700 onwards for more detail, although this is more focussed on the distinction for income rather than expenditure and so is more useful when considering income from exploiting intellectual property (see Chapter 6).

Key questions to determine revenue or capital for creation expenditure

3.38   Although there is no set criteria, there are a number of questions established through case law that are usually taken into account when considering whether expenditure on creating intellectual property is revenue or capital. No single answer is likely to be conclusive, but the overall trend of answers will usually indicate the type of expenditure. More of the questions are considered in Chapter 5, as they relate principally to acquisition expenditure, but the question that is likely to apply in considering expenditure on creating intellectual property is:

Did the expenditure create an asset?

3.39   If the intellectual property asset is created for permanent use in the business, to be used to enable the business to be carried on, the expenditure is more likely to be capital (*British Insulated and Helsby Cables v Atherton* (1926) 10 TC 155).

3.40   If, however, the asset created is to be sold as a specific product or service of the business, the expenditure is more likely to be revenue: the intellectual property created is similar to trading stock.

Example 3.4

A partnership may develop two types of software:

1   software that underlies the other types of software they produce, such as a graphics engine that is used to generate particular visual effects. This software may be licensed to other businesses, but such exploitation is not the purpose of development. Expenditure incurred in creating such software may be capital because it is used to enable the business to be carried on and creates an advantage for the business overall, even though it may not be capitalised in the accounts of the partnership; and

2   bespoke software for other businesses: expenditure incurred in creating
each piece of software is likely to be revenue because producing bespoke
software is the trade of the company, and they will be likely to retain (at
best) limited intellectual property rights in the software; the expenditure
is effectively the cost of sales.

3.41   Developing a brand name may be considered to be creation of an asset.
HMRC take the view that development of a brand name involves primarily
expenditure on advertising; that may be a rather simplistic view of the position.
Nevertheless, in deciding whether or not the expenditure involved in building
up a brand name is capital expenditure creating an asset, the following factors
will be relevant:

● does the product vary over time?

● is quality maintained?

● do customers tend to show brand loyalty that persists over substantial
periods?

● is the brand part of a portfolio in which the decline of established brands
and the creation of others is a continuing process?

● does the brand have a clear legal status which protects it from being
copied or imitated?

3.42   HMRC are generally reluctant to accept that a brand is a capital asset:
in practice, they will consider discrete elements of intellectual property (the
trademark, associated intellectual property etc) to be assets but are reluctant
to consider that these may together form an asset which is a brand with more
value than the discrete elements. In particular, they tend to the view that where
a brand 'is created it is transitory and not sufficiently durable to be regarded
as capital. This recognises that the consumer is often a fickle creature and can
change allegiance relatively quickly' (HMRC Manual BIM35640).

See Chapter 5 for more detail on the distinction between revenue and capital
when acquiring intellectual property.

Borderline cases

3.43   In borderline cases, case law indicates that the practical and business
effect of the expenditure should be considered, rather than a detailed analysis
of any legal rights acquired or surrendered (set out as part of a dissenting
judgment in *Hallstrom's Proprietary Ltd v The Federal Commissioner of
Taxation* 72CLR634: this is an Australian case, but the dissenting judgment
has been quoted with approval all the way up to what is now the Supreme
Court in the UK).

3.44 In this case, the taxpayer manufactured refrigerators using patents held by a competitor. The patents were about to expire, and the competitor applied for an extension of its patent. The taxpayer incurred costs opposing the extension. The dissenting judgement held that the expenditure by the taxpayer was of a capital nature, saying that

'What is an outgoing of capital and what is an outgoing on account of revenue depends on what the expenditure is calculated to effect from a practical and business point of view rather than upon the juristic classification of the legal rights, if any, secured, employed or exhausted in the process'.

REVENUE EXPENDITURE

3.45 Unlike capital expenditure, revenue expenditure is deductible in calculating the taxable profits for the accounting period in which it is incurred and so reduces the tax charge in that accounting period. There are general rules on the deductibility of revenue expenditure that will apply to the creators of intellectual property, as well as additional rules that specifically allow such creators to make particular deductions in circumstances where the general rules would not allow those deductions.

3.46 The primary key to deduction of revenue expenditure for tax purposes is that it must be incurred in connection with a trade, profession or vocation, taxable under ITTOIA 2005, Pt 2 (see above for the distinction between trading and non-trading, and a profession or vocation).

3.47 If an individual is not carrying on a trade, profession or vocation, then expenditure on creating intellectual property cannot, in general, be deducted as revenue when calculating tax due on income. There are some specific statutory exemptions to this, particularly with regard to fees relating to patents (see para **3.59**). However, if the intellectual property created is eventually sold or licensed, the expenditure of a non-trader may be deductible when computing income tax or capital gains tax on the exploitation or disposal of intellectual property (see Chapter 6 and Chapter 7).

General rules

3.48 Deduction of expenditure when calculating the profits of a trade for tax purposes is not something that is exhaustively defined by tax legislation, unsurprisingly, given the range of trades and expenditure that is possible.

3.49 Generally an item of expenditure is deductible in computing the profits of a trade chargeable if the deduction is justified by commercial accounting principles (ITTOIA 2005, s 25); however, tax statutes or case law may prohibit a deduction even where it is allowed by commercial accounting principles. As noted above, for example, entertainment expenditure is not deductible for tax purposes (as revenue or capital) even where it is allowed as a deduction in the business' profit and loss account (this is a general tax rule, rather than specific to intellectual property and so the details of this exclusion are outside the scope of this book).

3.50   For example, in *Lothian Chemical Co Ltd v Rogers* (1926) 11 TC 508 the court considered that '... in considering what is the true balance of profits and gains in the ... Tax Acts ... you deal in the main with ordinary principles of commercial accounting ... where these ordinary principles are not invaded by statute they must be allowed to prevail'.

3.51   While there is no exhaustive definition, a number of general principles can be established from the legislation and case law regarding deductibility of expenditure, so that expenditure must be:

- incurred by the taxpayer (*Peter Merchant Ltd v Stedford* (1948) 30 TC 496);

- incurred for the purposes of the trade (ITTOIA 2005, s 34(1));

- wholly and exclusively so incurred (ITTOIA 2005, s 34(1)); and

- of a revenue rather than a capital nature (*City of Dublin Steam Packet Co v O'Brien* (1912) 6 TC 101 and ITTOIA 2005, s 33): see above for details on the distinction.

3.52   The phrase 'wholly and exclusively for the purposes of the trade' requires three main questions to be answered:

- is the expenditure incurred for the purposes of the trade?

- is it wholly so incurred?

- is the trade purpose the exclusive purpose?

3.53   The question of exclusivity is the most difficult to determine—the trade questions are not generally difficult to determine. Motive is always harder to define.

Wholly and exclusively

3.54   Some guidance is available in *Strong & Co Ltd v Woodifield* (1906) 5 TC 215 on the general principles underlying the 'wholly and exclusively' test: the case is not specifically about intellectual property, but the principles hold good. The taxpayer ran an inn and claimed a deduction for damages paid to a guest who was injured on the premises. Judgment included the comment that:

'... the payment of these damages was not money expended "for the purpose of the trade" [because] ... it is not enough that the disbursement is made in the course of, or arises out of, or is connected with, the trade or is made out of the profits of the trade. It must be made for the purpose of earning the profits'.

3.55 It is, consequently, necessary for a company to include in the minutes of the directors' meeting which authorises the 'expenditure' some evidence as to the purpose of the expenditure. Whilst this is not incontrovertible evidence of exclusivity, it will support the premise.

Evidence

3.56 Some evidence will generally be required to satisfy the tests: in *Salt v Buckley (Insp of Taxes)* (2001) SpC 293 deductions for expenditure were denied because there was no evidence that the payments had actually been made, nor that they were incurred wholly and exclusively for business purposes. Salt conducted and published research into the characteristics of commercial film and television; in his income tax return for 1997–98, he deducted various expenses for services provided by unincorporated businesses through which he traded. The expense claims were denied on the grounds that the payments had not been made, or that if they had been made, they had not been made wholly and exclusively for those businesses.

Specific tax deductions for revenue expenditure on creating intellectual property

3.57 These additional rules specifically allow creators of particular types of intellectual property to make particular deductions in circumstances where the general rules would not allow them, or extend the deductions available under the general rules.

3.58 If no specific rules are available, the general rules will apply to the expenditure. For example:

- expenditure on the creation of know-how in the course of a trade is subject to the general rules only, so expenditure is likely to be revenue expenditure, particularly as the know-how is likely to develop over time rather than be created as a specific asset;

- expenditure on the creation of a trademark would generally be regarded as capital expenditure, as an enduring asset is created. However, for a brand where the lifetime can be shown to be finite and short, the creation costs could be eligible to be deducted as deferred revenue expenditure over the life of the brand.

Fees and expenses of registering intellectual property

3.59   In addition to the general rules on deductibility, ITTOIA 2005, ss 89–90 allow traders to deduct certain fees and expenses of registering intellectual property (applications and renewals) when calculating profits for tax purposes. Specifically, fees and expenses incurred can be deducted when obtaining for the purposes of the trade:

● the grant of a patent;

● the extension of the term of a patent;

● the registration of a design or trademark; and

● an extension of the time for which the right in a registered design exists.

In addition, fees and expenses incurred in connection with any rejected or abandoned application for a patent can also be deducted.

Note that the provisions of ss 89–90 apply only to trades and not to professions or vocations; the costs of registering a patent would not be tax deductible in calculating the profits of an artist working in metal sculptures, for example (even if the patent is related to something in the artist's work). The fees may be deductible in calculating his overall tax charge, as relief is available for hobbyist inventors (see below).

3.60   Specific relief is also available for registration expenses wholly and exclusively incurred by an inventor in devising an invention otherwise than in the course of a trade (ITTOIA 2005, s 601): see para **18.292** for more information on hobbyist inventors.

Non-trade intellectual property

3.61   Non-traders—generally, those holding intellectual property as an investment—can obtain a tax deduction (ITTOIA 2005, s 582) for expenses incurred in that same year wholly and exclusively in generating such royalties and income, but the deduction can only be from the royalties and other income so generated. Expenses that would not be deductible if the taxpayer were carrying on a trade (such as business entertainment) are similarly not deductible. There is no carry-forward of expenses against future royalties and income.

Computer software development

3.62   Almost all businesses will now use computer software; businesses with a particular emphasis on intellectual property creation may use software more than most. Ordinarily, the costs of a computer services department will

47

be deductible as revenue expenditure. However, where a business develops its own software, whether the expenditure (such as the salaries and associated costs of the staff who developed the software) is revenue or capital will largely depend on the economic function of the software within the business.

3.63   In general, expenditure on developing software for use in the business will be deductible as revenue where the software development project is not one that significantly impacts the business (either alone or as part of a larger series of projects) (see para **17.96** for more information).

3.64   Expenditure may also be deductible as revenue even where the software development project as a whole is considered to be capital (see para **3.84**).

Training courses

3.65   Training courses that are undertaken to provide new expertise, knowledge or skills are generally considered to create an intangible asset of enduring benefit to the business. The expenditure on attending the course will then be capital expenditure (see para **3.83**).

3.66   If the course is, instead, undertaken to maintain or update existing expertise, knowledge or skills, the expenditure on the course is generally accepted to be deductible as revenue expenditure, provided that it is incurred wholly and exclusively for the purposes of the trade (HMRC Manual BIM35660).

Employees—patents

3.67   Generally, a person who is employed as an inventor will not personally incur expenditure on creating intellectual property: the employer, instead, incurs the relevant expenditure in the form of the employee's salary, and equipment and consumables needed for the employee's work. The employee will receive a salary, possibly with bonuses, commissions, benefits-in-kind and other forms of employment income.

3.68   However, under the Patents Act (PA) 1977 an employee inventor may apply to the court (PA 1977, s 40) for an additional payment from the employer where that employee's work has created a patent of outstanding benefit to the employer.

3.69   Note that it is the *patent* that must be of outstanding benefit to the employer; the work done by the employee does not need to be of outstanding benefit, but the monopoly position granted to the employer by the patent must be of such benefit.

3.70   Few of these cases come to court: the employees who are likely to create a patent of outstanding benefit will generally be recognised as such by the employer to ensure that they are retained and remunerated accordingly; that remuneration would be taxed as employment income as usual. Paying appropriate remuneration will significantly reduce the risk of a claim as the employee's salary (together with any consideration for grant or assignment of the licence of the patent by the employee) will be relevant when the court considers whether to make an award, and how much the award should be.

3.71   Where an employer does make such a payment, the tax treatment of the expenditure on that payment will depend on the treatment of the expenditure on the overall project which gives rise to the patent; where it is part of qualifying R&D, for example, it should be possible to argue that this is part of the general earnings of the employee and so is within the scope of the deduction for staff costs.

CAPITAL EXPENDITURE

3.72   As stated above (see para **3.32**), capital expenditure cannot, in principle, be deducted in full in the year in which the expenditure is incurred. Instead, the expenditure is usually deductible either when the asset acquired is sold or, for qualifying expenditure, over a period of years. The deduction over time is given by capital allowances; these are the tax equivalent of the depreciation charges in a profit and loss account, allowing a taxpayer to deduct capital expenditure from taxable profits over a period of time, to reflect its use in generating those profits. The depreciation deductions in the accounts are not deductible when calculating the taxable profits of the company.

3.73   Capital expenditure incurred in creating intellectual property will usually be expenditure on specific assets: computers, laboratory equipment, office furniture, etc. However, as noted above, capital expenditure can also include the overall costs, including staff costs, of projects intended to create intellectual property assets for the trade to use. This is particularly the case with in-house development of software which is created for direct use in the trade, rather than to be licensed out to others (see below for more information on in-house development of software).

General capital expenditure

Plant and machinery

3.74   Capital allowances are available to anyone carrying on a trade, profession or vocation under the general rules for capital expenditure relating to plant and machinery (Capital Allowances Act (CAA) 2001). 'Plant' is not defined by statute, but case law has evolved a number of principles which can be used to determine whether something is plant and, in general, any apparatus which is used in carrying on a business will be plant. This does not include stock in trade, which is bought for sale, but will include anything kept for 'permanent employment in the business' (*Yarmouth v France* (1887) 19 QBD 647). The following is an outline of the way in which capital allowances work; a detailed explanation is outside the scope of this book where the allowances are not specific to intellectual property.

3.75   An accelerated form of capital allowance, called the annual investment allowance, is available to all businesses: this provides that the first £25,000 (from April 2012; the limit was higher in earlier years) of capital expenditure on plant and machinery is deductible in full in determining the business' profits and losses in the year of expenditure. A taxpayer with more than one trade is entitled to only one annual investment allowance, rather than one per trade.

3.76   Once the annual investment has been used up, a deduction of 18% per year (from April 2012; the rate was slightly higher in earlier years) is allowed, on a reducing balance basis, for expenditure on plant and machinery in that accounting period. This allowance is intended to reflect the use of the asset in the business, similar to depreciation in the accounts. There is also a lower rate of 8% (from April 2012; the rate was similarly slightly higher in earlier years) which applies to expenditure on items on a specific list of building-related assets; these are not items which are likely to be specific to creating intellectual property and so are not discussed further.

Example 3.5

Thomas, an architect with his own practice, buys a computer in 2013 to assist with the engineering load calculations needed as part of the research and development involved in projects that he undertakes.

The computer is built to order, to ensure that the calculations can be carried out faster than a normal desktop computer would manage, and costs £10,000.

In the same year, Thomas has acquired office furniture and other computers costing £20,000. As a result, only £5,000 of the cost of the new computer will qualify for the annual investment allowance. He can deduct this £5,000 (and the other £20,000 of expenditure) from his trading income in 2013 and so reduce his tax charge.

The remaining £5,000 of the cost of the computer will qualify for normal plant and machinery allowances so that, in the year of acquisition, Thomas can claim £900 of allowances (£5,000 @ 18%). This £900 can also be deducted from his 2013 trading income to reduce the tax charge. His total deductions in 2013 are therefore £25,900.

In 2014, he will be able to claim £738 of allowances (£4,100 @ 17% – the previous year's allowance is deducted each time, so that the amount on which allowances are claimed declines each year). As before, this £738 is deducted from his 2014 trading income to reduce the tax charge.

(Note: this is an outline example, demonstrating the principle in high level and assumes that the annual investment allowance amount, and the plant and machinery rate, remain at 2012 levels).

Research and development

3.77   A specific capital allowance deduction is available for expenditure by a trader on capital assets used in qualifying research and development; this is discussed in detail in Chapter 4.

3.78   This allowance is available to all taxpayers carrying on a trade (unlike the research and development tax reliefs for revenue expenditure, which are only available to companies) and should be claimed in preference to plant and machinery allowances where available.

Other capital allowances

3.79   Capital allowances were previously available for industrial buildings or structures; the allowances are no longer available for new acquisitions and are being phased out where they are presently being claimed by businesses. Buildings used for research and development may still qualify for the research and development allowance mentioned above.

3.80   Capital allowances are available for expenditure incurred in buying patent rights and know-how: these are discussed in Chapter 5.

Assets not qualifying for capital allowances

3.81   Where capital allowances are not available—usually because the asset acquired does not fall into one of the categories of assets on which allowances are given—the expenditure is only deductible from any taxable gain that is received when the asset is eventually disposed of. This will reduce the taxable gain on that asset so that relief is obtained for the expenditure, albeit with a higher cashflow cost to the business due to the time taken to obtain that relief.

Example 3.6

Joe buys an asset for his trade for £10,000. If it qualifies for capital allowances, he will be able to deduct £10,000 from his taxable profits in the year he buys it (assuming that he hasn't already used up his annual investment allowance). This will save him £4,000 if he's a 40% taxpayer.

If the asset doesn't qualify for capital allowances, however (for example, because it is a building that doesn't qualify for the research and development allowance) then there is no tax deduction available until Joe later sells the asset, and this could be many years later. The full cost is carried forward until the eventual sale.

3.82   The cashflow cost of not having capital allowances should not be underestimated, so businesses should be sure that they understand whether or not capital allowances will be available when spending substantial sums on equipment for creating intellectual property.

Specific capital expenditure on creating intellectual property

Training

3.83   The costs of training the owner of the business to develop new expertise, knowledge or skills will be capital because it creates an asset (the knowledge) which is of enduring benefit to the business (HMRC Manual BIM35660). As noted before (see para **3.65**), the costs of training to simply update expertise etc which the owner already has will be revenue.

Computer software development staff costs

3.84   Where a business develops its own software, some costs will clearly be capital in nature: computing equipment purchased for the project, for example. However, other expenditure such as the salaries and associated costs of the staff who developed the software may be regarded as either revenue or capital depending on the expected benefit from the software once developed (see para **3.63**). If it is capital, then capital allowances may be claimed in respect of this expenditure even though it includes recurring costs that would ordinarily be considered to be revenue. Whether the expenditure is revenue or capital will largely depend on the intended economic function of the resulting software within the business. See para **17.94** for more detail on the issues to consider when determining whether or not the expenditure is capital.

INCOME FROM ASSISTING WITH CREATING INTELLECTUAL PROPERTY

Casual income

3.85   In some cases, income may be paid to an individual for assisting in the creation of intellectual property, usually copyright works: for example, an individual may be paid by a publisher for providing information to a writer who then produces an article or book based on that information.

3.86   This income will generally be taxed as non-trading income from intellectual property (ITTOIA 2005, s 579), where there is no disposal of copyright by the individual (assuming that the individual is not carrying on a trade of providing such information).

3.87   Where the individual at the same time disposes of intellectual property (eg publication rights, or film rights), and the principal transaction is the disposal of the rights, then the payment may be treated as a capital receipt instead, subject to capital gains tax (see Chapter 7).

Employees—patents

3.88   Where an employee receives a payment under the Patents Act 1977 (see para **3.67**), in respect of an invention created for their employer, that payment is treated as earnings from the employment and will be subject to deduction of income tax (at up to 45% from April 2013) and National Insurance Contributions, accounted for by the employer through PAYE, in the same way as other income from the employment. As the tax treatment is the same as for any other employment income, further details are outside the scope of this book.

CHECKLIST

3.89

- Is the taxpayer carrying on (or intending to carry on) a trade, profession or vocation? If not, deductions for expenditure on creating intellectual property will be very limited.

- Has the taxpayer started trading yet? If not, deductions will be deferred until the trade actually commences.

- Is the trade carried on by a partnership with a corporate partner? If so, the taxable profits will need to be calculated twice, for income tax purposes and for corporation tax purposes: see Chapter 9 for details of tax deductions for corporation tax on creating intellectual property where the intellectual property is a post-1 April 2002 asset. The deductions may be different for the two sets of calculations.

- Is the expenditure capital or revenue? If revenue, it can be deducted from that year's income and so reduce taxable profits.

3.89 *Creating intellectual property*

- If revenue:

  — is it wholly and exclusively for the purposes of the trade, profession or vocation?

  — is it excluded from deduction by legislation (business entertainment, for example)?

  — does it fall within one of the specific deductions (registration costs, for example)?

- If capital, does the expenditure qualify for capital allowances (usually plant and machinery allowances, but possibly also research and development capital allowances: see Chapter 4).

Research and development allowances

Summary: Research and development allowances provide an accelerated tax deduction for expenditure on capital equipment, including buildings, used for qualifying research and development. Without the research and development allowances, deductions for equipment purchases would only be available through plant and machinery allowances, which take over 20 years before being fully deducted for tax purposes. Deduction in respect of purchases of buildings would only be available when the building was later sold.

Research and development allowances are available all traders—corporate and non-corporate—and provide a 100% deduction against taxable income for the expenditure incurred.

- Qualifying research and development (para **4.5**)

- Qualifying expenditure (para **4.6**)

- Tax deductions (para **4.14**)

- Tax charge on disposal (para **4.18**)

- Adjustments (para **4.21**)

INTRODUCTION

4.1   Research and development allowances are available on qualifying capital expenditure incurred by a trader (that is, not only a company but also individuals, partnerships and other unincorporated entities that are carrying on a trade, but are not available to any person carrying on a profession or vocation) for research and development (CAA 2001, s 437(1)).

4.2   Prior to CAA 2001 these allowances were known as scientific research allowances; the legislation was rewritten for inclusion in CAA 2001 but not substantially changed.

4.3   Where an item of expenditure could qualify for alternative capital allowances, the taxpayer needs to choose which allowance to take: the research and development allowance cannot be claimed in addition to other allowances on the same item.

4.4   Research and development allowances are specifically excluded from the changes to capital allowances in FA 2008 ('Business tax reform: capital allowances changes' consultation paper, July 2007, ¶ 2.8) and so continue to be given at 25%, instead of reducing to 20% and 18% with plant and machinery allowances.

QUALIFYING RESEARCH AND DEVELOPMENT

4.5   'Research and development' is defined as for the research and development revenue expenditure tax reliefs (see para **10.3** onwards for more details of the definition) although, for the research and development allowance, research and development in respect of oil and gas exploration and appraisal is specifically included in the definition of qualifying research and development (CAA 2001, s 437(2)).

QUALIFYING EXPENDITURE

4.6   Expenditure on research and development includes:

- expenditure incurred on capital assets used by employees carrying out research and development (for example: computers, tools, testing equipment); and

- expenditure incurred in providing facilities for carrying out research and development (such as the purchase of a laboratory, but not including the costs of the land on which the laboratory stands).

4.7   There are few restrictions on the type of assets that qualify for research and development allowance. However:

- as with other capital allowances, no allowance is available for the costs of acquisition of land; where property is acquired for research and development purposes, any element of the expenditure which relates to land (rather than the buildings on the land) must be excluded; and

- no allowance is given for dwellings, unless the dwelling is part of a building used for research and development purposes and no more than 25% of the cost of the building relates to the dwelling (note that this proportion is related to the costs, not the area of the building that comprises the dwelling).

Example 4.1

The RD Partnership spends £500,000 on a new building for laboratories. The research and development being carried on in the building requires the partnership to maintain a small flock of sheep in a field next to the building, as the product they are working on is a protein effectively manufactured within sheep's milk, and to employ someone to look after the animals. A small flat is made available to that employee as they are required to be on the premises overnight, and the flat is part of the new building. The £500,000 included:

- £100,000 for the land on which the new building is located and the adjoining field;

- £360,000 for the laboratory space; and

- £40,000 for the flat.

As the building costs of the flat are less than 25% of the total building costs (£400,000), all of the building costs qualify for the research and development allowance. The £100,000 spent on land will not qualify for the allowance and so relief for that expenditure will only be available if the land is sold in the future.

Existing assets

4.8   An existing asset historically used for other activities that begins to be used for research and development purposes does not qualify for research and development allowances, although it will continue to qualify for any normal capital allowances where these are already being taken.

By or on behalf of the trader

4.9   Expenditure qualifies for research and development allowances if it is capital expenditure which is incurred on research and development directly undertaken by the trader or work carried out on behalf of the trader (CAA 2001, s 439), provided that either:

- the trader incurs the expenditure on research and development connected with an existing trade; or

- a trade to which the research and development is connected is commenced after the expenditure has been incurred.

Expenditure connected with a trade

4.10   As with research and development relief (see Chapter 10), 'research and development connected with a trade' includes research and development which:

- may lead to or facilitate an extension of the trade; and

- is of a medical nature and which has a special relation to the welfare of workers employed in the trade.

4.11 If not also incurred in relation to the welfare of workers employed in the trade, expenditure on medical research and development undertaken for the benefit of the community as a whole will only be qualifying expenditure if it leads to or facilitates an extension of the trade (ie is carried out by a company with a medical trade, such as a pharmaceutical company).

Where a trader has more than one research and development trade, allowances may only be claimed once in respect of qualifying expenditure, even where the assets or facilities acquired with the expenditure are used in both trades—after all, the asset is only acquired once. The trader will need to choose which trade gets the benefit of the allowance.

Research and development trade

4.12 Where the trade consists solely of research and development (for example, where a group of companies includes a subsidiary set up to carry out research and development for the entire group), all of the assets of that trade will qualify for research and development allowances (unless the asset is one which is specifically excluded from qualifying).

Expenditure incurred on behalf of a trader

4.13 To qualify for research and development allowances, there must be a clear and close relationship between the trader and the research undertaken on behalf of the trader. The relationship need not be contractual, but must not be an agency relationship (or similar) (HMRC Manual CA60400). However, the fact that research undertaken by someone else is for a trader's benefit, or is in his interest, is not alone enough to classify the expenditure as being on behalf of the trader and so qualifying for research and development allowances (*Gaspet Ltd v Elliss* (1987) 60 TC 91).

TAX DEDUCTION

4.14 Research and development allowances provide a deduction of 100% (CAA 2001, s 441) in the period in which the expenditure is incurred, unless the taxpayer elects to deduct a smaller percentage (prior to CAA 2001, only the 100% deduction could be claimed as there was no option to take a smaller percentage. CAA 2001 applies from 5 April 2001 for income tax purposes and for accounting periods ending after 31 March 2001 for corporation tax purposes). Where a smaller deduction is taken, the balance cannot be deducted later; a balancing charge may also later arise in this case (see below). As a result, it is very unusual for a partial allowance to be claimed.

4.15 If the expenditure was incurred before the trade began, the allowance is given in the period in which trade commences.

4.16 As the allowance is only given in the accounting period of expenditure, there can be no balancing allowances (ie later tax deductions where the asset is sold at a loss) given in respect of research and development allowances.

Deduction adjustment for rapid disposals

4.17 If the asset is quickly disposed of, so that it is in fact disposed of in the same period in which it was acquired, the deduction is reduced so that the allowance given is 100% of the original expenditure less the disposal value. The tax charge on disposal (see below) does not also apply where there has been a rapid disposal.

Example 4.2

RDCo spends £100,000 on testing equipment for a research and development project in January 2008; the project and the expenditure qualify for research and development allowances. The project takes less time than anticipated and so RDCo sells the equipment in November 2008 for £75,000. RDCo's accounting period is the calendar year.

In 2008, therefore, RDCo will claim a research and development allowance of £25,000 (the difference between the acquisition price and the disposal proceeds).

TAX CHARGE ON DISPOSAL

4.18 A balancing charge (a tax cost) will be created and treated as a receipt of the trade if the asset or facility on which a research and development allowance has been claimed is disposed of (CAA 2001, s 442).

4.19 The balancing charge is the lesser of:

- the disposal value (or, if there is any unclaimed research and development allowance, the amount by which the disposal value exceeds that unclaimed research and development allowance); and

- the research and development allowance given.

The balancing charge is brought into account as a receipt in the accounting period in which there is a relevant disposal; if the trade has been discontinued before such disposal, the balancing charge is brought into account in the accounting period in which the trade is discontinued (CAA 2001, s 444).

Example 4.3

RDCo spends £100,000 on testing equipment for a research and development project in January 2008 and claims the full research and development allowance.

RDCo ceased trading on 31 December 2009, at the end of an accounting period, and later sold the equipment in November 2010 for £50,000.

RDCo will have a balancing charge on the disposal of the equipment of the lesser of:

- £50,000 (the excess of the disposal value, £50,000, over the unclaimed allowance, £0); and

- £70,000 (the allowance given).

RDCo will have a balancing charge of £50,000 on the disposal of the testing equipment in the accounting period ended 31 December 2009, as that is the period in which the company ceased trading, although the disposal in fact took place 11 months after the end of that period.

Example 4.4

If RDCo had not claimed the full allowance in Example 4.3 but had, instead, only claimed £70,000 of research and development allowance (so that £30,000 was unclaimed), the balancing charge on the disposal of the equipment would be the lesser of:

- £20,000 (the excess of the disposal value, £50,000, over the unclaimed allowance, £30,000); and

- £70,000 (the allowance given).

RDCo would have a balancing charge of £20,000 in this case.

Disposal events

4.20   The disposal events that could trigger a balancing charge are (CAA 2001, s 443):

- cessation of ownership of the asset, on the earlier of completion of the transfer or the date on which possession is taken up by the new owner, in which case the disposal value is the net proceeds, provided that the asset is sold at not less than market value, otherwise it is market value;

- demolition or destruction of ownership of the asset whilst still owned by the trader, in which case the disposal value is the net amount received following destruction/demolition, together with any insurance money or similar compensation received.

Costs of demolition are included in the total cost of the asset; where the demolition costs exceed the disposal value, and the asset had not passed into use for something other than qualifying research and development until demolition, research and development allowances equal to the excess are given (HMRC Manual CA60700).

There is no disposal event merely on the asset ceasing to be use for qualifying research and development.

ADJUSTMENTS

4.21   Acquisition of capital assets such as those qualifying for research and development allowances will usually involve some VAT cost. These VAT costs can usually be recovered (see para **15.5**) by most businesses. However, additional VAT can become due or repayable under the VAT Capital Goods Scheme, which applies to traders who make supplies that are partly exempt from VAT. The Scheme has recently been extended to cover assets acquired for partly non-business use: given that the research and development allowance requires the equipment to have been acquired for the trade, it is unlikely that this extension will significantly impact research and development equipment.

4.22   The Scheme applies to capital expenditure on certain types of assets, including computer equipment, buildings and refurbishments and fitting-out works which are not used wholly for making taxable supplies.

4.23   These assets can be used by a business over a number of years and so there can be some variation over the period of ownership in the extent to which the assets are used in making taxable supplies. The Scheme is a mechanism for adjusting the initial input VAT on the asset to reflect the use of the asset.

4.24   When an asset is acquired, the normal rules for claiming input tax apply:

- 100% of input VAT is recoverable if wholly used in making taxable supplies;

- 0% of input VAT is recoverable if wholly used in making exempt supplies; and

- a proportion of input VAT is recoverable if used for making taxable and exempt supplies, reflecting the ratio of such supplies.

4.25   If the taxable use of the asset changes within the five or ten years (depending on the type of asset: five years for computers and certain short leases, ten years for all other assets) after it is acquired, the input VAT has to be adjusted to reflect the change. If the taxable use increases more input VAT can be claimed form HMRC. If it decreases, some of the input VAT already claimed is repaid to HMRC. The adjustment is given by the formula:

VAT/A x P

where VAT is the input VAT originally claimed when the asset was acquired, A is the relevant period during which adjustments must be made (five or ten years) and P is the percentage change in taxable/exempt use of the asset.

4.26   Where some of the input VAT liability claimed has to be repaid by the business to HMRC, that repayment is deemed, for the purposes of research and development allowances, to be additional qualifying expenditure (CAA 2001, s 447) and so a research and development allowance can be claimed in respect of that liability in the accounting period in which the liability is incurred.

4.27   Where some more of the input VAT is reclaimed from HMRC, that repayment of VAT is deemed to be disposal proceeds and will create a balancing charge in the accounting period of repayment. Subsequent balancing charges, on disposal, will need to take any adjustments into account.

Example 4.5

RDCo has spent £117,500 on research and development equipment in January 2008. RDCo makes both taxable and exempt supplies of healthcare-related products. It plans to use the research and development equipment entirely for taxable supplies and so reclaims all of the input VAT (£17,500) from HMRC and claims the full research and development allowance on the net cost of the equipment of £100,000.

Two years later, RDCo begins to use the equipment for some exempt supplies, so that 25% of the use of the equipment is now for exempt supplies.

RDCo has to repay some of the VAT claimed to HMRC. The original input VAT claimed was £17,500, the adjustment period is ten years and the percentage change is 25%. The adjustment is therefore:

- 17,500/10 × 25% = £437.50.

This VAT adjustment is paid to HMRC and is treated as additional expenditure qualifying for research and development allowances, so RDCo can claim that £437.50 as an allowance in the accounting period in which it makes the repayment.

On a subsequent disposal of the asset for £50,000, the balancing charge is the lower of:

- £50,000 (the disposal value, as there is no unclaimed research and development allowance); and

- £100,437.50 (the original cost of the asset plus the additional VAT repaid).

Example 4.6

If RDCo in Example 4.5 had planned to use the research and development equipment entirely for exempt supplies it would not have been able to reclaim any of the input VAT (£17,500) from HMRC. It would have claimed the full research and development allowance on the total cost to RDCo of the equipment of £117,500.

Two years later, RDCo begins to use the equipment for some taxable supplies, so that 25% of the use of the equipment is now for taxable supplies.

RDCo can now reclaim some of the input VAT from HMRC. The original input VAT claimed was £17,500, the adjustment period is ten years and the percentage change is 25%. The adjustment is therefore:

- 17,500/10 × 25% = £437.50.

This VAT adjustment is reclaimed from HMRC and is treated as disposal proceeds, leading to a balancing charge of the lower of:

- £437.50 (the reclaimed VAT); and

- £117,500 (the original cost of the asset to RDCo as no VAT reclaim could be made).

On a later disposal of the asset for £50,000, the balancing charge on disposal is the lower of:

- £50,000 (the disposal value, as there is no unclaimed research and development allowance); and

- £117,062.50 (the original cost of the asset less the additional VAT reclaimed and in respect of which a disposal value has been taken into account).

CHECKLIST

4.28

- Is the expenditure incurred by a trader?
- Is the expenditure incurred on qualifying research and development?
- Is the expenditure qualifying?
  - Is the expenditure on a new asset?
  - Has it been incurred by or on behalf of the trader?
  - Is it connected with the trade?

4.28 *Research and development allowances*

- Has there been a disposal of equipment or a building on which research and development allowances were claimed?

  — If so, consider whether there is a balancing charge.

- Has there been a change of use of equipment or a building on which research and development allowances were claimed, and to which the Capital Goods Scheme applies?

  — If so, consider whether there needs to be a VAT adjustment.

Chapter 5

Acquiring intellectual property— individuals and non-corporates

Summary: On acquiring intellectual property, the key question (as with creating intellectual property) is: when can the expenditure on acquiring the intellectual property be deducted for tax purposes, to reduce tax costs?

When considering the expenditure, it is important to identify the type of intellectual property being acquired; whether it is a patent, a design right, copyright, know-how, or trademark, for example. There are some specific tax deductions available for expenditure on certain different types of intellectual property. Where there is no specific deduction for an item of expenditure, the general tax rules will apply.

In addition, it may be necessary to withhold tax from payments for acquisitions of intellectual property; there is more information in Chapter 16 on withholding tax, and the specific provisions are cross-referenced in this chapter.

- Acquisition expenditure – capital or revenue? (para **5.4**)
- General rules (para **5.17**)
- Patents (para **5.31**)
- Copyright (para **5.84**)
- Know-how and show-how (para **5.104**)

INTRODUCTION

5.1   Although this chapter applies primarily to acquisitions by individuals and non-corporates, it should be noted that these rules will also apply to companies acquiring intellectual property which was owned by a related party on or before 1 April 2002, and to any other intellectual property that is excluded from the corporate intangibles rules (see para **8.29** onwards for details of excluded intellectual property). However, to the extent that the acquisition is of a licence over intellectual property, rather than the outright acquisition of intellectual property, the royalties paid under that licence will nevertheless fall within the corporate intangibles rules (see Chapter 8). The following rules will only apply to companies which acquire outright pre-1 April 2002 intellectual property from related parties.

5.2   Not all businesses that use intellectual property will create their own intellectual property assets—it is far more usual for the intellectual property to be acquired from the original creator or another intermediate acquirer. There are substantial benefits to be gained from acquiring rather than creating:

- a business does not need to employ inventors, authors, programmers—creators of intellectual property—and can, instead, concentrate on exploiting that intellectual property rather than becoming involved in ancillary areas which may be better outsourced;

- the availability of support from a supplier of intellectual property can also be important for businesses, particularly in the area of information technology, reducing the need to maintain a large support function;

- the asset may be fully developed and immediately available for use in the business, without the need for the testing and tweaking that is involved in creating it from scratch;

- software for non-income producing business functions such as accounting, for example, can be brought into use immediately, rather than needing to go through the process of designing and creating the software; and

- even where the business is involved with developing intellectual property, it may be more effective to buy in external intellectual property to extend the functions of the core products of the business: for example, many websites use Google's search engine to provide complementary Internet search facilities; licensing Google's engine has allowed those sites to concentrate on developing the core elements of their business.

5.3   When creating intellectual property, the distinction between the different types of intellectual property is not of paramount importance: the tax implications are broadly similar with only a few specific rules on deducting expenditure, generally in respect of registration expenses. However, when acquiring intellectual property, it is important to identify the type of intellectual property being acquired; whether it is a patent, a design right, copyright, know-how, or trademark, for example. There are specific deductions available for different types of intellectual property, with general rules applying otherwise. To ensure that the correct deduction is obtained, therefore, it is essential to identify the intellectual property being acquired.

ACQUISITION EXPENDITURE

5.4   A person acquiring intellectual property will generate expenditure in doing so, either by payment of a lump sum, or by regular payments such as royalties for the use of the intellectual property. Whether or not this expenditure can be deducted for tax purposes depends on whether the expenditure is capital or revenue, and the capacity in which the acquirer incurred the expenditure: is the acquirer acting in the course of a trade, profession or vocation?

5.5   As discussed earlier in this book (see para **3.46**) revenue expenditure can be deducted as an expense immediately when calculating profits for tax purposes for the period in which the intellectual property is acquired. Similarly, taxpayers carrying on a trade, profession or vocation will generally be entitled to a wider range of deductions for acquisitions: for example, capital allowances are not available to hobbyists (see para **3.8** onwards for more detail on the distinction between trading and non-trading).

Capital or revenue

5.6   Capital expenditure cannot be immediately deducted in full: however, a deduction may be available through capital allowances, which allow expenditure on patents and industrial know-how (only) to be deducted over a period of time, to reflect the use of the intellectual property in the business (see paras **5.25**, **5.60** and **5.107**).

5.7   Intellectual property creates particular problems in distinguishing between capital and revenue because of the different types of rights that can be acquired. However, where intellectual property is acquired outright for use in the business, it is most likely to be a capital asset for that business.

5.8   More details on the distinction between capital and revenue are in para **3.37** onwards; the following sets out a number of tests that may be particularly relevant when acquiring intellectual property.

Does the expenditure create an enduring benefit for the business?

5.9   Business expenditure is generally made with the intention of getting some commercial advantage; part of the distinction between revenue and capital expenditure is the question of the effect of the advantage and how long it is expected to last.

5.10   The leading case in this area as it affects intellectual property (and other intangible assets), is *Strick v Regent Oil Co Ltd* (1965) 43TC1. The case considered assets whose value would not diminish through use, but only with the passage of time, which clearly covers intellectual property assets.

5.11   In *Strick*, Lord Reid distinguished between regular payments for the use of an asset and a lump sum paid to cover use over a period of several years:

'To help the conduct of his business a trader obtains a right to do something on someone else's property or an obligation by someone to do or refrain from doing something… And the right or obligation or the effect of the contract may endure for a short or a long period of years. The question then arises whether the sum which he has paid for that advantage is a capital or revenue expense…

Where the … asset is a right to some benefit for a period of years and the consideration given for it is the payment of an annual sum during the continuance of the right there is generally no difficulty. Rent payable under a lease or under an agreement for the hire of a machine is treated as a proper debit against incomings, and the same must, I think, apply to an annual (or quarterly or monthly) payment for a [right to use]. The difficulty begins to arise when a lump sum is paid to cover several years. If that is so then it is not so much the nature of the right acquired as the nature of the payment made for it that matters …'

5.12 Lord Wilberforce, in the same case, set out that there is no specific minimum or maximum period to be considered, but that the question has to be considered in the light of all the circumstances; a short period of benefit might point to the expenditure being revenue but, if the benefit is substantial, it may still be capital.

5.13 Although five years was considered sufficient in *Strick* to mean that the expenditure on the asset was to be treated as capital expenditure, the case makes it clear that no rule can be laid down for determining the capital or revenue question by reference to any particular period. It is necessary to consider the nature of the asset in the context of the trade in question.

Does the expenditure remove a restriction or obligation that was an obstacle to the business?

5.14 The costs of removing such an obstacle are likely to be capital, particularly where the expenditure enhances the value of the assets used in the business (*Collins v Joseph Adamson & Co* [1938] 1 KB 477).

Example 5.1

Fred develops software which he licences to other businesses; his main competitor is Harry, who sells software with similar functionality. If Fred were to buy Harry's intellectual property, and perhaps also require Harry to enter into a agreement not to compete with Fred for a period of time in that business sector, then the costs of the purchase and any amount paid for the agreement not to compete will be capital expenditure, even if that intellectual property is then left dormant, as it will improve Fred's access to the market by removing competition.

Does the expenditure reduce revenue expenditure that would otherwise be incurred in carrying on the business?

5.15   Such expenditure will generally be revenue: for example, where a payment is made to terminate an onerous agreement early, eliminating ongoing payments that would otherwise need to be made (*Vodafone Cellular Ltd v Shaw* (1997) 69 TC 376; in this case, a lump sum payment made by the company to relieve it of an obligation to pay annual sums for a period under the terms of an agreement for the supply of know-how was held to be revenue).

Is the expenditure a single lump sum payment or a recurring expense?

5.16   This is probably the least useful test in general terms; it may be used as a tie-breaker but is rarely helpful in isolation: for example, a lump sum may be payable over a period of time. Equally, capital expenditure on an asset which removes an obstacle to the business may be based on the use of the asset acquired and so be a recurring expense (for example, where a business has to acquire the rights to use certain intellectual property in order to complete its own intellectual property, such as a camera maker who licences the right to be able to have its cameras store photographs using a particular proprietary format, the intellectual property to which is owned by another entity).

GENERAL RULES

Revenue expenditure of a trade

5.17   The rules for deduction of revenue expenditure when calculating the profits of a trade for tax purposes are not exhaustively defined by tax legislation.

5.18   Generally an item of expenditure is deductible in computing the profits of a trade chargeable to tax if the deduction is justified by commercial accounting principles (ITTOIA 2005, s 25); however, in some instances, legislation or case law will prohibit a deduction even where it is justified by commercial accounting principles.

5.19   The general principles that all expenditure must satisfy to be deductible as revenue, unless covered by a specific statutory provision allowing its deduction in any event, require expenditure to be:

●   incurred by the taxpayer (*Peter Merchant Ltd v Stedford* (1948) 30 TC 496);

●   incurred for the purposes of the trade (ITTOIA 2005, s 34(1));

- wholly and exclusively so incurred (ITTOIA 2005, s 34(1)); and
- of a revenue rather than a capital nature (ITTOIA 2005, s 33).

5.20 The phrase 'wholly and exclusively for the purposes of the trade' is a question of law (*CIR v Dowdall O'Mahoney & Co Ltd* [1952] 33 TC 259), and requires three main questions to be answered:

- Is the expenditure incurred for the purposes of the trade?
- Is it wholly so incurred?
- Is the trade purpose the exclusive purpose?

The question of exclusivity of purpose is the most difficult to determine; the trade questions are not generally difficult to determine. Motive is always harder to define.

5.21 Where expenditure is incurred for more than one purpose, a deduction for tax purposes can still be taken where an identifiable proportion of the expenditure is incurred wholly and exclusively for the purposes of the trade (ITTOIA 2005, s 34(2)).

5.22 A more detailed exploration of the issues around the question of whether something is wholly and exclusively for the purposes of the trade are outside the scope of this book, as they are not specific to intellectual property.

Capital expenditure

5.23 Capital expenditure cannot immediately be deducted in full, so that there will be a limited reduction in tax on income as a result of the expenditure. However, a tax deduction may be available through capital allowances, which permit the expenditure to be deducted over a period of time, to (arguably) reflect the use of the intellectual property in the business. Unlike accounts amortisation, the deductions for capital allowances do not follow the useful economic life of the asset and so it can take considerably longer than the useful economic life for the cost to be deducted for tax purposes.

5.24 Where capital allowances are not available, the cost of acquiring the asset will not be deductible until it is eventually disposed of (see para **7.10** onwards).

Capital allowances

5.25 Intellectual property capital allowances may be given for capital expenditure incurred in acquiring intellectual property for the benefit of a trade; they are the tax equivalent of the depreciation charges in a profit and loss account, allowing a taxpayer to deduct the capital expenditure over a period of time, to reflect its use.

5.26   There are specific capital allowances for the acquisition of patents (see para **5.60**) and industrial know-how (see para **5.107**), but capital allowances may also be available for some other acquisitions.

5.27   When acquiring intellectual property, capital allowances will generally be given if that intellectual property is considered to be plant.

'Plant' is not defined by statute, but case law has evolved a number of principles that can be used to determine whether something is plant (see para **3.74**).

5.28   In terms of intellectual property, the type of intellectual property that may be acquired as plant may include the rights to software, or the rights to reproduce photographic images: for example, an advertising agency may acquire the rights to use photographs as dummy images or placeholders in mock-ups of campaigns. The photos will not be the actual images used in the final campaign and will be recycled from one campaign to another. The copyright acquired may qualify as plant as a result.

5.29   Capital allowances on plant and machinery are given at 18% per year on a reducing balance basis (see para **3.75** for more details of the system of capital allowances generally).

5.30   Expenditure on acquiring rights to research and development, or acquiring rights arising out of research and development does not qualify for research and development allowances, as these are specifically for expenditure on plant and machinery when undertaking qualifying research and development (see Chapter 4 for more information).

PATENTS

5.31   Patents have perhaps the most comprehensive set of taxation rules, both in legislation and in case law. Patent rights are defined for tax purposes (in various places, including ITTOIA 2005, s 587) as 'the right to do or authorise the doing of anything which would, but for that right, be an infringement of a patent'. There is no specific definition of 'patent rights' in ITA 2007 in respect of the reliefs below, but it is likely that the definition given in ITTOIA 2005 would apply to these reliefs as well.

Tax deducations for patent royalty payments

Deductions for individuals

5.32   Businesses will generally be able to deduct payments of patent royalties under the general rates rules where the royalty is an expense of the business in the accounts and is paid wholly and exclusively for the purposes of the business (ITTOIA 2005, s 25 and s 54).

5.33 Individuals paying royalties for patents for non-business reasons (unusual, but possibly where the patent was acquired as an investment rather than for use in a trade) previously had to rely on somewhat arcane rules relating to charges on income to be able to get a deduction. A specific relief was, however, introduced for such individuals in 2007.

5.34 Accordingly, the following sets out the tax treatment for royalties paid on or after 6 April 2007: see earlier editions of this book for the tax treatment (via annual payments etc) of royalties paid before 6 April 2007.

5.35 Relief is given for a payment of patent royalties (ITA 2007, s 448):

- made by an individual;

- which is a payment from which tax is required to be withheld on payment (under ITA 2007, s 900 or s 903) (see para **5.46**); and

- in respect of which no other deduction is available in calculating the individual's income from any source.

5.36 As a result, this relief is principally available for patent royalties that are not paid in the course of a trade, where tax is withheld from the royalty payment under s 903. Where tax is withheld under s 900, it is because the payment is made for commercial reasons relating to a trade, profession or vocation so that, in practice, a deduction for such a royalty payment would usually be available as an expense of the trade under ITTOIA 2005, s 25 and s 54 instead.

5.37 Where relief is available under s 448, the individual can claim relief equal to the lower of:

- the gross amount of the payment; and

- the individual's modified net income (ITA 2007, s 1025) for that year.

5.38 Relief is given by deducting the amount of the relief in calculating the individual's net income for income tax purposes in that year.

5.39 An individual's 'modified net income' is that individual's net income for the year (as calculated in ITA 2007, s 23), but excluding items such as:

- non-qualifying income (as defined in ITA 2007, s 1026);

- losses carried back from the following year;

- adjustments to profits through averaging (a relief for creative artists, and certain others—see para **18.267**).

See ITA 2007, s 1025 for the full list of exclusions.

5.40   This relief is specifically for patent royalties from which tax has to be deducted under ITA 2007, s 900 or s 903; where patent royalties are paid otherwise (ie where tax is deducted under ITA 2007, s 910 on payments for purchases of UK patents from non-UK resident vendors: see para **5.57**) there is no direct relief for purchasers who are not carrying on a trade.

Example 5.2

An individual, A, pays gross patent royalties of £4,700 in a tax year in which he has net income of £5,000.

Assuming that A's modified net income is the same as his net income, then A can claim relief on the entire amount of the patent royalties paid:

Net income   £5,000

Patent royalties   (£4,700)

Taxable   £300

If A's net income includes an upwards adjustment of £500 as a result of averaging profits received as a creative artist, A's modified net income will be £4,500. The relief for the patent royalties paid will be restricted in this case, as A's modified net income is less than the gross patent royalties paid:

Net income   £4,500

Patent royalties   (£4,500)

Taxable   £0

Relief for partnerships and other non-individuals

5.41   As with individuals, payments of patent royalties to non-UK residents will be deductible under the general rules where the payment is made wholly and exclusively for the purposes of a trade.

5.42   Where the payment is not made for the purpose of a trade, a similar relief to that for individuals is available for persons other than individuals (ie partnerships and non-corporate entities) who make a payment in respect of patent royalties that:

- is a payment in respect of which income tax needs to be withheld (under ITA 2007, s 901 or s 903);

- is not otherwise deductible in calculating that person's income from any source; and

- is not ineligible for relief.

5.43   Relief is given by deduction from net income for the year in the same way as for an individual (see above), relieving the lower of (ITA 2007, s 449):

● the gross amount of the payment; and

● the modified net income of that partnership (or other unincorporated entity) for the relevant tax year (see above for the meaning of modified net income).

5.44   A payment of patent royalties by a person other than an individual is ineligible for relief (ITA 2007, s 450) to the extent that:

● it can only be paid out of capital; or

● it can only be paid out of income that is exempt from income tax; or

● the payment is ultimately borne by a person other than that claiming the relief, unless

— the person who does make the payment is within the charge to income tax on an amount of money; and

— that person does not ultimately bear the cost of the patent royalty as a result of receiving, or having some interest in, that amount on which it is subject to tax.

5.45   Basically, relief is denied where the person making the payment does not pay income tax, as the relief is given to reflect the tax paid on the income from which the royalty is paid. Where the royalty is paid from a source that has not been subject to income tax, no relief is available.

Withholding tax

5.46   Tax is withheld from patent royalty payments by the payer, who then accounts for that tax to HMRC (directly or indirectly). Payments for acquisition of a UK patent from a non-UK resident person must also have tax withheld. These measures ensure that HMRC receive tax on payments which they might otherwise not be aware of.

5.47   Any agreement for paying royalties or other amounts in respect of patents without deduction of tax will not override the payer's obligation to deduct tax; the payer will still be required to account to HMRC for the tax that should have been deducted.

5.48   The rules of withholding tax from payments of royalties were substantially amended and rewritten into ITA 2007; the rules for withholding tax from royalties paid before 6 April 2007 can be found in earlier editions of this book.

UK recipient of patent royalties

5.49 There are requirements to withhold tax from payments of patent royalties which can apply even if the licensor is in the UK (ITA 2007, s 900, s 901 or s 903).

5.50 An individual who acquires a licence of a patent for commercial purposes is required to deduct income tax from any patent royalties which are qualifying annual payments (ITA 2007, s 900; see para **16.59**).

5.51 As a result, no income tax needs to be withheld where the patent royalty payment is made by an individual and is a qualifying annual payment (see para **16.61**) but the patent licence is not acquired for commercial purposes – this is likely to be a relatively rare occurrence.

5.52 Where the royalties are not qualifying annual payments (eg they are not pure income profit, or the royalties are included in the profits of a trade or profession – see para **16.63**), income tax must still be deducted where the payment will be subject to UK income tax or corporation tax (ITA 2007, s 903; see para **16.64**) regardless of whether the licence is acquired for commercial purposes and regardless of whether the payment is made by an individual or another person.

5.53 Income tax must be withheld by the licensee at the basic rate in force for the year in which the royalty becomes due (ITA 2007, s 903(5)(a)). The basic rate of income tax for 2012–13 is 20%. That withheld tax must be accounted for in the licensee's self-assessment return for the year of payment (ITA 2007, s 903(5)(b)) or, where the individual has insufficient income, by direct assessment (ITA 2007, s 963).

5.54 A similar deduction is required where a patent royalty which is a qualifying annual payment is made by a non-individual (such as a partnership); there is no requirement that the payment be made for commercial purposes (ITA 2007, s 901; para **16.59**). The withholding must be notified to HMRC, who will raise an assessment for the amount of tax withheld (ITA 2007, s 963).

Example 5.3

A (an individual) pays B patent royalties of £10,000 per annum; the royalties are a qualifying annual payment, and the licence is acquired for commercial reasons. For 2012–13, A is required to withhold tax of £2,000 (20%) from the payment, paying over the net £8,000 to B.

A is required to account for the £2,000 tax withheld to HMRC; she will report the tax withheld on her self-assessment tax return as an additional sum due to

HMRC in addition to any tax that she is required to pay on her net income and gains.

Non-UK resident recipient of patents royalties

5.55   Where the recipient of income from patents, including a patent royalty, is not resident in the UK there is still a requirement for the payer to withhold tax at the basic rate (20% for 2012–13) from patent royalties which are qualifying annual payments made for commercial purposes. However, a qualifying annual payment must be pure income profit (see para **16.63**). If the licensor also provides services as part of the patent licence, the payment will not be pure income profit (as the licensor will incur expenses in providing the services) and so, in these circumstances, it is arguable that no tax will need to be withheld. As HMRC will look to the payer to account for withholding tax, the payer should ensure that they are satisfied that no withholding will be required.

5.56   Where the royalties are not a qualifying annual payment, there is no requirement to withhold tax under ITA 2007, s 903 (see para **5.50**) as this withholding provision requires that the payment be subject to income tax or corporation tax in the UK; a payment received by non-UK resident recipient would not be subject to these taxes. Again, as the payer is responsible for any withholding tax, the payer should ensure that they are satisfied that the payment is not actually being made to a UK permanent establishment (see para **16.17**) which would be subject to UK tax, in which case withholding would still be required.

Non-UK vendor of UK patent

5.57   Where a UK patent (ie one granted under the Patent Act 1977) is acquired outright from a non-UK resident, the proceeds of sale are subject to UK tax (ITTOIA 2005, s 587 or CTA 2009, s 910; see paras **7.34** and **16.49**). This overrides the normal territorial nature of UK tax law. As it is difficult to ensure compliance with UK tax law by a non-resident (who may not even be aware of the tax charge), tax must be withheld from the payment by the UK purchaser (ITA 2007, s 910; see para **16.49**).

5.58   The amount withheld is not accounted for through the self-assessment return as above; instead, a non-corporate payer is required to notify HMRC 'without delay' (ITA 2007, s 963(2)). An assessment will be raised for income tax equal to the amount deducted from the payment (ITA 2007, s 963(3)).

Double tax treaties

5.59   Where the royalty recipient is resident in a country whose tax treaty with the UK provides an exemption or partial relief from UK tax of royalties, then the recipient can make a treaty claim to HMRC to allow the licensee acquiring the intellectual property (or the licensee's paying agent) to make the payment without deduction of tax or under deduction at a specified rate of tax. The mechanism for making a treaty claim may vary between countries, and details of the requirements are on the HMRC website; where a form is required, this can also usually be downloaded from the HMRC website. See para **16.173** for a wider discussion of tax treaty reliefs.

Patent capital allowances

5.60 Capital allowances provide a tax deduction for capital expenditure by a business, with the deduction being spread over a number of years (unlike accounts amortisation, though, the period of deduction has nothing to do with the economic life of the capital asset acquired). The deduction is front-loaded—the largest deduction is in the first year, with progressively smaller deductions in each following year.

5.61 Under the Capital Allowances Act 2001 (CAA), capital allowances are available if a person carrying on a business incurs 'qualifying expenditure' on the purchase of patent rights (CAA 2001, s 464(1)). The acquisition of a licence in respect of a patent is treated as a purchase of patent rights (CAA 2001, s 466(2)).

5.62 'Qualifying expenditure' is either 'qualifying trade expenditure' or 'qualifying non-trade expenditure' (CAA 2001, s 466(2)).

Qualifying trade expenditure (CAA 2001, s 468)

5.63 Qualifying trade expenditure is capital expenditure incurred on acquiring patent rights for the purposes of a trade. Qualifying expenditure incurred before the trade starts is treated as incurred on the date when the trade starts, unless all the patent rights are sold before the trade in fact starts.

5.64 Patent capital allowances given in respect of qualifying trade expenditure are treated as an expense of the trade in calculating profits for tax purposes (CAA 2001, s 478(a)) so that they can be deducted from any trading income of the business.

Qualifying non-trade expenditure (CAA 2001, s 469)

5.65 Qualifying non-trade expenditure is capital expenditure on acquiring patent rights that is not qualifying trade expenditure (generally, where the patents are acquired as an investment, or by a person not carrying on a trade) where any income that might be received in respect of the rights would be liable to tax.

5.66   Where the allowance is given in respect of qualifying non-trade expenditure, the allowance is given as far as possible by deduction from 'income from patents' for the chargeable period concerned (CAA 2001, ss 479–480). HMRC have confirmed that allowances are available *only* against patent income.

5.67   'Income from patents' is (CAA 2001, s 483):

● any royalty or other sum paid in respect of the user of a patent; and

● any capital sums in respect of patents which are taxable as income; and

● any balancing charge in respect of patent expenditure.

5.68   Where the allowances due for a year of assessment exceed the income from patents for that year, the excess is carried forward and can be deducted from the income from patents in future years of assessment.

Example 5.4

A acquires a patent from B for a single payment of £50,000. The patent is acquired by A for its potential future capital value, rather than for direct use by A, so that the patent is treated as an investment and the expenditure is qualifying non-trade expenditure.

The capital allowance available in the first year on the acquisition of the patent is £12,500 (25% of £50,000: see below).

A's income from patents in that year is £20,000 and so the full capital allowance can be taken as the income from patents is higher than the capital allowance claimed.

If, however, A's income from patents had been only £2,000 of patent royalties and a £4,000 capital sum on the sale of a patent (which is taxable as income), then the income from patents would—at £6,000—be less than the capital allowance in respect of the patent.

In this case, £6,000 would have been deducted from the income from patents as a capital allowance and the balancing £6,500 carried forwards to be deducted from future income from patents.

Connected persons

5.69   Capital allowances may be restricted where the patent rights are acquired from a connected person (as defined in CAA 2001, s 575; see para **18.66** for more details of who is a connected person for this purpose). Tax law imposes a number of restrictions on transactions between connected persons due to the risk that the connection between the parties may mean that the transaction is not necessarily on market terms.

5.70   As a result, where the patent rights are acquired from a connected person, patent allowances cannot be claimed on any excess of the purchase price over the amount determined by the following rules (CAA 2001, s 477(2)–(3)):

- where the vendor brings a disposal value into account, an amount equal to that disposal value;

- where the vendor receives on the sale a capital sum on which he is taxable as non-trading income, an amount equal to that sum;

- where neither of the above applies, the lowest of:

    — the market value of the rights at the date of acquisition;

    — the vendor's capital expenditure on his acquisition of the rights; and

    — the capital expenditure incurred by a person connected with the vendor on acquiring the rights.

These restrictions are intended to ensure that there is no tax advantage to the transaction.

Anti-avoidance

5.71   Allowances will also be denied or restricted as above where the sole or main benefit that appears to have been derived from a sale of patent rights (or a series of transactions including a sale) is the obtaining of an allowance (CAA 2001, s 481).

Rights to acquire patent rights

5.72   In some cases, the rights bought are not the patent rights themselves but, instead, the right to acquire the patent rights in an invention once the patent has been granted. Given the length of time involved in the patent application process, these rights to acquire are often traded. This ensures that the acquirer will have first call on the rights, rather than facing competition for them once the patent application has been made and competitors become aware of the invention from the publicly available patent application information.

5.73   Expenditure on such right to acquire is deemed to be expenditure on the acquisition of patent rights (CAA 2001, s 465) and, if the patent rights are subsequently acquired, is then deemed to be part of the expenditure on the acquisition of the actual patent rights.

Example 5.5

A pays B £20,000 for the right to acquire B's patent rights in respect of a new drug that will fit well within A's product portfolio. When the patent is finally granted, A acquires the patent from B for an additional £70,000.

A's acquisition expenditure in respect of the patent is a total of £90,000, being the £20,000 paid for the right to acquire, and the patent itself.

Capital allowances are available first on the £20,000 paid for the right to acquire, and later on the additional £70,000 paid for the patent.

Calculation of capital allowance

5.74   Allowances are calculated in a similar way to capital allowances for plant; a 'pool' of expenditure on patent rights is created in the same way (CAA 2001, s 470).

5.75   There is a separate pool:

● for each trade in respect of which there has been qualifying trade expenditure on patent rights; and

● for all non-trade expenditure on patent rights.

5.76   The allowance for each period is calculated separately for each pool and depends on:

● the available qualifying expenditure (AQE) in that pool for that period; and

● the total disposal receipts (TDR) to be brought into account in that pool for that period.

5.77   If AQE exceeds TDR, the taxpayer is entitled to a writing-down allowance for the period. The allowance is 25% of the amount by which AQE exceeds TDR (CAA 2001, s 472(1)). This rate has not been reduced in line with the reduction in the rate of plant and machinery allowances.

Example 5.6

Taking the example above, and assuming that A's purchases are regarded as trade expenditure, then on A's purchase of the right to acquire B's patent, the available qualifying expenditure is £20,000.

The capital allowance available in the first year is £5,000 (25% of £20,000). In the second year, it will be £3,750 (25% of £(20,000–5,000).

Available qualifying expenditure (AQE)

5.78   AQE consists of:

- qualifying expenditure allocated to the pool for that period in accordance with the allocation rules described below; plus

- any unrelieved qualifying expenditure carried forward in the pool from the previous chargeable period under the rules for such expenditure described below;

- unrelieved qualifying expenditure is available to carry forward is the excess less the writing-down allowance made for the period; or, if no writing-down allowance is claimed for the period, the entire excess.

5.79   Under the allocation rules referred to above, qualifying expenditure:

- cannot be allocated to the pool for a period if it has been taken into account in available qualifying expenditure for an earlier period;

- cannot be allocated to the pool for a period before that in which the expenditure is incurred; and

- cannot be allocated to the pool for a period if in any earlier period the rights to which it relates have come to an end without having been revived, or have been entirely disposed of.

Example 5.7

Following on from the example above, assuming that A has sufficient income from patents to fully utilise the capital allowances, the unrelieved qualifying expenditure carried forward to the second year is £15,000.

If A then purchases the patent rights themselves in the following year, the acquisition costs of £70,000 are added to the pool, giving a total available qualifying expenditure of £85,000.

The capital allowance available in the second year is £21,250 (25% of £85,000).

Assuming that A has sufficient income from patents to fully utilise the capital allowances, the unrelieved qualifying expenditure carried forwards is £63,750.

In the third year, if there are no subsequent acquisitions, the capital allowance available is £15,937.50 (25% of £63,750).

Total disposal receipts

5.80   Total disposal receipts are the proceeds of any disposal of the whole or part of the patents rights that are capital receipts, including the receipt of a lump sum from a finance lease in respect of a patent right (CAA 2001, s 476(2)).

Example 5.8

Following on from the example above, A disposes of the patent in the fourth year for £25,000.

The total disposal receipts are therefore £25,000.

The available qualifying expenditure is £47,812.50 (£63,750 less £15,937.50) and so AQE exceeds TDR by £22,812.50. The capital allowance available in the year of disposal is therefore £5,703.13 (25% of £22,812.50), and the AQE carried forwards is £17,109.37.

Reductions in allowancea

5.81   If the chargeable period is not 12 months, the amount of the allowance is proportionately increased or reduced.

5.82   If in the case of qualifying trade expenditure the trade has been carried on for only part of the chargeable period, the amount is proportionately reduced.

5.83   A taxpayer claiming a writing-down allowance can choose to have the allowance reduced to a specified amount (CAA 2001, s 472(4)): for example, to ensure that group relief can be maximised.

COPYRIGHT

Licensing copyright: tax relief on copyright royalty payments

5.84   The deductibility of a copyright royalty (which includes any other payment similar to a royalty) as a revenue expense has not generally been disputed where incurred as trade expenditure; it will usually be deductible as an expense of the trade (ITTOIA 2005, s 25 and s 54). Note that there is no relief for non-traders who acquire copyright licences; there is no equivalent to ITA 2007, s 448 (see para **5.35**) for copyrights.

Withholding tax on copyright royalties

5.85   As with patents, withholding taxes apply to payment of copyright royalties. Copyright royalties can include both periodical payments and lump sums but, where such lump sums represent advances on royalties or payments of the nature of royalties, they may not be capital in nature for the payer unless they can be shown to confer an enduring benefit and so, in practice, withholding tax can apply to lump sum payments for copyright as well as to periodic payments. This will be the case even where the lump sum is a capital receipt for the licensor (an unusual situation, see para **7.59**).

5.86 For example, in *IRC v Longmans Green & Co Ltd* (1932) 17 TC 272 it was held that a lump sum payment in advance for the right to translate and publish a fixed number of copies of a book by a non-resident French author was a copyright royalty in respect of which tax needed to be deducted by the licensee.

5.87 Note that HMRC take the view that payments to authors to create specific works will generally be treated as professional fees and so payments to non-UK residents may not be subject to withholding tax (see para **18.287**).

5.88 Any agreement for paying a copyright royalty without deduction of tax will not override the licensee's obligation to deduct tax; the licensee will still be required to account to HMRC for the tax that should have been deducted.

Deduction of income tax: UK licensors

5.89 The following applies to royalties paid on or after 6 April 2007; see earlier editions of this book for details of withholding tax obligations before 6 April 2007.

5.90 An individual who acquires intellectual property for commercial purposes is required to deduct income tax from copyright royalties which are qualifying annual payments (ITA 2007, s 900; see para **16.61**). As noted above, in practice, almost all copyright royalties will be paid for commercial purposes. This requirement to withhold tax applies regardless of the location of the owner or recipient of the payment.

5.91 A similar deduction is required where a copyright royalty which is a qualifying annual payment is made by a non-individual (such as a partnership); there is no requirement that the payment be made for commercial purposes (ITA 2007, s 901; see para **16.59**).

5.92 Income tax must be withheld by the licensee at the basic rate in force for the year in which the royalty becomes due (ITA 2007, s 903(5)(a)). That withheld tax must be accounted for in the licensee's self-assessment return for the year of payment (ITA 2007, s 903(5)(b)) or, where the individual has insufficient income, by direct assessment (ITA 2007, s 963).

5.93   Note that there is no equivalent of ITA 2007, s 903 (see para **5.52**) for copyright royalties. As a result, where the copyright royalty is not a qualifying annual payment (eg the royalty forms part of the profits of a trade or profession of the recipient, or the royalty is not a pure income profit: see para **16.63**), there is no requirement to withhold tax from the royalty. As most copyright royalties will be included in the profits of a trade or profession for tax purposes, this means that the requirement to withhold tax from UK recipients of copyright royalties is much more restricted than the requirement to withhold tax from UK recipients of patent royalties.

Withholding tax: non-UK recipient of copyright royalties

5.94   Tax must be withheld from payments of copyright royalties that are qualifying annual payments, where the payment is made by an individual who acquires the licence for commercial purposes (ITA 2007, s 900; see para **5.90**); there is no geographic restriction to this withholding requirement. Similarly, there is no geographic restriction for the withholding requirement for payments by non-individuals where the copyright royalty is a qualifying annual payment (ITA 2007, s 901; see para **5.91**).

5.95   Where tax does not need to be withheld under s 900 or s 901 (ie where the royalty is not a qualifying annual payment, see para **16.61**), there may still be a requirement to withhold tax from certain non-UK resident licensors who are nevertheless within the scope of UK tax (ITA 2007, s 906; see para **16.65**), usually where they are trading in the UK.

5.96   Certain payments are excluded from the withholding requirement even where the conditions for withhold are otherwise satisfied. These include (HMRC Manual INTM342530; this refers to the old rules but the principles should remain the same for the new withholding tax rules):

* royalties on copyright works exported for exploitation outside the UK;

* lump sum payments for an outright purchase of a copyright, or part of it (eg serial rights);

* payments to overseas contributors to newspapers and periodicals;

* royalties for film copyright payments (to the owner of the copyright in the film only, not to the copyright owner of the script or scenario on which the film is based);

* payments for a software licence allowing only a limited right to copy to facilitate use (HMRC Manual INTM34630).

5.97   As a result, where the recipient of a copyright royalty is not resident in the UK, withholding tax is required only where:

- the recipient is not a creative professional receiving a fee (see para **18.287**); and

- is chargeable to UK income tax or corporation tax; and

- the payment is not otherwise excluded from withholding tax.

This is likely to be relatively unusual for non-corporate entities but, as the payer is liable to account for withholding tax to HMRC, the payer should satisfy themselves that the recipient is not in fact chargeable to UK income tax or corporation tax.

5.98   The withheld tax must be notified to HMRC and will be accounted for by direct assessment (ITA 2007, s 963).

Agents' commission

5.99   If a copyright royalty is paid by or through a UK resident agent who is entitled to deduct commission from the payment, the requirement to deduct and account for tax applies to the payment as reduced by the agent's commission (ITA 2007, s 908; HMRC Manual INTM345230).

5.100   Where the amount of the commission is not known at the time when the payment is made, or the payer does not realise that a commission will be payable, tax must be deducted from the full amount of the payment (ITA 2007, s 908(2)). The owner of the royalties may be able to reclaim the tax relating to the commission element of the payment by submitting a UK tax return.

5.101   For all tax purposes a payment of copyright royalties from which tax needs to be deducted is treated as made at the time when it is made by the licensee, and not when it is paid by or through an agent (ITA 2007, s 909).

Example 5.9

A pays a royalty of £10,000 to C, a licensor resident outside the UK. The payment is made through C's agent, B. B takes a commission of 5% of the royalty before paying it to C.

If A is not aware that B will take a commission, or does not know the amount, A is required to withhold tax from the full payment, ie withhold £2,000 and account for that to HMRC. B can later apply to HMRC to recover the tax withheld on the commission element.

If A is aware that B will deduct 5% commission, then A can withhold tax on the net payment of £9,500 that C will receive (95% of £10,000). The tax withheld is then £1,900.

Double tax treaties

5.102   Where the royalty recipient is resident in a country whose tax treaty with the UK provides an exemption or partial relief from UK tax of royalties then the recipient can apply to HMRC to give notice enabling the licensee (or his paying agent) to make the payment without deduction of tax or under deduction at a specified rate of tax.

Withholding tax on design rights and other rights similar to copyright

5.103   The provisions requiring withholding from copyright royalties paid to an owner whose place of abode is not usually within the UK (see para **5.85** onwards) also apply to design rights and public lending rights. In summary, these require the deduction of tax from royalties or other sums paid periodically in respect of design rights or public lending rights, where the recipient is not UK resident but is still nevertheless subject to UK tax (ITA 2007, s 906). Where the recipient is in the UK, the royalty would have to be a qualifying annual payment and the arrangements fall into ITTOIA 2005, s 900 or s 901 (see paras **5.90–5.91**) for withholding to be required.

KNOW-HOW AND SHOW-HOW

5.104   A payment under a licence of know-how is generally deductible as revenue expenditure as a trading expense of a business in the usual way. Given the nature of know-how (see para **2.87**), it is not likely that know-how would be acquired for non-trade purposes.

Payments for know-how: tax relief

5.105   Payments for know-how and show-how are usually considered to be revenue expenditure, rather than capital, as the transaction is generally regarded as connected with the trade itself (particularly with regard to show-how), rather than a payment to acquire an asset of the trade.

5.106   In *British Sugar Manufacturers Ltd v Harris* (1938) 21 TC 528 a payment to obtain technical and financial knowledge and experience was held to be deductible as revenue for tax purposes.

Withholding tax

5.107   Payments for know-how may be annual payments (see *Delage v Nugget Polish Co Ltd* (1905) 92 LT 682, which held that payments of a percentage of receipts over a period of 40 years in exchange for the use of a secret process were annual payments). However, they are unlikely to be qualifying annual payments (see para **16.61**) as the definition requires that the payment be taxed as miscellaneous income of the recipient; a receipt for a licence of know-how will almost always be taxed as part of the profits of the trade from which it is licensed. If the payment is not a qualifying annual payment, the withholding requirements in ITA 2007, s 900 or s 901 (see paras **5.90–5.91**) will not apply.

Acquisition of industrial know-how: capital allowances

5.108   It is possible for a payment for know-how to be considered to be capital if, as part of the transaction, the licensor also agrees not to do business in a competing geographical area. The payment may be capital because the effect is to improve the position of the business to an extent which is of enduring benefit to the business. This can be considered to be a part-disposal of the asset by the licensor, as the licensor is limiting what it can do in the future.

5.109   Expenditure that is capital expenditure on the acquisition of know-how may qualify for specific know-how capital allowances which are similar to patent capital allowances (see above), if 'qualifying expenditure' is incurred on the acquisition of know-how for use in a trade carried on or to be carried on by the taxpayer.

5.110   The allowance is only available if relief is not otherwise available in respect of the expenditure (CAA 2001, s 455(1)). If the expenditure can be relieved as a trading expense then the know-how capital allowance is not available, and would not usually be preferred in any case: deduction as a trading expense gives a larger immediate tax deduction, not a deduction over time.

5.111   Know-how is defined, for the purposes of the allowance, as any industrial information or techniques likely to assist in (CAA 2001, s 452):

● manufacturing or processing goods or materials;

● working a source of mineral deposits; or

● carrying out any agricultural, forestry or fishing operations.

Payments between connected persons

5.112   Acquisition expenditure on know-how cannot be deducted where one party controls the other, or where both are under common control. This exclusion does not apply where one individual acquires know-how from another individual.

5.113   The control test will be met where (CAA 2001, s 575):

- the buyer is a body of persons (a company or partnership, generally) controlled by the seller; or

- the seller is a body of persons controlled by the buyer; or

- the same person controls both the buyer and the seller, where both buyer and seller are each a body of persons.

5.114   Control, for these purposes, means (CAA 2001, s 574):

- in the case of a company, the power to control how the company acts, through:

  — a share holding; or

  — voting power; or

  — the terms of the Articles of Association or similar document (such as a shareholders' agreement);

- in the case of a partnership, the right to more than half of the:

  — assets; or

  — income; and

  — partnership.

Commercial know-how

5.115   HMRC have stated that no capital allowances are available for expenditure on commercial know-how because it does not fall within the statutory definition of know-how (HMRC Manual CA70030).

5.116   Commercial know-how does not assist directly in the manufacturing and processing operations of a trade but is concerned primarily with the selling of the product once it has been manufactured. Commercial know-how includes information about marketing, packaging or distribution.

Acquisition of know-how with trade

5.117   Where there is an acquisition of a trade or part of a trade together with know-how used in it, the acquisition of know-how is treated as the acquisition of goodwill (ITTOIA 2005, s 194) and, therefore, within the capital gains tax provisions. In such circumstances the expenditure will not qualify for capital allowances because no capital allowances are available for expenditure on the acquisition of goodwill.

5.118   However, if both parties so elect, the know-how is not treated as goodwill and the purchase will then qualify for capital allowances. Such an election cannot be made if the parties are under common control. If the trade in which the know-how was used was carried on wholly outside the UK before the disposal and the vendor and purchaser are not under common control, the treatment of the consideration for the know-how as a payment for goodwill applies only to the vendor; the purchaser may therefore be able to claim capital allowances in respect of his expenditure.

Calculation of allowance

5.119   Allowances are calculated in a similar way to patent allowances for plant; a 'pool' of expenditure on know-how is created for each trade in respect of which the taxpayer has qualifying expenditure (CAA 2001, s 456). However, there is no pool for non-trading know-how because it is considered that know-how cannot be held for non-trading purposes.

5.120   The allowance for each period is calculated for each pool and depends on:

* the available qualifying expenditure (AQE) in that pool for that period; and

* the total disposal value (TDV) to be brought into account in that pool for that period.

5.121   If AQE exceeds TDV, the taxpayer is entitled to a writing-down allowance for the period. The allowance is 25% of the amount by which AQE exceeds TDV (CAA 2001, s 458(1); see paras **5.78–5.80** for details on determining AQE and TDV). As with patent allowances, this rate does not decline in line with the rate for plant and machinery allowances.

Example 5.10

A pays B £10,000 for know-how in respect of a particular process that B has developed; the purchase qualifies for capital allowances.

As this is A's first acquisition of know-how, a new special pool is set up for the know-how. The initial balance in the pool is £10,000 and, in the first year, a know-how capital allowance of £2,500 (25% of £10,000) is deducted. The unrelieved expenditure carried forward is £7,500.

In the second year, capital allowances of £1,875 are available (25% of £7,500) and unrelieved expenditure of £5,625 is carried forward.

A disposes of the know-how in the third year for a net disposal value of £5,000. The available qualifying expenditure is £5,625 and so AQE exceeds TDR by £625. The capital allowance available in the year of disposal is therefore £156.25 and the unrelieved expenditure carried forwards is £468.75.

Balancing charges and allowances

5.122   As with patent allowances (see para **5.81**), a balancing allowance deduction is only available for a know-how pool in the final chargeable period of the taxpayer business (CAA 2001, s 457) or when the pool's written down value reaches £1. Once know-how capital allowances have started to be claimed the taxpayer will continue to claim capital allowances on the declining balance of AQE in the know-how pool, even though the know-how has been disposed of, until the pool is exhausted (in which case the allowance is £1) or the taxpayer ceases to trade.

5.123   A balancing charge is made in any accounting period where the TDR exceeds the AQE; the amount of the balancing charge is the excess of TDR over AQE; the charge is treated as a taxable receipt of the trade.

Example 5.11

If, in Example 5.11, A had disposed of the know-how in the fourth year for £7,000, a balancing charge would have arisen:

The available qualifying expenditure for that accounting period was £5,625 and so TDR (£7,000) exceeds AQE by £1,375.

The balancing charge would be £1,375.

Reductions in allowance

5.124   As with patent allowances, if the chargeable period is not 12 months or the trade has been carried on for part only of the chargeable period, the amount of the allowance is proportionately increased or reduced.

A taxpayer claiming a know-how allowance can choose to reduce the allowance claimed to a specified amount (CAA 2001, s 458(4)): for example, to maximise group relief claims.

CHECKLIST

5.125

- Has the intellectual property been acquired for the purposes of a trade?
- Is the acquisition a capital transaction? If yes, is the acquisition of a patent or know-how?

— If yes, capital allowances should be available.

— If no, a tax deduction will generally only be available when the asset is eventually disposed of.

● Does tax need to be withheld from the payment for the acquisition?

— Is the recipient in the UK? Check ITA 2007, ss 900, 901 and 903.

— Is the recipient outside the UK? Check ITA 2007, s 906.

Chapter 6

Exploiting intellectual property

Summary: Intellectual property can be exploited through direct use, by licensing to others, or as protection against competition.

Income derived from direct use of intellectual property, in manufacturing or services, will be treated as income from the sale of manufactured goods, or from the supply of services and so will be taxed as trading income in the usual way. Income from licensing intellectual property will generally be taxed as trading income of a business, or miscellaneous income where the relevant activities do not amount to trading.

Where intellectual property is used to improve market access, by protecting against competition, the owner does not usually derive any income directly from the intellectual property unless litigation is required: in that case, the tax treatment will depend on the terms of any settlement or court award in respect of the intellectual property.

- Exploitation or disposal? (para **6.6**)
- Expenditure (para **6.14**)
- Receipts: general rules (para **6.16**)
- Revenue or capital? (para **6.23**)
- International aspects (para **6.35**)
- Patents (para **6.41**)
- Copyright (para **6.49**)
- Know-how (para **6.55**)

INTRODUCTION

6.1　　These rules apply to receipts from exploiting intellectual property which was created or acquired by an individual or partnership (or other non-corporate entity) at any time.

6.2　　The rules will not often apply to companies; although the corporate intangibles tax rules generally only apply to intellectual property assets that were created or acquired by the company or a related party before 1 April 2002, there is an exception in respect of royalties so that royalties received by a company will be within the corporate intangibles tax rules regardless of when the intellectual property fixed asset was created or acquired (see para **8.33**). However, these rules will still apply to intellectual property of companies which are excluded from the corporate intangibles tax rules (see para **8.29** onwards).

6.3   The rights relating to intellectual property are negative rather than positive: they allow the owner to stop others from using the protected property. From a tax and accounting perspective, intellectual property is generally only regarded as valuable for the owner to the extent that it creates economic benefits.

6.4   Economic benefits in relation to intellectual property can be derived:

•   by direct use of the intellectual property: where the owner uses the intellectual property as the basis for products and/or services which generate income;

•   by licensing the intellectual property to third parties, generating royalties and similar payments; or

•   as protection, preventing others from competing and so improving the owner's market access. This will not usually result in direct receipts for the owner but will, instead, improve income from the owner's business. It may also give rise to receipts under settlements or court awards, where the intellectual property needs to be enforced against others.

6.5   Direct use of intellectual property for the purposes of a business by individuals and other non-corporate entities is outside the scope of this book (apart from in respect of direct exploitation of patents by companies which qualifies for the patent box; see Chapter 13), as the expenditure and receipts incurred or received in direct use of intellectual property in fact relate to the goods and services being produced rather than the intellectual property itself: the general rules on such expenditure and receipts will apply for tax purposes, and not any specific rules relating to intellectual property.

EXPLOITATION OR DISPOSAL?

6.6   At first sight, the distinction between disposing of intellectual property as a capital asset and exploiting it to produce income should be straightforward. In practice, however, the distinction can be complicated, particularly when dealing with licences where the consideration mechanisms can include a number of different elements: for example: a one-off lump sum payment; milestone payments on reaching certain further development criteria;

and ongoing royalties for the use of the intellectual property on a percentage or per-item basis. The difficulty of ascribing an overall value to the intellectual property asset, especially where it has not already been used for the purposes of a trade, means that consideration can often involve participation in the success (or otherwise) of the use of that intellectual property by the licensee, to produce a more equitable form of consideration for both parties.

6.7   Accordingly, the tax treatment may depend on whether the intellectual property:

- will be exhausted or diminished in value by the transaction, or

- will retain its value for the owner despite the transaction (see Lord Reid's judgment in *Jeffrey v Rolls-Royce Ltd* (1962) 40 TC 443, further referred to in para **6.57**).

6.8   Where the copyright will be diminished in value, HMRC are more likely to accept that the transaction is capital. In this case, the accounts may assist where the intellectual property has been recognised on the balance sheet (generally, where it has been acquired by the business): if the balance sheet shows a reduction in value of the intellectual property (full or partial) then it is likely that a disposal or part-disposal of the asset has occurred for tax purposes.

6.9   An outright disposal (see Chapter 7) of intellectual property is not, for the purposes of this book, regarded as exploiting that intellectual property. 'Exploitation' is taken to indicate that the owner of the intellectual property may, concurrently or in another territory or in future, deal with the rights to that intellectual property again directly or by licensing it to other third parties.

Part disposals

6.10   Where the exploitation limits the rights of the owner of the relevant intellectual property—for example, on the sale of the film rights to a novel or on the grant of an exclusive licence in respect of software—the receipts are more likely to be capital because the licensor is giving up the rights to exploit within a territory (cf *Evans Medical Supplies Ltd v Moriarty* (1957) 37 TC 540). Although such exploitation will allow the owner of the intellectual property to retain overall ownership of that intellectual property, such a sale is effectively a part disposal of the intellectual property.

6.11   Part disposals are covered in more detail in Chapter 7.

Litigation awards and settlements

6.12   The receipts from successful litigation will, generally, be treated for tax purposes as derived from the specific elements of the award (eg where a licence is granted, the receipts relating to that licence will be taxed accordingly).

6.13   Where the receipt is compensation for damage to the intellectual property, the recipient is generally treated as having partly disposed of the intellectual property (see Chapter 7 and para **17.57**).

EXPENDITURE

6.14   The tax issues relating to exploitation of intellectual property will, usually, be related to income rather than expenditure. However, in order to continue to exploit the intellectual property, the owner will generally have to pay on-going maintenance costs, including:

● specific renewal costs for trademarks, design rights, and patents (ITTOIA 2005, ss 89–90; see para **3.59**); and

● staff (and/or external adviser) costs of continuing to maintain the registrations and manage the intellectual property (deductible as trading expenses under the general rules; see para **3.49**).

6.15   Other payments (eg in relation to litigation over the intellectual property) are likely to also be deductible as revenue expenditure under the general rules. Any payment that is intended to preserve the existing assets of a business, without addition or improvement, is generally considered to be income expenditure. For example, in *Southern v Borax Consolidated Ltd* (1940) 23 TC 597, Lawrence J held that:

'... the principle which is to be deduced from the cases is that ... if no alteration is made in the fixed capital asset by the payment, then it is properly attributable to revenue, being in substance a matter of maintenance, the maintenance of the capital structure or the capital assets of the company.'

RECEIPTS: GENERAL RULES

6.16   The general rule for receipts is that revenue receipts will be taxed as income, either of a trade (ITTOIA 2005, Pt 2) or as miscellaneous income from intellectual property (ITTOIA 2005, s 579).

6.17   Any capital receipts will be taxed as a capital gain; the net proceeds after any deductible costs of acquisition will be subject to capital gains tax for individuals (under TCGA 1992). This can be at a considerably lower tax rate than for revenue receipts (in 2012–13, the maximum rate of capital gains tax is 28% whereas the maximum published rate of income tax is 50%). Companies will be subject to corporation tax on capital gains; this will be at the same rate as income, as corporation tax is charged on both income and gains of companies. Where the recipient has brought-forward capital losses, the taxable gain can be reduced by the use of those losses.

6.18 As well as the general rules, there are some specific rules which will apply in certain circumstances, depending on the type of intellectual property involved. Where no specific rules apply, the transaction will need to be considered under the general rules described above.

Withholding tax: from UK payers

6.19 Royalties (including lump sums treated as income rather than capital) may have basic rate tax deducted from the payment by UK taxpayers (ITA 2007, ss 900, 901, 903; see Chapter 16). This is likely to be more usual for patent royalties, under s 903, than for royalties in general under s 900 or s 901.

6.20 The deduction is treated as income tax paid by the recipient so that it is set against the tax due from the recipient for that accounting period. However, HMRC can elect to recover tax from the recipient of the royalties if the licensee has failed to deduct tax (*Grosvenor Place Estates v Roberts* [1961] Ch 148).

6.21 Royalty (or similar) payments can be received gross in certain circumstances (see para **16.69**) when made by a corporate payer.

6.22 Individuals cannot receive payments of royalties gross from a UK payer where withholding is required by law, even if the payer believes that the individual is subject to UK income tax.

REVENUE OR CAPITAL?

6.23 The distinction between revenue receipts (taxed as income) and capital receipts (potentially subject to capital gains tax) is generally less important when considering the exploitation of intellectual property which is retained by the owner. Such receipts will almost always be taxed as income, either of a trade or as miscellaneous income of the UK owner, as the property is not disposed of.

Licensing as a trading activity

6.24 There is no requirement that an intellectual property owner use its intellectual property to produce goods and services directly; many biotechnology companies create intellectual property specifically to license it to others for their use. This can be taken to extremes, usually by acquirers of intellectual property rather than creators of intellectual property. The term 'patent troll' is sometimes used to describe an intellectual property owner that owns and enforces a patent portfolio in an unduly aggressive manner, usually with no intention of producing goods or services with the patents. Such owners will generally acquire their intellectual property on an opportunistic basis from businesses that have ceased trading.

6.25   Where intellectual property is regularly exploited by licensing to others, the owner will be assessed on profits from the exploitation of the intellectual property rights as trading income (ITTOIA 2005, Pt 2; where the intellectual property is a pre-1 April 2002 asset owned by a company, the income is taxed under CTA 2009, Pt 3), even if the receipt is a one-off payment.

6.26   This is supported in a know-how case, *British Dyestuffs Corpn (Blackley) Ltd v CIR* (1924) 12 TC 586, which related to an exchange of know-how for which the UK taxpayer was entitled to receive a sum of £25,000 each year for ten years. The Court of Appeal held that the receipt was revenue and not capital.

6.27   The court held that the test to apply was to identify whether the taxpayer was parting with any of its property for a purchase price or whether it was 'a method of trading by which it acquires this particular sum of money as part of the profits and gains of that trade'. If the transaction is an isolated occurrence, receipts are less likely to be revenue whereas if the business regularly licenses intellectual property to others the receipts are almost certain to be revenue (see Upjohn LJ's comments in *Jeffrey v Rolls-Royce Ltd* (1962) 40 TC 443).

6.28   Whether or not a business is carrying on a trade in exploiting intellectual property will be a question of fact, although there are a number of key areas that are taken into account when considering the question of whether a trade is being carried on (see para **3.8** onwards).

6.29   Where the business retains patents with the intention of exploiting those patents by granting licences, this will generally be regarded as a trading activity (cf *Noddy Subsidiary Rights Co Ltd v IRC* (1966) 43 TC 458), but see also para **3.12**; in this case the licensing was part of an on-going trade and not a one-off transaction).

Royalties

6.30   Licence payments received on a royalty basis for the use of the intellectual property are generally treated as income of the recipient for tax purposes. They may be taxed either as profits of a trade, profession or vocation income under the general rule in ITTOIA 2005, Pt 2 or as investment income under ITTOIA 2005, Pt 5 depending on whether or not the intellectual property is held for the purposes of a trade. In general, royalties and other income from intellectual property will be regarded as investment income if such income has not been included in the profits of a trade or profession (ITTOIA 2005, s 579).

6.31   As noted at the beginning of this chapter, royalty receipts of a company are now within the corporate intangibles tax rules even where the intellectual property is a pre-1 April 2002 asset, unless the company itself is excluded. Where the company itself is excluded from the corporate intangibles tax rules, the company will be treated in a similar way to unincorporated intellectual property owners, subject to tax on receipts either as trading income (CTA 2009, Pt 3) or miscellaneous income (CTA 2009, Pt 10).

Past and future use

6.32   If a payment is made retrospectively—and so relates primarily to the past use of an intellectual property right—it is likely to be considered to be income where the owner of the intellectual property has retained that asset (cf *Constantinesco v R* (1927) 11 TC 730).

6.33   However, where a one-off payment is made for the future use of intellectual property, it is more likely to be treated as capital where it also precludes the owner from using the asset (cf: *Desoutter Bros Ltd v J E Hanger & Co Ltd and Artificial Limb Makers Ltd* (1936) 15 ATC 49). In this case, the transaction is closer to a part-disposal of the intellectual property (see para **7.6**).

Miscellaneous receipts

6.34   Payments for non-competition covenants or keep-out clauses will generally be capital receipts, since they will usually involve the recipient giving up certain rights. In *Murray v ICI* (1966) 44 TC 175 a lump sum keep-out fee was agreed, payable by instalments. It was held to be capital, being ancillary to an exclusive patent licence where receipt of payments under the licence were also treated as capital (although note that, now, any receipts in respect of patents will be taxed as income in all cases; see para **7.34**).

INTERNATIONAL ASPECTS

6.35   The UK tax system generally imposes tax on either:

● the worldwide income of a UK resident taxpayer; or

● the UK source income of a foreign resident.

6.36 To determine whether a owner of intellectual property will be subject to UK income tax on the receipts from exploiting that intellectual property, it is necessary to consider:

- whether the owner is UK resident; and if not:;

- whether the intellectual property produces UK source income. HMRC take the view that intellectual property income has a UK source if a payment is made in the UK for UK exploitation of that intellectual property (HMRC Manual INTM 345230).

See para **2.5** for further details on the location of intellectual property for tax purposes, and para **16.182** for details of UK tax relief for taxes also paid or withheld overseas on the same intellectual property income.

Income of a non-trader

6.37 Income from exploiting intellectual property by a UK resident person who is not carrying on a trade or profession in this country is assessable as miscellaneous income under ITTOIA 2005, Pt 5 (ITTOIA 2005, s 579).

Withholding taxes: from international payers

6.38 Double tax treaties generally provide that royalties should be taxed in the recipient's country of residence. The recipient is usually the owner of the rights, so the location of the owner of the rights takes precedence over the location of the rights themselves if they are registered elsewhere. Nevertheless, most tax treaties also include a right for the country of origin of the payment to withhold tax on that payment.

Overseas licensor

6.39 Where a payment of royalties is received by a non-UK licensor from a UK licensee, basic rate UK income tax may have been deducted from those royalties (ITA 2007, ss 900, 901, 903, or 906; see Chapter 16). That withholding tax cannot be recovered from HMRC, but the licensor may have some tax relief for the withholding in their local jurisdiction: this will depend on the local laws.

UK licensor

6.40 Where the royalty is paid to a UK licensor from overseas, tax will often be withheld at the source of the payment. Relief is available against UK income tax due on the same payment (see para **16.174** for further details).

PATENTS

6.41   All receipts from the exploitation of patents are taxed as trading income (ITTOIA 2005, Pt 2) where it is exploited in the course of a trade, or otherwise as miscellaneous income (ITTOIA 2005, s 579), and will be taxed in full in the year of receipt.

Capital payments

6.42   A lump sum receipt for exploitation of patent rights will usually be capital where the rights licensed are for future use that is commercially equivalent to an outright disposal of those rights, including:

- exclusive use of the patent rights for all of the remaining life of the patent; or

- unlimited use of the patent rights for a specified term of years.

6.43   Essentially, where the terms of a licence include provisions that effectively restrain the licensor from using the invention, rather than simply undertaking not to enforce the right to complain of an infringement, a lump sum payment is likely to be regarded as a capital (cf *British Salmson Aero Engines v IRC* (1938) 22 TC 29) receipt for the part disposal of the patent rights.

6.44   For more details on the taxation of capital receipts on the disposal of patents, see para **7.33** onwards.

Spreading relief

6.45   Where payments in respect of patents are received for past use of the patent (eg on settlement of litigation for infringement (see para **17.55**), the recipient may claim relief (ITA 2007, s 461) if:

- the period of past use is two complete years or more;

- the payment is made in a lump sum; and

- the payment is one from which income is required to be withheld under ITA 2007, s 903 (see below).

6.46   For relevant corporate recipients, in relation to pre-1 April 2002 patents, a similar relief is available under TA 1988, s 527. This has not been rewritten into the updated Corporation Tax Acts of 2009 and 2010.

6.47   The relief enables the payments to be spread as follows:

- where the payment relates to a period of past use of at least six years, a claim can be made to spread the payment received and treat it as a royalty received in six equal annual instalments, the last of which was paid on the date on which the payment was in fact made.

● where the payment relates to a period of more than two but less than six complete years, a claim can be made to spread the payment received and treat it as a royalty received in as many equal annual instalments as there are complete years in that period of past use.

6.48   The relief is the difference between the tax payable in the year of receipt if no relief were given, and the total tax that would have been paid if the royalty had in fact been spread over the period of use. This relief is primarily of use for taxpayers with income below the higher rate of tax, where the royalties (if taxed solely in the year of receipt) would be taxed principally at the higher rate of tax; it will also be of use where the rate of income tax has increased during the period of use.

Example 6.1

A receives a gross royalty payment from B of £100,000 in August 2011; the payment is for B's use of A's patent over the past five years, as A has granted B a licence to cover B's previously unauthorised use of the patent. A's income has been fairly low over the previous five years, not least because of the success of B's patent-infringing product, and A's taxable income (after personal allowances and expenses) for those years has been as follows:

2010/11	£25,000
2009/10	£20,000
2008/09	£23,000
2007/08	£28,000

A's taxable income for 2011/12, before the royalty payment from B is taken into account, is £45,000. If A does not claim relief, then all of the royalty payment received from B will be sub five years, so that £20,000 is deemed to be received in each of 2008/09, 2009/10, 2009/10, 2010/11 and 2011/12. Given A's other income, the deemed royalty payment for each of the first four years will be taxed partly at basic rate and partly at the higher rate, as follows:

Year	at 22%/20%	at 40%	total tax due
2007/08 (22%)	£6,600	£13,400	£6,812
2008/09 (20%)	£11,800	£8,200	£5,640
2009/10 (20%)	£17,400	£2,600	£4,520
2010/11 (20%)	£12,400	£7,600	£5,520

In 2011/12, the entire £20,000 will be taxed at 40% (£8,000) as he is above the threshold for higher rate tax before receiving the royalty payment. The tax that would have been paid on the receipt if the payment had been received over the period of use is therefore £30,492.

A can claim relief of £(40,000 − 30,492) = £9,508 in 2011/12, being the difference between the tax due on the total in the year of receipt and the tax that would have been paid if the royalty had been paid over the period of use.

Note, that for the purposes of simplifying the illustration, no account has been taken of the fact that tax will be withheld at basic rate from the payment: the actual tax due to be paid by A will reflect any withholding made from the payment, but does not affect the calculation of the relief.

COPYRIGHT

6.49   Exploiting copyright generally results in royalties, but *any* receipts of a UK taxpayer whose profession or vocation involves the creation of copyrights are trading income, taxed under ITTOIA 2005, Pt 2 regardless of whether these are royalties or lump sums received in lieu of royalties (BIM 50710). (See also para **18.240** onwards: lump sums received on the sale of copyright by such a person will also be treated as income.)

Public lending rights payments

6.50   Public lending rights payments are treated in the same way as copyright royalties (ITA 2007, s 907 and BIM50755). Technically this only applies where the owner of the copyright is non-UK resident, but the BIM reference suggests that HMRC will apply the principle more widely. The public lending right scheme provides statutory compensation for authors whose books are available to public library borrowers to reflect the wider readership than a single sale to a library would indicate and compensate for the potential loss of sales to library readers.

Casual receipts

6.51   In general, copyright royalties received by a person who is resident but which are *not* derived from carrying on a trade, profession or vocation are taxable as miscellaneous income under ITTOIA 2005, s 579.

6.52   Any payments (including lump sum payments) for *services* rendered in relation to copyright will also usually be chargeable under ITTOIA 2005, Pt 5 as miscellaneous income from intellectual property (ITTOIA 2005, s 579). For example, in *Housden v Marshall* (1958) 38 TC 233 a jockey who worked with an author to produce newspaper articles about his racing days was taxable on the payment (then under the equivalent provision, Sch D, Case VI), as it was for services rendered to the newspaper.

Withholding tax: tax treatment of non-UK author

6.53   Where an overseas creative professional, such as an author, receives payment for creating a work there is no need to withhold tax from the payment even though the author is not UK tax resident. There is still some paperwork needed to ensure that no withholding is required (see para **18.287**).

Averaging relief for creative professionals

6.54   Because of the fluctuating nature of income from creative works, a form of averaging relief is available to 'smooth' the profits of authors, artists etc (see para **18.267** for more details).

KNOW-HOW

6.55   Know-how is generally exploited by licence, for the payment of royalties or a lump sum and taxed as trading income, under ITTOIA 2005, Pt 2. HMRC do not usually accept that know-how can be held for non-trading purposes, since know-how generally relates to trading activities.

Lump sum receipts from know-how

6.56   Lump sum receipts need to be identified as either capital or income receipts. Historically, the distinction has been made on the basis of case law.

6.57   The key cases relating to lump sums receipts of know-how are *Jeffrey v Rolls Royce Ltd* (1962) 40 TC 443 and *Evans Medical Supplies Ltd v Moriarty* (1957) 37 TC 540. The principal distinction in the cases relates to whether or not the licensor is restricted in its ability to exploit the know-how after the transaction has taken place.

6.58   In the *Rolls Royce* case, the know-how licence did not prohibit Rolls Royce from continuing to use the know-how in their own business: the lump sum receipt was held to be income, since it was simply an alternative source of income from a continuing asset of the business (the expertise).

6.59   In contrast, in the *Evans Medical Supplies* case, the licensor agreed not to use that know-how within a particular market (the know-how had been licensed to the Burmese government, and the company undertook not to exploit the know-how in Burma). The lump sum receipt under that licence was held to be for a part-disposal of the know-how and hence capital, since the company had restricted the way in which it could use the asset and this was not the way in which the company usually carried on business, even though the payment was calculated by reference to the use of the know-how.

6.60   Similarly, in *Musker v English Electric Co Ltd* (1964) 41 TC 556, the taxpayer acquired specialised information and techniques in engineering processes and later entered into agreements which, amongst other things, required that the techniques be passed on to licensees for specified payments. Viscount Radcliffe in the House of Lords held that:

'... in reality no sale takes place. The appellant had after the transaction what it had before it. There is no property right in "know-how" that can be transferred, even in the limited sense that there is a legally protected property interest in a secret process ... [but] imparting "know-how" for reward is not [a capital receipt] any more than a teacher sells his knowledge or skill to his pupil'.

6.61   Disposals of know-how will now generally be treated as income receipts where the vendor carries on a trade, and continues to carry on a trade after the know-how has been disposed of (see para **7.61** for more detail on the tax implications of disposing of know-how).

CHECKLIST

6.62

- Confirm that the transaction is one of exploitation, not part-disposal (or disposal):
  - Can the recipient of the payment continue to exploit the intellectual property? If not, the transaction is likely to be a part-disposal.
  - If the transaction is settlement, or an award, in respect of litigation consider the elements of the settlement or award on their own terms (see para **17.52**).
- Is the receipt income or capital?
  - Note that receipts in respect of patents will always be taxed as income.
  - Receipts of a creative professional will always be taxed as income.
  - Will transfer pricing or the connected parties rules apply to adjust the receipt for tax purposes?
- Withholding tax:
  - Make treaty claims to reduce wherever possible.
  - Consider a claim for unilateral relief where possible.

— Consider claiming an expense deduction for the relief if unilateral relief not available or appropriate.

- What type of intellectual property does the receipt relate to?

    — Patents:

        (i) Check whether UK income tax has been deducted.

        (ii) Consider whether spreading relief should be applied.

    — Copyright:

        (i) Creative professionals: consider whether averaging should be applied.

        (ii) Casual receipts: taxed as miscellaneous income.

    — Know-how:

        (i) Taxed as trading income if not a disposal.

Chapter 7

Disposing of intellectual property

Summary: Intellectual property may be disposed of by sale, or may expire at the end of a protection period. The tax treatment on the proceeds of disposal will depend on the nature of the intellectual property: disposals of copyright by authors are almost always taxed as income, for example. Where the receipt is a capital receipt, it will be subject to capital gains tax. Receipts on disposal of patents are always subject to income tax and may be subject to withholding tax even when paid by other UK taxpayers.

- Part-disposals (para **7.6**)

- Receipts: general rules (para **7.8**)

- Particular issues (para **7.23**)

- Patents (para **7.33**)

- Copyright (para **7.58**)

- Know-how (para **7.61**)

- Other unregistered intellectual property (para **7.72**)

INTRODUCTION

7.1   Intellectual property can be disposed of in two principal ways:

- it can be sold outright; and

- it can expire: patents, copyrights and associated intellectual property have a finite life. Trademarks may continue indefinitely, but do need to be renewed; where a renewal is not made, the trademark will come to an end. Know-how may also continue indefinitely.

7.2   For tax purposes, there can also be a part-disposal of intellectual property where the owner agrees to limit their rights in respect of the intellectual property.

7.3   These rules apply to disposals of intellectual property created or

106

acquired by an individual, a partnership or other non-corporate entity at any time.

7.4 The following rules also apply to disposals of intellectual property assets that were created or acquired by the disposing company before 1 April 2002, or otherwise excluded from the corporate intangibles tax rules, although, for simplicity, the text refers principally to individuals and other non-corporate entities, as corporate intellectual property assets are increasingly within the corporate tax rules described in Chapter 8 onwards.

7.5 Where expenditure on creating an asset was incurred by a company over the 31 March/1 April 2002 threshold, that asset is regarded as two separate assets for tax purposes: one in the old regime (reflecting pre-1 April 2002 expenditure) to which the following rules apply, and one in the corporate intellectual property tax rules (reflecting post-31 March 2002 expenditure), to which the rules later in this chapter apply.

PART-DISPOSALS

7.6 Where a transaction limits the rights of the owner of the relevant intellectual property, for example, on the sale of the film rights to a novel or on the grant of an exclusive licence in respect of software, the receipts are more likely to be capital than revenue. Although such exploitation will allow the owner of the intellectual property to retain overall ownership of that IP, such a sale is effectively a part-disposal of the intellectual property.

7.7 The treatment of income from such part-disposals will depend on the position of the owner of the intellectual property and the status of the intellectual property in question. In general, though, the excess of:

● the exploitation proceeds, over; and

● the relevant proportion of the expenditure incurred on acquiring or creating the asset,

will be treated as a capital receipt and taxed as such (although see below for taxation of lump sums received for copyright by creative artists, and for patents). See also para **6.10** for more information on part-disposals of intellectual property.

RECEIPTS: GENERAL RULES

7.8 The question as to whether the receipt is capital or revenue is of more concern on disposals than in exploitation, as it is more likely that a disposal receipt will be treated as capital. Any receipts that are treated as income will be subject to tax as trading income (ITTOIA 2005, Pt 2) where received by a trade, or as miscellaneous income (ITTOIA 2005, s 579) where received by a non-trader.

7.9   Where the receipt is capital, it will be taxed as a capital gain (except for capital receipts in respect of patents, which are always taxed as income: see para **7.33**). An individual (including a sole trader) will be subject to capital gains tax on capital gains (generally taxed at lower rates than income; for 2012–13, capital gains are taxed at 28% whereas income is taxed at up to 50%), and a company will be subject to corporation tax on capital gains (in 2012–13, at between 20% and 24%, depending on the level of profits overall). The disponor may also be able to set brought-forward capital losses from other transactions against the gain, to reduce the tax on the capital gain—this applies to both capital gains tax and corporation tax on gains; brought forward capital losses cannot be set against trading income.

Amount of capital gain

7.10   For an individual, the taxable gain on disposal of a fixed asset will generally be the proceeds of disposal less the original cost of the asset (unless capital allowances have been claimed; see paras **7.51–7.69**).

Deductible costs: wasting asset

7.11   Intellectual property will be a wasting asset (TCGA 1992, s 262(1)) where that intellectual property has a remaining life on acquisition of less than 50 years: for example, where more than 20 years have passed since the death of the author of copyright material, so that less than 50 years of the copyright period remains; copyright protection persists for 70 years after the death of the author.

7.12   Intellectual property such as trademarks, which can be renewed indefinitely, will not be wasting assets even though they would expire within the 50-year period if not renewed. A patent would always be a wasting asset, as the registration period is less than the wasting asset period—but gains on patents are taxed as income, not capital, so this is not an issue in practice (see para **7.33**).

7.13   Where intellectual property is a wasting asset, the acquisition expenditure (less any residual value) incurred on the intellectual property will be restricted pro rata when calculating any chargeable gain on the disposal or expiry of the asset.

Example 7.1

A copyright is acquired for £50,000 with 25 years unexpired. It has a residual value of £2,500. The copyright is sold 10 years later, when 15 years are left unexpired, for £20,000. The chargeable gain is:

	£	£
Disposal proceeds		20,000
Acquisition cost	50,000	
Less (50,000–2,500) × 15/25	(28,500)	
Allowable expenditure	21,500	(21,500)
Capital loss		(1,500)

General reliefs

7.14   There are few reliefs for capital gains on intellectual property for individuals; the principal relief available is entrepreneur's relief, available on the disposal of intellectual property assets as part of the disposal of a business (except in the case of patents; see para **7.37**). Entrepreneurs' relief can reduce the capital gain on disposal from 28% to 10%. As entrepreneurs' relief is a general tax relief, and not specifically for intellectual property, the details are outside the scope of this book.

7.15   For a company outside the corporate intangibles tax rules, indexation allowance may be available to reduce the gain. Indexation effectively gives relief for the impact of inflation over the period for which the intellectual property asset is held; as before, this is a general capital gains relief for companies and not specifically an intellectual property tax relief, so the details are outside the scope of this book.

Capital or revenue?

Purpose for which held

7.16   The tax treatment of the disposal of an intellectual property asset will depend on the purpose for which the intellectual property is held by the vendor. Intellectual property assets will most often be held as a capital asset used directly in the trade, but they can also be held as trading stock (by a person trading in the intellectual property directly, rather than using it in manufacturing goods or providing services), as an investment or for non-commercial purposes.

Used in business, profession or vocation

7.17   If the intellectual property being sold is used in the business which owns it—for example, the trademarks of the business, or the patent rights which are related to the goods produced by a manufacturing business (or relate to the process through which those goods are made)—a sale of that intellectual property will be the sale of a capital asset. The proceeds (if any) of a disposal of the intellectual property will be taxed as a capital receipt of the business rather than as income of the business. An outright sale of an intellectual property asset being used in an unincorporated business usually arises on the sale of the business as a whole (it is difficult to continue a business where the intellectual property rights used in the business are disposed of) or on securitisation of the intellectual property (where the purchaser grants a licence back to the vendor).

Trading stock

7.18   Where intellectual property is sold as trading stock—where the business carries on a trade of buying or creating intellectual property for resale, such as (for example) a dealer in broadcast rights—the vendor will be assessed to tax on the profits from the sale of the intellectual property rights as trading income under ITTOIA 2005, Pt 2.

7.19   Whether or not a business is carrying on a trade in the sale and purchase of intellectual property will be a question of fact, although there are a number of key areas that are taken into account when considering the question (see para **3.12**).

7.20   Note that copyright of a creative professional will not be regarded as trading stock, even though it could be argued that an author creates copyright works and then sells the copyright. The case of *Mason v Innes* [1967] 44 TC 326 confirmed that, where an individual produces a literary, artistic or other work in the exercise of the individual's profession, the work produced is not trading stock (see para **18.261** for more information on this point).

Investment

7.21   If the IP disposed of is held by the business but not used directly in the business (for example, a patent that has been superseded but is still valid), a disposal is likely to generate a capital receipt of the business. This is subject to specific rules in respect of disposals of patents (see below), which will always be taxed as trading income (ITTOIA 2005, Pt 2) or miscellaneous income (ITTOIA 2005, s 579).

Non-commercial purposes

7.22   Where the intellectual property is not held for trading purposes, nor as an investment of a business, a sale of that intellectual property will generally give rise to a capital receipt, taxed under general rules as a capital gain (or available as a capital loss, depending on the circumstances).

PARTICULAR ISSUES

Incorporation relief: capital gains

7.23   On a transfer of intellectual property from an individual to a new company in exchange for shares in that company (ie on incorporation of a business), CTA 2009, s 845 will apply. This provision deems transfers of intangible assets between related parties (the individual and his company will be related parties for these purposes: see para **18.69**) to take place at market value for the purposes of all Taxes Acts. Accordingly, the disposal of the intellectual property by the individual to the company will be deemed to take place at market value and a chargeable gain will arise accordingly (**except** in the case of transfers of patents, which are subject to income tax and outside the scope of capital gains tax; see para **7.33**). Care needs to be taken to ensure that the disposal on incorporation does not fall foul of the rules relating to sales of personal income (see para **18.282**).

7.24   If there is a capital gains tax charge on the transfer of intellectual property to a new company on incorporation then this tax charge can generally be mitigated by holdover relief (TCGA 1992, s 165), as the intellectual property is an asset used by the individual for the purposes of his profession. The holdover relief must be claimed, and on a claim the chargeable gain is reduced by the amount of the held-over gain on the disposal.

7.25   So that the gain is only deferred and not lost as a result of holdover relief, there is a provision (CTA 2009, s 849) which requires that the acquisition cost of the intellectual property for the company is reduced by the same amount that the taxable amount is reduced for the individual through holdover relief.

7.26   The effect of this will be that, if the individual is not to pay any capital gains tax on the transfer to the company, the company will have a minimal base cost and so will not be able to take a deduction for any material amounts of amortisation under CTA 2009, Pt 8 in respect of any post-2002 copyright assets acquired (see para **11.27**).

Expiry

7.27   The expiry of intellectual property is, technically, a disposal of the intellectual property, as the owner no longer has an asset: it is, however, a disposal at nil value and so will usually give rise to a capital loss and not a capital gain. For expired patents (and know-how with nil value, as it does not technically expire) where capital allowances have been claimed, this may give rise to a balancing allowance to be deducted from trading income for tax purposes (see para **7.57**).

Capital losses

7.28   For copyrights and other intellectual property, the expiry of the intellectual property may give rise to a capital loss (equivalent to the costs incurred on the acquisition of the asset, if any) which can be set against other capital gains. This loss may be restricted for intellectual property which is a wasting asset (generally, any intellectual property which has an expected useful life of less than 50 years when acquired; see para **7.11**).

7.29   This is a capital gains tax provision and so patents cannot be wasting assets for tax purposes, as the proceeds of disposal of patents are not subject to capital gains tax.

International aspects

7.30   The UK tax system generally imposes tax on either:

* the worldwide gains of a UK resident taxpayer; or

* the UK source gains of a foreign resident.

7.31   To determine whether a owner of intellectual property will be subject to UK income tax on the receipts from disposing of that intellectual property, it is necessary to consider:

* whether the owner is UK resident; and if not; then;

* whether the intellectual property produces UK source income.

See para **2.5** for further details on the location of intellectual property for tax purposes.

7.32   Receipts on disposals of intellectual property are not generally treated as royalties and so should (in the first analysis) not be subject to withholding tax; however, the structure of the payments may be such that tax is nevertheless withheld at source where the payer is obliged to withhold. Double tax relief is generally available in the UK to relieve some or all of the tax suffered overseas (see Chapter 16).

PATENTS

7.33   Profits from the sale of patent rights will be taxed under the specific provisions of ITTOIA 2005, s 587 even if the receipt is considered to be capital for tax purposes (corporate vendors of pre-1 April 2002 patents, and other patents excluded from the corporate rules, will be taxed under CTA 2009, s 912) provided that capital allowances have not been claimed on the acquisition expenditure on the patent (see para **7.51** for the tax treatment on disposal where capital allowances have been claimed).

7.34 Non-residents selling UK patents are also subject to UK tax on the gain on sale; a non-resident individual will be subject to tax under ITTOIA 2005, s 587, although tax will usually be withheld by a UK purchaser (see para **5.57**). A non-resident company will be subject to UK corporation tax on the sale of a UK patent (CTA 2009, s 912(2)); again, tax is likely to be withheld when paid by a UK purchaser, as for non-resident individuals.

7.35 The chargeable profits from the sale will be (ITTOIA 2005, s 588) the:

- capital sum received for the disposal, less:

- deductible costs, which will generally be the capital expenditure on acquiring the patent and any incidental costs of sale

Reliefs on disposal

7.36 The disposal of a patent will, therefore, always be subject to income tax for an individual disponor even where the receipt is considered to be capital in nature. This will limit the reliefs available to the disponor.

On sale of a business

7.37 Where the patent is disposed of as part of the sale of a business, the vendor will not be entitled to entrepreneur's relief on the disposal of the patent even where the rest of the assets are eligible for relief. Entrepreneur's relief is specifically a relief from capital gains tax (TCGA 1992, s 169H), reducing the rate of capital gains tax on business disposals from 28% to 10% in qualifying circumstances.

7.38 Any amounts which are taxed as income are specifically excluded from being taken into account for capital gains tax purposes (TCGA 1992, s 37). As a result, where the patent is a significant part of the value of the business, the owner may find that very little relief on disposal is available and that the majority of the disposal proceeds are subject to income tax at up to 50%.

Incorporation

7.39 Where a business is reliant upon one or more patents, the owner may want to consider incorporating the business to be able to sell the shares and obtain entrepreneurs' relief on the sale: this would need to be done well in advance of any sale, given the conditions for relief to be available, and preferably before significant value is attributable to the patents, as reliefs on incorporation (see para **7.23**) are, similarly, reliefs from capital gains tax only.

7.40   Incorporation may have other benefits, not only for entrepreneurs' relief but also for research and development relief (which is only available to companies: see Chapter 10) and the patent box relief (also available only to companies: see Chapter 13). The transfer of a patent to a company is unlikely to be caught by the sale of income from a personal occupation rules (see para **18.282**), as a business exploiting patents is unlikely to be regarded as a profession or vocation.

Spreading relief: UK residents

7.41   Where a capital sum is received on the disposal of a patent by a UK tax resident, the tax charge is spread across six years (ITTOIA 2005, s 590; the same relief is available to corporate vendors under CTA 2009, ss 914–915).

7.42   If not otherwise received in instalments, the chargeable profits (as above) are deemed to be divided into six equal amounts for tax purposes. The first one-sixth is brought into account for tax purposes for the tax year in which the payment is received and the remaining amounts are each brought into charge over the next five tax years.

7.43   Where the chargeable profits of disposal are received in instalments, one-sixth of each instalment is taxed in the year of receipt and each of the subsequent five years, requiring calculations for each year in which an instalment is actually received.

Example 7.2

A sells a patent for £12,000, to be received in four payments of £3,000 each. The first instalment is received on the date of sale, 1 December 2007 and the following three instalments are received on each of the three following anniversaries of sale. The amounts that need to be brought into account for tax are as follows:

2007 instalment:	£500 will be taxed in each of 2007/08, 2008/09, 2009/10, 2010/11, 2011/12 and 2012/13
2008 instalment:	£500 will be taxed in each of 2008/09, 2009/10, 2010/11, 2011/12 , 2012/13 and 2013/14
2009 instalment:	£500 will be taxed in each of 2009/10, 2010/11, 2011/12, 2012/13, 2013/14 and 2014/15
2010 instalment:	£500 will be taxed in each of 2010/11, 2011/12, 2012/13, 2013/14, 2014/15 and 2015/16

The total taxed in respect of this disposal in each tax year will, therefore, be:

2007/08	£500
2008/09	£1,000
2009/10	£1,500
2010/11	£2,000
2011/12	£2,000
2012/13	£2,000
2013/14	£1,500
2014/15	£1,000
2015/16	£500

7.44   The recipient can elect for the entire payment to be brought into account for tax purposes in the year the payment is actually received (ITTOIA 2005, s 590(3)) (or the years in which it is actually received if in fact paid in instalments). The election needs to be made by the first anniversary of the normal self-assessment filing date for the tax year in which the payment was received (ie in the self-assessment tax return or by amended return).

7.45   An election will be useful where the recipient has losses which can be used to eliminate the tax charge, to reduce the need to bring amounts into charge in future years, or where income projections mean that it is likely that income in future years will be taxed at a higher rate.

7.46   Where a lump sum receipt is being spread for tax purposes, if the recipient dies whilst the payment is being spread, the tax charge on the remaining instalments are accelerated and taxed in the period in which the death occurs (ITTOIA 2005, s 593; a similar provision applies where a company is wound up whilst taking the relief, under CTA 2009, s 918).

7.47   The personal representatives can require that the payments are reallocated equally over the years beginning with that in which the payment was received and ending with the year in which death occurred (ITTOIA 2005, s 593(2)) so that the tax charge can be spread backwards over several periods: this will generally be useful where the individual was not a higher rate taxpayer.

7.48   To elect for such treatment, the personal representatives need to notify HMRC by the first anniversary of the normal self-assessment filing date for the tax year of death (ITTOIA 2005, s 593(4)).

Spreading relief: non-residents

7.49   A non-resident recipient of a capital sum on disposal of a patent will also be taxed under ITTOIA 2005, s 587 on that receipt (a non-resident corporate recipient will be taxed under CTA 2009, s 912) but the spreading relief is not automatically available. A non-UK resident recipient can, however, elect that the spreading provisions detailed above be applied to reduce the amount charged in any one year (ITTOIA 2005, s 591; for corporate non-residents within the charge to UK tax, a similar election is available under CTA 2009, ss 916–917, and see para **16.40**).

7.50   The payment will already have had tax deducted by the payer (under ITA 2007, s 910); if one-sixth of the tax deducted is more than the tax liability of the recipient for any year to which the election applies, the excess deduction will be repaid when the liability for that year has been finalised (ITTOIA 2005, s 596).

Capital allowances

7.51   Where capital allowances have been claimed on the acquisition of patent rights (see para **5.60**), any capital receipt received on the disposal of those patent rights will be dealt with under the capital allowances rules to determine the amounts to be brought into account for tax purposes, before the rest of the gain (if any) is taxed under ITTOIA 2005 or CTA 2009.

7.52   Patent capital allowances are not affected by the changes to capital allowances for plant and machinery in FA 2008.

7.53   On receipt of a capital sum on disposal of a patent, a disposal value is deducted from the patent pool. The disposal value is the net capital proceeds from the disposal of the patent (CAA 2001, s 476(3)) subject to an overall maximum of the capital expenditure incurred on acquiring the patent (CAA 2001, s 477). Any excess over this amount is taxed as income under ITTOIA 2005 or CTA 2009, as above (see para **7.33**).

7.54   Where the disposal value is not greater than the written down value of the pool, and the patent is not the last patent in the pool, the patent pool will continue so that patent capital allowances will continue to be claimed on the declining balance of qualifying expenditure, as adjusted for the disposal, in the patent pool until the pool is exhausted (in which case the allowance is £1) or the taxpayer ceases to trade. There will be no balancing charge or allowance.

7.55   If the disposal value is greater than the written down capital allowances pool for patent rights, a balancing charge equal to the excess is brought into account for tax purposes.

Example 7.3

A buys a patent for £100,000 and claims capital allowances on that asset. Three years later, A sells the patent for £80,000.

If A has no other patents, the written down value of the patent pool prior to disposal is £42,187.50 (after three years of writing down).

The disposal value brought into account is £80,000 and so a balancing charge of £37,812.50 is brought into account for tax purposes in A's tax return for the year.

Example 7.4

If A had sold the patent for £120,000, the disposal value brought into account would be £100,000 (limited to the original capital expenditure) and so a balancing charge of £57,812.50 is brought into account as income for tax purposes in A's tax return for the year.

7.56   Where the patent rights disposed of were acquired from a connected person, or in a series of transactions between connected people, the limit on the disposal value for calculating a balancing allowance or charge is the greatest amount of capital expenditure incurred by any of those connected persons.

Example 7.5

A, B and C are connected: A buys patent rights for £50,000. He then sells them on to B for £45,000. B finally sells them to C for £47,000.

C sells the rights to an unconnected person for £60,000. His disposal value limit is £50,000, not the £47,000 that he paid for the rights.

Expiry of patent

7.57   Where a patent expires—when the rights come to an end without being renewed—a balancing allowance will be given on any unallowed expenditure (CAA 2001, s 99) if it is the last patent in the pool. The balancing allowance is a mop-up tax deduction, closing the patent pool. It is only available for a patent pool in the final chargeable period of the taxpayer business (CAA 2001, s 471) or, in practice, once the written down value of the pool falls below £1.

COPYRIGHT

7.58   Disposal of copyright is largely dealt with under the general rules; however, particular rules may apply to disposals by authors and creative artists (see also para **18.240**).

Capital treatment

7.59   In general, receipts on disposals of copyright will be treated as income unless the disponor can show that the copyright was held as an investment. For example, in *Shiner v Lindblom* (1960) 39 TC 367 an actor was required to sell film rights to a production company in order to ensure that it made the film, in which he also starred. He had bought the rights some time earlier, intending to hold them as an investment. The Revenue initially attempted to treat the payments for the rights as income from his profession as an actor, but the court disagreed. The judgment was that the actor's professional activities did not include the disposal of copyright, and the payment for the sale of the copyright was clearly distinct from his earnings as an actor. He was held to be realising an investment in making the sale and so the profits could not be attributed to his profession.

7.60   Alternatively, where the taxpayer can show that the copyright was disposed of as part of the disposal of a business, payments received may be treated as capital as part of the overall proceeds of disposal. In this case, entrepreneurs' relief may be available where the proceeds are subject to capital gains tax, reducing the capital gains tax charge from 28% to 10% (the rates for 2012–13).

KNOW-HOW

7.61   For tax purposes, a disposal of know-how includes both an outright disposal of the know-how and an agreement not to use particular know-how, restricting the activities of the individual receiving consideration (ITTOIA 2005, s 583). A lump sum receipt on the disposal of know-how will be taxed (ITTOIA 2005, s 584) as one of the following:

- the receipt of trading profits;

- capital receipt in respect of goodwill if disposed of as part of the disposal of all or part of a trade;

- royalties, where neither of the above apply (ITTOIA 2005, s 578);

- a balancing charge or allowance where capital allowances have been claimed; or

- as a disposal not otherwise subject to tax (ITTOIA 2005, s 583 or CTA 2009, s 908).

Deemed disposal of know-how, where business continues

7.62   Deemed disposals of know-how (for example, an agreement not to use know-how) will generally be treated as trading profits taxable under ITTOIA

2005, Pt 2 unless capital allowances have been claimed in respect of the know-how, where the vendor carries on a trade and continues to carry on that trade after the know-how has been disposed of (ITTOIA 2005, s 193; for corporate vendors of pre-1 April 2002 know-how, the relevant provision is CTA 2009, s 177). If capital allowances have been claimed, the capital allowances rules (see below) take precedence.

Know-how disposal as part of disposal of goodwill

7.63   Where there is a disposal of a trade or part of a trade together with know-how used in it, the disposal of know-how is treated as the disposal of goodwill, and in such circumstances the expenditure will not qualify for capital allowances for the purchaser and no disposal value can be brought into account in the vendor's pool unless the parties so elect (see below). The receipt will, instead, be taxed as a capital gain to the extent that a profit over acquisition or creation expenditure is realised (ITTOIA 2005, s 194 and TCGA 1992, s 261A; for corporate vendors of pre-1 April 2002 know-how the relevant provision is CTA 2009, s 178).

7.64   If the trade in which the know-how was used was carried on wholly outside the UK before the disposal and the vendor and purchaser are not under common control, the treatment of the consideration for the know-how as a payment for goodwill applies only to the vendor (ITTOIA 2005, s 194(4)).

Election

7.65   The parties may elect for this deemed goodwill treatment not to apply; the election must be made jointly by both parties within two years of the disposal (ITTOIA 2005, s 194(5)); it is recommended that any agreement for the transaction includes a provision that each party will enter into such an election, or includes a form of election to be entered into as a condition precedent to completion.

7.66   No election is possible where one party controls the other, or where both are under common control (ITTOIA 2005, s 195).

Disposals not otherwise taxable

7.67   Receipts for disposals of know-how that are not otherwise taxable (generally, where the know-how is held for non-trading purposes) are brought into account under ITTOIA 2005, s 583 (for individuals and other non-corporates) or CTA 2009, s908 (for companies) and taxed in the year of disposal.

7.68   Any expenditure incurred in acquiring and/or disposing of the know-how can be deducted to calculate the chargeable amount; however, if that expenditure can be deducted under another taxing provision (for example, where it is deductible under the general rules), it will not be deductible for s 583 purposes (ITTOIA 2005, s 585(1)).

Capital allowances

7.69   Where capital allowances have been claimed on the acquisition of know-how, any capital receipt received on the disposal of that know-how will be dealt with under the capital allowances rules. As noted above, however, where the deemed goodwill treatment applies, the capital allowances rules are overridden and no disposal value is deemed to arise.

7.70   On the sale of such know-how, a disposal value is deducted from the pool (CAA 2001, s 462). The disposal value is the net capital proceeds from the disposal of the know-how, subject to an overall maximum of the capital expenditure incurred on acquiring the know-how.

7.71   If the disposal value is greater than the written down capital allowances pool for know-how, a balancing charge equal to the excess is brought into account for tax purposes as a receipt of the trade under ITTOIA 2005, Pt 2. See Examples 7.4 and 7.5: the calculations are the same as for patent capital allowances.

OTHER UNREGISTERED INTELLECTUAL PROPERTY

7.72   Other unregistered intellectual property that is not capable of separate exploitation (such as unregistered trademarks) will, usually, be treated as part of the goodwill of the business and so HMRC generally take the view that it will not be capable of separate disposal without the rest of the goodwill which, in turn, can generally only be disposed of with the business (HMRC Manual CG68210).

CHECKLIST

7.73

> • Is the disposal of the entire asset, or a part-disposal such as the grant of an exclusive licence?
>
>   — If part-disposal, pro-rata acquisition expenditure to determine the taxable amount of the receipt.

- Is the receipt capital or revenue?

  — Receipts on the disposal of copyright by authors and other creative professionals are almost always revenue receipts, taxed as income:

    (i) receipts on the disposal of copyright as part of the disposal of a business are generally taxed as capital;

    (ii) note the particular issues relating to authors and other creative professionals (see para **18.231**), such as the sale of personal income rules

  — Receipts on disposals of non-patent investment intellectual property are treated as capital receipts, subject to capital gains tax.

  — Where intellectual property is a wasting asset, there will be restrictions on the deduction of acquisition expenditure when calculating any taxable capital gain.

  — Has tax been withheld from the payment?

    (i) Is double tax relief available if so?

- Patents

  — Receipts on disposals of patents are always subject to income tax:

    (i) consider whether the patent should be held in a company, to obtain reliefs such as entrepreneur's relief, R&D relief and the patent box relief.

    (ii) spreading relief may be available to minimise the impact on tax rates.

  — Where patent allowances have been claimed, a balancing charge or allowance may arise.

- Know-how:

  — Where know-how allowances have been claimed, a balancing charge or allowance may arise.

  — On disposal of a business, treated as disposal of goodwill unless elect otherwise.

IP tax: companies

Chapter 8

Corporate intangibles tax rules: introduction

Summary: The rules on taxation of intellectual property and other intangible assets (including goodwill) for companies changed substantially from 1 April 2002, with the introduction of a set of tax rules dealing specifically with corporate intangible fixed assets, including intellectual property.

The company must prepare GAAP-compliant accounts to be able to determine the amounts which will be taken into account for tax purposes, and must be able to determine whether the intellectual property is a qualifying intangible fixed asset for the purposes of the corporate intangibles tax rules.

Where the intellectual property is not a qualifying intangible fixed asset or is otherwise excluded, or the company holding the asset is excluded from the rules, the tax treatment of income and expenditure relating to that intellectual property will be defined by the same rules that apply to individuals and other non-corporate entities (see Chapters 3–7).

- GAAP-compliant accounts (para **8.7**)

- Intangible fixed assets (para **8.11**)

- Intellectual property excluded from the corporate intangibles tax rules (para **8.29**)

INTRODUCTION

8.1   The corporate intangibles tax rules in Part 8 of CTA 2009 closely follow the accounting treatment of the income and expenditure relating to intellectual property. In contrast with the general rules on the tax treatment of income and expenditure, the corporate intangibles tax rules require little adjustment to determine the tax credits and debits for intellectual property.

8.2   With the focus on the accounts, the requirement to distinguish between capital and revenue treatment of expenditure, with the resulting confusion over how to treat items of expenditure and which is the relevant tax, no longer applies in general to companies when creating new intellectual property assets.

8.3   This makes the tax position on creation of intellectual property very much simpler for companies than for non-corporate taxpayers as:

- there is no distinction made between the various types of intellectual property, as the same rules apply regardless of whether a copyright, a patent, or other intellectual property is being created;

- there is also no need to consider whether or not the expenditure is capital or revenue. The auditors will need to consider that, and it may be useful to discuss the treatment with them, but the tax treatment will depend upon the treatment in the accounts rather than needing to consider the case law and statutory distinctions.

8.4   Instead, the key questions for the corporate intangibles tax rules are:

- is there an intangible fixed asset (or will there be, once created)?

- is it excluded from the corporate intangible tax rules?

- how is it treated in the accounts?

8.5   Where there is an intangible fixed asset—and intellectual property assets will almost always be intangible fixed assets—and that asset is not excluded, the corporate intangibles rules will apply to receipts and expenditure relating to that asset.

8.6   Where there is an intangible fixed asset (or will be, once created), but it is excluded from the corporate intangibles tax rules, the tax rules in Chapter 3 onwards relating to individuals and partnerships will also generally apply to the asset (unless a different set of tax rules specifically applies) even though it is owned by a company.

GAAP-COMPLIANT ACCOUNTS

8.7   In order for the corporate intangibles tax rules to be applied, the company must have GAAP-compliant accounts or, where it does not, will have to prepare GAAP-compliant accounts, as the provisions of the corporate intangibles tax rules only apply to the amounts which would be recognised in GAAP-compliant accounts.

8.8   'Generally accepted accounting practice' (GAAP) is defined as being (CTA 2010, s 1127):

- UK generally accepted accounting practice, which is that used to produce accounts that give a 'true and fair view'—essentially, the practice

125

codified in Companies Act 2006 and the standards and statements of the UK's Accounting Standards Board; and

• generally accepted accounting practice in relation to international accounting standards (as defined by Regulation (EC) No 1606/2002 of the European Parliament and the Council of 19 July 2002), for companies that follow international accounting standards ('IAS').

8.9   If, for any reason, the company does not draw up accounts that follow generally accepted accounting practice ('correct accounts'), the expenditure that can be deducted for tax purposes is that which would have been deducted in the accounts if correct accounts had been produced (CTA 2009, s 717).

8.10   This requirement for 'correct accounts' will generally affect foreign companies with UK permanent establishments, whose accounts may not reflect either IAS or UK GAAP: those accounts will need to be restated for UK tax purposes to reflect 'correct accounts'. For example, accounts prepared under US GAAP may capitalise certain development costs that would be revenue expenditure in the profit and loss account under UK GAAP.

WHAT IS AN INTANGIBLE FIXED ASSET?

8.11   Part 8 of the Corporation Tax Act (CTA 2009) is a specific corporation tax regime that applies solely to the gains and losses of intangible fixed assets (CTA 2009, s 711). In practice, most intellectual property will be an intangible fixed asset. However, the specific definition may need to be considered, particularly where the intellectual property is closely linked with a tangible asset.

Tax definition

8.12   An 'intangible fixed asset' is an 'intangible asset created or acquired by a company for use on a continuing basis in the course of the company's activities' (CTA 2009, s 713(1)).

Fixed asset

8.13   As the asset must be a fixed asset—that is, used on a continuing basis (CTA 2009, s 713(1))—this will exclude intellectual property that is bought and sold by a company as trading stock (for example, where a company deals in intellectual property rights such as broadcasting rights). Such companies will be taxed on the income from those transactions under the general rules for trading income, the detailed rules of which are outside the scope of this book as they do not relate specifically to intellectual property.

8.14   The corporate intangibles tax regime also applies to any option (or similar right) to acquire intellectual property that would be a fixed asset if it were acquired, or any option or similar right to dispose of a fixed asset (CTA 2009, s 713(2)).

8.15   In addition, the tax definition specifically includes certain intangible fixed assets which have not been capitalised on the company's balance sheet (CTA 2009, s 713(3)). These will include most internally generated intellectual property fixed assets and licences where the consideration for the licence is solely in royalties (a licence may be capitalised where a lump sum is paid for the asset; a royalty-only licence will not generally be capitalised in the accounts).

There are also specific exclusions from the definition of intangible fixed assets (and hence from CTA 2009, Pt 8) (see para **8.29** onwards).

Intangible asset

8.16   An 'intangible asset' is defined for tax purposes (CTA 2009, s 712(1)) as having the same meaning that it does for accounting purposes. As noted above, either UK accounting standards or international accounting standards may be used and so the relevant definition should be considered.

Accounting definition: UK

8.17   'Intangible assets' are defined in Financial Reporting Standard 10 (FRS10) as 'non-financial fixed assets that do not have physical substance but are identifiable and are controlled by the entity through custody or legal rights'. Such assets can be created or acquired; where they are acquired, this may be either directly or as part of the acquisition of a business and its assets (FRS10, ¶2). In the case of intellectual property, a company will protect it either by registration or through other means (such as non-disclosure agreements) where registration is not available.

8.18   'Identifiable' means that the asset can be disposed of separately, without also disposing of the business of which it forms part.

8.19   Certain types of intellectual property may not qualify under this definition as they are not controlled by the entity through custody or legal rights; however, such intellectual property should be within the goodwill of the company, which is specifically included in the category of qualifying assets for the corporate intangibles tax rules.

Accounting definition: international

8.20   International Accounting Standard 38 (IAS38) has a similar definition, stating that an intangible asset is 'an identifiable non-monetary asset without physical substance'. IAS38 requires that a company be able to control an intellectual property asset and derive future economic benefits from it (such as income or reduced future costs) (IAS38, ¶8). It must be probable that economic benefits will be derived from the intellectual property before it can be recognised for IAS38 purposes.

8.21   'Identifiable' for IAS38 purposes is a wider definition than that in FRS10, as it means that the intellectual property can be:

● separated from the company and sold, transferred, licensed and otherwise exploited on its own or with other related assets or liabilities; or

● arises from legal rights, whether or not these are transferrable or separable from the company or other assets or liabilities (IAS38, ¶12).

8.22   The cost of the intellectual property must be able to be measured reliably. As with UK GAAP, some intellectual property may not fall within this definition but should be within the goodwill of the company and so included in the rules in that way.

Intellectual property

8.23   The corporate intangibles tax rules make it clear that 'intangible asset' specifically includes defined items of intellectual property: patents, trade marks (registered and unregistered), registered designs, copyrights, design rights, plant breeders' rights and plant variety rights, know-how and show-how (CTA 2009, s 712(2), (3)). The definition also includes any licence in respect of an item of intellectual property specifically included in the legislation (CTA 2009, s 712(3)(d)).

8.24   As intellectual property has been specifically included in the definition of 'intangible asset' this should mean that a change in accounting standards (for example) would not remove an intellectual property asset from the corporate intangibles tax regime.

8.25   The definition of intellectual property is not restricted to UK intellectual property, and similar foreign intellectual property will be within the definition (CTA 2009, s 712(3)(b)).

Goodwill

8.26   The corporate intangibles tax regime also applies to goodwill (CTA 2009, s 715). Goodwill has the same meaning it has for accounting purposes (CTA 2009, s 715(3)) and includes internally generated goodwill which cannot be capitalised under FRS10 (CTA 2009, s 713(3)). In practice, most intellectual property that would not fall within the accounting definition of an intangible asset would come within the corporate intangibles tax regime through this provision as such intellectual property would usually be regarded as part of the goodwill of the company.

Internally generated intellectual property

8.27   Internally generated intellectual property assets cannot usually be capitalised in a company's accounts and so will not appear as fixed assets, because it is not usually possible to state with sufficient certainty during development that the expenditure will provide an enduring benefit to the company, and so will not appear on the balance sheet. Such assets are, nevertheless, specifically regarded as intangible fixed assets for corporation tax purposes (CTA 2009, s 713(3)) so that income relating to the asset is dealt with under the corporate intangibles tax rules.

8.28   Similarly, a licence that is paid for solely through royalties will not usually appear on the company's balance sheet even if the licence is used by the company on a continuing basis, as the payments are deducted as revenue expenditure in the profit and loss account. A licence may be capitalised where a lump sum is paid for the asset; a royalty-only licence will not usually be capitalised under UK GAAP or IAS. Such licences will still be regarded as intellectual property assets under the corporate intangibles tax regime (CTA 2009, s 712(3)(d)).

WHEN IS INTELLECTUAL PROPERTY EXCLUDED FROM THE INTANGIBLES RULES?

8.29   There are some specific exclusions from the intangible fixed assets rules (CTA 2009, Pt 8, Ch 10). Where intellectual property is excluded from the corporate intangibles tax rules, income and expenditure relating to that intellectual property is dealt with under the same corporation tax rules as continue to apply for individuals and other non-corporate entities (see Chapters 3–7).

8.30   In some cases the intellectual property is excluded so that the specific rules can be applied instead (such as films, and intellectual property held by mutual trades, and life insurance businesses).

8.31   There are three types of exclusion (CTA 2009, s 800(2)):

● intellectual property wholly excluded;

● intellectual property excluded except as to royalties;

● intellectual property excluded to the extent specified in the rules.

Intellectual property wholly excluded

8.32   Some intellectual property assets are entirely excluded from the corporate intangibles tax regime, even if they are within the definition of an intangible fixed asset for accounting purposes, such as:

- intellectual property held for non-commercial purposes (CTA 2009, s 803): this is distinct from intellectual property held for non-trading purposes, and generally applies to intellectual property held for personal reasons of a company founder, for example;

- intellectual property previously treated as a tangible asset for which capital allowances were previously given (CTA 2009, s 804): intellectual property in websites is most likely to be caught by this, as UK accounting standards may capitalise some of the expenditure on the website, which is then eligible for plant and machinery allowances as software (see para **17.120** onwards);

- internally generated goodwill of a trade of a company (or a related party) that was carried on at any time before 1 April 2002: this may affect unregistered trademarks, for example, where they are treated as part of the goodwill of the company;

- film production expenditure, where the film incentive rules apply to the gains and losses of the production company (see para **18.237** onwards), unless the production company has elected out of the film incentive rules (CTA 2009, s 808).

Other assets are also excluded in CTA 2009, Pt 8, Ch 10 but, as these do not relate to intellectual property, they have not been listed here.

Intellectual property assets excluded except as to royalties

Pre-1 April 2002 intellectual property

8.33   The cut-off point for the corporate intangibles tax rules is 1 April 2002. Intellectual property will be regarded as created or acquired on or after that date where it is:

- created or acquired by the taxpayer company on or after 1 April 2002 (CTA 2009, s 882(1);

- acquired by the taxpayer company at any time where the asset was acquired from a related party (see para **18.69** for more information on related parties) and:

    –   was a post-1 April 2002 asset for that company; or

    –   was created by the related party after 1 April 2002; or

– was acquired by the related party after 1 April 2002, provided that it was not acquired from a related party.

Where the intellectual property is not created or acquired on or after 1 April 2002, it is a pre-1 April 2002 asset and the corporate intangibles rules only apply with regard to royalties recognised for accounts purposes on or after 1 April 2002 (CTA 2009, s 882(7), s 896). Transitional rules applied at the time the rules were introduced but, as this was now a decade ago, the rules are outside the scope of this book (see earlier editions for on these transitional rules).

8.34   Intellectual property created by the taxpayer company before 1 April 2002 is excluded from the corporate intangibles tax rules (as above), but an intellectual property asset created by the taxpayer may be treated as split into two for the purposes of these rules. Intellectual property creation involves ongoing expenditure; some projects necessarily crossed the 1 April 2002 threshold and may still be ongoing (for example, pharmaceutical products can take many years from initial development through clinical trials to reach the market). The general rule here is that such an asset is treated as though it is two assets, one created before 1 April 2002 and one created after 31 March 2002; the pre-1 April 2002 asset is subject to the rules otherwise applicable to unincorporated entities and the post-31 March 2002 asset is subject to the rules of the corporate regime (CTA 2009, s 883(5)).

Example 8.1

BioCo began developing WonderDrug2000 during 1998. The development process took 10 years to complete, with the drug finally reaching the market in 2008. For tax purposes, WonderDrug2000 will be treated as two assets: one, reflecting the expenditure between 1998 and 31 March 2002 will be subject to tax under the current individual/partnership intellectual property rules; and a second, reflecting the expenditure incurred between 1 April 2002 and the finalisation of the intellectual property, which will be subject to tax under the corporate intellectual property rules.

8.35   Expenditure should be apportioned between the two assets on a just and reasonable basis. In general, this will be the basis of the date on which the expenditure was incurred unless there is particular reason to spread the expenditure differently (CTA 2009, s 883(7)). New expenditure will be incurred on the post-1 April 2002 asset, as the expenditure on the pre-1 April 2002 asset has been frozen. The distinction between the two is more importance when considering receipts from exploitation or realisation of the asset.

8.36   Created goodwill is **not** split into two assets: the goodwill created on an ongoing basis by a company will be treated as a single pre-April 2002 asset (and hence continues to be dealt with under the tax rules otherwise applicable to individuals and partnerships) where the company existed on 31 March 2002, regardless of the fact that goodwill continues to be created after that date (CTA 2009, s 884). As noted above, this may affect unregistered trademarks and other intellectual property where it is treated as part of the goodwill of the company.

8.37   Anti-avoidance rules apply to prevent an asset being brought into the scope of the corporate intangibles tax regime as a result of transfers between related parties where the asset was owned by a related party at 31 March 2002 (CTA 2009, s 882(1)(c)).

8.38   There is no requirement that the asset be shown on the balance sheet of the company or a related party at 31 March 2002. Internally generated intellectual property created before that date will still be a pre-1 April 2002 asset (even where it is brought onto the balance sheet of a company on acquisition after April 2002: see *Greenbank Holidays Ltd v Revenue and Customs Commissioners* [2011] UKUT 155 (TC), [2011] STC 1582).

Example 8.2

A Ltd acquires an intellectual property asset from a partnership to which it is related; the partnership acquired the asset in 2005 from an individual who had created the intellectual property in 1999.

The intellectual property asset will be an excluded asset, outside the corporate intangibles tax rules, for A Ltd if either:

- the partnership is related to the individual (so that A Ltd is related to the individual through the relationship with the partnership); or

- A Ltd alone is related to the individual at the time of the acquisition

It is not necessary for the partnership and the individual to be related for the asset to be outside the rules; it is enough that A Ltd and the individual are related.

Mutual trade

8.39   The income and expenditure of a mutual trade are generally excluded from tax, but capital gains (including those in respect of intellectual property) remain subject to the capital gains rules and so intellectual property assets of a mutual trade are excluded from the intangible fixed assets regime to ensure that such gains remain subject to capital gains tax (CTA 2009, s 810).

Life insurance business

8.40 Life insurance businesses are subject to a separate tax regime and so any income or expenditure which relates to intellectual property (other than royalties) is excluded from the corporate intangibles tax regime (CTA 2009, s 902)

Software

8.41 Capital expenditure on computer software is excluded from the corporate intangibles tax rules where an election is made (see para **17.101**), but any receipts from such software remain within the rules. Making the election allows a company to claim plant and machinery capital allowances and so make a short life asset election in respect of the software, so that it can be written off more quickly than the accounts amortisation would allow (CTA 2009, s 815). The normal capital allowances rules (see para **3.74** onwards) usually mean that it can take more than 20 years to fully deduct the cost of a qualifying asset for tax purposes, even where the asset is disposed of or otherwise becomes worthless. Making a short life asset election means that, if the asset is sold or expires, the tax deduction can be claimed much faster (the precise details are outside the scope of this book, as short life asset elections are not limited to intellectual property).

Partial exclusion

8.42 Where an asset is only partly excluded (for example, where an asset is held both for commercial and non-commercial purposes) then the asset is treated as two separate assets, one of which is within the corporate intangibles tax regime and one of which is not (being the excluded element of the asset). Where an asset is partly excluded, apportionment of gains and losses in respect of that asset will need to be made on a just and reasonable basis (CTA 2009, s 802).

RELATED PARTIES

8.43 Where the parties to a transaction relating to intellectual property are related (see para **18.69** for the definition of related), the tax value of that transaction is subject to special rules which must be taken into account.

8.44 In particular, the related party rules have to be considered (CTA 2009, Pt 8, Ch 13):

- when determining whether an intellectual property asset is within the corporate intangibles rules, as an asset which was held by a related party before 1 April 2002 will not generally come into the corporate intangibles rules when it is acquired by the company after 1 April 2002 (see para **8.33**);

- on a transfer of an intellectual property asset, as a transfer between related parties usually takes place at market value (see para **11.16**);

- on part-realisation of a chargeable intellectual property asset, as no roll-over relief is available for any gain where the transfer is to a related party (see para **12.62**); and

- when considering the deductibility of a royalty paid to, or for the benefit of, a related party (see para **11.18**).

CHECKLIST

8.45

- Does the company have GAAP-compliant accounts?

  — If not, these will need to be prepared if the corporate intangibles tax rules apply.

- Is the intellectual property an intangible fixed asset?

  — If it is not, the same rules as for individuals and non-corporates will apply.

- Was it created or acquired by the company or a related party before 1 April 2002?

  — If so, the same rules as for individuals and non-corporates will apply.

- Is the intellectual property nevertheless excluded from the corporate intangibles tax rules?

  — If so, the same rules as for individuals and non-corporates will apply to the extent that the asset is excluded.

  — If only partially excluded, an apportionment will need to be made.

- is there a transaction with a related party?

  — if so, special rules apply to valuation.

Chapter 9

Creating intellectual property

Summary: Expenditure relating to the creation of intellectual property assets will be deductible for tax purposes when the expenditure is recognised in determining a company's profits and losses, provided that it is not specifically excluded from deduction.

The amount of the expenditure that can be deducted for tax purposes is the same as the amount recognised as a charge in the profit and loss account for accounting purposes.

Expenditure for trade purposes is treated as an expense of the trade; expenditure for non-trading purposes is pooled with any income from intellectual property held for non-trading purposes, and the use of net expenses is restricted.

- Relevant intellectual property assets (para **9.5**)

- Deductible expenditure (para **9.6**)

- Excluded expenditure (para **9.8**)

- How much is deductible? (para **9.19**)

- Effect of accounting debits on tax computation (para **9.23**)

INTRODUCTION

9.1 The following rules apply to qualifying intellectual property held by companies (see Chapter 8). Expenditure on the creation of intellectual property fixed assets depends entirely on how it is treated in the company's profit and loss account. That is, it is brought into account for tax purposes as and when it is recognised in the company's profit and loss account. It overrides the general computational rules in respect of capital and revenue expenditure on the creation of intangible assets.

9.2 As a result, compared to the rules on the tax treatment of expenditure on creation of intellectual property by non-corporate entities, the rules here are reasonably short and straightforward: there is no need to identify whether the payment is capital or revenue, or to identify the type of intellectual property being created.

9.3 These rules do not apply to expenditure on *tangible* assets acquired for intellectual property development projects; this expenditure is still treated as capital expenditure, regardless of the treatment in the accounts, and may be eligible for research and development allowances (see Chapter 4).

9.4 This chapter also does not cover the research and development reliefs available for expenditure on creating intellectual property, as these are excluded from the corporate intangibles rules. These reliefs are, instead, covered in Chapter 10.

RELEVANT INTELLECTUAL PROPERTY ASSETS

9.5 The intellectual property assets to which these rules apply are those that are created on or after 1 April 2002, and are not otherwise excluded (see para **8.29**).

DEDUCTIBLE EXPENDITURE

9.6 Expenditure relating to the creation of intellectual property assets will be deductible for tax purposes when the expenditure is recognised in determining a company's profits and losses (CTA 2009, Pt 8, Ch 3) under the corporate intangibles tax rules provided that the expenditure is not specifically excluded (see below).

9.7 If not excluded, expenditure on creating intellectual property will be deductible in computing taxable profits if it is:

- costs written off for accounting purposes as they are incurred, in creating intellectual property on or after 1 April 2002 (CTA 2009, s 728); or

- an amortisation deduction in respect of the capitalised costs of the created intellectual property (see paras **9.10** and **11.25** for more information on amortisation costs, as amortisation is more usually found where intellectual property is acquired rather than created) (CTA 2009, ss 729, 730).

EXCLUDED EXPENDITURE

Excluded under general rules

9.8 Expenditure that is specifically not deductible for tax purposes is still not deductible under the corporate intellectual property rules even if it is an expense in the company's profit and loss account: for example, entertainment expenditure incurred as part of a project to develop a brand will still be disallowed (CTA 2009, s 865), even though the purpose of the expenditure is to create an intangible asset and add value to (for example) a trademark.

9.9   Other typically excluded expenditure which could relate to creation of intellectual property would include payments in excess of an arm's length price under transfer pricing rules (see para **16.94** onwards).

Expenditure on capitalised created intellectual property

9.10   FRS10 does allow expenditure on internally generated intellectual property to be capitalised when it belongs to a homogenous population of assets that are equivalent in every respect and for which an active market exists, as evidenced by frequent transactions (14 FRS10, ¶2).

9.11   It is extremely rare for these conditions to be satisfied, and so most expenditure is written off to the profit and loss account as it is incurred.

9.12   However, if internally created intellectual property has been capitalised in the accounts, then a deduction is still available when a debit for tax purposes corresponding to the amortisation charged in the profit and loss account is brought into account; where an impairment review has been undertaken and has led to a write down over and above the normal annual amortisation charge, the whole impairment charge will be brought into account for tax purposes (CTA 2009, s 729) as a debit.

9.13   Detailed information on the tax treatment of capitalised intellectual property assets is covered in Chapter 11 as it will be more generally applicable on the acquisition of intellectual property assets rather than on the creation of such assets, given that it is very unusual for expenditure on creating intellectual property to qualify for capitalisation under FRS10.

Research and development expenditure

9.14   Research and development expenditure is specifically excluded from the corporate intangibles tax rules (CTA 2009, s 814). Instead, such expenditure is separately deducted in calculating the profits of the trade as an expense of the trade where it is revenue expenditure (CTA 2009, s 87), so that it is deducted for tax purposes as it is incurred, regardless of the treatment in the accounts. Where this expenditure is on qualifying research and development, the research and development tax reliefs may also be available. The exclusion is in fact intended to ensure that expenditure on qualifying research and development remains eligible for the enhanced deductions available under the research and development tax reliefs.

9.15   Capital expenditure on research and development cannot be deducted as an expense of the company's trade but may qualify for the research and development capital allowance (see Chapter 4).

9.16   This exclusion covers all expenditure that is within the accounting definitions of research and development in SSAP13 (UK GAAP) and IAS38 (international accounting standards) (CTA 2010, s 1138; see para **10.3** onwards for more information on these definitions of research and development).

Website development costs

9.17   Websites are principally copyright assets (with copyright in the content and in the software), created by many businesses, and the accounting treatment of the costs of development are not always straightforward to identify.

9.18   If the website can generate such revenue then at least some of the application and infrastructure development expenditure on the website will be capitalised as creating an enduring asset, with deductions taken over the useful economic life through amortisation, rather than written off as an expense as incurred (see para **17.120** onwards).

HOW MUCH IS DEDUCTIBLE?

9.19   The amount of the expenditure that can be deducted for tax purposes is the same as the amount recognised as a charge in the profit and loss account for accounting purposes.

9.20   As the accounting treatment of expenditure is key, it is worth outlining the way in which expenditure on creating intellectual property is dealt with for accounts purposes.

Accounting treatment of expenditure

9.21   The majority of expenditure on creating intellectual property will be written off through the profit and loss account of the company as it is incurred, as an immediate expense of the business as the accounting concept of prudence means that expenditure will not be recognised as capital until it is reasonable to conclude that there will be an identifiable enduring benefit to the company from the expenditure. This means that, in general, internally generated intellectual property is not reflected on the balance sheet of the company (arguably distorting the information on the value of the intellectual property in the business). The expenditure on creating that intellectual property is reported only at a single point in time—when it is spent—and the value of the intellectual property to the business is only accounted for when (or if) it later becomes the subject of a commercial transaction (ie when it is disposed of). A company with substantial, internally generated, intellectual property may appear to be worth nothing one day and then apparently suddenly create profits out of nothing when it sells or licenses the intellectual property (Licensing Executive Society, 2002).

9.22   FRS18 requires entities to prepare accounts on an accruals basis, so that the effect of transactions and other events should be reflected (as far as possible) in the accounting period in which the transaction or event occurs (FRS18, ¶27), rather than in the accounting period in which the expenditure is actually paid or the accounting periods in which income is expected to be received as a result of the expenditure. Where the expenditure is expected to create an asset that will be recognised on the balance sheet, then the expenditure is capitalised and will only be reflected in the profit and loss account through amortisation deductions (see para **11.24** for more details, as intellectual property assets are generally amortised on acquisition, rather than creation).

EFFECT OF ACCOUNTING DEBITS ON TAX COMPUTATION

9.23   The purpose for which the intellectual property is held will determine the way in which the related debits are dealt with for tax purposes.

Trading

9.24   Where the intellectual property is created and held for the purposes of the trade (CTA 2009, s 747), the debits in the profit and loss account relating to intellectual property (including the creation of intellectual property) are treated as expenses of the trade when calculating the taxable profits and losses of the business for tax purposes. If the expenses create a loss, it will be a trading loss which can be:

- set against other profits of the same accounting period (CTA 2010, s 37(3)(a));

- carried forward against future profits of the same trade (CTA 2010, s 45(4));

- carried back against profits of the previous accounting period (CTA 2010, s 37(3)(b));

- surrendered as group relief (CTA 2010, Part 5); or

- surrendered as consortium relief (CTA 2010, s 143).

Non-trading

9.25   Where the intellectual property is created and held for non-trade purposes (CTA 2009, s 751) (generally, where it is held as an investment, although not all investments qualify as relevant assets to which these rules apply), the debits in the profit and loss account relating to intellectual property are pooled.

9.26   An overall profit after pooling will be subject to corporation tax in the usual way, unless there are brought forward losses which can be used to absorb the non-trading profit.

9.27   If a non-trading loss arises—where there are only non-trading debits, or if the total non-trading debits exceed the total of non-trading credits received in respect of any intellectual property held as an investment—then the company can claim for that loss to be set against the total profits of the company for that period (CTA 2009, s 753). The claim must be made within two years of the end of the accounting period.

9.28   Where the loss is not absorbed by that period's profits, and is not surrendered by way of group relief, it can be carried forward to the next accounting period to be treated as a non-trading loss of that period and so on until fully utilised (CTA 2009, s 753(3)).

CHECKLIST

9.29

- Is the creation of the intellectual property an ongoing project that was in existence at 1 April 2002? If so, then there will be two assets deemed to have been created: one outside the corporate intangibles tax rules and one within the rules.

- Is the expenditure on an excluded asset? If so, the rules in Chapter 3 will apply.

- Is the expenditure on research and development, as defined by accounting standards? If so, the expenditure is deductible under CTA 2009, s 87 and research and development tax relief (see Chapter 10) may be available.

- Is the intellectual property created and held for the purposes of the trade? If not, deductions for expenditure may be restricted.

Chapter 10

Research and development expenditure

Summary: The principal intellectual property tax incentives in the UK are those relating to research and development. There are three forms of relief: the small companies' relief, a super-deduction of 225% on qualifying research and development revenue expenditure; the large companies' relief, a super-deduction of 130% on similar expenditure; and the repayable tax credit, available where the small companies' relief creates or increases a loss, which provides a repayment equivalent to up to 24.75% of qualifying expenditure in exchange for the surrender of the loss.

There is also a vaccine research relief for expenditure on specific vaccines, which can be claimed by large companies.

- Qualifying research and development? (para **10.3**)

- Research and development tax relief (para **10.62**)

- Payable tax credit (para **10.157**)

- Large companies' relief (para **10.176**)

- Refunds of expenditure (para **10.193**)

- Anti-avoidance (para **10.194**)

- Administration (para **10.197**)

- Vaccine research relief (para **10.199**)

INTRODUCTION

10.1   The tax rules for corporate expenditure on intellectual property specifically exclude research and development expenditure from their scope so that enhanced deductions can be claimed under the following rules (see para **9.14**).

10.2   Research and development tax relief is available for certain revenue expenditure on creating intellectual property, and also available for revenue expenditure on research and development that is added to the cost of an intangible asset in accordance with national or international accounting standards (FA 2004, s 53). Under IAS such expenditure could only be relieved as and when the cost of the intangible asset was amortised in the profits and loss account, and so specific measures were required to ensure that such expenditure could still qualify for the research and development tax reliefs. Where research and development tax reliefs have been claimed in respect of such expenditure, no tax deduction can be taken under CTA 2009, Part 8, for the subsequent amortisation of the capitalised expenditure in the accounts.

QUALIFYING 'RESEARCH AND DEVELOPMENT'?

10.3   'Research and development' has a specific meaning for tax purposes: it is not the narrow science-fiction image of people in laboratories in white coats, bent over test tubes. However, research and development (for tax purposes) is also not the broad phrase often used in business—covering market research, commercial product development and other such activities that do not qualify as relevant research and development for tax purposes.

Relevant to the trade

10.4   First, research and development expenditure is only qualifying expenditure for tax relief purposes if the research and development relates to a trade carried on by the company, including research and development that could lead to an extension of that trade (CTA 2009, s 1042). Broadly, most research and development expenditure incurred by a company is likely to be relevant expenditure as it is unusual for a company to spend money on pure 'blue sky' research and development with no thought as to how that might benefit the company (certain very large companies might have a development lab that encourages this: Google and Microsoft are, anecdotally, the sort of company that has such a lab and, possibly, the costs of such a lab may not be relevant expenditure if the lab work goes off at a complete tangent). An extension of the trade can be the possibility of licensing out any resulting intellectual property—it does not have to be used by the company in producing goods and services directly.

10.5   Where the trade of the company is the carrying out of research and development then HMRC take the view that the research and development carried out is still considered to be relevant to that trade. In addition, where (for example) a single group company carries out research and development on a subcontracted basis for other group companies, the research and development company and the payer company are (in effect) considered together when determining whether the research and development qualifies for relief (CTA 2009, s 1082).

10.6   Finally, relevant research and development expenditure will also include expenditure on medical research that is particularly relevant to the welfare of workers employed in the trade of the company. This will generally only apply to trades where there are specific risks to workers: for example, in the mining sector.

Accounting definition

10.7   Finance Act 2000 introduced a definition of 'research and development' for tax purposes, so that research and development for tax purposes has the same meaning that it does in generally accepted accounting practice (CTA 2010, s 1138 and ITA 2007, s 1006).

10.8   The corporate intangibles tax rules outsource the definition of research and development by ensuring that an activity will broadly qualify as research and development for tax purposes if it would be treated as research and development under generally accepted accounting practice for companies in the UK (under SSAP13 or the Financial Reporting Standards for Smaller Entities (FRSSE)).

UK GAAP

10.9   Under UK accounting practice, research and development is divided into:

- 'pure research', which is experimental work that seeks scientific or technological knowledge for its own sake;

- 'applied research', which is original or critical investigation undertaken to gain a new scientific or technical knowledge and directed towards a specific practical objective; and

- 'development', which is the application of scientific or technological knowledge to produce new or substantially improved products, materials, devices or services; also the installation of, or substantial improvement of already installed, new processes and systems prior to commencement of commercial production or application.

International accounting standards

10.10   International accounting standards' definition of research and development (IAS 38) is wider than the UK GAAP definition:

- 'research' is original and planned investigation undertaken with the prospect of gaining new scientific or technical knowledge and understanding; and

- 'development' is the application of research findings or other knowledge to a plan or design for the production of new or substantially improved materials, devices, products, processes, systems or services prior to the commencement of commercial production or use.

Tax definition of research and development

10.11   For tax purposes, the accounting practice definitions are modified by Guidelines (the 'Guidelines on the Meaning of Research and Development for Tax Purposes'), the latest edition of which were issued by the DTI in 2004. The 2004 Guidelines differ slightly in approach to the previous Guidelines (issued in 2000) and cover in some detail the meaning of 'research and development' with examples indicating what can and cannot qualify as research and development. HMRC have published their commentary and interpretation of the Guidelines in the Corporate and Intangibles Research and Development (CIRD) Manual, starting at CIRD81900.

10.12   The 2004 Guidelines take precedence over accounting definitions for tax purposes; activities that are research and development for accounting purposes may not, therefore, be regarded as research and development for tax purposes.

10.13   The principal distinctions between the tax definition and the UK accounting definition of research and development are in the area of development: pure and applied research (as defined for accounting purposes) should qualify as research and development for tax purposes. However, development will only qualify as research and development where it concerns *appreciable* (rather than substantial) improvements to products, materials, and devices, etc. Development related to installation of new processes and systems will generally not be research and development for tax purposes, under the 2004 Guidelines, unless there is also a technological uncertainty that needs to be resolved, advancing technology, in the process.

10.14   The tax definition of research and development is considerably narrower than the IAS definition: under IAS, there is no requirement either than any technological uncertainties be resolved, or that any advance in science or technology is sought.

10.15   The focus of the 2004 Guidelines is on activity, rather than attempting to formulate a definition of 'research and development'. Instead, research and development is described as activities that take place within a qualifying project.

Project

10.16   A project is defined by the Guidelines as a collection of 'activities conducted to a method or plan in order to achieve an advance in science or technology' (para 19). The beginning and end of a project are not always straightforward to determine, as projects may arise out of other projects and activities.

10.17   For the project to qualify as research and development for tax purposes the Guidelines state that it must seek to achieve an advance in science or technology (para 3). For example, periodic updating or modification of a product will not be research and development unless that updating or modification involves an appreciable element of innovation.

10.18   The project must seek to achieve the advance through resolution of scientific or technological uncertainty (para 4). This point was emphasised in the case of *BE Studios v Smith & Williamson* [2005] EWHC 1506 (Ch), [2006] STC 358, where the company claiming the relief could not show the necessary advance in scientific or technological knowledge. Merely being 'cutting edge' and 'innovative' was not sufficient; the research and development had to resolve some scientific or technological uncertainty.

10.19   A project is defined by the 2004 Guidelines as a collection of 'activities conducted to a method or plan in order to achieve an advance in science or technology' (¶19). Only some of these activities will qualify as research and development. The beginning and end of a project are not always straightforward to determine, as projects may arise out of other projects and activities.

10.20   For the project to qualify as including qualifying research and development for tax purposes the 2004 Guidelines state that it must seek to achieve an advance in science or technology (¶3). For example, periodic updating or modification of a product will not be research and development unless that updating or modification involves an appreciable element of innovation.

10.21   The project must seek to achieve the advance through resolution of scientific or technological uncertainty. It is the activities which seek to resolve this uncertainty which are qualifying research and development for tax purposes (¶4). This point was emphasised in the case of *BE Studios v Smith & Williamson* [2006] STC 358, where the company claiming the relief could not show the necessary advance in scientific or technological knowledge. Merely being 'cutting edge' and 'innovative' was not sufficient; the research and development had to resolve some scientific or technological uncertainty.

Activities

10.22   Research and development activities are those which directly contribute to attempting to resolve the underlying uncertainty which would lead to an advance in either science or technology (¶4, ¶26). These include:

- scientific or technological design, testing and analysis undertaken to resolve the scientific or technological uncertainty;

- scientific or technological planning activities; and

- activities to create or adapt software, materials or equipment needed to resolve the scientific or technological uncertainty, provided that the software, material or equipment is created or adapted solely for use in research and development (¶27).

10.23   Identifying when qualifying activities start is important to ensure that research and development tax relief is maximised: the qualifying activities begin when the work to resolve an uncertainty begins, once the uncertainty has been identified, and there is no qualifying research and development until that uncertainty has been identified (¶33).

10.24   The project will end either when the uncertainty has been resolved or the project is abandoned. Uncertainty will, generally, be considered to be resolved when the knowledge obtained from the qualifying activities can be expressed in a tangible form, perhaps as a prototype, or as a published document (¶34).

10.25   A project does not need to succeed in order for its activities to qualify as research and development (¶10): it is the intention of the project that is important, not the outcome. Arguably, a failure of the project can still be considered to be an advance in science or technology: by failing, the project has expanded the knowledge of what does not work.

Qualifying indirect activities

10.26   In addition to the activities which directly contribute to resolving the uncertainty, certain indirect activities are also regarded as research and development activities (¶5). The status of qualifying indirect activities has been in doubt from time to time, but HMRC have confirmed that qualifying indirect activities do constitute research and development for relief purposes (see, eg, HMRC Manual CIRD81300).

10.27   The Guidelines provide an exhaustive list (¶31). If an activity is not on this list, it is not a qualifying indirect activity (¶32):

- indirect supporting activities: maintenance, security, administration and clerical activities, and finance and personnel activities, insofar as undertaken for research and development;

- ancillary activities essential to the undertaking of research and development (eg taking on and paying staff, leasing laboratories and maintaining research and development equipment including computers used for research and development purposes);

- training required to directly support a research and development project;

- research by students and researchers carried out at universities;

- research (including related data collection) to devise new scientific or technological testing, survey, or sampling methods, where this research is not research and development in its own right;

- feasibility studies to determine the strategic direction of a specific research and development activity; and

- scientific and technical information services for the purpose of research and development support (eg the preparation of the original report of research and development findings).

Non-qualifying activities

10.28   The Guidelines also include a list of activities (¶28) which specifically do not directly contribute to the resolution of scientific or technological uncertainty and so will not be qualifying research and development. This list is not exhaustive; any activities which are not qualifying research and development, or qualifying indirect activities, will be non-qualifying:

- commercial and financial activities;

- non-scientific or non-technological aspects of a new or appreciably improved process, material, device, product or service;

- production and distribution of goods and services;

- administration and other supporting services;

- general support services; and

- qualifying indirect activities.

Science and technology

10.29   Science is defined in the Guidelines as 'the systematic study of the nature and behaviour of the physical and material universe' (¶15), and specifically excludes any study of the arts, humanities and social sciences. Included within science is work in physics, chemistry, engineering (civil, mechanical, etc). Arguably, mathematics is not included, as it is not specifically the study of the nature and behaviour of the physical and material universe. In practical terms, any commercial research and development project is unlikely to involve pure mathematics without also involving physics in particular, if not other sciences.

10.30   Technology is defined as 'the practical application of scientific principles and knowledge' (¶17).

10.31 It is the particular project that is important; the overall business need not be specifically focused on science or technology.

Example 10.1

A logistics trucking company develops a new low-cost refrigeration unit for its trucks, subcontracting much of the work. The project requires the resolution of an area of technological uncertainty with regard to the refrigeration material and the refrigeration material developed represents an advance in scientific knowledge.

The project will be qualifying research and development, although the principal business of the company (logistics, trucking goods around the country) does not initially appear likely to involve research and development.

Advance in science or technology

10.32 Activities may be research and development if the project they form part of is concerned with (¶6–12):

- the use of new scientific or technological principles in an existing area of investigation; or

- the adaptation of existing scientific or technological principles to a new area of investigation.

Advances in science or technology sought by a project must be advances in *overall* knowledge in that field, not simply in the company's knowledge. Overall knowledge is that which is publicly available or readily deducible by a competent professional in that field; companies are not expected to know their competitors' trade secrets, for example (¶20–22).

Uncertainty

10.33 The Guidelines do not specifically state what is or is not uncertainty; instead, it is considered to be present when certain factors exist (¶13–14):

- where the ability to achieve the scientific or technological objective is unknown;

- where the method of achieving that objective is not readily ascertainable;

- where a particular type of method of achieving an objective is not readily ascertainable, for example, producing a low-cost version, or improving reliability.

10.34 Uncertainty is more than simply a lack of knowledge; if the competent professional in the field could readily resolve the problem, then that problem is not considered to be uncertainty under the Guidelines.

Commercial development

10.35   Commercial development is excluded under the Guidelines; it may be difficult in some areas to decide whether development is commercial or not and the Guidelines suggest that what is important is the motive behind the development; if it is being carried on to test the viability of the research and development then it may be classed as research and development itself. For example, drug development may involve testing to ensure that the delivery mechanism (the tablet casing or bindings in which the active ingredients are bound to enable a patient to take the drug) does not interfere with the drug itself. The dyes used in a casing could potentially interfere with the drug, for example, so expenditure on establishing the colour of the final product may be qualifying research and development. Expenditure on establishing the best colour for a new type of mobile phone, however, is very unlikely to be qualifying research and development, even where the phone itself contains technology developed through qualifying research and development.

10.36   If the scientific or technology uncertainty which the research and development sought to overcome is no longer in question, the continued development is likely to be considered to be commercial; expenditure on commercial development will be dealt with under the general rules.

10.37   In some cases, research and development activities may overlap with non-research and development ones—for example, where work continues on resolving the scientific or technological uncertainties underlying a project to develop a particular product whilst, at the same time, carrying out market research to support work on the aesthetic development of the product.

10.38   Careful analysis of the various activities involved in a project is necessary to be able to support a claim for research and development tax relief; there is no single methodology that can be applied to distinguish qualifying activities from non-qualifying activities, so each project must be considered on its facts.

Particular cases

Prototypes

10.39   The boundary between experimental development (which is research and development for tax purposes) and pre-production activity (which is not) can be extremely grey in respect of prototypes in engineering work. The design, construction and testing of a prototype will generally involve qualifying research and development expenditure.

10.40   There can be more than one prototype before the research and development activities of a project are completed; either the initial prototype continues to be modified, or the project generates a series of prototypes. A series of prototypes will be produced where testing renders the previous prototype unusable, or where multiple models are required for field-testing. For example, electronic equipment used in racing cars is likely to need to be tested in races as part of the research and development process: the research and development will not be complete until it has been established that the electronics can perform in the harsh environment of a race; where the cars complete in a race series open to a variety of cars, the equipment will need to be tested in all the cars to ensure that it can operate not only in the conditions but also in each of the types of cars. Each of the prototypes will, at this stage, still be within qualifying research and development if the resolution of uncertainties is being tested (for example, to check whether a new type of anti-vibration system functions). It is generally not cost-effective to attempt to reproduce this type of race environment simply for testing purposes!

10.41   Once testing is satisfactorily completed and the uncertainty has been resolved, further work will be classed as pre-production and subsequent prototypes will be commercial development, which will not qualify for the enhanced relief.

Areas of difficulty

10.42   This has, historically, been an area of contention between taxpayers and HMRC. ¶28(c) of the 2004 Guidelines explicitly excludes production activity from the definition of research and development, and defines production as being activity undertaken with a view to producing goods or services for supply to customers. This is a rather wide definition.

10.43   The area of contention is around 'first in class' products and other one-off items that may be produced as prototypes but, if they work, would then be sold to a customer. It is not necessarily economically appropriate to scrap the prototype and rebuild it for sale, particularly where it is a bespoke item and there is no intention to produce any further quantities for sale. HMRC accepted that if the sole aim of producing the prototype was for use in research and development, but it was later sold to a customer, that would not change the nature of the activity in constructing the prototype. The particular problem was with projects where the intention was, on creation of a successful version, to sell that version to the customer: ie where the intention to sell arose later, after the research and development.

10.44   This did not entirely accord with other areas of the 2004 Guidelines, as ¶34 states that a research and development 'project ends … when a prototype or pilot plant with all the functional characteristics of the final process, material, device, product or service is produced'. That is, the research and development ends after the prototype/pilot has been produced and not before.

HMRC draft guidance on production and prototypes

10.45 After much discussion, HMRC have produced a revision to their manual section CIRD81350 (still in draft at the time of writing) which acknowledges that if the main aim of creating a prototype is experimentation to resolve an uncertainty, then part the costs of producing the prototype can still be part of research and development, even where it is successful and is intended to sold to a customer in the event of success.

10.46 The draft guidance indicates that HMRC do now accept that where production trials 'are necessary to test whether the scientific or technical advance has been made, the whole or part of the expenditure on such a trial may be on R&D, depending on the degree of uncertainty existing within the process at a particular time'.

10.47 This is not as helpful as it could be, but it is a reasonable step forward. It does mean more documentation: HMRC will be looking for information as to when in the production trial the uncertainty was resolved, for example, so some consideration of the point will need to be made and recorded. This does extend to bespoke products (or 'first in class' products, as HMRC refers to them), where part of the 'costs ... would qualify for R&D relief, even though the total build costs would not'. Again, the company will need to determine where in the process the uncertainty was resolved.

Computer software

10.48 Software development can be either the object of research and development or to produce a tool for use in a research and development project—a modelling system, for example, or data handling software (CIRD81960).

10.49 Qualifying software research and development includes theoretical computer science, the development of new operating systems and new languages, significant technical advances in algorithms, and artificial intelligence investigation.

10.50 However, routine software activities are not research and development. These include:

- supporting existing systems;
- converting or translating programming languages;
- de-bugging systems;

- adapting existing software; and

- producing user documentation.

10.51   Where software is used to achieve research and development, expenditure on the software element of the project may still qualify for enhanced research and development relief even though there is no technical advance to the software itself involved. The types of project that are likely to qualify would include:

- drug design; and

- aerospace innovation,

as both of these fields make extensive use of computer modelling. This will require expenditure on creating computer software to do the modelling and will be part of the qualifying research and development expenditure on the pharmaceutical or aerospace project, even where creating the software alone would not be qualifying research and development.

10.52   Using software simply to simulate aerodynamics or fluid dynamics, though, will probably not qualify as research and development expenditure. However, developing new software to provide such 'in silico' simulation might qualify (provided that the necessary advance in scientific or technological knowledge could be shown).

Capitalised software

10.53   Where internally developed software is classed as a tangible asset in the accounts—because it is software included within hardware costs as being 'directly attributable to bringing a computer system or other computer-operated machinery into working condition for its intended use within the business'— then the included software would not be within the intangibles regime and so the expenditure would not be able to be excluded from the regime to fall within the research and development reliefs. The overall capital expenditure on the system as a whole, including the software, would generally be eligible for plant and machinery capital allowances.

10.54   Other internal software development (not so linked to hardware) should be within SSAP13 and so expenditure on it is capable of being within the research and development reliefs even if it is capitalised, as the result should be an intangible fixed asset.

10.55   Expenditure on an intangible fixed asset that is qualifying research and development expenditure is excluded from the intangible fixed asset rules, even where the expenditure has been capitalised (CTA 2009, s 814) so that immediate tax deductions can be given for the expenditure within other tax rules on research and development, including these research and development reliefs.

10.56 Capitalisation of research and development under SSAP13 is an option even where the specific conditions are met, rather than a requirement, so it should be possible to ensure that the expenditure is not capitalised in the first place.

Pharmaceuticals

10.57 HMRC have issued additional guidance on the availability of research and development relief for activities in pharmaceutical research and development (HMRC Manual CIRD81920).

10.58 In practice, HMRC will generally accept research activities of discovery, pre-clinical development and Phase I–III clinical trials (required for licensing of medicines by a regulator) will usually be concerned with the resolution of scientific and technological uncertainty.

10.59 Phase IV clinical trials are carried out post-licensing and are focused on longer-term safety and efficacy; the scientific advance has generally been established by the time the licence for the medicine is granted and so HMRC will not expect companies to claim research and development relief for these trials; that said, they accept that in unusual circumstances qualifying research and development may be done in Phase IV trials—payments to volunteers will nevertheless be qualifying expenditure (see para **10.129**).

10.60 This does not override the general principles of what activities qualify as research and development: brand name research and development work, for example, will not qualify.

Generics

10.61 Once a patent on a pharmaceutical drug has expired, other companies can produce generic versions of that drug. To get a licence for a generic drug, the company generally only needs to demonstrate that their product is bio-equivalent and has equal clinical safety to the previously-patented product. Neither of these demonstrations is likely to involve the resolution of any scientific or technological uncertainty and so a generic drug manufacturer is unlikely to have qualifying research and development activities.

RESEARCH AND DEVELOPMENT TAX RELIEF

10.62 The relief was originally introduced for small- and medium-sized companies, applying from 1 April 2000. It was extended—with some modifications—to large companies in the 2002 Budget and has since been further modified by subsequent Finance Acts. There are, in effect, two reliefs: the small- and medium-sized companies' relief and the large companies' relief. Revenue expenditure of a small- and medium-sized enterprise (SME) that does not qualify for the SME relief may, in some circumstances, qualify for the large company relief. The rules are now contained in CTA 2009, Part 13.

10.63   The research and development reliefs are only available for companies, not partnerships, individuals or other non-corporate entities.

SME relief

10.64   The SME research and development relief is available to small and medium sized companies which have qualifying research and development expenditure and are either carrying on a trade, or preparing to trade.

10.65   The relief provides an enhanced deduction for tax purposes of an additional 125% (from 1 April 2012) of qualifying revenue expenditure on qualifying research and development, in addition to the 100% deduction already available for revenue expenditure under the normal tax rules (CTA 2009, s 1004(8), amended by Finance Act 2012, Sch 3, para 2). Before 1 April 2012, the additional deduction was: between 1 April 2011–31 March 2012, 100%; between 1 August 2008–31 March 2011, 75%; before 1 August 2008, 50%).

Example 10.2

SMECo carries out qualifying research and development, and its qualifying costs for the accounting period starting on 1 April 2012 are £150,000. It will be able to claim a total deduction in respect of research and development of £337,500:

Expenditure	£150,000
Research and development tax relief @ 125%	£187,500
Total deduction	£337,500

10.66   In some circumstances, an SME may only be able to claim an additional deduction equal to the large company relief (30%)—this will, in general, be in circumstances where the company does not qualify for the full SME relief (see para **10.141**).

Definition of small- and medium-sized (CTA 2009, ss 1119–1120)

10.67   Before 1 August 2008 the standard EU definition of an SME (EU Recommendation 2003/61) applied to establish the companies entitled to the

SME relief (see earlier editions of this book for more information). From that date (date appointed by SI 2008/1880), the small- and medium-sized companies' relief was extended to be available to 'larger SMEs' that have fewer than 500 employees in a year and either, or both of:

- an annual turnover not exceeding €100 million; and

- a period-end balance sheet total not exceeding €86 million.

10.68   These figures are double the normal SME thresholds; some companies that qualify as SMEs under this test will not normally consider themselves to be SMEs because they are used to dealing with the standard EU definition (this is particularly the case in the biotechnology/pharmaceutical sector, where there are a number of EU benefits for SMEs, so that the company status is generally kept under review). These companies may need to be convinced that they qualify for SME research and development relief!

10.69   The calculation of these limits may include the employees, turnover and balance sheet total of other enterprises, including partner enterprises and linked enterprises, if the company in question is not a standalone company. Note that, although only *companies* may claim research and development tax relief, the tests take into account *enterprises*, which may not be corporate entities: an enterprise is any entity carrying on an economic activity, regardless of its legal form, and so can include even an individual.

10.70   In all cases, to be an SME or larger SME, the company must be independent: that is, less than 25% of its capital or voting rights can be owned by one or more companies that are not SMEs (Art 3.1 EU Recommendation 2003/61) unless such companies are venture capital companies or institutional investors and public investment corporations, provided that they do not have actual control of the SME (Art 3.2, 3.3 EU Recommendation 2003/61 and CIRD91300).

10.71   The independence requirement does not mean that the SME cannot be part of a group; provided that the group as a whole meets the SME criteria then a subsidiary (including a subsidiary of an overseas company) can be a qualifying SME for the purposes of research and development relief.

Partner enterprises

10.72   Partner enterprises (Art 3.2, EU Recommendation 2003/61) are those in which one enterprise does not control another but where, either alone or in connection with linked enterprises, one enterprise owns 25% or more of the share capital or voting rights of the enterprise under consideration.

10.73   In this case, the limits are applied to the aggregate of the figures of the enterprise under consideration together with the appropriate percentage of the figures of the partner enterprises. However, note that venture capital companies, business angels, universities and institutional investors may own more than 25% (but not more than 50%) of the company without being considered to be a partner enterprise of the company (CIRD91700).

Linked enterprises

10.74   Linked enterprises are those in which one enterprise can exercise control, directly or indirectly, over the affairs of the other(s) (Art 3.3, EU Recommendation 2003/61, and CIRD91600) by having:

- more than 50% of the shareholders' or members' voting rights in another enterprise, either directly or as a result of provisions in a shareholder agreement;

- the right to appoint or remove a majority of the members of the administrative, management or supervisory body of that other enterprise;

- the right to exercise a dominant influence over another enterprise as a result of the terms of a contract entered into with that enterprise or as a result of a provision in its memorandum or Articles of Association.

10.75   Enterprises can also be linked if a relationship of the sort listed above exists through an individual or group of individuals acting together, but only if the enterprises are engaged (wholly or partly) in the same markets or adjacent markets in a vertical supply chain.

10.76   The limits are applied to the aggregate of the figures for *all* the enterprises with which the company under consideration is linked, together with those of the company itself.

Change in size

10.77   HMRC provide a 'year of grace' for companies which exceed the SME thresholds. Such a company will not change status from SME to large unless it exceeds the thresholds for two years in a row, in which case it will become large with effect from the second year (HMRC Manual CIRD92000).

10.78   This 'year of grace' only applies in respect of the staff, turnover and assets thresholds: if a company ceases to meet the SME thresholds because it no longer meets the independence requirement, the year of grace will not apply and the company will be treated as large from the beginning of the accounting period in which it was taken over.

Going concern

10.79 The accounts of an SME claiming the SME relief or the repayment credit must be prepared on a going concern basis (CTA 2009, s 1046 and s 1057), but this must not be only because it is expected that research and development relief will be received. There must be other reasons for enabling the accounts to be prepared on a going concern basis (CTA 2009, s 1106).

10.80 A company will not be a going concern at any time if it is in administration or liquidation (CTA 2009, s 1046; after amendment by FA 2012, Sch 3, para 9 with effect for claims for relief made on or after 1 April 2012). This amendment was introduced because a company's going concern status had been determined by the most recent set of accounts; these may have been prepared several months ago, and the company's financial position could have changed substantially in the meantime.

10.81 Note that where a company fails to qualify for the SME relief on a going concern basis, it will not be able to claim *any* research and development relief, either under the SME relief or the large company relief. Where a company fails to qualify for the SME relief for other reasons, it can usually claim an amount equal to the large company additional deduction instead (see para **10.141**). This option is not available to companies that fail to qualify on a going concern basis.

Qualifying expenditure

10.82 The expenditure that qualifies for relief (CTA 2009, ss 1052–1053) must:

- be revenue expenditure
- relevant to the trade of the SME
- relate to:
  - the cost of qualifying staff involved;
  - software and consumable items used;
  - qualifying subcontractor costs;
  - costs of externally provided workers (for expenditure incurred after 26 September 2003); and
  - payments to the subjects of clinical trials (for expenditure incurred after 1 August 2008).

Note that the expenditure does not need to be incurred in the UK. This is one of the more generous aspects of the UK research and development tax relief; many other countries restrict relief to expenditure incurred in that country alone.

10.83   There is no requirement for the research and development to be successful; after all, an advance in the state of knowledge of science and technology includes new knowledge as to what does *not* work.

10.84   Previously, where the research and development was successful, an SME had to own any resulting intellectual property; this requirement was abolished for expenditure incurred on or after 9 December 2009 (by FA(No3) Act 2010, s 13) although, in practice, if the SME does not own resulting intellectual property, HMRC are likely to query whether the SME is in fact acting as a subcontractor to the company that will own the intellectual property and so has only limited entitlement to research and development relief (see para **10.147**).

Minimum expenditure (historic)

10.85   For accounting periods beginning before 1 April 2012, there was a requirement that the company spend a minimum of £10,000 on research and development before being able to claim the relief (CTA 2009, s 1050—Finance Act 2012, Sch 3, para 3 sets out the removal). This minimum was tested against the aggregate of:

- qualifying expenditure on research and development undertaken by the company itself; and

- qualifying expenditure on research and development undertaken by sub-contractors; and

- additional qualifying SME expenditure (ie that which qualified only for the large company relief because, for example, a subsidy has been received for the project).

If the accounting period was more or less than 12 months, the minimum expenditure requirement was increased or reduced pro rata.

10.86   In practice, the costs of making an research and development relief claim may outweigh the benefits of the relief for very small claims so that this de minimis may continue in practice if not in law: the removal is likely to be most useful where a project continues over more than one year, with very small expenditure amounts in the last year. As most of the work involved in making a claim will be a repetition of work done in previous years, the costs of a final year claim may not be prohibitive compared to the relief claimed for small amounts of expenditure.

Example 10.3

ClaimCo spent the following amounts on research and development in 2012:

- £2,500 on staff costs on research and development;

- £5,000 on qualifying research and development that is subcontracted out

- £3,000 on a self-employed consultant assisting staff in research and development activities;

- £2,000 on a research and development project for which a subsidy has been received.

Total expenditure: £12,500

The costs of the consultant are not qualifying research and development expenditure and so, as the remaining expenditure was less than £10,000, ClaimCo could not claim research and development tax relief on the qualifying expenditure before the removal of the de minimis restriction.

If the consultant had been employed through a staff provider, so that the costs were capable of being categorised as expenditure on an externally provided worker, then the £10,000 de minimis would have been met and research and development tax relief could have been claimed on the full expenditure.

Revenue expenditure

10.87 For the expenditure to be eligible for research and development relief, it must be allowable as a deduction in calculating in the profits of the trade (CTA 2009, s 1044); ie it must be revenue expenditure of the company. The accounting treatment of the expenditure will be important in considering whether the expenditure can be deducted.

UK GAAP: accounting treatment of research costs

10.88 SSAP13 requires that pure and applied research costs are generally deducted immediately in the profit and loss account as they are incurred, because:

- the outcome of the research will usually be uncertain for much of the project. As a result, it would not be prudent to carry the costs forward as it may not be possible to match them against future economic value arising from the expenditure. Expenditure is generally only capitalised where future economic benefit can be identified, and is then written off (through amortisation) over the period for which it is expected to generate economic benefits. In this way, the expenditure is effectively matched to the income which it generates;

- even where the research has advanced to a point where it is reasonable to expect that the carried forward costs will be able to be matched to related income, the receipts of income will remain uncertain (as to when they will arise, and the total expected income). It would still be impractical to try and calculate the accounting periods that will benefit from the research work (the useful economic life of the created intellectual property). In practice it could be very difficult to clearly link any one piece of research work to an income stream, particularly where (for example) multiple research projects over time have contributed to a number of products and different income streams;

- the capitalisation of pure or applied research is specifically disallowed by company law.

10.89   Where the outcome of a project can be identified and the company can identify both the expenditure on the project and the resources to complete the project, then it may be possible to capitalise the expenditure on creating the intellectual property rather than writing the expenditure off immediately through the profit and loss account. In practice this will not happen often, given the inherent uncertainties over intellectual property research.

10.90   A business may prefer the immediate writing off of the expenditure through the profit and loss account in any case, as such a write-off will reduce taxable profits being made elsewhere in the business.

UK GAAP: accounting treatment of development costs

10.91   Development activities are considered to be easier to identify for accounting purposes, and easier to match to actual or potential future revenues. SSAP 13 states that 'expenditure on such development is normally undertaken with a reasonable expectation of specific commercial success and of future benefits arising from the work, either from increased revenue and related profits or from reduced costs'.

10.92   However, even at a development stage there can often still be areas of uncertainty over features of a project, including:

- its technical feasibility; and
- its ultimate commercial viability considered in the light of factors such as:

    — likely market conditions (including competing products or services);

    — public opinion; and

    — consumer and environmental legislation,

and so, given the accounting concept of prudence, development costs will still be deducted in the profit and loss account if the future economic benefit is not sufficiently certain.

10.93   Note, however, that only development which still relates to scientific or technical uncertainties will be qualifying research and development for tax purposes (see para **10.22**).

International accounting standards

10.94 The basic principle in IAS 38 is that all research costs should be expensed (IAS 38.54), and that development costs can be capitalised only once the technical and commercial feasibility of the asset for sale or use has been confirmed (IAS 38.57).

10.95 Where it is not clear whether the research phase has completed and the development phase has begun, IAS 38 requires expenditure to be expensed and not attributed to an asset; HMRC will not be so forgiving when it comes to research and development tax relief and so the fact that research and development expenditure is expensed under IAS 38 will not automatically mean that the expenditure (assuming it is a qualifying project) will qualify for relief.

10.96 Note that a research and development project acquired in a business combination is treated as an asset, even where part of the cost of the project is research. Any subsequent expenditure on that project is accounted for as any other research and development cost, so subsequent research expenditure will be expensed (IAS 38.34).

Capitalised expenditure

10.97 Where development expenditure has been capitalised in the accounts, then it may still be possible to obtain research and development relief for that expenditure. This will usually be where the company has adopted international accounting standards, as IAS38 requires the capitalisation of development costs, but there is still scientific or technological uncertainty so that the activities remain within the scope of qualifying expenditure for research and development relief purposes. This will be unusual; as noted above, IAS38 requires capitalisation where the technical feasibility of the asset has been confirmed, which would usually be after the point at which scientific or technological uncertainties had been resolved.

10.98 In this case, research and development tax reliefs and vaccine research tax relief (for large companies only from 1 April 2012) are available for qualifying revenue expenditure on research which is added to the capitalised costs of an intangible asset in the accounts in accordance with UK GAAP or IAS (FA 2004, s 53; HMRC Manual CIRD 98500).

10.99 Where research and development and vaccine research reliefs are claimed for such expenditure, no tax deduction can be taken for any subsequent amortisation of the capitalised asset in the accounts (see para **11.25** for more details).

Qualifying staff

10.100   Qualifying staff are employees (generally, someone with whom the company claiming the relief has an employment contract (CIRD83000)) and directors who are directly and actively involved in the research and development: researchers, managers, etc, who organise and carry out or support the research and development activity (CTA 2009, s 1124).

10.101   Any support function must still be directly and actively involved to qualify: for example, directing technical activity will qualify for the relief but long-term strategic planning and contract administration will not qualify, and neither will equipment maintenance. It is the actual activity that is important and not the title of the individual. The staff costs must be apportioned for staff members who are not involved full time with the research and development activity. Remember, in particular, that directors and managers may have administrative and other functions that are not related to qualifying research and development. It may be useful to have staff complete time sheets for a representative period to determine the proportion of time spent on qualifying research and development.

10.102   The allowable staff costs (CTA 2009, s 1123) include:

- emoluments paid by the company, including all salaries, wages, bonuses and other perquisites, but *not* benefits-in-kind;

- secondary Class 1 NICs paid by the company; and

- pension fund contributions paid by the company.

Example 10.4

RD Co has three employees, including the managing director. Total staff costs are £110,000 per annum. One employee, a researcher, is paid £30,000 per annum and spends all his time on research and development activities. The managing director is paid £65,000 per annum and spends 50% of her time on research and development activities, 35% of her time maintaining investor relationships and seeking new funding, and 15% of her time on other general administration activities. The third employee, paid £25,000 per annum, supports both of the others and spends around 75% of his time on research and development activities.

The qualifying staff costs are therefore:

Researcher: 100% of £30,000	£30,000
MD: 50% of £60,000	£30,000
Assistant: 75% of £20,000	£15,000
Total qualifying staff costs:	£75,000

10.103 The exclusion of benefits-in-kind can be an issue for small technology companies that reward staff with share options, to participate in the growth in the company, and can only afford to pay small salaries: only the salaries will count as research and development expenditure. The share options are benefits-in-kind and so are not qualifying staff costs.

10.104 Where staff are seconded intra-group and salary costs incurred by another group company are recharged to the research and development company, these are not qualifying staff costs for the purposes of research and development relief although they may qualify as costs of externally provided workers (see para **10.116** onwards).

Software and consumable or transformable material

10.105 Consumable items include supplies directly used up in the research and development activity—essentially materials and equipment, but only where the equipment has a short useful life. Consumable items also include utilities such as power, water and fuel (CTA 2009, ss 1125–1126).

10.106 HMRC will accept claims for relief on expenditure on materials (such as chemicals) that are recycled provided that the materials are actually used in the first place and (in practice, although not stated in guidance) will generally accept expenditure on catalyst materials which, by their nature, are not transformed or used up (HMRC Manual CIRD82400).

10.107 If the software, materials or utilities are only partly used for research and development, an apportionment needs to be made: any practical apportionment can be made, such as by floor area or staff headcount, between research and development activity utilisation and non-research and development activity utilisation. Where a research and development function makes heavy use of utilities, it may be cost-effective to have separate metering for the research and development areas to evidence that utilisation.

Example 10.5

TechCo has electricity bills of £250,000 per annum for the building in which its offices and labs are based. The labs make up 60% of the area of the building and so TechCo makes a research and development claim for 60% of £250,000 = £150,000 in respect of the power costs.

As noted above, TechCo should consider whether it would be better to have separate meters for the labs area and the administration area if the research and development activity is an intensive user of power, as apportionment by area may not adequately reflect the research and development element of the power costs.

TechCo has also spent £100,000 on a software licence. The software is used by one administration employee (not for qualifying indirect activities) and 12 research and development workers. In this case, one-thirteenth of the licence cost will not qualify but the balance of £92,308 will qualify for research and development relief.

Capital equipment: research and development allowances only

10.108   Equipment that is expected to have an enduring benefit to the company is capital expenditure and does not qualify for the research and development tax relief, but it should qualify for the 100% research and development allowance (see Chapter 4).

Subcontracted research and development

10.109   Expenditure on subcontracted qualifying research and development will qualify for research and development relief for the SME, and the subcontractor to an SME cannot claim research and development relief on its costs (CTA 2009, ss 1065–1068), even where that subcontractor is another SME.

10.110   The subcontractor does not have to be a small- or medium-sized company for the relief to be available to the claimant and it need not be in the UK. The work done by a subcontractor need not, on its own, qualify for research and development relief provided that it is part of a larger project of the SME that will qualify.

10.111   For example, some testing procedures are better outsourced than done in house by a claimant because it would not be cost-effective for the claimant company to purchase the equipment needed for testing. The testing procedure alone would not be considered to be research and development because it does not involve any innovation. However, where it is a part of an activity that does meet the definition of research and development, the costs of the subcontract will be part of the qualifying research and development costs for relief.

10.112   Where the company and the subcontractor are connected persons (as defined in CTA 2010, s 1122; see para **18.66**) the company can claim relief on the lower of:

● the costs which the subcontractor includes in his year-end accounts in respect of staff and consumables costs relating to the work done;

● the amount of the company's payment to the subcontractor (CTA 2009, s 1134).

10.113   If the company and the subcontractor are not connected, they may still elect to use the connected person's treatment (CTA 2009, s 1135). The election needs to be made within two years of the end of the accounting period of the company in which the subcontract is entered into. As the election needs to be joint, the company should ensure that any contract relating to the subcontract work requires the subcontractor to sign such an election when requested to do so.

10.114 This election also, in effect, requires the subcontractor to disclose to the research and development company information that would indicate the profit being made on the contract: the subcontractor may be reluctant to provide this information and so may not agree to enter into the election.

10.115 If the joint election is not made, the company can claim relief on 65% of the payment made to the subcontractor (CTA 2009, s 1136).

Example 10.6

RD Co subcontracts a specialist testing routine to Sub Co for a payment of £100,000. The two companies are not connected.

Sub Co's accounts show qualifying costs in respect of that subcontracted test of £75,000; the rest of the charge to RD Co reflects the use of equipment, which is not a qualifying cost, and a profit margin.

If no election is made, RD Co can claim 65% of the payment made, ie £65,000.

If RD Co and Sub Co make the election, RD Co can claim the lower of its actual payment (£100,000) and Sub Co's costs (£75,000). RD Co would be better making the election, if it can persuade SubCo to do so, as this will enable it to claim £75,000 rather than being restricted to the 65% (£65,000) otherwise available.

Externally provided workers

10.116 Relief is available for workers who are not employed by the company carrying out the SME but, instead, are employed by an intermediary company to provide services to the SME (CTA 2009, s 1127). A staff provider may also include another company within the same group as the company carrying out research and development.

10.117 There are strict requirements that must be met for the expenditure to be eligible (CTA 2009, s 1128), requiring that the worker:

- must be an individual;

- cannot be a director or employee of research and development company (this was confirmed in *Gripple Ltd v Revenue and Customs Commissioners* [2010] EWHC 1609 (Ch), [2010] STC 228);

- must provide services through a staff provider;

- must be subject to the control of the research and development company; and

- must personally provide services to the research and development company through a contract between the worker and *someone other than the research and development company* (amendment introduced in Finance Act 2012, Sch 3, para 4. For expenditure prior to 1 April 2012, the contract had to be directly with the staff provider. This change allows for other intermediaries to be included in the chain, such as a personal service company).

10.118   The requirement to provide services personally to the research and development company under the contract means that general temporary staff costs will not usually be eligible, as they are not usually contracted to provide services to a specific company. This can also be an area where group employment companies can fail to qualify, where employee contracts simply require them to work for the group as a whole and not for the specific research and development company.

10.119   The external workers must be directly and actively engaged in relevant research and development (CTA 2009, s 1052(3)). Where only a proportion of the external workers' time is spent on relevant research and development activities, relief is available for only that proportion of the costs.

10.120   As a result of these requirements, research and development relief is *not* available for the costs of self-employed consultants (although, of course, the normal revenue deduction will still be available), as the staff provider must be a company. This can be resolved if the consultant operates through a personal service company, as the relief should then be available, provided that the contracts are properly structured.

10.121   Where the external worker is self-employed through a personal service company where the arrangements are such that the provisions of IR35 (see below) do not apply to that personal service company, no research and development relief will be available for the costs of that external worker as the control requirement at para **10.115** will not be met if the arrangements mean that the IR35 provisions do not apply.

10.122   The IR35 provisions are a set of rules that are intended to ensure that employment is not disguised by the use of a worker's personal service company. They do not affect the engager company directly although, as noted above, where the personal service company is outside IR35, the engager company will not be able to claim research and development relief in respect of the costs under the externally provided worker heading.

10.123 In outline, where the rules apply the worker's personal service company is required to account for income tax and national insurance contributions via PAYE on 95% of the income from the engagement. The tests as to whether IR35 applies are broadly the same as the normal employment status tests; the detail of these is outside the scope of this book but, in brief, where the engaging company (the research and development company in this case) has the degree of control over the worker required for the research and development relief deduction as an externally provided worker, it is likely that the IR35 rules will apply to the personal service company. The worker would normally want to ensure that the IR35 rules do *not* apply.

10.124 The deduction which can be made for the research and development tax relief in respect of expenditure on externally provided workers is calculated in a similar way to expenditure on subcontractors.

10.125 Where the research and development company and the staff provider are not connected, the SME can claim research and development relief on 65% of the qualifying payments to the staff provider (CTA 2009, s 1131).

10.126 Where the company and the intermediary are connected (see para **18.66**), the qualifying expenditure is the lower of:

- the costs which the intermediary includes in his year-end accounts in respect of remuneration incurred in providing the company with the staff (ie not including any ancillary costs, such as recruitment costs incurred by the intermediary); and

- the amount of the company's payment to the intermediary (CTA 2009, s 1129).

10.127 If the company and the intermediary are not connected, they may still elect to use the connected person's treatment (CTA 2009, s 1130). The election needs to be made within two years of the end of the accounting period of the company in which the contract is entered into. As the election needs to be joint, the company should ensure that the contract relating to the externally provided workers requires the intermediary to sign such an election when requested to do so.

10.128 If the joint election is not made and the parties are not connected, the company can claim relief on 65% of the payment made to the intermediary.

Example 10.7

ContractCo engages WorkCo to provide two researchers for six months, at a cost to ContractCo of £50,000. The two companies are not connected.

WorkCo's accounts show that it incurred remuneration costs of £30,000 in supplying those researchers to ContractCo; the rest of the charge to ContractCo covers administration costs and profit.

If no election is made, ContractCo can claim the tax credit on 65% of the £50,000 payment made, ie £32,500.

If ContractCo and WorkCo make the election, ContractCo could only claim £30,000 (WorkCo's costs) and so, in this case, there would be no point in making the election.

Clinical trials payments

10.129   Finance Act 2006 introduced relief for payments made to human subjects in clinical trials undertaken in connection with the development of a health care treatment or practice. As these subjects are volunteers, and not employees or externally provided workers, such payments would not otherwise qualify. Research and development relief is specifically available for such payments made by SMEs after 1 August 2008 (FA 2006, Sch 28, para 2 given effect by SI 2008/1878).

Pre-trading expenditure

10.130   Where a company is undertaking research and development in order to be able to trade, but is not yet doing so as part of a taxable trade, there are specific rules to allow the company to claim the SME research and development tax relief immediately in respect of qualifying expenditure (CTA 2009, s 1045). Without such rules, the company could not claim relief until it began trading, when such expenditure would be treated as having been incurred on the first day of trading.

10.131   The company can elect to be treated as having incurred a trading loss for the accounting period equal to 225% (from 1 April 2012; the amount was 200% for the period 1 April 2011–31 March 2012, 175% for the period 1 August 2008–31 March 2011, and 150% before 1 August 2008) of the amount of its qualifying expenditure in that period (FA 2012, Sch 3, para 3).

10.132   The company can therefore surrender the deemed loss and claim the payable research and development tax credit immediately (see below), to assist with cash flow through the pre-trading period. The usual pre-trading rules are disapplied in respect of that expenditure so that it is not brought into account again on the first day of trading.

10.133   The deemed trading loss cannot be carried back against any profits that may have been made by the company in the preceding accounting period, unless the company had research and development pre-trading expenditure in that earlier period although it can be used for group relief or carried forward if not surrendered for repayment (CTA 2009, s 1048).

10.134 If an election is made to treat the expenditure as a deemed trading loss, it must be made in respect of *all* of the qualifying research and development expenditure for that accounting period (CTA 2009, s 1045(7)). An election cannot be made in respect of part only of that expenditure.

10.135 The election must be made in writing to HMRC within two years of the end of the relevant accounting period. The election must specify the accounting period for which it is made, as a separate election is required for each accounting period in which pre-trading research and development expenditure is to be treated as a trading loss (CTA 2009, s 1047).

10.136 Where the company does not yet have an accounting period, it is treated for these purposes as though an accounting period began when the relevant research and development activity began.

Form of the SME research and development relief

10.137 Provided that the SME is carrying on a trade, the relief is taken as an expense, a deduction for tax purposes (CTA 2009, s 1044) reducing a profit or increasing a loss (to reduce future profits) then, if the business is loss-making, the additional loss arising from the relief can be surrendered in exchange for an immediate repayment from HMRC ('the payable research and development tax credit') (CTA 2009, s 1054).

Deduction from profits

10.138 The relief is given by allowing a business to deduct 125% (for expenditure from 1 April 2012; see para **10.65** for rates before that date) of its qualifying expenditure when calculating profits/losses for tax purposes, in addition to the 100% deduction already available under the general rules. See para **10.141** for details of restrictions on the amount of relief given.

10.139 For a tax-paying company, this will reduce the tax liability. For a loss-making company it will increase the loss available to carry forwards or backwards, use against other income of the period, or surrender as group relief.

Example 10.8

Net Co spends £40,000 of qualifying expenditure on relevant research and development activity in a year. The company can deduct £90,000

$(£40,000 + (£40,000 \times 125\%))$

from turnover when calculating its profits/losses for that year.

Claiming the relief

10.140 The relief must be claimed within two years of the end of the accounting period to which the claim relates (FA 1998, Sch 18, para 83B (as amended)). The relief should be claimed on the company's self-assessment return or by an amended return.

See earlier editions of this book for claim periods for accounting periods ending on or before 30 March 2006.

Reduced relief for SMEs

10.141 In various circumstances, an SME is restricted in the amount of relief it can claim: in these circumstances the full SME relief is not available but an amount equal to the large company additional deduction (30%) can be deducted in calculating taxable profits, in addition to the 100% deduction already available under the general rules. The SME can, therefore, deduct only 130% in respect of such expenditure, rather than 225% under the SME relief. This reduced relief is available in respect of capped expenditure, certain subcontracted work, and expenditure covered by grants and subsidies.

10.142 An SME claiming restricted relief will be subject to tax on any refunds of expenditure on which this restricted relief has been claimed. 30% of the refund is treated as trading income of the company (CTA 2009, s 1083).

10.143 Note that no repayment credit (see para **10.157**) is available for an SME in respect of this restricted relief.

Capped relief

10.144 An SME can only claim research and development relief to the extent the total combined research and development relief and vaccine research relief (prior to 1 April 2012, see para **10.203**) claimed for expenditure on a particular project does not exceed €7.5 million in total. This is a lifetime limit on relief for each project (CTA 2009, s 1113).

10.145 There is a formula to calculate the total research and development relief received to date, to identify whether the cap has been reached, and a recalculation is required each year (CTA 2009, s 1114).

10.146 Where the cap is reached for a particular project the SME can no longer claim SME relief on the expenditure in excess of the cap, but it can deduct an amount equal to the large company additional deduction of 30% (CTA 2009, 1068(5)(b)) in respect of any qualifying research and development expenditure in excess of the threshold.

Relief for expenditure on work subcontracted to an SME by a non-SME

10.147 An SME can claim an amount equal to the large company additional deduction (30%) where the company incurs qualifying expenditure on research and development that has been subcontracted to it by either:

- a large company; or

- any person otherwise than in the course of a UK taxable trade, profession or vocation (broadly, such persons are likely to be foreign companies) (CTA 2009, s 1063).

An SME cannot claim *any* research and development relief on work subcontracted to it by another SME within the scope of UK corporation tax as, in that case, the subcontracting company will be able to claim the relief itself.

10.148 The reason for this exception is that, otherwise, all research and development relief would be lost in respect of such subcontracted research and development because a large company cannot claim research and development relief on work that it subcontracts to others. A foreign company could, in theory, set up a UK subsidiary to carry out research and development; that subsidiary would be able to claim research and development relief on qualifying expenditure. In each case, an SME to which the work is subcontracted can claim the large company relief on its expenditure so that some relief is therefore granted. Large companies, in particular, should take note of this and endeavour to negotiate the costs of the contract accordingly, taking into account the enhanced relief that the SME will receive as a result of the subcontract.

State Aid grants

10.149 Where a notified State Aid is received in connection with a research and development project *none* of the expenditure on that project will qualify for the full SME research and development tax relief (CTA 2009, s 1138; HMRC Manual CIRD81670), even if the State Aid grant is intended to cover capital expenditure. This is because the SME research and development relief is a State Aid, and EU rules do not permit the accumulation of State Aid. Most government/EU funding is also a State Aid.

10.150 Where the receipt of a State Aid grant means that the company cannot claim the SME research and development relief, an amount equal to the large company additional deduction (30%) can be claimed for the research and development expenditure on the project instead (CTA 2009, s 1068(5)(a)).

10.151 'Project' is not defined and HMRC state that each case depends on its own merits; in practice, good documentation prepared to establish the scope of a project and supporting the independence of that project from others carried on by the company will assist in any queries that HMRC may raise over the allocation of expenditure between grant-supported and non-supported projects.

10.152 An SME carrying out qualifying research and development should, therefore, take care to establish the effect of the receipt of a grant before applying as it may be considerably less advantageous to accept the grant. The large company relief is given at a lower rate, does not cover subcontracted expenditure, and perhaps most importantly to many SME companies involved in research and development, no repayment credit is available.

Example 10.9

R&D Co has two projects underway. It is considering making an application to the local RDA for a grant for research and development in respect of one of those projects.

The budget for the project in question is £1.5m; the maximum grant for which the company qualifies is £200,000.

If the company does not make the application, it will be able to claim SME research and development relief on the expenditure; assuming that all the expenditure qualifies, the additional research and development relief deduction available during the life of the project will be:

125% of £1.5m = £1,875,000

Assuming that the company is loss-making, this relief can be surrendered (together with the trading loss in respect of the expenditure) in exchange for a repayable tax credit. The overall repayment credit available over the life of the project will be (see para **10.157** onwards):

11% of (£1,500,000+£1,875,000) = £371,250

Net effect if no grant received: £371,250 repayment available, no loss carried forward

In comparison, if the company decides to apply for—and receives—the grant, it will only be able to claim the large company relief in respect of that project (see para **10.150** and note that any research and development relief claim in respect of the other project, for which no grant is claimed, is not affected by the grant received for this project, provided they are independent projects). The additional research and development relief deduction available will be:

30% of £1.5m = £450,000

This assumes that all of the expenditure is incurred in-house: if, for example, £500,000 of the £1.5m project expenditure is subcontracted costs, the research and development relief deduction will only be:

130% of £1m = £300,000

None of this can be surrendered for a repayment.

Net effect of receipt of grant: £200,000 immediately available (from grant), overall loss carried forward from project of £1,950,000 (ie £1.5m plus the research and development relief of £450,000, or less, where work is subcontracted), available for set-off against future profits.

The loss carried forward could, eventually, be worth £429,000 (at an eventual corporation tax rate of 22%) but, for many SMEs involved in research and development, the impact on cashflow of the 'loss' of £171,250 from being unable to claim repayment may be more important than a future deduction against profits.

Other subsidies

10.153   Other grants and subsidies—which do not amount to State Aid—will reduce qualifying expenditure for the purposes of the SME research and development relief but will not disqualify all expenditure on the project (CTA 2009, s 1052; HMRC Manual CIRD81650).

10.154   For that part of the project expenditure that is covered by a grant or subsidy, an amount equal to the large company additional deduction (30%) will be available (CTA 2009, s 1068(4)); SME relief continues to be available for expenditure on the project that is not covered by the non-State Aid grant or subsidy.

10.155   Funding from financial institutions, etc, is not automatically considered to be a subsidy; the nature of the funding and any associated benefits will need to be taken into account. Most funding from financial and similar institutions is in the form of loans or equity investment which will not be considered to be a subsidy.

10.156   In practice, most non-State Aid and subsidies are given for capital expenditure which is not covered by the research and development relief and, where this is the case, they will have no effect on the research and development relief.

PAYABLE RESEARCH AND DEVELOPMENT TAX CREDIT

10.157   If the SME is loss-making once the research and development relief has been deducted, the option of surrendering the loss relating to the SME research and development tax relief and qualifying expenditure and taking the credit as immediate cash is available, but the payment from HMRC is less than the tax ultimately saved if the relief is carried forward as a loss. The repayment option may be preferable for a company that has cash flow issues, where the longer-term financial disadvantage is less important than the short-term need for cash.

10.158 In exchange for surrendering the loss relating to the SME research and development tax relief and qualifying expenditure, the company can claim a repayment that is effectively up to 24.5% of the qualifying costs, calculated according to the loss surrendered and the PAYE and NICs paid by the company.

10.159 Any trading loss carried forward arising in the relevant accounting period is reduced by the loss surrendered to obtain the tax credit repayment.

Surrenderable loss

10.160 The company can surrender a loss equal to the lower of (CTA 2009, s 1055):

- the research and development reduction: 225% (from 1 April 2012) of the qualifying research and development expenditure;
- the total loss of the trade, less:
  - any claim made, or which could be made, to set the loss against other profits or gains of the same accounting period; and
  - any other relief claimed in respect of the losses, including losses carried back to an earlier accounting period or surrendered by group or consortium relief.

10.161 Once the surrenderable loss has been determined, the company can claim a maximum repayment of (CTA 2009, s 1058) 11% of the surrendered loss (previously, the repayment rate was 12.5% from 1 April 2011–31 March 2012; 14% from 1 August 2008–31 March 2011; 16% prior to 1 August 2008). This equates to 24.75% of the qualifying research and development expenditure (25% from 1 April 2011–31 March 2012; 24.5% from 1 August 2008–31 March 2011; 24% prior to 1 August 2008).

10.162 The company is not required to surrender the maximum amount possible; part of the loss arising from the SME research and development tax relief can be retained to carry forwards and, where the full research and development relief cannot be surrendered, must be retained to carry forward to set against future profits.

Example 10.10

LossCo, an SME, spends £250,000 of qualifying expenditure on research and development activity in a year, incurs other losses of £500,000 and has taxable income of £100,000 in that same year from subletting part of its office space.

LossCo's total deduction for research and development is:

£250,000 + (£250,000 × 125%) = £562,500

LossCo can surrender the lower of:

- research and development deduction: £562,500

- total losses: £(500,000 + 562,500 − 100,000) = £837,500 (the total loss of the company after setting losses against income)

As the research and development deduction is less than the total losses, LossCo can surrender the whole of the research and development deduction (£562,500) to obtain a repayment.

PAYE/NIC limitation (historic)

10.163   For expenditure prior to 1 April 2012, the repayment was limited to the total amount of relevant PAYE and Class 1 NICs paid by the company for PAYE periods ending in the relevant accounting period (CTA 2009, s 1059; repealed by FA 2012, Sch 3, para 15).

10.164   The relevant PAYE and Class 1 NICs were:

- the total amount of income tax for which the company is required to account to HMRC for that period under the PAYE regulations, before any deductions authorised in respect of the working families' tax credit (WFTC) or the disabled persons' tax credit (DPTC); and

- the company's Class 1 NICs for which the company is required to account to HMRC for that period, before any deductions authorised in respect of statutory sick pay (SSP), maternity pay or the WFTC and DPTC.

These PAYE and Class 1 NIC amounts were those for which the company is required to account in respect of *all* staff, not only those involved in qualifying research and development activity.

10.165   PAYE periods end on the fifth day of the month, and the relevant PAYE and NICs were those *paid* in the accounting period, not liabilities accrued to the end of the accounting period. Where a company had, for example, an accounting period ending on 31 December, the relevant PAYE and NICs were those actually paid in the 12 PAYE periods ending on 5 December (or the four quarterly periods ended on that date, if the company was a small employer and has elected to make quarterly payments).

Claiming the repayment

10.166   The repayment credit must be claimed within two years of the end of the accounting period to which the claim relates, and must be made in the company's corporation tax return or by amended return (FA 1998, Sch 18, para 10(2) (as amended)). The claim must be quantified when it is made.

10.167 Although HMRC generally pay the repayment credit to the company soon after receipt of the claim, that payment can be withheld if the corporation tax return for that period is subject to enquiry before the research and development repayment has been made.

10.168 No payment will be made until the company has paid all the PAYE and Class 1 NICs for the accounting period of claim. In addition, HMRC can use the repayment credit to discharge any corporation tax liabilities of the company (CTA 2009, s 1060).

10.169 Overpayments of the research and development credit are recovered by HMRC through the existing rules for recovery of excessive repayments and interest (FA 1998, Sch 18, para 52 and CIRD90700). Losses cannot be used to reduce the overpayment (to avoid having to actually pay money back to HMRC) as the repayment credit is not considered to be taxable 'profit' against which losses can be set. Penalties not exceeding the excess credit claimed will be applied to fraudulent or negligent claims, and for failure to remedy otherwise incorrect claims without unreasonable delay (FA 1998, Sch 18, para 83F).

Deduction or repayment: which is more useful?

10.170 To make the decision between taking a repayment and keeping a deduction, the company will need to consider the cost of the capital employed in the business (the interest cost, any returns due on preference shares, etc), and balance that cost against the benefit of a loss going forwards. If a deduction is taken, no benefit as such is received until the business moves into profit, when it will defer the point at which the business exhausts its losses and begins to pay tax on profits.

10.171 The company therefore needs to be funded until it moves into profit and becomes self-sustaining; if the deduction is taken more funds (either raised by borrowing or from the sale of equity) will be needed than if a repayment is taken. If the cost of that additional borrowing or equity sale, less the future tax saving, is more than the difference between the repayment and the future tax saving then it is likely to be better to take the repayment and have the cash immediately, reducing the funding requirement.

Example 10.11

RD Co Ltd carries on research and development, incurring a surrenderable loss of £100,000 in one accounting period. RD Co is loss making and does not expect to have to start paying tax on profits within the next five years.

If the loss is in fact surrendered, RD Co will receive £11,000 back from the HMRC.

If the loss is not surrendered, it will be carried forward until RD Co moves into profit. If, at the point where the loss is utilised against profits, RD Co's tax rate is 20%, a tax saving of £20,000 will be achieved.

The eventual tax saving would be £9,000 more than the repayment.

If, however, by taking the repayment RD Co can avoid the need for additional capital which would, over the anticipated five years until the tax saving is achieved, have support costs with a net present impact of, say, £10,000 (in interest and fund raising costs etc, as well as the potential dilution effect on existing shareholders) it would be more beneficial to take the repayment.

Group relief

10.172 Alternatively, the SME may be able to surrender to the loss to another, profitable, UK group company by way of group relief (CTA 2010, Part 5), although note that the entire group must be within the definition of an SME for the research and development company to qualify for research and development relief.

10.173 A surrender of losses through group relief will reduce the profits of the other company so that the group as a whole benefits more than it would have done if the research and development company had surrendered the loss for a repayment. Where there are cashflow issues for the research and development company, the profitable company to which the loss is surrendered can pay the research and development company for the surrendered loss; such a payment is ignored for corporation tax purposes provided that it does not exceed the corporation tax saved (CTA 2010, s 183).

Example 10.12

If RD Co Ltd in the example above was a member of a group, it could pass the £100,000 of research and development loss by group relief to another group company with profits of more than £100,000. If that company pays tax at the small companies' rate (20%), it will save tax of £20,000.

If the group company pays RD Co Ltd £11,000 for that £20,000 saving for the group relief, RD Co Ltd will be in the same position that it would have been if it had claimed a repayment from HMRC, but the group as a whole has an additional benefit of the extra £9,000 also saved by the profitable group company.

No consortium relief

10.174 An SME may be owned by a consortium rather than a group. A company will be owned by a consortium where at least 75% of its ordinary share capital is owned by two or more companies, each of which owns at least 5% of the share capital (CTA 2010, s 153). Provided that such companies were also SMEs, a company could be owned by a consortium and still qualify as an SME itself (see the independence test at para **10.70** onwards).

10.175 A company can surrender trading losses to consortium members (CTA 2010, s 143) but, where an SME is owned by a consortium, it cannot surrender any research and development relief losses to the consortium members (CTA 2009, s 1049).

LARGE COMPANIES' RELIEF

10.176 A large company is any company that does not meet the definition of a small- or medium-sized company.

Large company relief

10.177 The large company research and development relief provides an enhanced deduction of 30% (25% prior to 1 April 2008) in addition to the standard 100% deduction for revenue expenditure (CTA 2009, s 1074). Changes to the large company relief are under consultation at the time of writing (see para **10.191**).

Example 10.13

LargeCo carries out qualifying research and development, and its qualifying costs for the accounting period starting 1 April 2012 are £150,000. It will be able to claim a total deduction in respect of research and development of £195,000:

Expenditure	£150,000
Research and development tax relief @ 30%	£45,000
Total deduction	£195,000

Qualifying expenditure

10.178 Expenditure that qualifies for the large companies' research and development tax relief is largely the same as that which qualifies for the small- and medium-sized companies relief (see para **10.82**), with the following modifications.

Research and development subcontracted by a large company

10.179 Expenditure by large companies on research and development that is subcontracted *to* another party will not be eligible for research and development relief for the large company, unless the work is subcontracted to one of the following (CTA 2009, s 1078):

- a qualifying body:
    - universities and other higher education institutions;
    - charities;
    - scientific research organisations;
    - NHS bodies; and
- individuals or partnerships of individuals.

10.180 A qualifying body does not have to be based in the UK, but must be approved by HMRC before payments will qualify. A list of already-approved non-UK qualifying bodies is maintained by HMRC (HMRC Manual CIRD82250). If the body in question is not on the list then approval should be sought from HMRC for the body to be designated as qualifying; the enquiry can be made to the appropriate research and development specialist office (see para **10.198**), who will refer it to the CT International and Anti-Avoidance (Technical) department.

10.181 The reason for allowing relief in these specific cases is that, if work is subcontracted by a large company, no research and development relief would be otherwise available to anyone as these entities cannot claim research and development relief on their own account.

10.182 Where work is subcontracted to an SME, that SME can claim an amount equal to the large company additional deduction on the expenditure it incurs in performing the subcontracted work (see para **10.145**) and so no research and development relief can be claimed by the large company commissioning the work. If the work is subcontracted to another large company, that company can claim relief (see below). Note that, in both cases, for a claim for relief to be successful, the activities carried out by the subcontractor will need to be qualifying research and development for the subcontractor—that is, it must be relevant to the trade of the subcontractor (see para **10.4**), not the trade of the large company subcontracting the work. Unless the subcontractor's trade is carrying out research and development, it may not be able to claim the relief. Nevertheless, because the subcontractor could in theory obtain the relief, the large company subcontracting the work will not be able to make a claim.

10.183 Where the large company relief can be claimed on the costs of subcontracting, the full costs can be eligible for relief: there is no requirement to take only 65%, or use connected parties relief, as there is for the SME relief (CTA 2009, s 1078).

Research and development subcontracted to a large company

10.184 Where a large company has work subcontracted *to* it, expenditure by the company on the research and development can be qualify for research and development relief where the work has been subcontracted by either:

- another large company; or

- any person otherwise than in the course of a UK taxable trade, profession, vocation (principally where the work is sub-contracted to the company from overseas)

10.185 The activities subcontracted to the large company must still be qualifying research and development (see para **10.3** onwards) for the company on a stand-alone basis (see para **10.182** and para **10.4**).

10.186 This requirement is modified where the work is subcontracted to the company by another group company which pays for the work, the activities of the two group companies are considered together to determine whether the activities are qualifying research and development. Where the aggregate activities are qualifying research and development, the company carrying out the work will be able to claim the large company research and development relief even if the specific activities would not qualify as research and development expenditure on a stand-alone basis (CTA 2009, s 1082).

10.187 Where work is subcontracted by an SME to a large company, the large company will not be able to claim any relief, to prevent double relief being claimed, as the SME can usually claim the SME research and development relief on some or all of the expenditure it incurs in commissioning that subcontracted work (see para **10.109**).

Contributions to independent research

10.188 Payments to any of the qualifying bodies listed above (see para **10.179**) in respect of their research will also be deductible where the work is not actually subcontracted, ie where the company does not receive the benefit of the work done by the organisation (CTA 2009, s 1079). However, for the expenditure to qualify, the research and development carried out by the organisation must still be relevant to the trade of the company (see para **10.4**). Where the contribution is made to an individual or a partnership, the company must not be connected to the individual or to any member of a partnership.

Grants and subsidies

10.189 Unlike the SME relief, subsidies do not restrict the large company relief as it is not a State Aid. Qualifying expenditure continues to qualify for full large company even where a grant or other subsidy has been received.

Form of the large company research and development relief

10.190 The research and development tax relief for large companies is given by allowing the company to deduct 30% of its qualifying expenditure on research and development, in addition to the 100% deduction given under the normal rules, when calculating its profits for tax purposes; this will either reduce the tax payable by the company or, if it is loss-making, increase the loss available to the company (CTA 2009, s 1074). The deduction was 25% for expenditure incurred prior to 1 April 2008.

Example 10.14

If a company spends £100,000 on qualifying research and development, it can deduct £130,000: £100,000 is deducted under the normal rules and £30,000 is deducted under the research and development tax relief:

- if the company is tax paying, this will reduce tax by up to £7,800 (at the 24% rate of corporation tax, on the £30,000 research and development tax relief); or

- if the company is loss-making, the additional loss can be used as a trading loss of the period and either carried forward or, if appropriate, set against other income of the period, carried back to earlier periods or surrendered as group relief.

Consultation on alterations to the large company relief

10.191 At the time of writing, HM Treasury has launched a consultation on changing the research and development relief for large companies to an *above the line* credit, which would be potentially repayable. As this consultation is at a very early stage, it is outside the scope of this book: updates will be available on the author's blog (http://www.ip-tax.com).

Claiming the large company relief

10.192 As with the SME research and development tax relief, a claim must be made within two years of the end of the accounting period in which the qualifying expenditure was incurred. The claim is made either in the company's corporation tax return or by way of amended return (see para **10.140**).

REFUNDS OF EXPENDITURE

10.193   Where research and development relief has been claimed on:

- contributions to independent research (see para **10.188**);

- research and development subcontracted to individuals, partnerships or qualifying bodies (see para **10.179**);

and these payments are subsequently refunded to the company, that refund is treated as taxable trading income of the company (CTA 2009, s 1083). 30% of the refund is also treated as taxable trading income of the company

ANTI-AVOIDANCE

10.194   There are anti-avoidance provisions attached to the research and development tax relief, both for the SME relief and the large company relief (CTA 2009, s 1084).

10.195   If the transaction leading to the relief is connected with arrangements undertaken wholly or mainly for a disqualifying purpose, that transaction is not taken into account when determining the amount of research and development relief (including pre-trading relief).

10.196   A disqualifying purpose is one in which the main object, or objects, of the arrangements is to enable the company to obtain an amount (or an increased amount) of research and development relief than that which it would otherwise be entitled to; in other words, the research and development is entered into purely to obtain the tax relief and not for the purposes of the trade.

ADMINISTRATION

10.197   HMRC have seven specialist research and development offices to deal with all corporation tax returns containing research and development claims, apart from the returns dealt with by:

- Large Business Service;

- Charities Division;

- Pharmaceutical Case Offices; and

- Small Company Enterprise Centres.

10.198   These specialist centres are based in:

● Cambridge;

● Cardiff (for claims from Wales, Scotland and Northern Ireland);

● Croydon;

● Leicester;

● Maidstone;

● Manchester; and

● Portsmouth.

Full addresses for these units are in HMRC Manual CIRD80350. The purpose of the specialist units is to improve the handling of research and development claims, particularly with regard to consistency from HMRC. A company tax return containing a claim for research and development relief should be sent to the appropriate R&D unit; the units are allocated by postcode (see HMRC Manual CIRD80360 for details of the postcode/unit mapping).

VACCINE RESEARCH RELIEF

10.199   Finance Act 2002, Schs 13 and 14 introduced a specific tax relief (now in CTA 2009, Part 13, Chapter 7) for qualifying expenditure on research and development relating to vaccines and medicines for the prevention and treatment of:

● tuberculosis;

● malaria;

● AIDS; and

● vaccines to prevent HIV infection from certain specific strains of the virus (CTA 2009, s 1086).

10.200   The HIV virus strains that qualify are those found in the developing world. The research must be specific to those strains of virus; research into vaccines and medicines that are not virus-specific will not qualify for the research (HMRC Manual CIRD76200).

10.201   Two areas of research will qualify:

● direct vaccine research, carried out by the company; and

● subcontracted vaccine research (CTA 2009, s 1098)

Until 1 August 2008, claims could also be made for contributions to vaccine research carried out by an independent body (such as a charity, university or scientific research organisation). Such contributions no longer qualify for vaccine research relief; see earlier editions of this book for more details of claims for such contributions.

10.202   Vaccine research relief is given *in addition to* research and development relief, not instead of it (see Example 10.16 below).

Eligible companies

10.203   For expenditure up to 31 March 2012, vaccine research relief could be claimed by SMEs and large companies, although the SME relief was halved for the period 1 April 2011–31 March 2012.

10.204   For expenditure incurred on or after 1 April 2012, vaccine research relief can only be claimed by large companies (CTA 2009, s 1085(1); FA 2012, Sch 3, para 16). In practical terms, this is unlikely to have a significant impact. As noted above, the relief is only available for a very restricted range of vaccines and only 10 claims for relief have been made each year that the relief has been available.

SME vaccine research relief (expenditure up to 31 March 2012 only)

10.205   Small- and medium-sized companies could:

- deduct an additional 20% of qualifying expenditure when calculating profits for tax purposes; ie in addition to the 100% deduction already available for revenue expenditure. The deduction was previously 40% between 1 August 2008 and 31 March 2011; 50% prior to 1 August 2008 (CTA 2009, s 1089 before repeal); and

- if loss-making, chose to surrender the loss arising from the relief in return for the payment of a tax credit of 16% of the vaccine research relief loss (CTA 2009, s 1103 before repeal).

10.206   An SME could, therefore, claim a total deduction of 220% of expenditure qualifying for both the SME research and development tax relief and vaccine research relief (100% normal deduction, 100% research and development tax relief and 20% vaccine research relief) during the 2011/12 tax year.

Example 10.15

VaccineSMECo spent £100,000 of qualifying expenditure on research and development into a vaccine for malaria in 2011/12. It could claim:

- the standard deduction of £100,000, plus

- research and development relief of 100% (for 2011/12) of £100,000 = £100,000, plus

- vaccine research relief of 20% of £100,000 = £20,000

giving a total deduction of £220,000 in respect of that qualifying expenditure. The actual cost of that £100,000 of expenditure was, therefore, £56,000 to a profit-making company (as the total deduction reduced corporation tax by £44,000, assuming the company paid tax at 20%).

10.207 As the SME vaccine research relief has now been abolished, see earlier editions of this book for more details of the SME vaccine research relief (although note that the relief was reduced to 20% for expenditure incurred on or after 1 April 2011, by Finance Act 2001, s 43).

Large company relief (CTA 2009, Pt 13, Chapter 7)

10.208 Large companies (that is, those that do not qualify as SMEs) are and continue to be entitled to the additional 40% (50% prior to 1 April 2008) deduction of qualifying expenditure (CTA 2009, s 1091), but can only take the relief as a deduction when calculating profits for tax purposes, to reduce profits or increase a loss. There is no repayment tax credit for large companies.

10.209 If a large company cannot deduct its qualifying vaccine research relief expenditure in computing taxable profits (eg because it has been capitalised), that company can claim to treat 140% of the qualifying expenditure as if it was so deductible (CTA 2009, s 1091(4)).

10.210 As the vaccine research credit is given in addition to the research and development tax credit, a large company can, in total, claim a deduction of 170% (175% prior to 1 April 2008) of such expenditure—ie 100% deduction under the general rules, 30% large company research and development tax relief and 40% vaccine research relief

---

Example 10.16

LargeCo spends £500,000 of qualifying expenditure on research and development into a vaccine for a relevant HIV strain. LargeCo can claim:

- the standard deduction of £500,000, plus

- research and development relief of 30% of £500,000 = £150,000, plus

- vaccine research relief of 40% of £500,000 = £200,000

giving a total deduction of £850,000 in respect of that qualifying expenditure.

Qualifying expenditure

10.211 Qualifying expenditure is calculated in much the same way as the research and development tax relief described above (see para **10.82** onwards), provided always that the qualifying expenditure is incurred on qualifying vaccine research. The range of qualifying expenditure is wider than that for large company research and development relief, as it includes expenditure on subcontracted research and development.

10.212 Accordingly, qualifying expenditure will be that incurred on:

- staff costs (CTA 2009, s 1101(4)(a));

- costs of externally provided workers, limited where the parties are connected (CTA 2009, s 1101(4)(c));

- software and consumables (CTA 2009, s 1101(4)(b));

- subcontracted costs, limited where the parties are connected (CTA 2009, s 1102); and

- clinical trials payments (CTA 2009, s 1101(4)(d)).

10.213 Vaccine research relief is also available for qualifying expenditure which is capitalised as an intangible asset in accordance with national or international accounting standards (FA 2004, s 53; see para **10.97**).

Grants and subsidies

10.214 Vaccine research relief will be limited where a subsidy is received, as no relief is available expenditure covered by a subsidy (CTA 2009, s 1101(6); CTA 2009, s 1102(5)).

Claiming vaccine research relief

10.215 A claim for vaccine research relief must be made in the company's tax return for that accounting period or by amendment of that return (FA 1998, Sch 18, para 83B, as amended). A claim must, therefore, be made within two years of the end of the accounting period for which the claim is made—the same time limit as for research and development relief claims. Amendment or withdrawal of the claim must be made within the same time period; later amendment can only be made with the permission of HMRC. The claim must specify the amount of relief claimed.

Anti-avoidance

10.216 Vaccine research relief anti-avoidance rules mirror those applying to the research and development tax reliefs (CTA 2009, s 1112; see para **10.196**).

RESEARCH AND DEVELOPMENT ALLOWANCES

10.217 The research and development and vaccine research reliefs are not available for expenditure on capital assets and the provision of facilities for research and development; instead, this expenditure will generally qualify for research and development capital allowances, which provide an immediate deduction for the expenditure for tax purposes (see Chapter 4 for details of this capital allowance).

CHECKLIST

10.218

- Must be qualifying research and development.

  — Consider accounts treatment, and research and development Guidelines.

  — Does the project seek an advance in overall knowledge in an area of science or technology by resolving an uncertainty that is not readily resolved by a competent professional in the field?

- Must be relevant to the trade carried on, or to be carried on, by the company.

- Must be revenue expenditure on:

  — Staff costs.

  — Externally provided workers.

  — Software and consumables.

  — Clinical trials volunteers payments.

  — Payments to subcontractors (very limited for large company relief).

- Capital expenditure may be eligible for research and development allowances instead.

- SME research and development relief:

  — Check size, double the usual thresholds apply.

  — Must be a going concern.

  — Must not receive another State Aid in respect of the project.

  — Total deduction: 225% of qualifying expenditure.

  — Repayment credit: up to 24.75% of qualifying expenditure.

10.218 *Research and development expenditure*

- Large company relief:
  - — Total deduction: 130% of qualifying expenditure.
  - — No repayment credit available.
  - — Limited subcontractor deductions.
  - — Can be claimed by SME where fail to qualify for SME relief other than on going concern basis.
- Vaccine research relief:
  - — Must be qualifying vaccine.
  - — Large companies only.
  - — Same expenditure as for research and development relief (but subcontractor costs not limited in the same way as for large company relief).
  - — Total deduction: 140% of qualifying expenditure.
- Aggregate research and development and vaccine research relief deduction of 170% if both reliefs claimed on the same expenditure.

Chapter 11

Acquisition of intellectual property by companies

Summary: The amount of expenditure recognised for tax purposes usually follows the accounts, but may vary in specific cases. In particular, market value is imposed where the intellectual property is acquired from a related party.

Expenditure on the acquisition of intellectual property fixed assets under the corporate intangibles tax rules depends entirely on how that expenditure is treated in the company's profit and loss account. That is, it is deducted for tax purposes as and when it is recognised in the company's profit and loss account.

Accordingly, deductions are available for the amortisation deduction in the accounts, or on a fixed basis where no amortisation is available.

Tax may need to be withheld from the payment where it amounts to a royalty.

- Relevant intellectual property (para **11.3**)

- Expenditure (para **11.9**)

- Capitalised costs – amortisation (para **11.24**)

- Effect of debits on computation (para **11.42**)

- Withholding taxes (para **11.47**)

INTRODUCTION

11.1 Acquisition of intellectual property covers a wide range of transactions, from purchasing a simple licence to use a photograph from an online stock library to acquiring the patents and know-how related to a biotechnology product. The intellectual property may differ, but there is no distinction in the corporate tax rules between the various types of intellectual property: the same rules apply regardless of whether a copyright, a patent, or other intellectual property is acquired. Options and other rights to acquire any intellectual property that would be a fixed asset of the company on acquisition are also included within the regime (CTA 2009, s 713).

Stamp duty

11.2   The UK abolished stamp duty on intangible assets, including intellectual property, in the 2000 Budget so that a person acquiring intellectual property in the UK will not pay any transfer taxes on acquisition. Where acquiring intellectual property assets outside the UK, note that other jurisdictions may still apply similar taxes or duties.

RELEVANT INTELLECTUAL PROPERTY

11.3   The following rules apply to acquisitions of qualifying intellectual property held by companies (see Chapter 8 for more detail on qualifying intellectual property). In particular, note that the intellectual property asset acquired must be treated as a fixed asset of the company in the accounts; not all licences of intellectual property will qualify as fixed assets. This is a matter for discussion, generally, with the auditors preparing the accounts.

11.4   Where the acquisition is of an excluded asset (for example, intellectual property held by a related party on or before 31 March 2002), then the rules in Chapter 5 continue to apply to the asset so that—for example—amortisation deductions are not available to the acquirer.

Computer software

Acquisition as part of hardware

11.5   Where software is bundled with related hardware, the cost of that software (eg operating systems) is, for accounting purposes, generally considered to be part of the cost of the hardware (FRS10 ¶2, see para **17.119**).

11.6   In this case, there is no debit taken into account each year to write down the expenditure (CTA 2009, s 813). Instead, the software may be eligible for deduction via capital allowances given for the bundled cost of hardware and software.

11.7   However, where ongoing royalties are payable in respect of that acquired software, those royalties do fall within the provisions of these rules (CTA 2009, s 813) and will generally be deductible for tax purposes as incurred.

Election for capital allowances treatment

11.8   Companies can elect to opt out of these rules in respect of computer software acquisitions (CTA 2009, s 815). The effect of the election is to exclude the acquisition of the software from the corporate intangibles tax rules (see para **8.41** for more information on this election).

EXPENDITURE

11.9 Expenditure on the acquisition of intellectual property fixed assets under the corporate intangibles tax rules depends entirely on how that expenditure is treated in the company's profit and loss account. That is, expenditure is deducted for tax purposes as and when it is recognised in the company's profit and loss account. The expenditure will either be written off immediately (generally, where royalties are paid in respect of a licence) or amortised over time (where the acquisition creates an enduring benefit for the company). This overrides the general computational rules in respect of capital and revenue expenditure on the acquisition of intangible assets (CTA 2009, s 728).

Deductions

11.10 Accordingly, deductions arise when the net carrying value of the relevant intellectual property asset (the capitalised cost less any amounts previously written off) is written down either:

● on an accounting basis (CTA 2009, s 729); or

● on a fixed basis (CTA 2009, s 730).

11.11 Debits may also be brought into account for tax purposes in respect of expenditure that is written off when incurred on:

● abortive expenditure (CTA 2009, s 727(1)); or

● royalties paid for the use of intellectual property (CTA 2009, s 727(1)(b)).

11.12 Any acquisition expenditure that is specifically not deductible under the general rules remains excluded, for example, expenditure on gifts is still disallowed (CTA 2009, s 865).

Grants

11.13 Where the company receives a grant to meet some or all of the expenditure on the acquisition of an intellectual property asset, the grant is to be treated as a receipt in respect of the asset for tax purposes (CTA 2009, s 852) (see Chapter 12 and Chapter 13 for more information on the tax treatment of receipts) rather than a reduction in the expenditure on the asset.

Trading stock

11.14   Bear in mind the capacity in which the company is acquiring the intellectual property. In particular, note that expenditure on acquiring intellectual property for trading purposes may be deducted as an expense of the company, where the intellectual property is regarded as trading stock and so is written off as incurred rather than capitalised. Such intellectual property is not a fixed asset of the business and so is outside the corporate intangibles tax rules (see para **8.13**).

Example 11.1

RadCo buys and sells the rights to broadcast music events, acting as a broker between producers and broadcasters. It acquires a wide licence over broadcasting rights for a specific event and then on-licences the broadcasting rights for specific territories to separate broadcasters. The acquisitions of the rights will generally be treated as purchases of trading stock in the accounts, rather than as an acquisition of capital assets of the company, not least because the rights may have a very short useful economic life.

Special rules for expenditure

Deemed expenditure

11.15   Assets may be deemed to be acquired, and expenditure incurred, on the following occasions:

- as a result of an intellectual property asset coming within the scope of UK corporation tax when (CTA 2009, s 863):

    — a company becomes UK resident; or

    — an intellectual property asset begins to be held for the purposes of a trade carried on in the UK by a branch or agency;

    in which case, the asset is treated as acquired immediately after it comes within the scope of UK corporation tax, and the acquisition expenditure is the accounting value at the time;

- when a foreign company comes within the controlled foreign companies rules (CTA 2009, s 870) in which case the intellectual property assets are treated as:

    — acquired at the beginning of the accounting period in which the rules first apply; and

    — having been acquired for their book value at that time;

provided in all cases that the asset is not excluded from the corporate intangibles tax rules (for example, where it was held by the company or a related party before 1 April 2002).

Acquisition from a related party

11.16 Where there is a transfer of a chargeable intangible asset between a company and a related party, the transfer is usually treated for tax purposes as taking place at market value (see para **18.63**). The actual consideration is ignored (CTA 2009, s 845) and the market value is used instead for tax purposes.

11.17 Where the asset transferred has nil book value for accounts purposes (such as most internally generated intellectual property), amortisation is still available and calculated as if the market value had been the accounting transfer value (CTA 2009, s 857); this can allow for tax deductions for acquisition even where the accounts do not provide for it.

11.18 Where the intellectual property is licensed, rather than acquired outright, from a related party, the royalty paid can only be deducted for tax purposes when it is paid if the related party is not subject to these rules *and* the royalty is not paid within twelve months of the end of the accounting period in which it is recognised in the accounts (CTA 2009, s851). Broadly, this is intended to stop companies getting the benefit of a deduction earlier than the receipt is recognised for tax purposes in the hands of the licensor (eg: where the licensor is taxed on a receipts basis under the general rules).

11.19 The circumstances in which a person can be a related party of a company are set out in detail in para **18.69**.

11.20 The market value rule does not apply where:

- the transfer is subject to the transfer pricing rules (TIOPA 2010, Part 4, see para **16.94** onwards) in which case the transfer pricing rules have precedence; and

- the transfer is a tax neutral transfer between group companies, under the provisions set out in para **18.162**.

11.21 In addition, the market value rule will be modified where:

- the transfer could be taxed as a distribution or as employment income: the market value is not used to calculate the tax on the distribution or employment income, but it does still apply for the purposes of the corporate intangibles rules; or

- capital gains tax gifts hold-over relief (see para **7.24**) is claimed: the acquisition cost for the company, for corporate intangibles tax purposes, is market value less the amount of the held over gain; or

- the intangible asset has been held for the purposes of an exempt foreign permanent establishment (under tax reliefs outside the scope of this book; see para **16.17** for more details on permanent establishments), in which case a formula is applied to calculate the transfer value (CTA 2009, ss 847, 849, 848A).

Assets acquired together

11.22   Where assets are acquired together in one transaction, the value of each asset is that allocated to the asset (CTA 2009, s 856):

- in accordance with generally accepted accounting principles; or
- where no allocation has been made in the accounts, on a just and reasonable apportionment of the expenditure.

11.23   Assets are acquired together where they are acquired as part of a single transaction even where separate prices are agreed for the various assets included in the transaction or where the transaction purports to be several separate acquisitions in relation to the assets.

Acquisitions from UK group companies

11.24   Acquisitions from UK group companies are, generally, treated as taking place on a tax neutral basis (see para **18.162** for more information).

CAPITALISED COSTS

11.25   Expenditure on acquiring intellectual property is brought into account for tax purposes when it appears in the profit and loss account. Generally, on acquisition, UK GAAP and IAS will require that the intellectual property asset will be capitalised where it has a readily ascertainable market value (see para **11.30** onwards); the costs of acquisition will then be written off through the accounts in stages over the useful economic life of the intellectual property.

11.26   Where the asset is capitalised, the tax deduction available will be the accounts amortisation charge each year in respect of that asset. Where there is no accounts amortisation, an election is available to provide a fixed tax deduction over 25 years in respect of that acquisition.

Writing down on accounts basis

11.27   There are two types of charge that may appear in the accounts in relation to capitalised costs of intellectual property; the amortisation charge for the period (the most usual charge) or a charge as a result of an impairment review.

11.28 Normally the tax and accounting debits will be the same; however, there are some occasions when the two will differ: this will generally be the case where roll-over relief is claimed to defer a gain on disposal of an asset (if roll-over relief is claimed, the cost of the related new asset acquired is reduced: see para **14.32** for more information about the operation of this relief) or on the re-valuation of the intellectual property.

11.29 Although the intention of these rules was to bring accounting practice and tax practice closer together, there will still be occasions when they diverge; this is one of them.

Amortisation

11.30 FRS10 recommends that intangible assets, including intellectual property, are amortised on a straight line basis over their useful economic life (¶15): this will rarely be more than 20 years (¶19), so the rate of amortisation will usually be at least 5% per year. 'Useful economic life' is generally matched to some aspect of the asset: patent or licence life, or historic replacement intervals. The asset may well, therefore, be written off more slowly than it would have been under the 25% writing down capital allowances previously given for capital expenditure on patents and industrial known (see paras **5.60** and **5.108**).

Impairment reviews

11.31 FRS10 ¶34 requires impairment reviews to be carried out on each item of intellectual property, generally at the end of the first full financial year since acquisition. Additional reviews can be carried out if events or circumstantial changes suggest that the carrying value may not be recoverable but the rate of such reviews will depend on the industry sector (for example, in the technology sector reviews may be frequent, occurring each time competing patents are generated). Regardless of the sector, where the intellectual property item has an amortisation period of more than 20 years (a copyright acquired from an author, for example) impairment reviews are required at the end of every accounts period.

11.32 If the review concludes that the carrying value needs to be written down, the amount of the write-down needs to be taken to the profit and loss account; an equivalent debit is brought into account for tax purposes (CTA 2009, s 729). From then on, the amortisation spreads the net carrying value of the asset over its remaining useful economic life (FRS10 ¶41).

Calculation of the amortisation deduction for tax purposes

On capitalisation

11.33   The amount of the debit for tax purposes, in the accounting period in which the intellectual property is capitalised, is (CTA 2009, s 729(3)):

$$\frac{AL \times TC}{AC}$$

where:

- AL = the amount recognised in the profit and loss account (the amortisation deduction or impairment review deduction);

- TC = the expenditure on the intellectual property recognised for tax purposes; and

- AC = the expenditure capitalised in the accounts.

TC and AC will usually be the same, unless roll-over relief has been claimed (see para **14.32**) or market value has been substituted in a related party transaction (see para **11.16**).

Subsequent periods

11.34   The amount of the debit in subsequent accounting periods is (CTA 2009, s 729(5)):

$$\frac{AL \times TV}{AV}$$

where:

- AL = the amount recognised in the profit and loss account;

- TV = the tax written down value of the asset immediately before the amortisation charge is made (or before an impairment review); and

- AV = the value of the asset for accounting purposes immediately before the amortisation charge is made (or before an impairment review).

As above, TV and AV are likely to be the same unless a relief has been claimed, or a related party transaction has arisen

Tax written down value

11.35   The tax written down value of the intellectual property is (CTA 2009, s 742):

Tax cost – debits + credits

The tax cost is the cost of acquiring the intellectual property that is recognised for tax purposes. Debits includes all debits previously brought into account for tax purposes (ie previous periods' writing down), and credits includes any credits previously brought into account for tax purposes on a revaluation. In effect, the tax written down value is the original tax cost less net tax deductions to date (including amortisation deductions).

Example 11.2

AcCo acquires a patent for £50,000. The patent is amortised over a period of 10 years, that period being in accordance with UK GAAP as the remaining useful economic life of the patent.

Provided that no roll-over relief has been claimed, the tax written down value and the accounts written down value of the asset are the same and so the full amount of £5,000 recognised in the profit and loss account will be brought into account for tax purposes.

If, however, AcCo takes the opportunity to use the acquisition to roll over a gain on the disposal of a trademark, the expenditure on the intellectual property recognised for tax purposes will be less than that recognised for accounts purposes.

If, for example, AcCo's roll-over relief claim reduces the cost of the patent to £30,000 for tax purposes, the debit for tax purposes on the amortisation of that patent will be restricted to £3,000, being:

$$\frac{5,000 \times 30,000}{50,000}$$

Fixed rate writing down election

11.36 FRS10, ¶17 indicates that an asset with an indefinite useful economic life should not be amortised. Whilst it is very rare that an acquired asset is not amortised, it may be the case with acquired goodwill under FRS10 where it is considered to have an indefinite life. IAS38 will not generally allow any amortisation on acquired goodwill (IAS 38.97), including any unregistered intellectual property that is considered to be part of goodwill.

11.37 This would generally mean that the company could not get any tax relief on the acquisition other than through impairment review deductions, and so the regime specifically allows a company to elect for the cost of an intellectual property asset to be written down over 25 years at a fixed rate of 4% for tax purposes (CTA 2009, s 730).

11.38 The election is fairly wide-ranging, as it can be made regardless of whether, or for how long, expenditure is amortised in the accounts (note:

where the asset is amortised in the accounts, it will almost always be more tax effective to take the amortisation deductions rather than make this election).

11.39 Once an election is made, the debit that can be brought into account for tax purposes is the lower of:

- 4% of the expenditure on the intellectual property asset recognised for tax purposes; and

- the balance of the tax written down value (being the final debit brought into account).

This amount must be proportionately reduced if the accounting period is less than 12 months.

11.40 No impairment review deductions can be brought into account where the fixed basis election is made, as the calculation is determined by tax law rather than the accounts.

Tax written down value

11.41 The tax written down value for the purposes of a deduction under this election is slightly different to that for a deduction for amortisation (CTA 2009, s 743) as no revaluation is possible for tax purposes:

Tax cost: debits

11.42 The tax cost is the cost of acquiring the intellectual property that is recognised for tax purposes. Debits include all debits previously brought into account for tax purposes (ie previous periods' writing down) (CTA 2009, s 743).

11.43 The election must be made within two years of the end of the accounting period in which the asset is acquired, and is made in respect of all the expenditure that is capitalised for accounting purposes. The election is irrevocable (CTA 2009, s 730).

Effect of debits on computation

11.44 The reason for which the intellectual property is held will determine the way in which the corresponding debits are dealt with in a computation. Where an intellectual property asset is held for more than one purpose, a just and reasonable apportionment of the debits is required (CTA 2009, s 750).

Trading

11.45 Where the intellectual property is acquired and held for the purposes of the trade, any written off costs and the amortisation or impairment debits are treated as expenses of the trade (CTA 2009, 747) when calculating the profits of the business for tax purposes.

Non-trading

11.46   Where the intellectual property is acquired and held for non-trade purposes (generally, where it is held as an investment, although not all investments qualify as relevant assets to which these rules apply), the debits are pooled and a non-trading loss arises where there are only non-trading debits, or if the total non-trading debits exceed the total of non-trading credits received (in respect of any intellectual property held as an investment) (CTA 2009, s 751).

11.47   A company that has a non-trading loss in an accounting period can claim for that loss to be set against the total profits of the company for that period (CTA 2009, s 753). The claim must be made within two years of the end of the accounting period.

11.48   Where the loss is not absorbed by that period's profits, and is not surrendered by way of group relief, it can be carried forward to the next accounting period to be treated as a non-trading loss of that period (CTA 2009, s 753(3)).

WITHHOLDING TAX

11.49   Companies will be required to withhold tax from licence payments on acquisition of intellectual property in a number of circumstances; this is one area of intellectual property taxation that has not been particularly modernised for companies, as payments may be made to individual and other non-corporate entities. In this case, it is necessary to consider the type of intellectual property for which licence payments are being made.

11.50   The UK withholding tax rules are covered in detail in Chapter 16. In summary, an acquirer of intellectual property is required to deduct basic rate income tax from any intellectual property royalties which are qualifying annual payments (ITA 2007, s 901), from certain overseas intellectual property royalties (ITA 2007, s 906) and from patent royalties which are not annual payments where the recipient is within the charge to UK income tax or corporation tax (ITA 2007, s 903). In addition, basic rate income tax must be withheld where UK patent rights are acquired outright and the vendor is chargeable to income tax or corporation tax (ITA 2007, s 910).

11.51   Income tax must be withheld by the licensee at the basic rate in force for the year in which the royalty becomes due (20% for 2012–13). That withheld tax must generally be accounted for in the licensee's corporate self-assessment return for the year of payment (see Chapter 16 for more details).

Payments to UK companies

11.52 No tax needs to be withheld where:

- the person beneficially entitled to the royalty is either:

    — a UK resident company (ITA 2007, s 933); or

    — a partnership, each member of which is a UK resident company or a local authority (ITA 2007; s 932);

    or

- the person beneficially entitled to the income in respect of which the payment is made is a non-resident company which (ITA 2007, s 934):

    — carries on a trade in the UK through a permanent establishment; and

    — takes the royalty into account in computing its UK chargeable profits.

This exemption is not available where a company makes a payment as trustee or agent for another person (ITA 2007, s 930(4)).

Payments to associated companies in EU Member States

11.53 Similarly, payments of royalties to associated companies in EU Member States will be made without deduction of tax (ITTOIA 2005, ss 757–767). Two companies will be associated for this purpose where one of them directly holds at least 25% of the capital or voting rights in the other company, or where a third company directly holds at least 25% of the capital or voting rights in both companies (ITTOIA 2005, s 761).

11.54 Any agreement for paying a patent royalty without deduction of tax will not override the licensee's obligation to deduct tax; the licensee will still be required to account to HMRC for the tax that should have been deducted.

Double tax treaties

11.55 A royalty recipient in a jurisdiction which has a tax treaty with the UK can apply to HMRC to give notice enabling the licensee (or his paying agent) to make the payment without deduction of tax or under deduction at a specified rate of tax.

11.56 UK companies can pay royalties with tax withheld at the treaty withholding rate, rather than the income tax basic rate, without prior clearance from HMRC, where the company has a reasonable belief that the non-resident is entitled to treaty relief (see para **16.69**). If treaty relief is not in fact available, the paying company will be liable for the tax that should have been withheld, together with interest.

CHECKLIST

11.57

> - Is the asset being acquired a qualifying intangible fixed asset?
> - Is the expenditure subject to special rules?
>   - Is there deemed expenditure by a foreign company?
>   - Has the asset been acquired from a related party?
>   - Has the asset been acquired from a group company?
>   - Has the asset been acquired as part of a bundle of assets, so that the value needs to be arrived at by apportionment?
> - Acquisition may enable roll-over of a gain: see para **14.32**.
> - Is there an amortisation deduction in respect of the asset in the accounts?
>   - If not, consider making an election for the fixed rate deduction instead.
> - Check whether tax needs to be withheld from the expenditure when paid to the licensor or vendor.

Chapter 12

Exploitation of intellectual property by companies

Summary: Intellectual property can be exploited through direct use, by licencing to others, or as protection against competition. Income derived from direct use of intellectual property, in manufacturing or services, will be treated as income from the sale of manufactured goods, or from the supply services and so will be taxed as trading income in the usual way.

Direct exploitation of the intellectual property, particularly through licensing, will follow the accounts rules for a corporate owner of intellectual property; the tax deduction will depend on when the revenue is recognised in the accounts. Receipts may be adjusted through transfer pricing or the related parties transaction rules. Where withholding tax has been deducted from payments, relief will be available against corporation tax.

The patent box, to be introduced in 2013, will provide corporation tax relief for income from derived from patents.

- Revenue recognition (para **12.8**)
- Receipts (para **12.46**)
- Part-realisation: exclusive licences (para **12.53**)
- Effect of debits and credits on computation (para **12.68**)
- Double tax relief (para **12.75**)

INTRODUCTION

12.1   Exploitation of intellectual property will generally take the form of licensing that intellectual property to others; where a company exploits intellectual property on its own account (in manufacturing, or providing services, for sale) then the income from that exploitation is treated as general trading income for tax purposes and is not subject to the rules on corporate intangible assets.

12.2   The distinction between exploitation and disposal is not always entirely clear-cut (see para **6.6** for more details on the distinction), but the accounts focus of the corporate intangibles tax rules means that, for intellectual property that is within the rules (broadly, post-1 April 2002 assets that are not excluded: para **8.29** onwards), the matter is mostly academic as the tax treatment will generally be governed by the accounts treatment. In addition, as companies pay the same rate of tax on gains as income, the distinction has less importance than it does for individuals and other unincorporated entities where the income tax and capital gains tax rates can be very different.

12.3   The principal issue in considering the tax treatment of exploitation receipts is determining when they should be recognised in the accounts, as this will determine when and to what extent they are recognised for tax purposes, subject to certain over-riding provisions.

Not trading receipts

12.4   These rules do not apply to receipts from a trade in dealing in intellectual property (ie buying and selling intellectual property) as such intellectual property would not be a fixed asset of the company—it would be trading stock and so outside the corporate intangible tax rules (see para **8.13**). Such receipts continue to be dealt with as trading (ie revenue) receipts in the same way as the receipts from the sale of any other trading stock.

Litigation

12.5   Any amounts derived from litigation in respect of intellectual property will be taxed according to their form: where a licence is granted in settlement or through an award in court, the receipts from that licence will be treated for tax in the same way as receipts from any other licence (see para **17.1** onwards for further details).

12.6   Where the amount is compensation for damage to the intellectual property, this will be treated for tax purposes as a part-disposal of the intellectual property (see para **17.57** for further details).

Patent box

12.7   In 2013 the UK will introduce the patent box relief from corporation tax, for income from the exploitation of patents by companies: this will apply to income from the direct exploitation of patents (by licensing, for example) and also to trading income from the internal exploitation of patents. It applies primarily to patents (as is clear from the name) but will also apply to other, similar, intellectual property. See Chapter 13 for more details on this tax relief;

as it is a substantial element of the UK intellectual property tax regime, it has been considered in a separate chapter.

REVENUE RECOGNITION

12.8   Receipts from exploiting intellectual property will be brought into account by a company for tax purposes as they accrue, when they are recognised in the profit and loss account (FA 2002, Sch 29, paras 1 and 13). As the corporate intangibles tax rules are accounts based, the amount recognised for tax purposes will generally be the same as that recognised for accounting purposes.

Accounting rules

12.9   The following is intended only as an overview of the accounting concept of 'revenue recognition', which determines when receipts are brought into accounting in the profit and loss account.

12.10   The specific circumstances of each case will be considered by the auditors to determine whether a business's proposed treatment is appropriate. If a situation appears to be capable of interpretation in a number of ways, advice should be sought from the business's auditor on the appropriate treatment as part of any consideration of the impact on the business's tax position.

12.11   For many businesses, revenue recognition is not too much more of a problem than working out whether the sale is recognised when the invoice is raised or when the cash is received. Where intellectual property forms the basis of products and services, however, the problem can be much more difficult and the process of deciding when to recognise sales as revenue is complex and, in parts, rather esoteric.

12.12   The implications of different approaches on the tax position of a business are all too obvious which means that HMRC are particularly likely to be interested in the policies and treatment adopted by companies with substantial intellectual property.

Background

12.13   There are a series of concepts that underpin the way that accounting works. One of those is the concept of matching (referred to by FRS 18 as the accruals concept) which states that costs and directly-related revenues should be recognised in the same period. The practicalities of that statement are that:

● if costs are incurred in one period and the related revenues in the next then the costs should be carried forward in the balance sheet at the end of the first period and set against the revenues in the next period;

- if invoices are issued at the start of a process then the revenues should be spread across periods so as to match the costs as they are incurred.

Revenue recognition therefore becomes a two-part process that involves identifying both the quantum of the revenue and the timing of its recognition.

Quantum

12.14 Not all revenue is easy to quantify. Invoices for fixed sums are obvious enough but other arrangements such as funded research, milestone payments based on levels of functionality (for example, speed of action), or royalty arrangements may be more difficult to identify.

12.15 Likewise, on projects where the revenue recognition is spread over a number of periods, the difficulty can be in working out how much revenue to recognise in each period. Indeed, on long-term contracts the revenue recognised will be an estimate right up to the period of completion and even beyond that if there are system-performance or other criteria in the contract.

Timing

12.16 Timing is the element that creates the biggest headache for accountants. The matching concept seems reasonable enough but, in practice, the relationship between costs and revenues may not be that clear. An example is maintenance or other support arrangements. The contract may run for a number of years with fixed amounts payable by the customer, but the associated costs will not be clear until the end of the period. A simple application of the matching concept is therefore difficult as, without a known cost, how can the costs and revenues be matched?

12.17 One answer in this case is to spread the revenues evenly over the period of the contract and to recognise the costs as they arise. However, if the profile of costs is known or can be estimated with reasonable certainty then the revenue should be spread so as to evenly match the costs.

12.18 A more fundamental issue can arise with the simple question: what triggers the revenue anyway? This is generally an area that gives rise to commercial disputes between customer and supplier as well and some industries have set up or accepted practices to address the problem. The construction industry, for example, has a system whereby a qualified quantity surveyor signs off the work done at different stages and this sign-off forms the basis of the invoicing. Other industries do not have such well-defined systems.

12.19 Intellectual property-based businesses tend to fall into this second category. The major exception is the drug development sector. Here the external approval process forms the basis of contractual terms and hence revenue timing. For example, the licence agreement between a biotech company and a pharmaceutical business for a compound to be used in a particular disease area will often include milestone payments to be made to the biotech company. These may well be tied to regulatory milestones, such as approval to move into the next clinical trials phase or successful completion of a clinical trials phase.

12.20 Other intellectual property-based businesses, such as the software industry, attempt to use similar milestone approaches but these can still lead to dispute, as there is no independent third party involved in the assessment process.

Accounting policies

12.21 These issues are addressed by the adoption of a standard accounting policy by the business that is intended to provide the rules for recognising both quantum and timing. The combination of legal requirements sets out the framework into which the accounting policies and the accounting treatments must fall. These legal requirements are contained chiefly in the Companies Act 2006, Companies Act 1985 (as revised), accounting standards and other pronouncements, such as those of the UK Accounting Standards Board's Urgent Issues Task Force. This combined weight of regulation and standard setting is referred to as 'Generally Accepted Accounting Practice' or GAAP.

12.22 GAAP varies from country to country. There are three major sets of GAAP:

- international: based on the developing set of International Accounting Standards produced by the International Accounting Standards Committee;

- US GAAP;

- UK GAAP.

Each has its own philosophy of reporting based, in the case of UK and US GAAP, on historical practice and local legislative frameworks.

12.23 Historically UK GAAP has been the most accommodating on revenue recognition. This has led to some companies adopting relatively aggressive accounting policies.

12.24 An aggressive accounting policy is one where any benefit is recognised early and downside is recognised in the future. Whilst this may seem short-termist in outlook, for public companies—with more than half an eye on their share prices—adopting an aggressive accounting policy may be tactically important now (for example as part of a defence against a takeover).

12.25 The range of available approaches can lead to confusion and certainly does not assist in comparing different companies' financial performance.

Addressing the issue

12.26 This is a problem that standard setters have recognised for some time. Whilst there is no standard in UK GAAP dealing with revenue recognition, UTIF 40 on Revenue Recognition and Service Contracts may provide some assistance.

12.27 However, readers should, as ever with these technical issues, seek advice from the business's auditors on the application of GAAP to specific situations. It is further stressed that the comments do not necessarily represent either current practice or the final requirements that may appear in a any new accounting standard.

What is revenue?

12.28 The basis of accounting for revenue is not going to change significantly. However, the role of the underlying contract between supplier and customer is emphasised, and underpins the proposed approach.

When can you recognise it?

12.29 Building on the importance of the contract, the driver for recognition becomes 'has the (selling) company performed its duties under the contract?'.

12.30 As ever this appears to be a simple question. However, below are just some of the potential pitfalls:

- completion of the contract is yet to occur: as in a long-term development arrangement or any form of contract which falls into two or more accounting periods;
- rights of return and options;
- linked services;
- valuation/measurement.

12.31 Performance is an obvious starting point for considering recognition and has underpinned practice for a long time. The basic rule is that simply entering into a contract is not enough to be a revenue event. Similarly, settlement of the consideration by the buyer does not necessarily indicate when the seller has actually provided benefit to the other party, for example an up-front rent payment does not of itself show that the tenant has gained an economic benefit of the lease.

Incomplete performance

12.32 The problem here is whether enough has been done for part of the revenue to be taken. The answer given is that some benefit needs to have accrued to the customer. Again, the construction industry approach with the involvement of a quantity surveyor contrasts with arrangements such as a bundled hardware and software sale.

12.33 Two basic situations arise: supply of a non-task specific system and installation of a bespoke package. A further question arises as to whether any associated hardware sale could be recognised before the software is fully installed. For a non-task specific system, it is relatively easy to break the contract into distinct parts and recognise revenue on completion of the hardware installation before the whole contract is complete.

12.34 The second scenario presents a more difficult problem. If the components are inextricably linked (and they would probably include training), can they really be separated? Alternatively, is there another approach to calculating the quantum of revenue to be recognised? Reliable valuation of revenues is going to be difficult but the discussion paper does allow for a portion of revenue to be taken during the contract. That said, if the contract requires full performance before payment then the accounting treatment will need to follow in the same way.

Compared to the US, the UK Accounting Standard's Board proposals still allow a little more flexibility.

Multiple part contracts

12.35 Internet Service Providers and telecoms companies, amongst others, often charge connection fees at the start of a supply contract. This contract would then require future services to be provided by the seller.

12.36 Currently, an aggressive but probably allowable policy would be to take the connection fee as revenue immediately. The proposed treatment suggests that the future services are conditional on the connection fee, likening the initial fee to a call option for future services. If the connection is for a specified period, then the proposal is that revenue should be spread over the contract term. Difficulties arise when the contract is open-ended, as is often the case with telecoms companies. In such a case, the revenue should be spread over an estimate of the probable term. Measures of customer 'turnover' could therefore become quite important in the calculation of revenue in any one period.

12.37 Of course, costs will need to be considered carefully in this. Where significant costs are incurred in connecting a customer, consideration ought to be given to whether benefit has passed to the customer at the point of connection. If it has, then revenue could be taken, but contract terms may need to be reviewed and careful thought will be required in reaching such conclusion on the timing of revenue recognition.

Valuation

12.38 A common theme running through most of these examples is calculation of quantum or more simply valuing the revenue to be recognised. Where elements of a contract require assessment for revenue recognition purposes, estimates will probably be needed. Unlike the construction industry it is doubtful that there is an industry recognised valuation methodology for most scenarios.

12.39 As is becoming the norm in financial reporting, fair values are the suggested solution for measurement problems, with an acknowledgement that these can be difficult to establish.

12.40 A fair value is basically the value that the open market would place on the item. Hence, judgment will still play a part in setting the policy and undertaking the calculations.

Contract

12.41 The overriding theme in all of this is the importance of the contract, and performance against it. The opportunity should be taken now to consider revenue streams, particularly new ones, and the policy adopted in recognising them. For new revenues, adopting an appropriate policy now could avoid the need for a future restatement of results and the investor uncertainty and confusion that could follow.

12.42 Further, as happened in the US with the introduction of new accounting requirements, licences and other agreements may change in form. As the contract is becoming more and more the arbiter of revenue recognition, it follows that companies, sensitive to their reported financial results, will attempt to adjust their contracts to provide the best outcome.

12.43 Interestingly, for presentational purposes this may not be to allow early recognition but may err more towards allowing a spreading of revenue over time. Spreading revenues helps to avoid the peaks and the often accompanying troughs in revenue and hence profitability, that disorient and disconcert investors.

12.44   As stated earlier, revenue recognition is an area of developing practice for UK GAAP and one where advice on an ongoing basis will be required from accountants and, if changes to contractual terms for future deals are involved, lawyers as well.

12.45   Further, it is important to understand the implications of the final standard for your business to ensure that you can explain the position and any impact on period results to staff, investors and your bank.

RECEIPTS

Royalties

12.46   These rules for taxation of intellectual property and other intangible fixed assets generally only apply to such assets where they are acquired or created by companies only on or after 1 April 2002 (see Chapter 8).

12.47   The exception to this is in respect of royalties: royalty payments received on or after 1 April 2002 are taxed under these rules, regardless of when the intellectual property to which they relate was acquired or created (CTA 2009, s 896).

12.48   In effect, since 1 April 2002, the timing of the tax charge for royalties received by companies has been related to the accounting treatment. As a result, the accounting rules (see above) are the primary consideration, together with the deemed receipt rules (see below).

12.49   To ensure that royalties would only be brought into account once for tax purposes (FA 2002, Sch 29, para 119(2)–(3), before repeal by CTA 2009) transitional rules applied for payments made over the 31 March 2002/1 April 2002 threshold (see earlier editions of this book for more details).

Deemed receipts: transactions with a related party

12.50   Where there is a transaction between a company and a related party (see para **18.69**), the transaction is usually treated for tax purposes as taking place at market value. The actual consideration is ignored (CTA 2009, s 845). This can result in a deemed receipt where the intellectual property is (for example) licensed at less than market value.

12.51   The market value rule does not apply where the transaction is subject to the transfer pricing rules (TIOPA 2010, Part 4; see para **16.94** onwards) as the transfer pricing rules have precedence in determining the amount deemed to have been received for tax purposes.

12.52   The market value rule also does not apply to transfers between group companies which are tax neutral (see para **18.162**) or on reorganisations to which tax relief applies (see para **17.71** onwards).

PART-REALISATION: EXCLUSIVE LICENCES

12.53   The exploitation of intellectual property by licensing will result in either:

- royalties, taxed as above;
- a part-realisation of the asset.

12.54   A part-realisation of an intellectual property asset will arise when there is a reduction in the accounting value of the asset (CTA 2009, s 734), usually on the grant of an exclusive licence. This is a rather clearer definition, for tax purposes, than the need to determine the effect of a transaction (as is required for exploitation by non-corporate entities, and in respect of pre-1 April 2002 corporate assets: see para **6.6**).

Example 12.1

PatentCo owns a patent which it has licensed to a number of other companies. Most of the licences are non-exclusive, time-limited, licences for which PatentCo receives royalties which are based on the number of goods which the licensees make which incorporate the patented technology. Receipts from these licences will be general receipts, brought into account for tax purposes as they are recognised in the profit and loss account under the normal revenue recognition rules (see para **12.9** onwards).

In one particular territory, however, PatentCo has granted an exclusive licence over use of the patent in that territory to a single licensor. The licence term runs until the end of the patent term, so PatentCo has effectively given up its rights over the patent in that territory as it will not be able to grant another licence in that territory and will not be able to exploit the patent itself in that territory. In this case, it is likely that the accounting value of the patent will be reduced to reflect the diminution in value of the patent to PatentCo. For tax purposes, this will create a part-realisation of the patent by PatentCo.

Written down intellectual property

12.55 Where the intellectual property asset has been acquired and the tax value has been written down under the corporate intellectual property tax rules for intellectual property (see para **11.25** onwards) either on an accounting basis or under a fixed rate election, the amount that needs to be brought into account for tax purposes on a part-realisation is as follows (CTA 2009, s 735):

- where the proceeds of the part-realisation exceed the appropriate portion of the tax written down value of the asset: a credit equal to the excess;

- where the proceeds of the part-realisation are less than the appropriate portion (see below) of the tax written down value of the asset: a debit equal to the shortfall;

- where there are no proceeds from the part-realisation (eg on a licence that is given away for no consideration): a debit equal to the appropriate portion of the tax written down value (see para **11.34** or **11.41** for details of how to calculate the relevant tax written down value).

12.56 The tax written down value on which the appropriate value is calculated is the written down value immediately before the part-realisation.

Example 12.2

In the example above, if the appropriate portion of the tax written down value is £500,000, then if the proceeds of the part-realisation are:

- £700,000: there is a credit for tax purposes of £200,000;

- £300,000: there is a debit for tax purposes of £200,000;

- £0: there is a debit for tax purposes of £500,000.

Intellectual property not written down

12.57 Where the intellectual property is shown on the company's balance sheet but has not been written down for tax purposes (usually where it is licensed soon after acquisition), then the amount brought into account for tax purposes (CTA 2009, s 736) is:

- where the proceeds of the part-realisation exceed the appropriate portion of the cost of the asset: a credit equal to the excess;

- where the proceeds of the part-realisation are less than the appropriate portion of the cost of the asset: a debit equal to the shortfall;

- where there are no proceeds from the part-realisation (eg on a licence donated to charity): a debit equal to the appropriate portion of the cost of the asset.

Example 12.3

In Example 12.2, if the carrying value had not been written down, and the appropriate portion of the cost is £200,000, then if the proceeds of the part-realisation are:

- £300,000: there is a credit for tax purposes of £100,000;

- £50,000: there is a debit for tax purposes of £150,000;

- £0: there is a debit for tax purposes of £200,000.

The cost of the asset is that recognised for tax purposes.

Proceeds of realisation

12.58   The proceeds of the part-realisation are:

- the amount recognised for accounting purposes as the proceeds of the part-realisation, less

- any amount recognised for incidental costs of realisation (CTA 2009, s 739).

Appropriate portion

12.59   The appropriate portion of the tax written down value or cost on a part-realisation is a proportion of the accounting value given by the following formula (CTA 2009, s 737):

$$\frac{(AVB-AVA)}{AVB}$$

where:

- AVB is the accounting value immediately before the part-realisation; and

- AVA is the accounting value immediately after the part-realisation.

Example 12.4

BrandCo has a trademark with a accounts value of £750,000. On 1 January 2009, it grants a licence to a third party to use the trademark in a particular territory and the terms of the licence are such that it is a part-disposal of the trademark.

After the licence is granted, the accounts value is adjusted to £650,000 to reflect the reduction in value as a result of the licence.

The appropriate portion of the tax written down value to be taken into account in calculating the tax debit or credit is:

$$\frac{(750,000 - 650,000}{750,000}$$

Effect of part-realisation

12.60   The effect of a part-realisation of an intellectual property asset under these rules is to deduct an amount from the tax written down value of the asset so that immediately after the part-realisation occurs, the tax written value is given by (CTA 2009, s 744):

$$\frac{WDVB \times AVA}{AVB}$$

Where, in relation to the asset:

- WDVB is the tax written down value immediately before the part-realisation; and

- AVA is the accounting value immediately after the part-realisation; and

- AVB is the accounting value immediately before the part-realisation.

12.61   This effectively 'resets' the tax written down value of the asset, so that calculations of the tax written down value in future only take account of:

- this value; and

- any capitalised enhancement expenditure incurred after the part-realisation; and

- any debits or credits brought into account for tax purposes after the part-realisation (CTA 2009, s 744(5)).

Example 12.5

In the example above, BrandCo had taken used roll-over relief (see para **12.62**) to defer a gain into the trademark when it acquired that trademark and so the tax written down value of the trademark before the part-realisation was lower than the accounts value, at £600,000.

After the part-realisation, the tax written down value of the trademark is £520,000, calculated as:

$$\frac{600,000 \times 650,000}{750,000}$$

The appropriate portion of the tax written down value is £80,000 (applying the calculation in para **12.59** to the tax written down value of the asset prior to the part-disposal).

Debits and credits that were brought into account in relation to periods before the part-realisation are no longer taken into account for tax purposes.

Roll-over relief

12.62   Roll-over relief (see para **14.32**) is available for gains on part-disposals of intellectual property where new intellectual property is acquired in the specified time period, in the same way as for full disposals. There is, however, *no* rollover relief available on the part-disposal of an intangible asset, including intellectual property, to a related party (CTA 2009, s 850; see para **18.69** for the definition of a related party), or where a related party acquires an asset derived from the part-disposed-of asset. This is a form of anti-avoidance, as the distinction between exploitation and part-disposal is capable of manipulation; these rules are intended to ensure that related parties cannot get roll-over relief for what is, in effect, income from intellectual property exploitation and not a gain on part-disposal of intellectual property.

12.63   The net proceeds of part-realisation are compared to the appropriate portion of the cost of the original asset to establish the relief.

12.64   The appropriate portion of the cost of the original asset is given by (CTA 2009, s 759):

$$\frac{AVB \times AVA}{AVB}$$

where:

- AVB is the accounting value immediately before the part-realisation; and

- AVA is the accounting value immediately after the part-realisation.

12.65   Where the original asset was subject to a previous part-realisation, or had its tax cost otherwise adjusted, it is the adjusted tax cost that is used to calculate the appropriate portion (CTA 2009, s 759(2)).

Example 12.6

ZCo has a patent which it acquired for £50,000. It has previously granted an exclusive licence over the patent which was treated as a part-realisation of the patent; the appropriate portion of the original cost which was taken into account at that time was £10,000. It now grants a further exclusive licence, again a part-realisation of the patent. Neither grant is to a related party.

In this case, the cost of the asset from which the appropriate proportion is established will be (£50,000–£10,000) = £40,000, deducting the amount taken into account on the previous part-realisation.

12.66   The effect of the roll-over relief is to reduce the gain (credit) brought into account for tax purposes on the part-realisation, so reducing the tax charge on the part-realisation and also reducing the tax cost recognised for the new asset. This in turn will reduce the amortisation deductions available (see para **11.33**) and increase the tax charge on the eventual disposal of this new asset, if no further roll-over claim is made (see para **14.42**).

12.67   The general requirements for roll-over relief (see para **14.33** onwards) apply on part-realisation as they to do realisations of the entire asset, so that the relief is restricted where the net proceeds of realisation are not fully invested, and the original and new assets must meet certain criteria.

EFFECTS OF DEBITS AND CREDITS ON COMPUTATION

12.68   The nature of the intellectual property to which debits and credits on exploitation relate will determine the way in which they are dealt with in a computation.

Trading debits and credits

12.69   Where the intellectual property is acquired and held for the purposes of the trade, the credits received for exploiting the intellectual property are treated as receipts of the trade when calculating the profits of the business for tax purposes (CTA 2009, s747).

Non-trading debits and credits

12.70   Where the intellectual property is acquired and held for non-trade purposes (generally, where it is held as an investment, although not all investments qualify as relevant assets to which the new regime applies) the debits and credits are pooled (CTA 2009, s 751) so that:

- a non-trading loss arises where:

    — there are only non-trading debits; or

    — if the total non-trading debits exceed the total of non-trading credits received (in respect of any intellectual property held as an investment);

- a non-trading gain arises where:

  — there are only non-trading credits; or

  — if the total non-trading credits exceed the total of non-trading debits received.

12.71 If the accounting period is not the same as the period of account for tax purposes, the gain or loss will need to be adjusted, generally on a time basis (CTA 2010, s 1172).

12.72 Where a company has a non-trading gain for the period, it is charged to tax as investment income (CTA 2009, s 752).

12.73 A company that has a non-trading loss in an accounting period can claim for that loss to be set against the total profits of the company for that period. The claim must be made within two years of the end of the accounting period in the corporate self-assessment return, or by amended return (CTA 2009, s 753).

12.74 Where the loss is not absorbed by that period's profits, and is not surrendered by way of group relief, it can be carried forward to the next accounting period to be treated as a non-trading loss of that period but can only be set against non-trading profits from intellectual property and intangible assets; the set off against total profits is only available in the accounting period in which the loss is incurred (CTA 2009,s 753(3)).

DOUBLE TAX RELIEF

12.75 Payments of royalties made between UK corporate tax payers are generally made without deduction of tax (ITA 2007, ss 933, 934), but exploitation of intellectual property overseas may mean that the UK recipient of royalties suffers withholding tax in the jurisdiction where the payer is located (see para **16.88**).

Concession for payments by non-resident persons

12.76 This rule is mitigated by a concession relating to copyrights, patents, designs, secret processes or formulae, trademarks 'or other like property' (ESC B8).

12.77 Where payments are:

- received from a non-resident by a person carrying on a trade in the UK; and

- those payments are consideration for the use of the intellectual property in the overseas country,

the payments are treated as income arising outside the UK even where the intellectual property is registered in the UK, so that double tax relief can be claimed on any overseas tax withheld. Where the payments include an element of consideration for services also supplied, where that element is more than incidental, the concession will not apply to that element.

Unilateral relief

12.78   Where a UK taxpayer receives a royalty that is subject to tax in the UK and has also suffered withholding tax in the country of source, the UK taxpayer will be entitled to unilateral relief from UK tax in respect of that withholding tax (TIOPA 2010, ss 8–17; see para **16.184** for more details).

Expensed relief

12.79   A taxpayer can also elect to treat any unrelieved tax as an expense of the business (TIOPA 2010, s 112; see para **16.186** for more details); this is not as generous a relief, as UK tax relief will only be a percentage of the withheld tax, but it does provide some relief for loss-making businesses, or where the tax withheld is more than the UK tax on the same income.

CHECKLIST

12.80

- Confirm that the transaction is one of exploitation:

  — Can the recipient of the payment continue to exploit the intellectual property? If not, the transaction is likely to be a part-disposal.

    (i)   Consider whether roll-over relief is available for a part-disposal.

  — If the transaction is settlement, or an award, in respect of litigation consider the elements of the settlement or award on their own terms.

- Will transfer pricing or the related parties rules require an adjustment to the receipt for tax purposes?

- Withholding tax:

  — Make treaty claims to reduce wherever possible.

— Consider a claim for unilateral relief where possible.

— Consider claiming an expense deduction for the relief if unilateral relief not available or appropriate.

Chapter 13

The patent box

The UK has had incentives for companies to perform research and development for over a decade now; what has been significantly missing has been any tax incentives for UK companies to exploit intellectual property. This is now being rectified in the form of a 'patent box', which is intended to make the UK more competitive, although it should be noted that the UK is playing catch-up with a number of other European jurisdictions that have had similar incentives in place for a number of years (particularly the Benelux countries).

A 'patent box' is a relief from corporation tax on income derived from patents; the name is apparently derived from the need to tick a box on a corporation tax form to claim the relief.

- Who can claim? (para **13.4**)

- Qualifying intellectual property (para **13.12**)

- Qualifying companies (para **13.21**)

- Calculating the patent box relief (para **13.61**)

- Patent box losses (para **13.174**)

- Anti-avoidance (para **13.197**)

INTRODUCTION

13.1   Following a long consultation period, legislation has been introduced in Finance Act 2012, inserting a new Part 8A in CTA 2010, to create a patent box in the UK, providing a relief from corporation tax that is equivalent to a 10% tax rate on qualifying net income from patents (establishing using a specific calculation). The relief is available on income derived from patents, whether as royalties, or income from manufacturing products covered by a patent, or income from services using patented processes.

13.2   The UK patent box relief will, on election into the regime, effectively reduce the corporate tax rate on relevant net income derived from patents to

10%, with effect from 1 April 2013. The relief is to be phased in: only 60% of the relief will be able to be claimed in 2013–14, the year of introduction. The amount that can be claimed will be increased by 10% each until the full relief becomes available in 2017–18.

13.3 In addition to patents, the relief will also be available for income derived from similar intellectual property: data exclusivity, supplementary protection certificates, and plant variety rights (see Chapter 2 for more details of these).

WHO CAN CLAIM?

Companies

13.4 The relief is available to companies within the scope of UK corporation tax which have patent income, regardless of size. It is a corporation tax relief only and so is not available to individuals or other unincorporated entities (CTA 2010, s 357A(1)). A corporate partner in a partnership can also obtain the patent box relief (see para **13.11**).

Election

13.5 The patent box rules are not mandatory, and any company that wants to claim the relief will be required to elect into the regime (CTA 2010, s 357A).

13.6 The election is made by giving notice to an officer of HMRC (in writing). The notice must specify the first accounting period to which it applies, and must be given within two years of the end of that accounting period (CTA 2010, s 357G). In practice, this means that the election should be sent with the tax return (or amended return) on which the patent box relief is first claimed.

13.7 The election applies to all of the trades of the company; it is not possible to elect in respect of one trade only or to pick and choose between qualifying intellectual property (see para **13.12**), where the company has more than one trade (CTA 2010, s 357G(4)). Where this is likely to be an issue (for example, where one trade would give rise to a patent box loss, reducing the benefit of the patent box profits in another trade in the same company: see para **13.181** for details) then pre-election structuring should be considered, to separate out into new group companies the trade (or trades) for which the patent box rules would not be beneficial.

13.8 An election by one group company does not affect any other group company: each must make its own election.

13.9   An election will apply to subsequent accounting periods unless and until it is revoked (CTA 2010, s 357G(5)). To revoke an election, another notice is required (CTA 2010, s 357GA). This must, as with the original election, be in writing to an officer of HMRC. The notice must specify the first accounting period from which the revocation will have effect, and must be given within two years of the end of that accounting period.

13.10   Once a company has revoked an election in respect of the patent box regime, it cannot re-elect into the regime for any accounting period that begins within five years of the day after the last day of the accounting period from which the revocation has effect (ie the company must be out of the regime for at least six years before it can elect back in) (CTA 2010, s 357GA(5)).

Partnerships

13.11   Only the corporate partners of a trading partnership (such as in a cost-sharing arrangement or other joint venture structured as a partnership) can elect into the patent box regime; each corporate partner must make a separate election in respect of their share of the relevant intellectual property profits of the partnership, where the partnership meets the necessary requirements (CTA 2010, s 357GB). An election by one corporate partner does not affect the calculation of the profit share of any other corporate partner. Similarly, any revocation of an election by one corporate partner does not affect the elections of any other corporate partner. There is no requirement that the partnership have only corporate partners, but any non-corporate partners cannot make an election. Where not all partners do, or can, elect into the patent box regime, the partnership profit will need to be calculated separately to establish the profits for partners inside, and outside, the patent box rules.

QUALIFYING INTELLECTUAL PROPERTY

13.12   Only income from qualifying intellectual property rights and items covered by qualifying intellectual property will be eligible for the patent box relief. The intellectual property rights which are eligible are (CTA 2010, s 357BB):

- UK patents, granted under the Patents Act 1977;

- patents granted under the European Patent Convention (ie granted through the European Patent Office, *not* patents of the individual European countries, although some of these may be eligible separately: see below). On grant, a European patent can be validated in European countries – this will not prevent it from qualifying, even if the local national patent would not be qualifying intellectual property;

- inventions which are not granted a patent solely because the application contains information prejudicial to national security or safety (ie where the inventor is notified under the Patents Act 1977, s 18(4));

- plant breeders' rights, granted under the Plant Varieties Act 1997 or EC Regulation 2100/94;

- supplementary protection certificates (issued under EC Regulations 469/2009 (medicines) or 160/96 (plants));

- EU marketing authorisations (data exclusivity for medicinal products for human use, orphan medicinal products and veterinary products).

These last two types of rights are effectively connected to patents. They can extend the effective protection period for products which require extensive testing and which, as a result, may not come to market until well into the normal patent protection period.

13.13 The range of qualifying intellectual property can be extended by Treasury Order (published in draft in December 2011 but not enacted at the time of writing) and, so far, patents granted by the patent offices of a number of European countries are set to be included so that they can qualify as qualifying intellectual property:

- Austria

- Bulgaria

- The Czech Republic

- Denmark

- Estonia

- Finland

- Germany

- Hungary

- Poland

- Portugal

- Romania

- Slovakia

- Sweden.

13.14 Other intellectual property (copyrights, trademarks etc) does *not* qualify for relief although, arguably, the way in which qualifying income is calculated means that at least some income from such intellectual property could qualify. For example, where a company receives licence fees for the grant of a licence over a patent and associated know-how, the income from the know-how will qualify (assuming that it was granted for the same purpose as the patent: CTA 2010, s 357CC(6)(c)).

13.15   In the case of items covered by a qualifying intellectual property right, there only needs to be *a* qualifying intellectual property right. If the company also has non-qualifying patents covering the item, there is no restriction on the patent box relief (but see below for information with regard to the position on exclusive and non-exclusive licences).

Exclusive licence

13.16   An exclusive licence is a licence (see para **17.1** for more information on licences) which meets specific criteria for the purposes of the patent box rules (CTA 2010, s 357BA). It is a licence which:

- is granted by the person who holds either the qualifying intellectual property rights, or holds an exclusive licence to those rights; *and*

- gives the licensee (alone or with others authorised by the licensee) specific rights over the qualifying intellectual property rights.

13.17   These specific rights are (CTA 2010, s 357BA(2)):

- one or more rights to the exclusion of all others in a particular area of business, including the grantor, in at least one country; and

- the right to bring proceedings for infringement of the rights without consent of the grantor or any other person; and

- the right to receive the whole (or greater part) of any damages awarded in respect of any infringement.

The territorial rights must cover at least one entire national territory, not just part of a country.

13.18   A right will only be regarded as exclusive if it will, in effect, give commercial exclusivity in a particular market (Technical Note of 29 March 2012, para 2.20). Where a licence gives exclusivity over a particular application of the relevant intellectual property, it will not be treated as exclusive for the purposes of the patent box if a subsequent licence granted over another application of the intellectual property would allow competition in that market between the licensees.

13.19   In contrast to the position with regard to intellectual property owned outright, care may be needed where the item is protected by intellectual property which has been licensed in by the company. Income from the exploitation of exclusive licences is within the scope of the patent box rules; income from the exploitation of a *non-exclusive* licence is not. Where a company has an exclusive licence in one jurisdiction but a non-exclusive licence in another jurisdiction, the income from exploiting the non-exclusive licence in the latter jurisdiction is not within the patent box rules. The company will need to be able to identify the income relating to the non-exclusive licence to ensure that it is excluded; in practice, this income is likely to be that derived from the territory in which the non-exclusive licence is held.

Groups

13.20   The requirement to include specific rights is relaxed for licences between group companies. In particular, where the licence is granted by one group company to another, it will still be regarded as exclusive where the group as a whole has all the necessary rights (CTA 2010, s 357(4), (5)). This allows the group intellectual holding company, for example, to retain the rights to enforce, assign or licence the intellectual property so that it can continue to manage the intellectual property portfolio of the group as a whole.

QUALIFYING COMPANIES

13.21   A qualifying company for the purposes of the patent box is one which meets the relevant ownership conditions (CTA 2010, s 357B; see below), *and* which meets the development condition (CTA 2010, s 357BC; see **13.35**), in respect of the qualifying intellectual property.

13.22   There is no restriction on the size of company which can elect into the patent box regime, and the only other requirement is (of course) that the company be within the scope of UK corporation tax. A UK permanent establishment (see para **16.17**) of a foreign company could, therefore, claim the patent box where it has qualifying intellectual property and income attributable to the permanent establishment from that intellectual property.

13.23   Any company considering electing should carefully review the likely benefit of the relief and the likely costs of calculating that relief to ensure that it will be cost-effective to make the election.

Ownership condition

13.24   To qualify for the patent box regime, a company must meet *one* of two ownership conditions (either current ownership or prior ownership). A group company must *also* meet the active ownership condition (CTA 2010, s 357B).

Current ownership

13.25   A company will meet the current ownership condition for a particular accounting period where, during that accounting period, it either (CTA 2010, s 357B(2)):

- owns (alone, or jointly with others) qualifying intellectual property rights (see para **13.12**); or

- has an exclusive licence in respect of qualifying intellectual property rights (see para **13.6**).

Prior ownership

13.26 A company will meet the prior ownership condition for an accounting period where it has income during the accounting period which is derived from a qualifying intellectual property right which the company previously owned, or to which it previously had an exclusive licence (CTA 2010, s 357B(3)).

13.27 However, the income must be derived from an event which occurred when the company:

- owned or had an exclusive licence to the intellectual property; *and*

- had elected into the patent box regime.

13.28 As a result, the patent box relief will not be available for income from patents which were sold or expired before the patent box rules come into force on 1 April 2013: no election can be made before that date.

Example 13.1

For example, a biotechnology company may receive milestone payments in respect of a patent which it has sold; the sale price for such a patent is likely to be paid in instalments, conditional on reaching specific milestones (eg successful clinical trials stages). These milestone payments may be received years after the patent has been sold.

Provided that the company had elected into the patent box regime in the accounting period in which the patent was sold, the subsequent milestone payments could be subject to patent box relief. The sale is the 'event' from which the later milestone payments are derived.

Active ownership (group companies only)

13.29 This condition must be met in addition to either the current ownership condition or the prior ownership condition, but applies to group companies only: it is intended to ensure that the company owning the intellectual property is not simply a passive holding company within the group. There is no need for this condition to apply to companies which are not in a group because they must meet the development condition (see para **13.34**) on their own account.

13.30 In order to fulfil the active ownership condition for an accounting period, all or almost all of the qualifying intellectual property held by the company must be intellectual property for which the company either (CTA 2010, s 357BE):

• carries out a significant amount of management activity; *or*

• carries out the development itself (ie the development condition is not met by attribution of another group company's activity: see para **13.46** onwards).

13.31 'Management activity' means 'formulating plans and making decisions in relation to the development or exploitation of the rights' (CTA 2010, s 357BE(3)), particularly 'deciding on whether to maintain protection in particular jurisdictions, grant licences, research alternative applications for the innovation or licensing others to do so' (Technical Note of 29 March 2012, para 2.68).

13.32 It is only the management activity in respect of the qualifying intellectual property that counts in determining whether the activity is significant; any management activity for other intellectual property is not taken into account.

13.33 As elsewhere, 'significant' is not defined; whether activity is significant will depend on all the relevant circumstances, including the resources and responsibilities of the company within the group. Ultimate decisions may need to be taken at group board level, to meet corporate governance requirements, but the company with the qualifying intellectual property must be actively involved in planning and have clear decision-making responsibilities. The activity does not have to be extensive in every accounting period if not commercially necessary; for example, if a licence is granted that lasts for several years, the company would not be expected to carry on extensive management activity in respect of that licence during the period of the licence (Technical Note of 29 March 2012, para 2.70).

13.34 'Almost all' is also not defined, and there is no guidance as to its meaning. In practice, it is likely that this will mean at least 90% of the qualifying intellectual property will need to be actively managed or have been developed by the group company owning it.

Development condition

13.35 A company must meet the development condition by carrying on qualifying development in respect of the intellectual property in order to be able to claim patent box relief on income derived from that intellectual property. This is intended to ensure that companies which acquire intellectual property from others as an investment will not be able to claim the patent box relief; the Treasury intends the relief to apply only to those companies which have either contributed substantially to the creation of the intellectual property, or to the development of that intellectual property and/or products and processes created using that intellectual property (CTA 2010, s 357BC).

13.36   The company is not required to meet the development condition for all intellectual property which it owns, but it must meet the condition for any intellectual property for which patent box relief is claimed on the income derived from that intellectual property.

Qualifying development

13.37   The development must be 'qualifying development', meaning that the company has either (CTA 2010, s 357BD):

- created, or significantly contributed to the creation of, the intellectual property, or

- performed a significant amount of activity for the purposes of developing the intellectual property or any item or process incorporating the intellectual property.

13.38   'Significant' is, again, not defined but—as for the active ownership condition—all relevant circumstances need to be taken into account. Merely applying for a patent in respect of acquired rights, or acquiring the rights to and marketing a fully developed patent or invention, or product incorporating the invention, will not be 'significant' activity (Technical Note of 29 March 2012, para 2.38).

13.39   Some guidance is also given (in the Technical Note of 29 March 2012), so that the following should all be taken into account when considering whether the company has significantly contributed to the development:

- costs, time or effort incurred; or

- value or impact of the contribution; or

- work to test or enhance the viability or usefulness of the idea; or

- having the idea for the intellectual property in the first place.

13.40   Where the company acquired intellectual property that is fully developed on acquisition, there may still be qualifying development activity where the company has to carry out further work to develop the product or process which is to incorporate that intellectual property, or where it has previously carried on development activity in respect of the product before acquiring the intellectual property to complete the product. This has to be more than mere commercialisation: where the acquisition is of a fully developed product, the development condition is unlikely to be met.

13.41   Note that the development has to be *in respect of* the intellectual property rights or products derived from those rights: there is no particular requirement that it be carried out before the registration or acquisition of intellectual property rights by the company. There is also no requirement that the development specifically led to the creation of the relevant intellectual property rights in order to be qualifying. For example, the 29 March 2012 Technical Note includes an example of a company carrying on development activity to create a better light bulb; after significant research and development has taken place, the company discovers that a third party has already obtained a patent that covers the work that they have been doing. The company acquires this patent. The development activity will be qualifying development even though it did not lead to the intellectual property rights; it is enough that the development relates to a product which incorporates those acquired intellectual property rights (Technical Note of 29 March 2012, para 2.41).

Meeting the development condition

13.42   A company can meet the development condition through *one* of four ways; two require the company itself to have carried out the qualifying development and two operate by attributing group qualifying development to the company.

Condition A (CTA 2010, s 357BC(2))

13.43   Condition A: The company has carried out the qualifying development activity at any time and has not since joined or left a group.

This is the basic condition, where the company both owns intellectual property and has developed it.

Condition B (CTA 2010, s 357BC(3))

13.44   Condition B: The company previously carried out qualifying development activity, has since left or joined a group, but has continued to carry out development activity of the same description for at least 12 months after leaving or joining the group.

13.45   The intention behind condition B is, principally, to ensure that groups and acquirers cannot get around the development condition by acquiring a company with qualifying intellectual property where there is no further development of the patented invention after acquisition of the company.

13.46   Where the intellectual property requires no further development, condition B can still be met where the acquired company continues to carry on similar research and development activities for at least 12 months after acquisition, for example, where the company continues to look for ways to make a product cheaper or easier to manufacture.

Condition C (group) (CTA 2010, s 357(4))

13.47   Condition C: The qualifying development activity was carried out by another company which was a member of the same group at the time it carried out the development.

This will allow group companies owning intellectual property to qualify for the patent box where the group includes a dedicated research and development company.

13.48   The definition of 'group' is very wide (see para **13.57** for more details), so that this condition may be met where (for example) the qualifying development activity was carried out by a controlled foreign company (see para **16.139** onwards for more information on controlled foreign companies).

Condition D (group) (CTA 2010, s 357(5))

13.49   Condition D: The qualifying development activity was carried out by another company which at some point in time was a member of the same group and that other company continued to carry out development activities for at least 12 months after joining the group and did not leave the group during that time.

13.50   This allows group intellectual property to qualify where a company is acquired which has carried on qualifying development but then transferred the intellectual property to (for example) a group intellectual property holding company. Provided that the acquired company continues to carry on similar development activity (eg research and development work into the same area), then the company now owning the intellectual property will meet condition D.

Special cases

13.51   Companies may enter into partnership to develop intellectual property by way of joint venture, or a cost-sharing arrangement. Regardless of the structure, a claimant must own the intellectual property (jointly or singly) or have an exclusive licence to the intellectual property in order for a claim for patent box relief to succeed.

Partnerships

13.52   A partnership will meet the development condition in respect of qualifying intellectual property if it has itself carried out qualifying development

230

in relation to the right, or if a relevant corporate partner (one that is entitled to at least a 40% share of profits or losses of the partnership) has done so (CTA 2010, s 357GB(7)).

13.53 The active ownership condition will be met by the partnership if the development condition is satisfied by the partnership, but not if it is satisfied by a relevant corporate partner only (CTA 2010, s 357GB(10)).

Cost-sharing arrangements

13.54 A cost-sharing arrangement is one in which one or more companies together agree to share the costs of developing intellectual property, and subsequently share the resulting intellectual property.

13.55 The arrangement can take various forms (see para **18.24**). Where the cost-sharing arrangements are contractual, the intellectual property is usually owned by one of the parties to the arrangement and licensed to the others, or the parties all share in the income from exploitation of the intellectual property rights. In such a case, any parties to the arrangement that do not directly own the intellectual property might fail to meet the ownership criteria for the patent box regime.

13.56 In order to ensure that such parties can benefit from the regime, ownership of the intellectual property rights resulting from the development to which they contributed is attributed to each of the parties (for the purposes of the patent box rules only) so that they are treated as having qualifying ownership of the patent rights (CTA 2010, s 357GC).

GROUP COMPANIES

13.57 The patent box regime has several provisions which apply to group members, particularly:

- determining whether the active ownership condition is met (see para **13.28**);

- determining whether the development condition is met (see para **13.42–13.50**);

- determining whether the requirements for an exclusive licence are met (see para **13.20**);

- calculating the amount of routine expenses to bring into account (see para **13.112**); and

- the use of set-off amounts (see para **13.181**).

13.58   The definition of a group for the purposes of the patent box regime is rather different to other tax definitions of a group (see para **18.154**): 'a company ("company A") is a member of a group at any time if any other company is at that time associated with company A' (CTA 2010, s 357GD(1)) (see para **18.159** for more information on how companies are grouped for patent box purposes).

13.59   This definition is extremely wide, and has no geographical restriction, so the various routes through which companies can be associated will include worldwide companies. It will bring into the definition joint ventures and smaller groups that would not normally be caught by group arrangements.

13.60   This clearly has an advantage for some measures, making it easier to meet the active ownership condition or the development condition, for example, as there is a wider pool of companies to draw on for support.

13.61   However, the definition may create considerable difficulty in determining the amount of routine expenses which must be brought into account, or establishing the use of set-off amounts, particularly for smaller companies which may find it easy to obtain the relevant information from other companies which would not necessarily consider themselves to be part of the same group.

CALCULATING THE PATENT BOX RELIEF

13.62   The patent box relief is not, unfortunately, a straightforward 10% tax rate on income from patents. The calculation of the relief is a multi-step process (at least five steps). There are two routes through the calculation:

● the standard calculation (CTA 2010, s 357C); and

● the alternative streaming calculation (CTA 2010, s 357D) which may be chosen by a company or required by HMRC in certain circumstances (see para **13.160** for more details).

13.63   Where the calculation produces a patent box loss (ie a negative figure is calculated at step 4; there may be no actual tax losses in the company) then further steps are required to establish whether any patent box relief is available in that or following accounting periods (CTA 2010, s 357E; see para **13.175** for details).

13.64   A separate calculation is required for each trade of the company (remember that an election into the patent box regime will apply to all of the trades of a company: see para **13.7**).

STANDARD CALCULATION

Summary

13.65 Steps 1–3 calculate the pro-rata profits of the trade that relate to qualifying intellectual property (see para **13.66**). Separate calculations are required for each trade of the company.

Step 4 deducts a 'routine return' that HMRC consider all companies will make, regardless of the type of business. The result establishes whether there is a qualifying patent box profit or whether there is a patent box loss (see para **13.113**).

If there is a patent box loss, Steps 5–6 are ignored.

Steps 5 or 6 (these are alternatives) are intended to eliminate any element of the patent box profit that relates to brand intellectual property (trademarks etc) (see para **13.124**).

Step 7 is optional, and allows a company to get some relief for pre-grant qualifying intellectual property income (see para **13.148**).

Any patent box losses must be taken into account once a patent box profit is calculated (see para **13.175**).

The final calculated profit is then subject to a formula to determine the deduction from total taxable profits before calculating corporation tax (see para **13.153**).

Step 1: calculate 'TI'

Gross trade income for the accounting period

13.66 'Gross trade income' of a company includes (CTA 2010, s 357CA):

- all income recognised as revenue under GAAP which is brought into account in calculating the trading profits for tax purposes; and

- damages, insurance proceeds and other compensation relating to the intellectual property which is not included above; and

- any receipts that are brought into account as receipts under CTA 2009, s 181 (ie where there has been a change of accounting policy and an amount falls out of GAAP recognition); and

- any amounts brought into account as a credit on the sale of intangible assets under the corporate intangibles tax rules, if not already included (see Chapter 14 for details); and

- profits from the sale of patent rights held for the purposes of the trade which are not within the corporate intangibles tax rules (generally, pre-1 April 2002 assets: see Chapter 7).

13.67   'Gross trade income' specifically does *not* include (CTA 2010, s 357CB):

- finance income (ie income from loan relationships); and

- amounts recognised as derived from a financial asset under GAAP; and

- amounts which are economically equivalent to interest; and

- credits in respect of derivative contracts (eg forex hedging).

These will need to be deducted from the amounts established above, in order to calculate gross trade income. If the company does not use GAAP for accounts purposes then it will be required to establish the relevant amounts that would have qualified, or had to have been deducted, under GAAP.

Example 13.1

Radcliffe Limited has elected into the patent box rules. In this accounting period, the company has total income recognised in the accounts of £2,500,000, and has received income of £200,000.

Radcliffe's gross trade income is therefore £2,300,000 (being £2,500,00–£200,000).

Step 2: calculate X%, being RIPI/TI x 100

13.68   Having established TI in Step 1, it is now necessary to calculate the company's RIPI and then calculate X%: the percentage of total income that relates to relevant intellectual property income.

'RIPI': the relevant intellectual property income of the trade for the accounting period

13.69   RIPI is initially defined as 'so much of the total gross income of the trade for the accounting period as is relevant intellectual property income' (CTA 2010, s 357C(1)), and is refined by the definition of 'relevant intellectual property income' in s 357CC.

13.70   Relevant intellectual property income is income falling within any of five specific 'heads' set out in s 357CC(2)–(9) which is not excluded. It can also, on election, include a notional royalty amount (see para **13.91**) where the qualifying intellectual property is used in a way that means that the income derived from the right is not RIPI (eg where the intellectual property covers a patented process and does not produce patented items).

Income excluded from RIPI

13.71   'Total gross income of the trade' has already been defined as excluding finance income (see para **13.67**), so RIPI cannot include any finance income, even if such income could fall within the definition otherwise.

13.72 In addition, two types of income which might qualify are also specifically excluded (CTA 2010, s 357CE):

- income from oil extraction activities or oil rights; and

- income from exploiting non-exclusive licences

13.73 Where a licence has some exclusive rights as well as non-exclusive elements, that licence will be treated as two separate licences - one exclusive (see para **13.20**), and one non-exclusive. The income from the licence needs to be appropriated between these two deemed licences on a just and reasonable basis (s 357CE(3)): only that relating to the deemed exclusive licence will be considered to be within RIPI.

Head 1: sales income (CTA 2010, s 257CC(2))

13.74 This covers income from the sale of:

- qualifying items (ie those which are wholly or partly protected by a qualifying intellectual property right. In the case of a patent, the qualifying item will be the invention specified in the patent); and

- items which incorporate a qualifying item, or designed to incorporate a qualifying item which is sold with that item at a single price, eg printer including a cartridge covered by a patent); and

- items which are wholly or mainly designed to be incorporated in items included above (ie spare parts, such as unpatented printer cartridges to be used in a printer covered by a patent).

13.75 Even though qualifying intellectual property rights will only (in general) provide protection with the EU at most), income from worldwide sales is included in this head. The fact that such income could include income derived from non-qualifying intellectual property (eg US patents) does not matter, provided that the item is covered by at least *one* qualifying intellectual property right (see para **13.15**).

13.76 It may be necessary to carry out a mapping exercise to match patents to products, to ensure that patent box relief is not claimed on items which are not covered by patents; this will probably be a straightforward matter in a smaller company.

Packaging

13.77 Packaging is specifically excluded, even where it can be regarded as incorporated, unless it has a function beyond the normal function of packaging so that it is essential for the use of the item, for the purposes for which it is intended to be used (CTA 2010, s 357CC(3), (4)). As a result, if the only patent is in the packaging of an item, the income from the sale of that item will not be included under this Head unless the packaging itself is qualifying.

13.78   Examples of qualifying packaging include the canister of gas in an asthma inhaler: if the gas is protected by patent, income from the sale of the canister together with the gas will be within the scope of the patent box relief even if the canister itself is not covered by a patent (Technical Note of 29 March 2012, para 3.34).

Mixed income

13.79   Where an item protected by qualifying intellectual property is sold as part of a larger unit, or as part of a package in a single agreement, with other non-patented items, the income from that sale is treated as 'mixed income' or 'income under a mixed agreement' and must be apportioned between the qualifying and non-qualifying items on a just and reasonable basis (CTA 2010, s 357CF).

13.80   If the non-qualifying amount is trivial then it can be ignored. As usual, 'trivial' is not defined in the legislation but HMRC suggest that, in practice, the amount would be trivial where the costs of establishing a just and reasonable apportionment would be 'disproportionate to the likely impact on the patent box calculation' and an amount of less than 5% of the total would probably be trivial (Technical Note of 29 March 2012, para 3.79).

Head 2: income from licensing qualifying intellectual property (CTA 2010, s 357CC(6))

13.81   This includes licence fees or royalties for granting rights over:

- qualifying intellectual property rights (including rights out of an exclusive licence);

- a qualifying item or process (eg where the non-UK/EPO patents over that item or process are licensed to third parties);

- and other associated intellectual property rights under an agreement granting one or more of the rights above.

13.82   Other associated intellectual property rights are those rights which are granted for the same purpose as those over the qualifying intellectual property rights. For example, where an owner of a patent licences the patent together with know-how that allows the licensee to use the patent effectively, the income from the licence over the know-how will be RIPI in the same way as the income from the patent licence (Technical Note of 29 March 2012, para 3.39). Note that, in general, this will cover know-how – a trademark licence is unlikely to be regarded as granted for the same purpose as a patent licence.

Head 3: proceeds of sale etc of qualifying intellectual property (CTA 2010, s 357CC(7))

13.83   This covers income from the sale, realisation or other disposal of qualifying intellectual property rights, or from the sale etc of a qualifying exclusive licence.

13.84   This covers intellectual property within the corporate intangibles tax regime, where the income will generally be the credit which is the excess of the proceeds of realisation over the amortised value of that intellectual property (see Chapter 14). It also covers income from the disposals of pre-1 April 2002 assets (see Chapter 7). Where the company can choose to spread the profits on such a disposal over a period of six years (see para **7.41**), the RIPI will be the amount actually brought into charge for the relevant accounting period (Technical Note of 29 March 2012, para 3.43).

13.85   This head does not include any income from the sale or other disposal of non-qualifying intellectual property rights, even if they are sold as part of the same agreement.

Head 4: infringement income (CTA 2010, s 357CC(8))

13.86   This covers amounts received by the company as compensation for infringement (awarded by a court) or alleged infringement (under a settlement agreement) of qualifying intellectual property rights.

13.87   The company does not have to own the intellectual property in the period in which the infringement income is received, provided that it owned it when the infringement took place and had elected into the patent box at that time (see para **13.26**).

13.88   Where the period for which the compensation is paid includes a period in which the intellectual property rights and/or the company were not qualifying (see para **13.21**: usually this will be periods where the company had not elected into the patent box regime, or before the rules came into effect on 1 April 2013) then an apportionment between the qualifying and non-qualifying periods must be made on a just and reasonable basis (Technical Note of 29 March 2012, para 3.49).

Head 5: damages, insurance etc (CTA 2010, s 357CC(9))

13.89 This covers income which is not directly related to infringement of the qualifying intellectual property and so does not fall within head 4. It covers damages, compensation etc relating to items which, if sold, the income would be within head 1, or which represents lost income which would (if it had been received) be RIPI.

13.90 This, in general, will cover pays for infringement of non-qualifying intellectual property. For example, where a company has a UK patent and a US patent both covering an item, income from the sale of that item will be within head 1 regardless of whether it comes from UK sales or US sales. If the patents are infringed, so that a competitor produces items sold in the UK and the US, and the owner takes action over the infringement, the amounts received for infringement will be:

- within head 4, for the UK patent infringement; and

- within head 5, for the US patent infringement (as the income from US sales would have been within head 1, as there is a qualifying patent—the UK patent—over the item).

Head 6: Notional royalty: on election (CTA 2010, s 357CD)

13.91 The notional royalty provisions are available to companies who use patents in their processes, so that such companies can calculate income that can be treated as RIPI for patent box relief purposes. This is needed because, for example, where a patent covers a process rather than a product, that patent will generate income for the company through the sale of the products created through the process or services delivered using the patented process but none of that income will fall within head 1 above, as the products or services supplied by the company will not themselves be covered by a patent. Where a patent includes both a product and a method, it may be necessary to apportion the income to allocate some to Head 1, reflecting the sale of the product, and to calculate (on election) an amount under Head 6 to reflect the income derived from the method. This is a point which is likely to be the subject of guidance in future; it is not covered in the rules at the time of writing.

13.92 Although the legislation refers to 'qualifying intellectual property rights', HMRC expect that only patents will be covered by the notional royalty provisions, that the other types of qualifying intellectual property right will not generate income in this way (Technical Note of 29 March 2012, para 3.57).

13.93 An election is required in order to use the notional royalty; it is not automatically within the calculation of patent box profits (CTA 2010, s 357CD(3)).

13.94   A company that has elected to bring in a notional royalty can include in RIPI an 'appropriate percentage' of the income derived from the use of the qualifying intellectual property.

13.95   The 'appropriate percentage' is the proportion of any intellectual property-derived income which the company would pay a third party on an arm's length basis for the use of the intellectual property, if it did not already have the right to use the intellectual property—an arm's length royalty, calculated (broadly; some assumptions and adjustments are required) on a transfer pricing basis in accordance with Article 9 of the OECD Model Tax Convention and the OECD Transfer Pricing Guidelines (CTA 2010, s 357CD(8). Any enquiries into the notional royalty will be subject to HMRC's governance processes on transfer pricing in the International Manual (Technical Note of 29 March 2012, para 3.69).

13.96   Broadly, this should be the full amount that the company would pay to a third party in an arm's length transaction. The third party is not defined, and so there is no need to establish what a particular third party would be prepared to sell the rights for, and no need to consider any relative bargaining positions (Technical Note of 29 March 2012, para 3.61). The assumptions that do need to be taken into account (s 357CD(6)) are that:

- the transaction is at arm's length;

- the company will have exclusive rights to exploit the intellectual property;

- the company will otherwise have the same rights over the intellectual property as it actually has;

- the relevant intellectual property rights are granted at the beginning of the accounting period of claim (or, if the rights were actually granted during the accounting period, on the date the rights were granted: Technical Note of 29 March 2012, para 3.64);

- the appropriate percentage is calculated at the beginning of the accounting period (although, in practice, no change should be needed if the rights and circumstances have not changed—where intellectual property is still being developed, adjustments may be needed);

- the appropriate percentage will continue to apply for each following accounting period for which the company holds the rights; and

- the company will not derive any income that is otherwise qualifying RIPI or excluded income (see para **13.71**) from the exploitation of the qualifying intellectual property (to avoid double-counting).

13.97   The notional royalty calculated will be a fixed-rate periodic royalty, to match the deemed payments with the period for which the company owns the qualifying intellectual property rights and derives income from them; in particular, the calculation cannot result in deemed lump sum or milestone payments, or other deemed payments which could distort the patent box profits/losses (Technical Note of 29 March 2012, para 3.66).

13.98 The cost of establishing the notional royalty should not be underestimated. It is likely to require the involvement of valuation specialists with experience in calculating royalty rates and access to the appropriate transfer pricing databases and similar information.

Example 13.2

Continuing with Radcliffe Limited: in the accounting period in question, Radcliffe had received £1,500,000 from the sale of items protected by qualifying intellectual property. It had also received £200,000 from licensing out non-core intellectual property which it did not use. The company uses no patented processes, and has not disposed of any intellectual property.

Radcliffe's RIPI for the accounting period is therefore £1,700,00 (£1,500,000 + £200,000).

Radcliffe's X% for the accounting period is 1,700,000/2,300,000 x 100 = 74% (rounded up to make the examples easier!)

Step 3: calculate X% of the profits of the trade for the accounting period

13.99 The percentage established at Step 2 needs to be applied to the *adjusted* profits of the trade, to determine how much of those profits is considered to relate to relevant intellectual property income. It is this step which may make it more appropriate for a company to use the streaming calculation (see para **13.160**): if the intellectual property is significantly more profitable than the other trade elements, the percentage calculated at this step may not properly reflect the profits derived from the intellectual property. If there are no profits, calculate X% of the adjusted losses of the trade.

Adjusted profits of the trade (CTA 2010, s 357CG)

13.100 The taxable profits of the trade must be adjusted under the patent box rules, to account for excluded income and to allow research and development relief to be available at the company's normal corporate tax rate. Losses are adjusted in the same way.

Added back to profits (or deducted from losses), increasing the profits attributed to intellectual property income:

- debits relating to loan relationships and derivative contracts (as these are excluded);

- the *additional deduction* from research and development relief (ie 125% for SMEs, 30% for large companies or SMEs claiming the 30% relief: see Chapter 10); and

- any research and development shortfall (in the first four years: see below).

Deducted from profits (or added to losses), reducing profits attributed to intellectual property:

- credits relating to finance income (as these are excluded); and

any research and development shortfall (in the first four years: see below)

Note that these adjustments are **only** for the purposes of calculating the patent box relief: the actual profits of the trade for tax purposes are not adjusted by these amounts.

Research and development shortfall deduction (CTA 2010, s 357CH)

13.101 This deduction relates to actual research and development expenditure of the company (ie the amount recognised in the accounts as research and development expenditure; CTA 2010, s 357CG(6)), **not** the additional deduction available under the research and development relief rules.

13.102 This adjustment is intended to bring into the patent box expenses relating to earlier research and development costs, where the expenses of the company in the current accounting period do not properly reflect the development costs of the items etc from which patent box income is derived.

13.103 This is meant to ensure that the company does not receive disproportionately more patent box relief by electing into the regime only once all research and development has been completed, thereby getting relief for research and development expenditure at the full corporation tax rate in earlier years, and then claiming patent box relief on higher profits in later years when no research and development expenditure is offset against that income (remember that accounting standards require most research and development expenditure to be written off as incurred: see para **10.88** onwards). This shortfall deduction effectively claws back some of that corporation tax relief received before the patent box election is made.

13.104 The shortfall deduction must be considered in the first accounting period in which the company elects into the patent box regime, and then in each accounting period that begins within the four years that begin with that accounting period (generally, the first four accounting periods of the company where the company's accounting periods are 12 months long) (CTA 2010, s 357CH(6)).

13.105   There will be a shortfall where the actual research and development expenditure (ie **not** the amount of the research and development relief) in the accounting period in which the patent box relief is claimed is less than 75% of the average annual research and development expenditure over the four years before the company elects into the patent box regime (CTA 2010, s 357CH(1)).

13.106   'Research and development expenditure' is that brought into account in calculating the profits of the trade, ie that recognised as such under UK GAAP or IAS (CTA 2010, s 357CH(3)(a) and see para **10.7** onwards). There is no requirement that the expenditure relate to research and development on the qualifying intellectual property rights for which patent box relief is being claimed, this could be research and development on non-qualifying intellectual property, or development of items not protected by qualifying intellectual property.

3.107   Where the company has not traded for four years before electing into the patent box regime, the average expenditure is calculated over the length of time that the company has traded prior to the accounting period in which it elects into the patent box regime (CTA 2010, s 357CH(5)). A company which elects into the patent box regime immediately on beginning trading will have no average to compare against, but in this case all research and development costs will be reflected in the patent box profits and so there could be no advantage to the company.

Adjustment to deduction

13.108   In calculating the deduction, the actual research and development expenditure during the first four years *after* the company elects into the patent box regime must be considered: any expenditure in those years above the average must be carried forward and used to add to future accounting periods in which expenditure below 75% of average before any adjustment is made (CTA 2010, s 357CH(8)).

13.109   Where the company's actual research and development expenditure, after adding in any brought-forward above-average expenditure from the first four years within the patent box regime is less than 75% of the average research and development expenditure during the four years before election into the regime, then the amount added back in adjusting the profits to which X% is applied in this step is the difference between:

- the total of actual and any brought-forward; and
- 75% of the pre-patent box average.

13.110 Where the brought-forward above-average expenditure is more than required to bring up the actual expenditure to 75% of the pre-patent box average, the excess over that requirement is carried forward again.

13.111 Where the actual research and development expenditure together with any brought-forward amounts is still less than 75% of the average pre-patent box expenditure, the amount added back is deemed to be 75% of the average research and development expenditure.

Example 13.3

In the four years before entering into the patent box regime, Radcliffe Ltd has an average annual research and development expenditure of £100,000; 75% of this is £75,000.

In the first four accounting periods (each 12 months) in which Radcliffe Ltd is elected into the patent box regime, it spends the following amounts on research and development:

— *AP 1*: £65,000 (below average expenditure and below 75% of average; £10,000 adjustment to profits required to bring up to 75% of average);

— *AP 2*: £120,000 (above average expenditure; £20,000 excess above the average carried forward);

— *AP 3*: £70,000 (below 75% of average; add £5,000 of brought forward amount to actual expenditure to bring total added back to 75% of average, carry forward remaining £15,000 of brought forward amount);

— *AP 4*: £60,000 (below 75% of average; add remaining £15,000 brought forward to actual expenditure to add back to bring up to average).

Radcliffe Limited has profits of £750,000 in the current accounting period; assuming that this is accounting period 1, these need to be adjusted to take account of the shortfall in research and development expenditure, as above. The total profits are therefore £740,000.

Applying X% to the adjusted profits gives patent box profits of £547,600 (£740,000 x 74%)

Step 4: deduct the routine return

13.112 The patent box rules assume that all companies will make a 'routine return', ie an amount of profit that a company would make regardless of whether or not the company has qualifying intellectual property. This is a policy decision: a biotechnology company, for example, which has only income from the licensing and sale of patents will not exist without qualifying intellectual property let alone make any sort of profit, routine or otherwise. That said, the exclusion of qualifying research and development expenditure (see below) will reduce such a company's routine return figure.

13.113 The routine return is calculated as X% of 10% of specific expenses ('routine expenses') (CTA 2010, s 357CI), to isolate the percentage of the routine expenses applicable to intellectual property. It would (arguably) make more sense to have deducted the 10% of specific expenses as an additional adjustment to taxable profits at Step 3 before calculating X% of the adjusted profits but that is not the way the legislation is written.

Routine expenses (CTA 2010, s 357CJ)

13.114 There are six categories of routine expenses:

- capital allowances deducted in calculating taxable profits;

- premises costs (rent, rates, repair, water, fuel, power etc);

- staff costs (costs of employing directors and employees, and costs of externally provided workers, as defined for research and development relief purposes);

- plant and machinery costs (other than capital allowances: includes leasing costs, construction and modification costs, maintenance, services, operations etc);

- professional services (consultancy, professional fees, administration and management);

- other services (software, telecoms, post, transport, waste etc).

Group expenses

13.115 Where some or all of these expenses are incurred by another group company on behalf of the company claiming the patent box, the expenses are included in the calculation as if they had been incurred by the patent box claimant (CTA 2010, s 357CI(3)).

13.116 Where the other company provides services to the patent box company, however, the expenses of the group company are not treated as routine expenses of the patent company: instead, the cost of the service provided will itself be included if it qualifies as a routine expense (Technical Note of 29 March 2012, para 3.104).

Research and development expenses excluded

13.117 The routine return is calculated as X% of 10% of specific expenses ('routine expenses') (CTA 2010, s 357CI), to isolate the percentage of the routine expenses applicable to intellectual property. It would (arguably) make more sense to have deducted the 10% of specific expenses as an additional adjustment to taxable profits at Step 3 before calculating X% of the adjusted profits but that is not the way the legislation is written.

13.118 Research and development capital allowances (see Chapter 4) and patent allowances (see para **5.60**) are also excluded (but *not* know-how allowances). The reasoning for this is that such expenditure is specifically related to the qualifying intellectual property rights and so would not be expected to contribute to a routine return. This does not entirely help the biotechnology company in the example above, as some of the expenses will not qualify for research and development relief (particularly many of the plant and machinery costs, rent and rates, and the professional services).

13.119 Deductions allowed for employee share acquisitions are also excluded from the routine expenses calculation where the employee is wholly or partly engaged in relevant research and development (ie qualifying research and development for research and development relief purposes: see para **10.7**). The amount excluded is the proportion of the staff costs that qualify for research and development relief (see para **10.101**).

Other excluded expenses

13.120 Debits relating to loan relationships are also excluded, as the income from loan relationships is not taken into account in the patent box relief.

Deduction

13.121 Once the routine expenses have been established, the routine return is calculated as being 10% of the routine expenses, and then X% of this figure is calculated to arrive at the amount to be deducted from the profits attributed to relevant intellectual property income (calculated at Step 3).

13.122 If the result is a profit then this is termed the qualifying residual profit ('QRP') of the company, and further adjustments are required to establish the amount of the patent box relief.

13.123 Where the result is negative (or nil) then there is a patent box loss and no further adjustment is needed: the next step in the calculation for a patent box loss is Step 7, if relevant (see para **13.147**).

Example 13.4

Radcliffe Ltd has total routine expenses categories of £250,000, but £150,000 of these expenses are qualifying research and development expenditure and so must be excluded from the calculation in calculating the routine expenses.

Assuming that all non-research and development expenditure is routine expenses, the overall routine return is 10% x (250,000–150,000) = £10,000.

This is then allocated between intellectual property profits and other profits of the trade, using X%, so that only £7,400 of the routine return is deducted from the profit attributed to relevant intellectual property income.

Radcliffe Ltd's qualifying residual profit is therefore £547,600–£7,400 = £540,200.

Steps 5 or 6: exclude profits relating to non-qualifying intellectual property

13.124   All income from qualifying items etc will be included in the patent box calculation (see para **13.70**): in many cases, this income will include an element of profit relating to non-qualifying intellectual property, particularly brand-related intellectual property such as trademarks and other marketing assets.

For example, an element of the profit on the sale of an Apple iPad will relate to the brand-related intellectual property and marketing intangibles attaching to 'Apple' and 'iPad'.

13.125   As the patent box relief is intended to give relief on income from a limited range of intellectual property only, these Steps 5 or 6 (they are alternatives) will deduct an amount intended to adjust for the value of that brand-related intellectual property.

13.126   Step 5 is a simplified calculation of the contribution of brand and marketing intangibles which can be used by election, provided that a company meets specific conditions (the 'small claims treatment'). Where the company does not meet the conditions, or chooses not to elect to use Step 5, then the more detailed calculation at Step 6 must be used instead.

Step 5: small claims election (CTA 2010, s 357CL)

13.127   A company can elect to use the small claims treatment where it meets *one* of two conditions (CTA 2010, s 357CL(1)–(3)):

- the QRP for all the trades of the company in aggregate does not exceed £1,000,000 (patent box losses are ignored in the aggregate); or

- the aggregate QRP of the trades of the company does not exceed the relevant maximum (see below) *and* the company has not used used the

Step 6 calculation method for excluding non-qualifying intellectual property in the previous four years.

13.128 The 'relevant maximum' is calculated as:

$$\frac{£3,000,000}{1+N}$$

where N is the number of associated companies of the company in the relevant period. 'Associated' means that the companies are grouped for patent box purposes (see para **13.57**) (CTA 2010, s 357CL(6)) and which have elected into the patent box regime.

13.129 As a result, for a solo company with a single trade, the options are:

- QRP < £1m: can always elect to use Step 5

- QRP > £3m: can never elect to use Step 5

- QRP ≥ £1m and ≤ £3m: will be able to elect if it has not used the Step 6 calculation method in the previous four years (for any accounting period beginning in the four years immediately preceding the start of the current accounting period).

This last requirement means that, once a company has elected to use the Step 6 calculation method, it will not be able to use the Step 5 method again (even where it has low profits) until it has had at least four years of patent box losses, or has elected out of the patent box and then elected back in again more than five years later.

Example 13.5

Radcliffe Limited has qualifying residual profits (QRP) of £540,200: Radcliffe Limited can therefore choose to use the small claims treatment as it has QRP of less than £1m provided that it has not used the Step 6 calculation method in the previous four years.

Radcliffe has 1 associated company so that, if Radcliffe Limited's QRP had been over £1.5m (£3m/2), the company would not have been able to use the small claims treatment (Radcliffe + 1 associated company = 2).

13.130 Where a patent box election has been made by a corporate partner, the number of associated companies to take into account is the number associated with the specific corporate partner and not for the partnership as a whole (CTA 2010, s 357GB(11), even though the patent box calculation is otherwise generally carried out as if the patent box rules applied to the partnership rather than a company (CTA 2010, s 357GB(2): see para **13.11**).

13.131 *The patent box*

13.131 Where the accounting period is less than 12 months, the relevant maximum is reduced accordingly (CTA 2010, s 357CL(7)).

Calculation (CTA 2010, s 357CM)

13.132 Where the company meets one of the conditions and elects to use the small claims treatment then the relevant intellectual property profits ('RIPP') amount on which the patent box relief is based is the *lower* of:

- 75% of QRP for the trade (as calculated in Step 4); and

- the small claims threshold for the company divided by the number of trades of the company.

13.133 The small claims threshold is:

£1,000,000/ (1+N)

where N is, again, the number of companies associated with the company in the relevant period which have elected into the patent box regime. Where the accounting period is less than 12 months, the small claims threshold is reduced pro-rata (CTA 2010, s 357CM(6)).

Example 13.6

The small claims threshold for Radcliffe Limited will be £500,000 as it has one associated company. Assuming that Radcliffe Limited has only one trade, the RIPP for Radcliffe Limited will be the lower of:

- 75% of QRP = £405,150; and

- £500,000.

So the RIPP for Radcliffe Limited, using the small claims treatment, will be £405,150. This is a reduction of £135,050 from the QRP. If Radcliffe Limited believes that there is little or no contribution to its QRP from brand/marketing intangibles, it can elect to use Step 6 (below) instead (bearing in mind that it will have to continue to do so in future accounting periods, given the limitation in para **13.129**).

Step 6: marketing assets return (CTA 2010, ss 357CN–357CP)

13.134 Where a company does not qualify for Step 5, or does not elect to use Step 5 where it qualifies, the company must calculate a 'marketing assets return' amount to deduct from QRP to establish the relevant intellectual property profits (RIPP) of the company.

Marketing assets return amount

13.135 The marketing assets return is the difference between (CTA 2010, s 357CN(1)):

- the notional marketing royalty of the company (see below); and

- any actual marketing royalty paid by the company (see below).

13.136 However, no deduction is made from QRP (CTA 2010, s 357CN(2)) where the marketing assets return amount is:

- negative (ie the actual marketing royalty exceeds the notional marketing royalty); or

- less than 10% of the QRP for the accounting period.

13.137 This is supposed to assist companies, so that they aren't required to undertake an expensive valuation exercise where the contribution from the marketing royalties is small (Technical Note of 29 March 2012, para 3.127). The Technical Note states, at para 3.130 that

'[w]here it is reasonable to conclude from a high-level consideration that [the deduction will be nil], a pragmatic and common-sense approach should be taken and it should not be necessary to insist that a computation of notional marketing royalty be undertaken merely to prove that the 10% threshold is not breached'.

Example 13.7

Paladin Limited is a biotechnology company, carrying out research and development. Its income comes only from licensing or selling the rights to patents which it develops.

Paladin Limited should be able to argue that it has no relevant marketing assets (see the definition below) so that no deduction from QRP needs to be made.

13.138 It is to be hoped that HMRC will in fact take the recommended pragmatic and common-sense approach. A company which believes that it will be within the limits so that no deduction is required should record the basis on which it has made the 'high-level consideration' referred to, in order to minimise any risk of penalties for careless error if HMRC later challenge the position.

Notional marketing royalty (CTA 2010, s 357CO)

13.139 This is the percentage of relevant intellectual property income for the accounting period (as calculated at Step 2) that the company would

13.140 *The patent box*

pay to a third party on an arm's length basis in order to be able to use the brand/marketing intangibles if the company did not already own those intangibles.

13.140 The brand/marketing intangibles which need to be considered are (CTA 2010, s 357CO(7)):

- anything for which an action for passing off (ie misrepresentation damaging goodwill) could be brought;

- equivalent rights under foreign law;

- signs or indications of geographic origin of goods or services; or

- customer information used for marketing purposes (but not for product development purposes)

Effectively, this covers trademarks (registered and unregistered), design rights (also registered and unregistered) and similar assets.

13.141 The notional marketing royalty is calculated using OECD principles on the same basis as the notional royalty that is included in the calculation of RIPI (see para **13.91**; CTA 2010, s 357CO(6)), using the same assumptions. As with the notional royalty, this is likely to require the assistance of valuation specialists. HMRC enquiries will, again, be subject to the transfer pricing governance process in their International Manual (Technical Note of 29 March 2012, para 3.153).

13.142 In addition, it should be assumed that the notional marketing royalty is only paid in respect of use on products qualifying for the patent box. For example, if the company uses a global trademark for all its products, the notional marketing royalty is not what it would pay to use the trademark on all products but only what it would pay to use it on the patented product in isolation (CTA 2010, s 357CO(4)(g); Technical Note of 29 March 2012, para 3.154).

13.143 As with the notional royalty, the notional marketing royalty should be assessed in each accounting period, although it is likely to stay the same in respect of a stable product. In contrast, where a company is actively promoting a new product which has an associated trademark (for example), the notional marketing royalty in respect of that product is likely to increase year-on-year if the trademark becomes more valuable with the success of the product.

13.144 Where the product is well-established, a high-level consideration should be all that is needed to assess whether circumstances have changed enough to require a detailed review of the notional marketing royalty (Technical Note of 29 March 2012, para 3.156).

Actual marketing royalty (CTA 2010, s 357CP)

13.145 In comparison, the actual marketing royalty is reasonably straightforward to calculate: this is a proportion of the royalties actually paid by the company to use brand/marketing intangibles (as defined above).

13.146 The proportion is X%, and the amount paid is: the aggregate royalties and other sums paid to acquire or exploit the relevant marketing assets, provided that they have been brought into account in calculating taxable profits. This will include amortisation deductions where the marketing asset was acquired outright and is being amortised over its useful economic life (see para **11.25** onwards).

13.147 Where the streaming calculation has been used, with the alternative Steps 1–4 (see para **13.160** onwards), then there is no need to take X%. Instead, the amount of the actual marketing royalty is that which has been allocated to the RIPI stream on a just and reasonable basis (CTA 2010, s 357DA(6)).

Step 7: additional relief for pre-grant profits (CTA 2010, s 357CQ)

13.148 This step is another elective step, rather than a compulsory element of the calculation. It can take a considerable time between application and grant of qualifying intellectual property rights (patents in particular), and the company can use or create the invention which is the subject of the patent in the meantime. This step is intended to provide a measure of patent box relief for profits which a company makes from a product etc before a patent over that product is actually granted. This step can be used by companies that make a loss in the first accounting period after election into the regime.

13.149 The company can look back up to six years before the grant, but can only take into consideration accounting periods in which it had elected into the patent box regime: there will be no lookback to periods before 1 April 2013 as a result. The company must also be a qualifying company in each accounting period. It will be treated as a qualifying company if the only reason that it does not qualify is that the patent has not yet been granted (CTA 2010, s 357CQ(8)). It is advisable to include in the corporation tax return white space a note to this effect.

13.150 Even where the company has disposed of the patent before the date of grant (ie where it sells the patent application rights), it can still elect to look back under this section if it has income from the patent in the accounting period in which the patent is granted.

13.151 The amount which can be added for relief purposes is the difference between:

- the actual aggregate RIPP for each accounting period whilst the patent application was pending (to a maximum of six years before grant); and

- the aggregate RIPP which would been calculated for those accounting periods if the patent had been granted at the date of application.

13.152 The effect of this additional amount is (in effect, through the calculation mechanism) a corresponding decrease in the non-RIPP profit of the company, so that less is taxed at the mainstream corporation tax rate; in effect, recovering a proportion of the tax which was paid on the relevant income when it actually arose.

Example 13.8

Radcliffe Ltd has made an election under s 357CP as a patent has only recently been granted, although it was applied for over six years ago.

Radcliffe Ltd determines that the difference between actual RIPP in the previous six years and the recalculated RIPP for those years is £450,000; it has elected for those years and would be a qualifying company for those years if the patent had been granted.

As a result, the RIPP for the current accounting period is increased to £450,000 + £405,150 = £855,150. This effectively grants retrospective relief on the pre-grant profits.

Deduction from tax (CTA 2010, s 357A(3))

13.153 At the end of the calculation, the calculated RIPP of the trade is adjusted to take into account any patent box losses (see para **13.175**). If there is still a profit following that adjustment, the patent box relief is given as an additional deduction in calculating the profits of the trade for corporation tax purposes.

13.154 This deduction is:

$$\frac{RP \times (MR-IPR)}{MR}$$

where

- RP is the RIPP of the trade after adjusting for patent box losses;

- MR is the main rate of corporation tax (23% for 2013–14); and

- IPR is the patent box tax rate (10%)

13.155 Where the company has more than one trade, the patent relief must be calculated separately for each trade (see para **13.65**) so there may be a series of deductions (one for each trade).

Example 13.9

Radcliffe Ltd has only one trade, and has no patent box losses. Its corporation tax rate is 23%. The patent box deduction which it can deduct (ignoring phasing in: see below) is therefore:

$$\frac{£855,150 \times (23-10)}{23} = £483,346$$

Its taxable profits are, therefore, £750,000–£483,346 = £266,654. Corporation tax at 23% on this figure is £61,330.

Note that the pre-grant relief at Step 7 has skewed these results considerably. If Radcliffe Limited had not claimed pre-grant relief, its RIPP would be £405,150 so that the deduction would be (ignoring phasing in):

$$\frac{£405,150 \times (23-10)}{23} = £228,998$$

Its taxable profits would be £750,000 – £228,998 = £521,002. Corporation tax on this figure would be £119,830.

For comparison, corporation tax on the pre-patent box profits of £750,000 would be £172,500 (at 23%).

13.156 The relief is given by way of deduction from profits to get around problems that might otherwise arise with losses and other reliefs. It also reduces the changes required to redesign the corporation tax return.

Phasing in (Finance Act 2012, Sch 2, Pt 3)

13.157 The entire patent box relief is not available immediately on introduction in 2013; instead, the relief will be phased in over four years to compensate for the extension of the relief to all qualifying intellectual property rights regardless of when they were granted (the original proposals had restricted the range of qualifying intellectual property rights initially to those granted after a particular date, and then to those commercialised after a particular date).

13.158 The relief is phased by applying a percentage to the RIPP (after adjustment for patent box losses) to reduce it before the patent box relief is calculated. The percentages are:

— 2013: 60%

— 2014: 70%

— 2015: 80%

— 2016: 90%

13.159 The full relief will be available from 2017. Where the accounting period straddles a tax year, the relief must be pro-rated and the relevant percentage applied.

Example 13.10

In practice, Radcliffe Ltd will have to take into account the requirement to phase in profits: assuming that the accounting period in the example is 1 January 2014 to 31 December 2014, the RIPP on which patent box relief is available will not be £855,150 but will, instead, be reduced as follows:

Profits in 2013/2014:

$$\frac{90}{365} \times £855,150 = £210,859$$

@ 60% = £126,353

Profits in 2014/2015:

$$\frac{275}{365} \times £855,150 = £644,291$$

@ 70% = £451,004

The total adjusted RIPP for the accounting period is therefore £210,859 + £451,004 = £661,863, and the patent box deduction from taxable profits is calculated using this figure. The phased-in deduction is, therefore:

$$\frac{£661,863 \times (23-10)}{23} = £374,096$$

so that Radcliffe Ltd's taxable profits would be £750,000 - £374,096 = £375,904

At 23%, the tax charge for Radcliffe for the accounting period would be £86,458.

This ignores the reduction in corporation tax to 22% in 2014, to avoid making the example unnecessarily complicated.

STREAMING CALCULATION

Elective streaming (CTA 2010, s 357D(1))

13.160 In some cases, a company's income and profits are such that a straightforward apportionment of profits between intellectual property income and non-intellectual property income does not give a reasonable approximation of the actual profits that arise from exploitation of qualifying intellectual property rights, so that the profits attributed to qualifying intellectual property in the standard calculation (at Step 3) are much lower than actually is the case.

13.161   In this case a company can elect to use streaming to allocate profits, to allocate expenses and profits to income streams on a just and reasonable basis. Once an election is made, it will continue to apply until the company elects otherwise.

Example 13.11 (derived from the Technical Note of 29 March 2012)

Block Ltd manufactures non-patented products and also separately licenses out qualifying intellectual property rights. It has total trade income of £1m, made up of £900,000 from the sale of products and £100,000 from the licensing activity. The expenses relating to the products are £850,000 so that it only makes profits of £50,000 on these products. In contrast, the licensing activity has no associated expenses so that all of the £100,000 income is profit.

Block Ltd therefore has profits of £150,000. Using the standard calculation would apportion these profits in the same ratio as income, so that only £100,000/£1m of the profits (ie £15,000) would qualify as relevant intellectual property income (see para **13.12** onwards) for the patent box. Using the streaming calculation, a significantly higher proportion would qualify as the product income and expenses would (in effect) be ignored.

In this case, Block Ltd would be likely to elect for the streaming basis in order to bring more of the licensing profits within the patent box regime.

Mandatory streaming (CTA 2010, s 357D(4))

13.162   The streaming calculation *must* be used (CTA 2010, s 357DC) where any one of three conditions are met:

- Condition A: the gross income of the trade includes a substantial amount of credits brought into account in calculating taxable trade profits, but not fully recognised as revenue under GAAP (eg transfer pricing adjustments); or

- Condition B: the gross income of the trade include a substantial amount of licensing income that is not relevant intellectual property income (eg trademark licensing etc: this type of licensing is generally almost pure profit and could skew the patent box results in the opposite way to the Block Limited example above, so that too much non-qualifying income is apportioned to the patent box under the standard calculation)

- Condition C: the trade generates income that is not relevant intellectual property income and the company also receives a substantial amount of relevant intellectual property income from licences granted, where those licenses are granted out of exclusive licences held by the company (eg conduit arrangements: these may generate little profit over all, but the amount could skew profits as above, so that too much non-qualifying income would be apportioned to the patent box under the standard calculation)

13.163   In this case, 'substantial' has been defined. Licensing income from non-qualifying intellectual property rights will be substantial if it is more than:

- £2m; or
- (if lower) 20% of the gross income of the trade for that accounting period.

There is a de minimis level so that, if the licensing income from non-qualifying intellectual property rights is no more than £50,000, it will not be regarded as substantial even where it is more than 20% of gross income.

Summary

13.164   Steps 1–3 calculate the profits of the trade that relate to qualifying intellectual property (see para **13.165**).

Step 4 deducts a 'routine return' that HMRC consider all companies will make, regardless of the type of business. The result establishes whether there is a qualifying patent box profit or whether there is a patent box loss (see para **13.171**).

The rest of the calculation and deduction is the same as with the standard calculation:

- if there is a patent box loss, Steps 5–6 are ignored;
- Steps 5–7 are the same as for the standard calculation (see para **13.124** onwards), subject to minor modification in calculating the actual marketing royalty in Step 6 (see para **13.147**);
- any patent box losses must be taken into account once a patent box profit is calculated (see para **13.175**); and
- the final calculated profit is then subject to a formula to determine the deduction from total taxable profits before calculating corporation tax (see para **13.153**).

Step 1: identify the streams of income (CTA 2009, s 357DA(1))

13.165   The taxable income of the trade (ie all amounts brought in as taxable credits), after deduction of finance income, must be apportioned into two streams of income:

- relevant intellectual property (RIPI) income (this is the same as the RIPI established at Step 2 of the standard calculation, using the principles in CTA 2010, ss 357CC–357DD; see para **13.74**) and

• all other income.

13.166 Where the company uses a patented process to create products or provide services, the streaming calculation may be particularly useful if the expenses relating to the patented processes are proportionately less than those relating to the rest of the business. The notional royalty relating to the process (CTA 2010, s 357CD; see para **13.95**) would be the RIPI stream in this case, as the income from the products or services would not be fall within one of the five heads of qualifying income (see para **13.74**).

Step 2: allocate expenses between the two income streams (CTA 2010, s 357DA(1))

13.167 First, it is necessary to establish the amount to be allocated. This will be the expenses of the trade (ie all debits deducted in calculating taxable profits) except:

• certain finance (loan relationships and derivative contracts) debits;

• the additional research and development relief deduction,

together with any research and development shortfall amount (see para **13.105**).

Example 13.12

Stiles Limited is an SME with total debits in an accounting period of £200,000. Of these, £10,000 relate to a loan relationship. Also included is £20,000 of qualifying expenditure on research and development in the accounting period and has an additional research and development relief deduction of £25,000 (125% of the qualifying expenditure: see Chapter 10). There is no research and development shortfall adjustment required, as Stiles Limited's research and development expenditure is increasing.

The amount to be allocated is:

£200,000–£10,000–£25,000 = £165,000

Note that the basic research and development expenditure (£20,000) must be allocated between the income streams (see below); it is only the additional deduction that is excluded.

13.168 The resulting amounts are allocated to the income stream to which they relate, on a just and reasonable basis. This should result in the RIPI stream having intellectual property-related expenses allocated to it and all other expenses allocated to the non-RIPI stream. All debits must be allocated to one of the two streams.

Just and reasonable allocation (CTA 2010, s 357DB)

13.169 What is 'just and reasonable' will depend on the company's particular circumstances and, once established, the same method of allocation must be used in each accounting period unless there is a change of circumstances relating to the trade of the company which makes the method inappropriate.

13.170 Where the allocation method is no longer appropriate, the company can either chose a different method or elect out of the streaming calculation where it is not mandatory. There is no restriction on a company later electing back into the streaming calculation in a later accounting period, if it becomes appropriate again.

13.171 The just and reasonable requirement may need to be considered carefully for research and development expenses where the company has a mixture of qualifying and non-qualifying intellectual property in development.

Example 13.13

Avery Limited manufactures a range of products which it then sells. Some of the products are covered by current patents (and so are qualifying items, and related income of £300,000 is the RIPI stream) and some which are no longer covered by patents (and so are not qualifying items, and the related income of £100,000 is the non-RIPI stream).

The research and development expenses in the current accounting period are likely to relate to future products, rather than those currently generating income for the trade. As the trade is one of creating and developing such products, it can be said that the research and development expenditure relates to the trade as a whole and so the expenditure could be apportioned between the two streams on a pro-rata basis relating to the amount of income in each stream. In this case, 75% would be allocated to the RIPI stream and 25% would be allocated to the non-RIPI stream, as total turnover is £400,000 and £300,000 of that is the RIPI stream.

If, however, part of Avery Limited's manufacturing was on a contract basis for third parties and the products which Avery Limited manufactured on its own account were all qualifying products (ie covered by a current patent) then research and development expenditure could be allocated entirely to the RIPI stream.

Step 3: calculate the net relevant intellectual property income amount (CTA 2010, s 357DA(1))

13.172 This is the easy step: deduct the amount calculated in Step 2 from the amount calculated at Step 1.

Step 4: deduct the routine return (CTA 2010, s 3537DA(1))

13.173   The routine return is 10% of the routine expenses which are included in the RIPI stream. 'Routine expenses' are the same as those for the standard calculation (see para **13.114**). There is no need to calculate X% in the streaming calculation because only those expenses attributable to RIPI are taken into account, as a result of the streaming.

13.174   Deducting the routine return from the net relevant intellectual property income calculated at Step 3 gives either:

- the qualifying residual profit (QRP) of the trade, in which case the calculation then follows the same route as the standard calculation, picking up at Step 5 or 6, depending on whether the company has elected to use the small claims treatment or not (see para **13.124**); or

- a patent box loss, in which case no further calculation is required (unless pre-grant profits are to be taken into account; see para **13.152**) and the loss is taken into account in calculating any other patent box profits of the company or group (see para **13.175**).

As noted in the summary (para **13.164**), the rest of the calculation follows the same steps as the standard calculation.

PATENT BOX LOSSES

13.175   Patent box losses (relevant intellectual property losses, or 'RIPL') are a product of the patent box calculation, whether standard (see para **13.64** onwards) or streaming (see para **13.164** onwards), and can arise in otherwise profitable companies. Broadly, a patent box loss will arise where the expenses relating to relevant intellectual property income exceed that income.

13.176   The patent box loss is described in the legislation as a 'set-off amount', equal to that loss (CTA 2010, s 357E). For clarity, the term 'patent box loss' is used in this chapter.

13.177   Where a trade generates a patent box loss, that loss *must* be set against patent box profits (as calculated at the end of step 7: see para **13.152**) of (in order):

- other trades of the company;

- other group companies;

- future accounting periods of the company or other group companies

before the relief is calculated (see para **13.153**).

13.178 Essentially, a company cannot have the benefit of the patent box relief until all patent box losses of that company or any of its group companies have been utilised—and remember that 'group' has a wide definition for the purposes of the patent box (see para **13.57**).

13.179 Any patent box loss set off against patent box profits will reduce the amount of the patent box deduction in calculating the taxable profits of the company.

Set off against other trades (CTA 2010, s 357EA)

13.180 An election into the patent box regime by a company applies to all the trades of the company (see para **13.7**). Where the company has more than one trade to which the patent box relates (considered an unlikely scenario by HMRC: Technical Note of 29 March 2012, para 5.4), then a patent box loss in one trade must be set against any patent box profits in the other trade(s) of the company.

Example 13.14

Masters Ltd has two patent box trades. In one accounting period it has patent box profits in one trade of £50,000 and patent box loses in the other trade of £20,000, giving a set-off amount of £20,000.

Without offset, Masters Limited would have patent box relief of £50,000 × (2–10/22) = £27,273 to deduct from its taxable profits (assuming a 22% tax rate).

Masters Ltd is required to offset the losses, so the profits to which the patent box relief applies will be reduced to £30,000. As this fully uses up the patent box loss, Masters Limited will have no patent box losses to set-off elsewhere or carry forward.

As a result, Masters Limited's actual patent box relief deducted from taxable profits will be £30,000 × (22–10/22) = £16,364.

Set off against group companies (CTA 2010, s 357EB)

13.181 Where the patent box loss is not completely set off against patent box profits of other trades of the company, it *must* be set against any patent box profits of relevant group companies in that accounting period. This is not optional; the company cannot choose to carry forward the patent box losses if there are relevant group companies with patent box profits.

13.182 The order of set-off between group companies is up to the group although, if the group does not determine the order of set-off, then the patent box losses will be set off in the company with the most patent box profits, then in the company with the second largest and so on.

13.183 A *relevant accounting period* for the company with the patent box loss is any accounting period that ends at the same time or within an accounting period of another group company.

13.184 A *relevant group company* is one which has elected into the patent box regime for that accounting period.

Planning

13.185 Clearly a company will need to identify the companies with which it is grouped for patent box purposes (see para **13.57**) in order to be able to determine whether it:

- must offset its patent box losses against patent box profits in one or more of those companies; or
- will have its patent box profits offset by patent box losses in one or more of those companies.

13.186 Where a company is in a group, deciding whether to elect into the patent box regime should take into account the possibility of patent box losses and set the risk of these against the potential benefit of being within the regime for future income.

Example 13.15

Dumas Limited is considering electing into the patent box regime. It has two group companies, Dunn Limited and Durrell Limited, both of which have elected into the patent box regime. Both Dunn and Durrell are expected to make patent box profits, but Dumas expects to make a patent box loss in the next two years if it is within the regime.

At first glance, it would seem appropriate for Dumas to wait for two years before making an election, so that it does not have patent box losses to reduce the patent box profits of Dunn and Durrell.

However, in both years, Dumas expects to sell patents which will give rise to income through milestone payments in future years. This income will not be within the patent box unless Dumas has elected into the patent box regime in the accounting period in which it sells the patent (see para **13.25**).

If the expected income is sufficiently large (and sufficiently certain), it may be more beneficial for the group as a whole for Dumas to elect into the patent box regime in order to get the relief in future, where the immediate costs (the set off of patent box losses) are reasonably expected to be less than the value of that relief.

Payments for group set-off (CTA 2010, s 357EF)

13.187   A company which is required to set off its patent box losses against the patent box profits of another group company can agree to make a compensating payment to that group company. As the set off is compulsory, this could be particularly advantageous for companies which are grouped for patent box purposes but otherwise do not have the benefit of group tax provisions.

13.188   Provided that the payment does not exceed the amount of the *losses* set off, the payment will not be taken into accounting in calculating the profits of either company, and will not be treated as a distribution.

13.189   As the payment limit is connected to the losses set off, and not to the increased corporation tax payment resulting from the set off, the payment could be more valuable to the recipient than the reduction in profits. This point should be considered carefully in negotiating any agreement to make a compensating payment.

Carried forward patent box losses (CTA 2010, s 357EC)

13.190   If the patent box losses are not fully used up in set off against patent box profits of other trades and other group companies, they are carried forward to future accounting periods and *must* be used:

- first, against any patent box profits of the company for the next accounting period; then

- if not used up, against any patent box profits of group companies for that next accounting period.

13.191   Any remaining patent box losses still not set off are carried forward again on the same basis until they are fully used against patent box profits.

13.192   In summary: a group of companies will not get tax relief under the patent box regime unless and until all patent box losses arising within the group have been set off against patent box profits within the group.

Cessation of business etc (CTA 2010, ss 357ED–357EE)

13.193   The patent box losses of a company are not necessarily extinguished by the company:

- ceasing to trade; or

- revoking its election into the patent box regime (see para **13.9**); or

- ceasing to be within the corporation tax charge.

13.194 If there are any patent box losses in a company when one of these events occurs, those losses must be transferred to any other group company that has elected into the patent box regime at that time (CTA 2010, s 357ED).

13.195 The patent box losses must be allocated between those qualifying group members which have patent box profits. The allocation is at the choice of the group although, if no allocation is made, the losses will be allocated to the group company with the largest patent box profits, then to that with the second-largest patent box profits etc. If no qualifying group companies have patent box profits, then the patent box losses go to the group member with the largest set-off amount of its own.

13.196 Only if there are no other group companies elected into the patent box are the patent box losses extinguished if the company ceases to trade etc.

Transfer of trade between group companies (CTA 2010, s 357EE)

13.197 The patent box losses also cannot be extinguished by transferring the trade of the company to another group company: the patent box losses will follow the trade.

ANTI-AVOIDANCE

Principal anti-avoidance rule

13.198 The main anti-avoidance rules applies where a company which has elected into the patent box regime is party to a scheme, one of the main purposes of which is to obtain a relevant tax advantage (CTA 2010, s 357FB).

13.199 A 'relevant tax advantage' is obtained where:

- RIPP is increased as a result of the scheme; and

- the scheme is one of the following specified types:

  — designed to avoid the application of any part of the patent box rules; or

  — designed to create a mismatch between expenses and income relating to a qualifying intellectual property right (eg where a company enters a group);

    —   designed to recognise non-intellectual property income as something other than revenue (to increase the proportion of intellectual property income).

Anti-avoidance: exclusivity

13.200 Where a licence is made exclusive and the main purpose (or one of the main purposes) of the exclusivity is to get the benefit of the patent box, the patent box relief will not be available (CTA 2010, s 357F). That is, exclusivity in a licence should be commercially justifiable for income derived from that licence to qualify for the patent box relief.

Anti-avoidance: incorporation of patented items

13.201 An anti-avoidance rule also applies where a patented item is incorporated into a product simply to bring the sale of the product within the patent box regime. There must be some commercial reason for the inclusion of the patented item within the overall product (CTA 2010, s 357FA).

SUMMARY

Does the patent box make the UK more competitive?

13.202 The patent box regime in the UK is, in some aspects, very wide—it certainly covers a wider range of income than many other patent box regimes. Ultimately, the restrictions on the patent box mean that, realistically, the patent box is most competitive for UK companies and groups with insufficient overseas activities to warrant serious consideration of a non-UK intellectual property holding structure.

13.203 For example, the patent box is limited principally to patents but companies do not limit their intellectual property to patents. Indeed, a company may prefer not to patent an invention in order to maintain secrecy (a patent application requires publication of a substantial amount of information that a company may prefer not to disclose to competitors). Other countries, such as Luxembourg, have implemented an 'innovation box', reducing the tax rate on royalties from a wider range of intellectual property. The rates in other countries are also substantially lower than the UK, with an effective tax rate on royalties of 5–7% in the Benelux countries, or 2% in Cyprus and 0% in Malta (albeit on royalty income only).

13.204 A non-UK group setting up operations in Europe would not pick the UK as an intellectual property holding location specifically for the patent box rate: there may be other reasons to pick the UK, and the patent box rate should be considered as part of the overall deliberations on locations, but—considered alone—it does not seriously compete with similar incentives in other European countries. In that sense, this is primarily a tax cut for UK companies that are already investing in patents.

CHECKLIST

13.205

- Ensure exclusive licences meet the requirements of the patent box rules.

- Elect into regime:

  — If not already elected, and not within five years of a revocation of an election.

  — Within two years of the end of the accounting period.

  — Consider what group companies exist, and whether they have elected into the regime. Consider whether patent box losses are likely, and the impact of these on the group's overall tax position.

- Step 1:

  — *Standard*: establish total gross income of the trade (TI).

  — *Streaming*: establish relevant intellectual property stream of the trade:

    (i) divide total gross income of the trade between relevant intellectual property stream and a stream for all other income.

- Step 2:

  — *Standard*: establish relevant intellectual property income (RIPI) of the trade and calculate X% as RIPI/TI x 100.

  — *Streaming*: Allocate expenses between streams on a just and reasonable basis.

- Step 3:

  — *Standard*: calculate intellectual property profits as X% of total trade profits.

  — *Streaming*: establish net relevant intellectual property stream (income at Step 1, less deductions allocated at Step 2).

- Step 4:

  — *Standard*: calculate X% of 10% of routine expenses to give routine return.

  — *Streaming*: calculate 10% of intellectual property stream routine expenses to give routine return.

  — *Both*: deduct routine return from result from result at Step 3:

    (i)   if positive: this is the qualifying residual profit (QRP);

    (ii) if negative, this is a patent box loss, *go to Step 7*.

- From here on, the steps are the same as for both calculation methods.

- Step 5 (if not using Step 6):

  — Elect for small claims treatment if qualify OR go to Step 6.

  — On election, exclude profits from non-qualifying intellectual property:

    (i)   calculation qualifying profits using formula: lower of 75% of QRP or small claims threshold.

  — Result is relevant intellectual property profits (RIPP).

  — *Go to Step 7.*

- Step 6 (if not using Step 5):

  — Exclude profits from non-qualifying intellectual property by comparing:

    (i)   notional marketing royalty;

    (ii) actual marketing royalty.

  — Deduct difference between notional and actual from QRP to calculate relevant intellectual property profits (RIPP). Note: difference is nil where actual is greater than notional, or the difference is less than 10% of QRP

- Step 7 (on election):

  — Elect to claim pre-patent relief OR go to calculation.

  — Calculate difference between:

    (i)   actual aggregate RIPP since patent application (max six years); and

    (ii) aggregate RIPP which would have been calculated if patent had been granted.

  — Add to RIPP or RIPL to establish adjusted RIPP or RIPL.

- Calculation:
  - — If the result is a loss (RIPL):
    - (i)   set off against any RIPP of another trade, if any; then
    - (ii)   set off against group RIPP, if any; then
    - (iii) carry forward and set off against future own and/or group RIPP
    - (iv)   until fully utilised.
  - — If the result is a profit (RIPP):
    - (i)   calculate deduction from taxable profits using formula;
    - (ii)   if accounting period starts before 1 April 2017, calculate phase-in deduction;
    - (iii) deduct result from taxable profits before applying appropriate corporation tax rate.

Chapter 14

Disposals of intellectual property by companies

Summary: Intellectual property can be disposed of for tax purposes by sale, by expiry, or by damage: broadly, it will be disposed of when it is no longer recognised on the balance sheet. Where the company receives any proceeds from the disposal (generally on sale, or as compensation for damage to the value of the intellectual property) then it will be subject to tax on the difference between the tax value of the asset and the amount actually received. Relief from this tax charge may be available where the gain is reinvested, or where the transaction is with another group company, or where it takes place as part of a reorganisation of the company.

- Disposal or realisation (para **14.1**)

- Deemed disposal or realisation (para **14.5**)

- General rules (para **14.7**)

- Specific situations (para **14.25**)

- Roll-over relief (para **14.32**)

DISPOSAL OR REALISATION

14.1   Most intellectual property can, generally, be sold outright (certain unregistered rights (such as unregistered trademarks) which cannot be separated from the goodwill of the business of the company cannot be sold); this is clearly a disposal of the intellectual property. There are other circumstances in which intellectual property is, in effect, disposed of for tax purposes: this will principally be when protection expires, or when it otherwise ceases to have any value.

14.2   The corporate tax rules recognise this by referring to 'realisation' of intellectual property assets, rather than disposals, covering a wider range of transactions than a sale of the asset. An intellectual property asset will be realised for tax purposes when it ceases to be recognised in the company's balance sheet (CTA 2009, s 734) and a credit or debit will be brought into account for tax purposes on that realisation. Note that the proceeds of realisation of a patent may then qualify for the patent box relief (see Chapter 13).

14.3   As a reminder, these rules do not apply to sales of intellectual property by a trade in dealing in intellectual property: those continue to be dealt with as trading (ie revenue) receipts (as the intellectual property will not be a fixed asset of the company; see para **8.13**). In addition, the following rules do not apply to disposals of pre-1 April 2002 assets (see para **8.33**), or to excluded assets (see para **8.38** onwards). Such assets continue to be dealt with under the same rules as those used for disposals by individuals and other unincorporated entities (see Chapter 7).

14.4   The starting point for calculating the taxable credit will be the accounts information, although any alterations in amortisation (for example, after roll-over relief claims: see para **14.32**) will need to be taken into account.

DEEMED DISPOSAL OR REALISATION

14.5   Besides sale, expiry or loss of value, an intellectual property asset may be treated as having been disposed of for tax purposes by a company as a result of:

- the company ceasing to be UK resident (generally, where a company is non-UK registered and central management and control is moved away from the UK); and

- the asset beginning to be held for the purposes of a mutual trade or business.

In these cases there is a deemed realisation and reacquisition of the asset at market value immediately before the asset ceases to be chargeable (CTA 2009, s 859).

14.6   A gain on the deemed realisation may be deferred if the disposal is as a result of the company ceasing to be UK resident whilst continuing to be a 75% subsidiary of a UK resident company (CTA 2009, s 860).

GENERAL RULES

Disposal of amortised intellectual property

14.7   Where the intellectual property asset has been written down under the corporate tax rules (see para **11.25** onwards) either on an accounting basis or under a fixed-rate election, the amount that needs to be brought into account for tax purposes on a realisation is as follows (CTA 2009, s 735):

- where the proceeds of the realisation (see para **14.12**) exceed the tax written down value of the asset, a credit equal to the excess;

- where the proceeds of the realisation are less than the tax written down value of the asset, a debit equal to the shortfall;

- where there are no proceeds from the realisation (eg when a patent expires), a debit equal to the tax written down value of the asset.

14.8   The tax written down value is that value immediately before the realisation (see para **11.35** for details of the calculation of the tax written down value). The effect of this is (broadly) to bring into account the amortisation deductions previously given for tax purposes whilst the intellectual property is owned by the company.

Example 14.1

DrugCo buys a patent for £1,600,000. A few years later, it sells the patent when it has a tax written down value of £800,000. It has claimed £800,000 of amortisation deductions in that time.

If the proceeds of the realisation are:

- £1,000,000: there is a credit for tax purposes of £200,000

- £400,000: there is a debit for tax purposes of £400,000

- £0: there is a debit for tax purposes of £800,000.

In effect, if the patent is sold for £1,000,000 then there is a clawback of £200,000 of the amortisation deductions given. Compared to the acquisition cost, DrugCo has sold the patent at a loss but the amortisation deductions given in earlier accounting periods have effectively already provided the company with tax relief of more than that loss, so the excess deductions are recovered through the calculated credit that must be brought into account for tax purposes.

Disposal of unamortised intellectual property

14.9   Where the intellectual property is shown on the company's balance sheet but has not been written down for tax purposes then the amount brought into account for tax purposes (CTA 2009, s 736) is:

- where the proceeds of the realisation exceed the cost of the asset, a credit equal to the excess;

- where the proceeds of the realisation are less than the cost of the asset, a debit equal to the shortfall;

- where there are no proceeds from the realisation (eg on a gift of the asset), a debit equal to the cost of the asset.

14.10   The cost of the asset is that recognised for tax purposes.

Example 14.2

In Example 14.1, if the carrying value had not been written down, and the acquisition cost of the asset was £1,000,000, then if the proceeds of the realisation are:

● £1,200,000: there is a credit for tax purposes of £200,000;

● £500,000: there is a debit for tax purposes of £500,000;

● £0: there is a debit for tax purposes of £1,000,000.

14.11   If the asset is not amortised then no tax relief has been given for the decline in value before the asset is disposed of or otherwise realised, so the full loss or gain should be taken into account.

Proceeds of realisation

14.12   The proceeds of the realisation are the amount recognised for accounting purposes as the proceeds of the realisation, less any amount recognised for incidental costs of realisation (CTA 2009, s 739).

14.13   Broadly, the proceeds of realisation will be amounts such as:

● the consideration for a transfer of the intellectual property; and

● compensation in settlement of, or awarded on success in, litigation over damage to the value of intellectual property.

Deemed proceeds: related parties

14.14   Where an intellectual property is transferred to a related party, and is a chargeable asset of the transferor and transferee, the consideration for the transfer is treated as being at market value for both parties (see para **11.16**).

14.15   This will not apply, however, where:

● the transfer is a tax-neutral between group companies (see para **18.162**); or

● the consideration for the transfer is dealt with under the transfer pricing regulations (see para **16.94**).

Tax reliefs for credits on realisation of intellectual property

14.16   There are a number of tax reliefs which may be available to reduce a credit arising on the disposal or other realisation of intellectual property. These are covered in more detail below and in other chapters but, in outline, are:

- roll-over relief, where a replacement asset is acquired (see para **14.32**);

- group relief, on intra-group transfers (see para **18.162**);

- reconstruction reliefs, on the transfer of a trade where there is no substantial change in ownership (see para **17.71**); and

- patent box relief, for qualifying intellectual property and companies (see Chapter 13).

Effects of debits and credits on computation

14.17   The status of the intellectual property to which debits and credits on realisation relate will determine the way in which they are dealt with in computing the taxable profits of the company.

Trading debits and credits

14.18   Where the intellectual property was acquired and held for the purposes of the trade, any debits and credits on disposal are treated as expenses and receipts of the trade, respectively, when calculating the profits of the business for tax purposes (CTA 2009, s 747).

Non-trading debits and credits

14.19   Where the intellectual property was acquired and held for non-trade purposes (generally, where it was held as an investment which qualifies as a relevant asset to which the corporate intellectual property tax rules apply), the debits and credits are pooled (CTA 2009, s 751) so that:

- a non-trading loss arises where:

  — there are only non-trading debits; or

  — if the total non-trading debits exceed the total of non-trading credits received (in respect of any intellectual property held as an investment);

- a non-trading gain arises where:

  — there are only non-trading credits; or

  — if the total non-trading credits exceed the total of non-trading debits received.

If the accounting period is not the same as the period of account for tax purposes, the gain or loss will need to be adjusted, generally on a time basis (CTA 2010, s 1172).

14.20 Where a company has a non-trading gain for the period, it is charged to tax as investment income (CTA 2009, s 752) in the year it arises.

14.21 A company that has a non-trading loss in an accounting period can claim for that loss to be set against the total profits of the company for that period. The claim must be made within two years of the end of the accounting period (CTA 2009, s 753).

14.22 Where the loss is not absorbed by that period's profits, and is not surrendered by way of group relief, it can be carried forward to the next accounting period to be treated as a non-trading loss of that period (CTA 2009, s 753(3)). A company can also choose to carry forward the non-trading loss without offsetting it against current profits or by group relief.

14.23 Only current year non-trading losses can be surrendered for group relief to reduce the taxable profits of group companies. Carried-forward non-trading loss cannot be surrendered (CTA 2010, s 104).

14.24 The use of such carried-forward non-trading losses may also be restricted, in common with other non-trading losses (CTA 2010, s 681), where there is a change in ownership of the company and there is:

- a major change in the nature or conduct of the business of the company; or
- a significant increase in the capital of the company; or
- the company's activities are minimal before the change in ownership and increase substantially after that change.

SPECIFIC SITUATIONS

Uncompleted disposals

14.25 In some cases a company can incur costs in connection with a disposal of an asset without that disposal transaction in fact taking place (where the transaction is aborted for some reason); the costs of that aborted transaction will be deductible as a debit for tax purposes to the extend that the costs are recognised by the company for accounting purposes (CTA 2009, s 743).

Disposal of asset not on balance sheet

14.26 Certain intellectual property assets will not be shown on the balance sheet (such as internally created goodwill); where these assets are sold, a credit equal to the proceeds of realisation will be brought into account for tax purposes (CTA 2009, s 738) because the costs will have already been deducted, either:

- as they were incurred and recognised in the profit and loss account (see para **9.21**); or

- where the expenditure was on research and development; because expenditure on research and development is outside the corporate intangibles tax regime, no deduction for previous expenditure on research and development is available when the products of the research and development are disposed of, as relief has already been obtained by deduction under the research and development relief rules or as a standard revenue deduction (CTA 2009, s 814).

Part-realisations

14.27   Where the intellectual property is retained by the owner, but a transaction means that the amount recognised in the balance sheet for that asset is reduced (eg on grant of an exclusive licence), there will be a part-realisation of the asset.

14.28   As part-realisations are more likely to occur as part of exploitation of the intellectual property, the tax consequences of part-realisations are covered in para **12.53** onwards.

Value shifting

14.29   There are anti-avoidance provisions that will apply where the value of the shares or securities of a company are materially reduced in order to obtain a tax advantage (TCGA 1992, s 31). This can interact with intellectual property where the reduction in value is achieved through a transaction involving that intellectual property—for example, a transfer of assets intra-group at an undervalue (less than both market value and acquisition cost of that asset)—which correspondingly reduces the value of the shares in the disposing company and so reduces the tax on sale of those shares.

14.30   The rules on value shifting were substantially simplified for disposals on or after 19 July 2011; the previous rules were a complex set of rules and have been replaced with the motive test in the paragraph above.

14.31   Where a transaction is caught by the value shifting rules, the proceeds of realisation of the intellectual property are deemed to be adjusted an amount that is just and reasonable in the circumstances (ie to counter the tax advantage).

ROLL-OVER RELIEF

14.32 The corporate intangibles tax rules provide a similar relief to the roll-over relief that is available for capital gains on certain type of business asset. The relief allows a company to effectively postpone a gain (a credit, see para **14.7**) on the disposal of an intellectual property asset where the company also acquires an intellectual property asset within a specific period of time.

Note: the HMRC CIRD manual refers to this relief as 'reinvestment relief' (CIRD20000 onwards), presumably to distinguish it from capital gains roll-over relief. Nevertheless, the legislation refers to it as 'roll-over relief' and so it is referred to as 'roll-over relief' in this book.

Qualifying conditions

14.33 Where there is a gain on a realisation of an intellectual property asset (the 'original asset'), the proceeds of that realisation may qualify for roll-over relief to reduce the taxable credit on the realisation (CTA 2009, Pt 8, Ch 7) where a number of conditions are met, as follows. That reduction in the taxable credit is mirrored by a reduction in the cost (for tax purposes) of the replacement asset so that, on a later realisation of the replacement asset, the taxable credit at that time is larger than it would be if roll-over relief had not been claimed. In addition, the amortisation charge available for deduction in respect of the new asset will be reduced. As a result, this relief effectively defers the gain: the gain will gradually be brought into the tax charge through the reduced amortisation (see Example 14.6).

Qualifying original asset

14.34 The asset realised must have been a chargeable intangible asset of the company (ie post-1 April 2002 intellectual property, but not excluded assets) at the time of realisation (CTA 2009, s 755(1)). There is no requirement that the asset has been used for the purposes of a trade, so roll-over relief can be claimed for disposals of investment intellectual property, although note that, to be a chargeable intangible asset, the intellectual property must have been held for business or commercial purposes (see para **8.32**; note that investment can be a business or commercial purpose).

14.35 A modified form of the relief is available where the asset is a pre-1 April 2002 asset, excluded from the corporate intangible tax rules only because it was acquired or created by the company before 1 April 2002 (see para **8.33**).

Ownership period

14.36 If the asset was a chargeable asset throughout the period in which it was owned, then all of the realisation gain will qualify for relief.

14.37   If the asset was only a chargeable asset for a substantial part of the period in which it was owned, then the asset is treated for the purposes of this relief as two assets: one representing the period in which it was chargeable; and one representing the remaining period (CTA 2009, s 755(5), (6)). Intellectual property may fall into this where it is held for part of the ownership period for non-business purposes and so is an excluded asset for that time (see para **8.32**).

14.38   Only the gain on the realisation of the asset representing the chargeable period will qualify for the relief. The apportionment between chargeable and non-chargeable period should be done on a just and reasonable basis (CTA 2009, s 755(7)).

14.39   'Substantial' is not defined and the HMRC manuals provide no particular assistance. Neither have there been any cases directly on the point. In practice it should be possible to argue that an apportionment is appropriate where the asset qualifies for at least 50% of the ownership period, but it may be possible to argue for lower percentages (after all, a 'substantial shareholding' for the purposes of that exemption is one of 10% or more).

Excluded gains

14.40   The gain on the asset cannot have arisen through a deemed disposal (eg on emigration of a company), other than on de-grouping (CTA 2009, s 763; see para **18.172**).

14.41   Similarly, the gain cannot have arisen on a part-realisation to a related party (CTA 2009, s 850; see para **12.62**). These gains are excluded because HMRC consider that such part-disposals could include transactions which might, between non-related parties, be structured as revenue receipts: roll-over relief is intended to relieve only gains of a capital nature. For example, a licence between related parties could be structured as an exclusive licence and treated as a part-disposal for accounts (and tax) purposes where the transaction is economically closer to exploitation.

Proceeds of realisation exceed cost of original asset

14.42   The proceeds of realisation must exceed the tax cost of the asset disposed of (ie the asset cannot have been disposed of at a loss) (CTA 2009, s 755). This condition is necessarily met where the asset is created in-house and so has no balance sheet cost.

14.43   This might seem an obvious point, as the relief is for gains and not for losses. The reference though is to the 'tax cost' of the asset disposed of. This will not always be the actual acquisition expenditure. For example, if the acquisition of the asset was used to claim roll-over relief on an earlier gain, the tax cost of the asset could be considerably lower than its acquisition cost.

14.44 Where the asset has been previously part-realised on exploitation, the cost of the asset is the adjusted cost of the asset after the part-realisation (CTA 2009, s 755(2)(b)).

Qualifying new assets

14.45 The new intangible assets into which the gain is rolled over are acquired in the period (CTA 2009, s 756(1)):

- beginning 12 months before the date of realisation (ie the date the original asset ceases to be recognised in the accounts); and

- ending three years after the date of realisation.

HMRC do have power to extend these time limits (CTA 2009, s 756(1)), as they do for capital gains roll-over relief. In practice, that power is rarely exercised.

14.46 The new asset must be:

- capitalised for accounting purposes (CTA 2009, s 756(2); expenditure on creating new intellectual property will not qualify where it is written off in the profit and loss account: see paras **11.10** and **11.25**); and

- chargeable intangible assets (ie post-1 April 2002 intellectual property, not excluded) of the company immediately after acquisition (CTA 2009, s 756(3)).

14.47 A new asset must be acquired; relief is not available through a deemed acquisition or deemed reacquisition of an asset (CTA 2009, s 763).

14.48 Where an asset is disposed of and then reacquired (an actual reacquisition, not a deemed reacquisition), the reacquisition is treated as giving rise to a new asset (CTA 2009, s 762), and relief can be available. Where the disposal and reacquisition is for a commercial purpose, HMRC will not challenge the relief. However, if the transaction is for tax avoidance, HMRC are likely to invoke the anti-avoidance provisions in the corporate intangibles tax rules (see HMRC Manual CIRD20140).

Amount of relief

14.49 The amount available for relief (CTA 2009, s 758(2), (3)) is:

- where the qualifying expenditure on the acquired intangible assets is more than the net proceeds of realisation, the amount by which the proceeds of realisation exceed the cost of the original asset; and

14.50   *Disposals of intellectual property by companies*

- where the qualifying expenditure on the acquired intangible assets is less than the net proceeds of realisation, the amount by which the qualifying expenditure exceeds the cost of the original asset.

The 'cost of the old asset' is the total capitalised expenditure recognised for tax purposes on that asset, ignoring any amortisation deductions previously given, but taking into account any gain deferred by roll-over relief on the acquisition of the asset.

14.50   Where the related party rules (see para **18.69**) or transfer pricing (see para **16.94**) require an adjustment to any expenditure or proceeds of realisation, it is the adjusted amount that is used for relief purposes.

Example 14.3

If PatentCo sells a patent for £300,000 in February 2012, having acquired it for £150,000, the net proceeds of realisation are £150,000. If PatentCo then acquires a new patent in March 2013 for £500,000, the amount available for relief would be £150,000, as the qualifying expenditure is more than the proceeds of realisation.

If PatentCo had instead acquired the new patent for £50,000 the amount available for relief would be limited to £50,000, as the qualifying expenditure is less than the net proceeds of realisation.

Amount of relief: earlier part-realisations

14.51   Relief is also available for part-realisations of intellectual property (eg exclusive licences: see para **12.53**).

14.52   Where there has been an earlier part-realisation, the cost of the original asset which is taken into account when establishing the roll-over relief on the eventual disposal of the intellectual property needs to take the prior part-realisation into account. The cost is reduced by any amounts already taken into account in calculating roll-over relief on the previous part-realisations.

Example 14.4

TradeCo has a design right over which it grants an exclusive licence, creating a part-realisation of the design right. The original cost of the design right was £25,000. At the time of the part-realisation, the proportion of the cost of the design right which was taken into account in calculating the relief (see para **12.59**) was £5,000.

On an eventual disposal of the design right, the original cost of the asset (£25,000) must be reduced by the £5,000 already taken into account on the part-realisation, so that the cost of the original asset for roll-over relief purposes is now £20,000 (£25,000–£5,000).

Restricted relief: proceeds not fully reinvested

14.53   The amount available for relief is subject to restriction where the net proceeds of realisation are not fully reinvested (CTA 2009, s 758(3)). In this case, the relief is limited to the excess of the expenditure over the tax cost of the original asset.

Example 14.5

SoftCo acquires an intellectual property asset for £100,000 and later sells it for £150,000. If the expenditure on replacement intellectual property is £110,000, the relief is limited to the excess of the expenditure over the original cost of the original asset (£100,000) so that the relief is limited to £10,000.

Relief given by deduction

14.54   The relief is given by deducting the amount of the relief (CTA 2009, s 758(1)) from:

- the proceeds of realisation of the old asset; and

- the cost recognised for tax purposes of the acquired intangible assets.

Example 14.6

Continuing the PatentCo example above, assuming that PatentCo acquired the new patent in March 2013 for £500,000 (so that relief of £150,000 is available), the effect of PatentCo's claim to defer the gain by roll-over relief is that:

- the proceeds of realisation of the old patent are reduced to £150,000 (£300,000–£150,000); and

- the cost recognised for tax purposes of the new patent is £350,000 (£500,000–£150,000).

As a result, the amortisation deduction (see para **11.27** onwards) available to PatentCo will be reduced. Assuming that the new patent is amortised in the accounts over ten years:

- without a rollover relief claim, PatentCo would have been able to deduct amortisation of £50,000 per year in respect of the new patent (but would have paid tax on the gain on sale of the old patent);

- with a rollover relief claim, PatentCo does not immediately pay any tax on the gain on sale of the old patent, but the amortisation deduction available on the new patent is reduced to £30,500 per year (£350,000 over 10 years).

PatentCo, in effect, pays tax on the amount of rollover relief over the ten year amortisation period as a result of the reduction in the amortisation deduction.

Effect of relief on tax charge

14.55   The roll-over relief will not eliminate the tax charge on the disposal completely, as the relief is established by comparing the proceeds of realisation with the original cost (see para **14.49**), whereas the tax charge is calculated by comparing the proceeds of realisation with the tax written down value of the asset (see para **14.7**).

Example 14.7

Continuing the PatentCo example, if the tax written down value (ie after deductions of amortisation etc) of the original patent was £100,000 at the date of realisation, PatentCo will have a taxable credit of £200,000 (the proceeds of realisation less the tax written down value) before relief is given.

The effect of the relief is to reduce the proceeds of realisation to £150,000, so that the taxable credit becomes £50,000 (the revised proceeds of realisation, less the tax written down value).

Modified relief for disposals of pre-1 April 2002 intellectual property

14.56   This is one of the few areas where the non-corporate and corporate tax rules on intellectual property can interact; roll-over relief can be obtained under the corporate intellectual property tax rules for the disposal of an intangible asset under the old regime where reinvestment is made in an intangible asset under the corporate intellectual property tax rules (CTA 2009, s 898).

14.57   Various modifications are made to the requirements for qualifying assets to accommodate the fact that the asset disposed of is not in the corporate intangibles tax regime, but the effect is broadly similar to that above.

Qualifying asset

14.58   The original asset must have been within the scope of UK corporation tax on gains throughout the period of ownership (ie the entity realising the gain must have been a UK resident company or a UK permanent establishment of a non-UK company, not exempted from UK tax on gains under a treaty, throughout the period of ownership) (CTA 2009, s 899(3)).

14.59   The net proceeds of disposal must exceed the original cost of the asset recognised for capital gains purposes (CTA 2009, s 898(2)).

Relief mechanism

14.60   The relief is given by (CTA 2009, s 758 as modified by ss 898–900):

- reducing the net disposal proceeds of the asset for capital gains purposes (after indexation, see para **7.15**) by the amount of the relief; and

- deduction of the amount of the relief from the cost recognised for the purposes of the corporate intangibles tax rules of the acquired intangible assets (reducing amortisation, as before).

Example 14.8

If BrandCo sells a registered design which it originally acquired in 2000 it can claim roll-over relief under the corporate intellectual property tax rules if it acquires a new intellectual property asset within the 12 months before, or three years after, the sale of the design.

Assuming that £200,000 of relief is available on a sale of the design for £300,000, and a new intellectual property asset is acquired at a cost of £500,000, the effect of BrandCo's claim to defer the gain by roll-over relief is that:

- the consideration received for the sale of the design is reduced to £100,000 (£300,000–£200,000) for capital purposes; and

- the cost recognised for tax purposes of the new intellectual property asset is £300,000 (£500,000–£200,000), reducing amortisation deductions.

Cashflow, not deferral

14.61   For corporation tax on capital gains on *non*-intangible assets, roll-over relief is an absolute deferral of the tax due. The tax deferred only becomes chargeable when a replacement asset is sold without further rollover relief being claimed. For corporation tax on corporate intangible assets, the roll-over relief is not an absolute deferral; instead, the relief is clawed back over the useful economic life of the asset. The relief provides only a cashflow benefit on gains relating to intangible assets such as intellectual property.

14.62   This clawback is because the relief requires the company to deduct the relief from the acquisition cost of the new asset. This recalculated acquisition cost (ie after deduction of the roll-over relief) is then used to calculate the tax deduction for amortisation. After claiming roll-over relief, the company will not be able to claim the accounts amortisation, based on the full acquisition cost (see para **11.25**), but will, instead, base the amortisation on this revised acquisition cost.

Example 14.9

ZZ Ltd disposes of a patent, realising a gain of £50,000. It acquires another patent in the appropriate time period, spending £100,000 on the new patent. The new patent has a useful economic life of 10 years.

If ZZ Ltd *does not* claim roll-over relief then it will pay tax on the £50,000 gain in the year of disposal. It will then claim amortisation deductions of £10,000 each year for the new patent.

If ZZ Ltd *does* claim roll-over relief then it will pay no tax on the gain because the disposal proceeds will be reduced to nil by the relief. A corresponding £50,000 will be deducted from the acquisition cost of the new patent, so that its cost for tax purposes is £50,000.

The tax deduction for amortisation over the 10 year economic life is based on this revised cost, so that ZZ Ltd can only claim amortisation deductions of £5,000 each year for the new patent. Over the course of the economic life of the patent, the tax saved on the £50,000 gain on disposal is clawed back through these reduced amortisation deductions.

14.63   A company can not only defer gains on realisations by acquiring other intellectual property assets but can also defer such gains by utilising relevant acquisitions of other group companies (see para **18.199** onwards).

Claim for relief

14.64   Roll-over relief needs to be claimed in the tax return for the accounting period in which the realisation takes place (CTA 2009, s 757). The claim must specify:

- the old assets to which the claim relates; and
- in relation to each of those assets:
  - the expenditure on other assets as a result of which relief is claimed; and
  - the amount of the relief claimed.

Provisional entitlement to relief

14.65   The assets acquired to enable the relief to be claimed need not have been acquired by the date on which the vendor company needs to submit its tax return with the claim for roll-over relief (the assets may be purchased up to three years after the realisation). Where such assets have not been acquired by the date of submission, the company can make a declaration of provisional entitlement to roll-over relief on the disposal in the tax return (CTA 2009, s 761).

14.66   The declaration needs to state that the company:

- has realised an intangible asset; and

- intends to meet the conditions for relief; and

- is entitled to relief of a specified amount.

14.67   The declaration remains in force, and the relief applies, until:

- the declaration is withdrawn; or

- it is superseded by a claim for relief; or

- four years have elapsed, without the declaration being withdrawn or superseded, since the end of the accounting period in which the realisation occurred.

If the declaration is withdrawn or runs out of time, the return with the declaration will need to be adjusted to reflect the fact that relief was not given.

OTHER RELIEFS

14.68   The group relief provisions for disposals of intellectual property between group members, including roll-over group relief provisions, are covered in detail in para **18.161** onwards. Reconstructions reliefs are covered in para **17.71** onwards.

CHECKLIST

14.69

- Is the asset pre-1 April 2002?

    — If so, gains on disposal taxed under the old rules (see Chapter 7).

    — Modified roll-over relief may still be available.

14.69 *Disposals of intellectual property by companies*

- Calculate the credit or debit on disposal:
  - If asset was amortised, compare to tax written down value.
  - Proceeds of realisation may need to be adjusted where the transaction is between related parties.
- Are any tax reliefs available?
  - Roll-over relief.
  - Group relief.
  - Reconstruction reliefs.
  - Patent box relief.
- Trading debits and credits:
  - Treat as expenses or receipts of the trade.
- Non-trading debits and credits:
  - Pool to establish whether a non-trading gain or loss.
  - Non-trading gain is taxable as a receipt.
  - Non-trading loss can be set against profits of the total accounting period or carried forward (but beware restrictions).

Chapter 15

Value Added Tax

Summary: Value Added Tax (VAT) is a tax charged on supplies of intellectual property. The requirement to charge depends on the nature of the supply, the supplier and their customer—and the location of the supply.

- Charging VAT (para **15.8**)

- Supplies to UK businesses from outside the UK (the reverse charge) (para **15.45**)

- Supplies to UK consumers from outside the UK (para **15.48**)

- Licences to consumers (para **15.56**)

- Research and development (para **15.69**)

INTRODUCTION

15.1   Value Added Tax (VAT) is an indirect tax which arrived in the UK via the European Union: adoption of VAT was one of the conditions of the UK's entry to the EEC (as it then was) in 1972.

15.2   VAT has fundamentally different principles to corporation tax, income tax and capital gains tax: it is, in effect, a tax on purchases which is collected by the supplier, throughout the business chain. The supplier has to account to HMRC for VAT which it has collected (also known as output VAT). Business purchasers that are registered for VAT can recover from HMRC VAT that they have paid on purchases (also known as input VAT). It makes no difference whether the business is a company or unincorporated; the VAT obligations are the same for both.

15.3   Other taxes apply only where a profit or gain is made (in broad terms), but VAT applies to the purchase price of good or services, not to the margin. The distinction in VAT is not whether a profit is made but, instead, whether the purchase is within the scope of VAT (see para **15.8**) and, if it is, whether it is exempt from VAT (see para **15.11**).

15.4   In practice, a business will usually be both a supplier and a purchaser (eg licensing intellectual property and buying research and development services from a subcontractor). As a result, a VAT-registered business is only required to account to HMRC for the net VAT for the business overall, ie output VAT less input VAT. In some cases, such as in the start-up phase or in certain types of business, there may be a net recovery of VAT from HMRC where input VAT has exceeded output VAT.

15.5   As a result, VAT is not usually an absolute cost to businesses: the supplier will charge VAT to its customers and business customers will usually be able to recover that VAT either by set-off against their own output VAT or alternatively by recovering it from HMRC. There are some exceptions for certain types of business which make exempt supplies (eg banks, and see para **15.11**) or are not registered for VAT.

15.6   In contrast, VAT is an absolute cost to consumers, and to business which have not registered for VAT, as the VAT paid on purchases cannot be recovered where the goods/services are purchased for non-business purposes.

15.7   VAT is dealt with on a quarterly basis, with a return made each quarter and the net output VAT arising in that quarter paid at the same time. The exact cycle will depend on when the business registers for VAT; not all business are on the same VAT cycle. Note that a separate return is required for sales made to businesses in the EU. This return is called an EC Sales List; it is also due on a quarterly basis but—unhelpfully—this is on a standard quarter basis (March, June, September and December) and not necessarily the same quarterly basis as the VAT return.

Example 15.1

Knight Limited is a university spin-out company; it is principally focussed on developing patents to license to others but is still at an early stage of that development cycle. It has a very small amount of income from providing research and development services to others, but most has expenses connected with the development of the patents. Assuming that it has, in the VAT quarter, supplied services worth £10,000 plus VAT of £2,000 and incurred expenses of £50,000 plus VAT of £10,000, Knight Limited will be able to *recover* VAT of £8,000 (£2,000 charged less £10,000 paid) from HMRC (in principle: note that HMRC may well want to check the circumstances of the company before making such a repayment, at least for the first time).

In contrast, Ellis Limited is a company that has been in business for a considerable time. It sells research and development services to other companies, such as testing and similar services. It supplies £100,000 of services, and charges £20,000 of VAT on those services, in the quarter. In the same VAT quarter, it makes purchases of £60,000 and pays VAT of £12,000 on those purchases.

Ellis Limited will have to *pay* £8,000 of VAT to HMRC (the £20,000 VAT charged to its customers, less £12,000 VAT paid to suppliers).

CHARGING VAT

15.8   The general rule is that VAT must be charged on any supply of goods or services that is:

- made (or is treated as made: see para **15.25**) in the UK

- by a taxable person (see below)

- in the course or furtherance of a business carried on by that person (see below)

- for consideration (see below),

(VAT Act (VATA) 1994, s 4).

15.9   The UK standard rate of VAT is currently 20%. Although VAT is a cost to the purchaser, it is the supplier (the taxable person) who has to account to HMRC for VAT on supplies made. HMRC will expect VAT to have been charged on those supplies, whether or not it actually has been charged, and will require the supplier to account for that VAT. The 'VAT-free' sales that occasionally appear at retailers are not VAT-free in reality: they are discounts by another name. The supplier still has to account for VAT on the sale. VAT must be accounted for on the earliest of one of three events: when a VAT invoice is issued or, when payment is received for the services or when the services are actually delivered (VATA 1994, s 6).

15.10   Given the supplier's liability, it is very important to ensure that the VAT treatment of intellectual property transactions is correct. If it is not, then the licensor/vendor (or other supplier of intellectual property) will be liable to HMRC for VAT that will come directly out of the licensor/vendor's profit margin, unless the contract allows for it to be recouped from the licensee/ purchaser.

Exempt supplies

15.11   Certain types of supplies are exempt from VAT (VATA 1994, Sch 9). In practice, these are narrowly defined and a supply of intellectual property is unlikely to be an exempt supply in its own right: even the licensing of exam-marking software has been held to be a taxable, not exempt, supply (*RM Education plc v HM Revenue & Customs* [2009] UKVAT V20911), as it is not covered by the exemption for certain types of education supply. An exempt supply may require intellectual property (eg the provision of clinical healthcare) but the transaction is not specifically the transfer, assignment or license of intellectual property.

15.12   Exempt supplies are nevertheless important in intellectual property transactions because the exemption from VAT means that a business which makes exempt supplies cannot recover input VAT on purchases or licenses that are related to those exempt supplies. As a result, the input VAT on supplies of intellectual property to a business that makes exempt supplies may be an absolute cost to the purchaser.

15.13   As above, it is important to ensure that the VAT treatment is correct to avoid a tax liability where VAT has been incorrectly charged and/or reclaimed.

Zero-rated supplies

15.14   In addition to the standard rate of VAT at 20%, the UK also has a reduced rate of 5% (applicable to specific supplies such as energy) and a 0% rate of VAT. This 0% rate of VAT can apply to certain intellectual property-derived supplies, such as the sale of physical books. Note that e-books (and other digitised goods) are regarded as the supply of a service—the supply of a licence over intellectual property—and so will be subject to VAT at the standard rate and *not* zero-rated because they are not taxed at the same rate as their physical equivalent (this is a point that the EU is consulting over at the time of writing).

15.15   It is important to distinguish between exempt supplies (as above) and zero-rated supplies of intellectual property, even though they may appear to have the same effect from the point of view of supplies made. Zero-rated supplies do not affect the ability of a taxable person to recover input VAT; the supplies are still regarded as being subject to VAT, albeit at a reduced rate, and so input VAT relating to those supplies is still recoverable.

Intellectual property: goods or services?

15.16   At first consideration, intellectual property would not seem to be either a good or a service (in general). However, VAT is binary: if a supply made in the course of business is not a supply of goods then it is a supply of services (VATA 1994, s 5), so that the definition of 'services' is effectively 'not goods'.

15.17   As a result, any transaction involving intellectual property is potentially a supply of services, including transfers and assignments of copyright, patents, trademarks and other intellectual property rights, and the grant of a licence over any of these. Provided that the other requirements (ie supplied in the UK, by a taxable person, in the course of business, for consideration) are met, the supply will be a taxable supply for services for the purposes of VAT.

15.18   The VAT rules do not distinguish between different types of intellectual property, regardless of whether the taxable person is a company or unincorporated.

Taxable person

15.19   In the UK, 'taxable person' is a person who is, or is required to be, registered for VAT purposes (VATA 1994, s 3). 'Person' means any natural or legal person (Interpretation Act 1978, Sch 1) and so includes individuals, companies, and unincorporated entities such as partnerships and associations. It will also include national and local government authorities. It can include a non-UK resident person, where they are making supplies in the UK (see below).

15.20   The EU legislation underlying VAT rules in the UK has a slightly different definition of 'taxable person': a person independently carrying on specific economic activities (Directive 2006/112/EC, art 9(1)). References to a 'taxable person' in this book are to the UK definition unless otherwise stated.

15.21   A person is required to be registered for VAT purposes in the UK if, at the end of any month, either:

●   that person has made taxable supplies exceeding the VAT threshold in the preceding 12 months; or

●   there are reasonable grounds for believing that the taxable supplies to be made in the next 30 days will exceed the VAT threshold.

15.22   The VAT threshold for 2012–13 is £77,000. Note that a person is required to register for VAT once the value of *supplies made*—not profits—exceeds the threshold. A company can be loss-making, or in a repayment position, and still be required to register for VAT.

Example 15.2

Mason Limited manufactures widgets using a patented process and has only recently started manufacturing. At the end of November 2012, Mason Limited's total supplies in the preceding 12 months had a value of £60,000 and so there was no requirement for Mason Limited to register for VAT. However, during December 2012, Mason Limited unexpectedly receives a large order worth £30,000, so that at the end of December 2012, its total supplies for the preceding 12 months have a value of £80,000 (the £10,000 of supplies in December 2011 are no longer in the calculation). Mason Limited is therefore required to register for VAT, and is a taxable person, from the end of December 2012.

Example 15.3

Fred, an author, has royalty income of around £1,000 most months and so has not needed to register for VAT as his income on a rolling 12 month basis is well under the VAT threshold. He wins a major book prize (which carries a very small monetary award, but is very prestigious) and, as a result, the advance agreed for his next book is £100,000 as it is expected to sell well as a result of the award. Fred will be required to register for VAT in the month before receiving the award, and will be a taxable person as the advance will mean that he expects his taxable supplies in the next 30 days to exceed the VAT threshold.

In the course of business

15.23 A 'business' in this context is any economic activity. It is wider than simply a trade, profession or vocation and does not even have to be carried on with a view to a profit (Directive 2006/112/EC, Art 9(1)).

15.24 Even if no profit motive is required, there must still be some form of economic activity for a 'business' to exist for VAT purposes. The mere holding of intellectual property as an investment is unlikely to be a business so that, for example, where a copyright which has been licensed to others is inherited, the copyright holder may not be required to be registered even if the royalties from that copyright exceed the VAT threshold. In such a case, the royalties should be regarded as being derived from the ownership of the copyright rather than from an economic activity. However, if the copyright holder later undertakes any activity in respect of that copyright—for example, granting a new licence—that may be sufficient to bring royalties within the scope of VAT. This will be more likely where the business actively manages the intellectual property (for example, monitoring the use of the licences).

Supply made in the UK

Business

15.25 The general rule for the place of supply of services to businesses, including intellectual property, is that the services are supplied where the customer 'belongs' (VATA 1994, s 7A(2)(a)).

15.26 The VATA 1994 contains detailed rules to determine where a person belongs. A supplier will belong in the UK if:

- it has its only business establishment or fixed establishment in the UK; or

- where the supplier has business establishments or fixed establishments in more than one country, it will be treated as belonging in the UK if this is the country which is most directly concerned with the supply in question; or

- if the supplier has no business establishment or fixed place of business anywhere, it is treated as belonging in the UK if that is where the supplier has its usual place of residence.

15.27 Similar rules apply to determine where the recipient of the supply belongs. Where the recipient belongs in the UK, a UK supplier of intellectual property will need to charge UK VAT on the licence, transfer of assignment of the intellectual property unless the 'use and enjoyment' provisions (see para **15.53**) override this.

Consumers

15.28 Where services are supplied to consumers (ie individuals receiving the supply in their personal capacity, not for the purposes of a business) belonging in the EU, the supply is treated as made where the *supplier* belongs (VATA 1994, s 7A(2)(b)). All supplies of intellectual property by a UK taxable person to EU consumers will, therefore, be subject to UK VAT. Consumer supplies of intellectual property are most likely to be electronic services such as downloaded software, music and e-books, as these 'digitised goods' are limited licences of copyright. Note that this rule, as to where the place of supply is located, will change from 2015 (see para **15.59**).

15.29 Similarly, supplies of intellectual property made to UK consumers by EU businesses will be charged at the supplier country rate of VAT. This is why many businesses supplying music, software etc over the internet are based in Luxembourg, which has the lowest EU VAT rate of 15%, and (at the time of writing) has a VAT rate of 3% applying to digitised goods such as e-books. This reduced rate is being challenge by the European Union. These supplies of 'digitised goods' are treated as licences of intellectual property (see para **15.14**).

15.30 Certain supplies of intellectual property (electronic services: see para **15.52**) to UK consumers by non-EU business are treated as supplied in the UK and so the supplier is required to charge and account for UK VAT at 20% on these supplies. Compliance with this requirement is not universal (see para **15.64**).

15.31 Supplies of intellectual property to consumers belonging outside the EU are outside the scope of VAT (VATA 1994, Sch 4A, para 16).

Non-UK business purchasers

15.32 A supply of intellectual property—whether a transfer, assignment or licence etc—by a UK taxable person to a business in another EU Member State is therefore supplied outside the UK (as the supply is treated as made where the customer is based). As a result, that UK supplier will not be required to charge UK VAT on that supply of intellectual property as the supply is not in the UK unless the 'use and enjoyment' provisions (see para **15.50**) override this.

15.33 The recipient will be required to effectively self-assess for local VAT under the reverse charge provisions. Where a UK business receives such a supply from outside the UK, it will similarly be required to self-assess for UK VAT under the reverse charge provisions (see para **15.45**). The UK licensor must complete a separate return (the EC Sales List) for HMRC each quarter detailing the supplies made to VAT registered EU businesses. The EC Sales List entries must include the licensee's VAT number. This must be the EU format VAT number; in some countries, VAT returns are completed using the local tax number of the business. Such businesses must be asked to provide their EU (sometimes referred to as 'international') VAT number. The validity of VAT numbers can be checked on an EU database at http://ec.europa.eu/taxation customs/vies/. Note that the EC Sales List must be completed each *calendar* quarter: March, June, September and December. This may not necessarily coincide with the licensor's VAT quarter reporting. The information on the EU Sales List is exchanged with tax authorities in the other EU Member States; this allows the tax authorities in each state to check whether the business recipients have complied with the reverse charge requirements in respect of these supplies.

15.34 Supplies to non-EU business purchasers are also considered to be supplied outside the UK and so are outside the scope of UK VAT unless the 'use and enjoyment' provisions (see para **15.53**) override this.

15.35 Where a UK business is licensing, transferring or assignment intellectual property to another business, it will need to determine where the business is located for VAT purposes. In practice, evidence such as confirmation of the recipient's VAT number will be sufficient to demonstrate that the recipient is a business and is located outside the UK. Where the recipient is a business but is not VAT registered (eg because its supplies are below the local threshold for registration in the country where it belongs) then other commercial evidence (such as a business letterhead) may be required.

Exceptions

15.36 There are, however, important exceptions to the general rule. In particular, 'use and enjoyment" provisions may apply to change the place of supply of services in certain circumstances. The UK has relatively limited use and enjoyment provisions (these are primarily in connection with telecoms and broadcasting, where the EU has set out the provisions) but other Member States have made more extensive provisions which may result in a change in the place of supply. Although this could affect any supply of services, it is in connection with intellectual property and similar intangible services that use and enjoyment are most often applied.

For consideration

15.37 Consideration can be in monetary or non-monetary form and includes everything received in return for the supply. VAT is charged on the 'value' of the supply: the amount which, with the addition of VAT thereon, equals the consideration given.

Example 15.4

Wilcox Limited grants a licence over a patent. The agreement is silent as to the consideration, but Wilcox Limited receives a lump sum of £120,000 from the licensee. The total consideration is therefore taken to be £120,000, made up of £100,000 as the value of the supply and £20,000 VAT at 20% on the value of the supply.

15.38 Where the consideration for the grant of a right takes the form of royalties, there is a separate supply of services on each occasion when payment is received or, if earlier, when an invoice is issued (VAT Regulations, SI 1995/2518, reg 89).

Outside the scope of VAT: when VAT is not charged

15.39 There are certain transactions to which VAT does not apply, some of which may encompass intellectual property.

Transfer of a business as a going concern

15.40 Where a business (or part of a business) is transferred as a going concern (broadly, that it is actively operating as a business), and certain conditions are fulfilled, the transfer of the assets of the business is treated as outside the scope of VAT (literally, as neither the supply of goods nor the supply of services) even though the transfer is regarded as being in the course of business (Value Added Tax (Special Provisions) Order 1995, SI 1995/1268, art 5(1)–(3)). This will apply to any intellectual property transferred as part of the transfer as a going concern, including unregistered intellectual property within the goodwill of the business.

Supplies between companies in the same VAT group

15.41 UK companies that are in a group for tax purposes (see para **18.127**) can register to be treated as a VAT group (VATA 1994, s 43). Where a VAT group exists, supplies between different members of the VAT group are disregarded for VAT purposes. The group representative member accounts to HMRC for VAT based on the group input and output VAT relating to transactions with non-group entities only.

15.42   Licenses and transfers of intellectual property, or supplies of research and development services, between such VAT group companies are therefore outside the scope of VAT.

Donations to charity

15.43   Donations to charity are specifically outside the scope of VAT so that no VAT is charged on the donation (gifts in general will be outside the scope of VAT where there is genuinely no consideration). Where, for example, research services are provided to a charity, no VAT will be charged on those services unless the donor receives some consideration, eg an interest in any resulting intellectual property.

Temporary imports

15.44   Where intellectual property is imported into the UK for a temporary purpose, that import may be outside the scope of VAT, depending on the terms of the importation. This is most likely to be relevant to works of art imported for an exhibition, for example, where there is no intention of selling the artwork in the UK.

SUPPLIES TO UK BUSINESSES FROM OUTSIDE THE UK: THE REVERSE CHARGE

15.45   As noted above (see para **15.25**), a supply of intellectual property to a business is supplied where the recipient is based. Where intellectual property is supplied by a UK business to a UK recipient, the supply is in the UK and the supplier is required to charge UK VAT on the supply. Where the recipient is a taxable person (see para **15.19**) they will usually be able to recover the VAT charge, either by set-off against their own output VAT or on repayment by HMRC.

15.46   Where the supplier is a person outside the UK, the supply will still be in the UK but the supplier—not being a UK taxable person—is not required to charge VAT on the supply. Instead, where the intellectual property is supplied to a UK taxable person for the purposes of their business, the supply is subject to a 'reverse charge'.

15.47   The 'reverse charge' rules treat the recipient as if it had supplied the services in the UK in the course or furtherance of its business and the supply were a taxable supply. If the recipient is a taxable person, he is both liable to account for output tax and eligible for input tax credit (to the extent that the services which are the subject matter of the reverse supply are attributable to taxable supplies). The reverse charge is therefore effectively neutral for businesses that do not make exempt supplies (see para **15.11** for more information on exempt supplies).

Example 15.5

Austen Limited is a publishing company which is granted a licence to publish a book by an author who belongs abroad. Austen Limited will have to pay VAT on the consideration for the licence but (assuming the company is entitled to full credit for its input tax) will also be able to recover the VAT as input tax in exactly the same way as if the VAT had been charged by a third-party supplier.

SUPPLIES TO UK CONSUMERS FROM OUTSIDE THE UK

15.48   Supplies to UK consumers by EU businesses will be subject to VAT at the supplier country rate of VAT until 31 December 2014. From 1 January 2015, EU businesses will be required to identify where their consumer customers belong and apply the consumer country rate of VAT (see para **15.59**).

15.49   Supplies to UK consumers by non-EU businesses are generally outside the scope of VAT. However, where a non-EU business supplies an EU consumer with digitised goods (e-books, downloaded music, software etc), that non-EU business is required to charge VAT at the consumer country rate of VAT and account for that VAT to the relevant country (see para **15.60**).

USE AND ENJOYMENT

15.50   In some circumstances, and for certain types of intellectual property, the place of supply rules (see para **15.25** onwards) can be overridden where the 'use and enjoyment' of the intellectual property is deemed to be in a different country to that which in which the intellectual property would otherwise be regarded as supplied (VATA 1994, Sch 4A, para 9).

15.51   The 'use and enjoyment' override only applies to business-to-business supplies, not to supplies to consumers, and so that where there is a UK supplier of relevant intellectual property:

● where the place of supply would normally be in the UK (because the customer belongs in the UK) but the intellectual property is used and enjoyed outside the EU, no UK VAT needs to be charged; or

- where the place of supply would normally be outside the EU (because the customer belongs outside the EU) but the intellectual property is used and enjoyed in the UK, UK VAT must be charged.

Relevant intellectual property

15.52 These rules do not apply to all supplies of intellectual property, only to a specific range of 'electronically supplied services' which are generally licences of intellectual property or related services. These include:

- website supply, web-hosting and distance maintenance of programmes and equipment;

- the supply of software and the updating of software;

- the supply of images, text and information, and the making available of databases;

- the supply of music, films and games (including games of chance and gambling games); and

- the supply of political, cultural, artistic, sporting, scientific, educational or entertainment broadcasts (including broadcasts of events)

in all cases, only where the supply is made electronically. The supply of software on CD, for example, is not within the scope of these provisions (in fact, the supply of software on CD is generally treated as a supply of goods for VAT purposes even though it is, in legal terms, a licence of that software).

What is 'use and enjoyment'

15.53 This electronically supplied intellectual property is 'used and enjoyed' where the recipient business actually uses the intellectual property, not where the licence is entered into, or where the contracting parties are based.

Example 15.6

Hobson Limited, a UK company, acquires a licence for software to be downloaded from the licensor's servers. The licensor is based in the UK for VAT purposes. The software is to be used only by Hobson Limited's branch in Dubai, and will not be used by the company in the UK. Normally, a licence of software from one UK company to another UK company would be subject to UK VAT but, in these circumstances, the licensor is not required to charge UK VAT on the software licence fees as the use and enjoyment provisions override the normal place of supply rules (see para **15.25**) and the recipient is treated as being outside the EU.

Example 15.7

Hogarth Inc, a US bank, licences images from a UK online stock photo library for use by its London branches in marketing their services in the UK. The licence of the images would usually be outside the scope of VAT where they are licensed to a non-EU business but, as the images are to be used in the UK, the stock library will need to charge UK VAT on the licence fees.

Practical points

15.54   A supplier of these types of intellectual property therefore needs to know not only where the recipient belongs for VAT purposes (see para **15.27**) but also where the services are to be 'used and enjoyed'. Where the purchaser appears to be in the UK, it is in the purchaser's interests to demonstrate that the intellectual property is actually used and enjoyed outside the EU in order to be outside the scope of VAT. A licence that grants rights to use the intellectual property only outside the EU should be sufficient to demonstrate that the intellectual property will be used and enjoyed outside the EU.

15.55   Where the recipient appears to be outside the EU, the UK supplier should take steps to obtain confirmation that the intellectual property will not be used and enjoyed in the UK, to make sure that there is no requirement to charge UK VAT. A warranty to this effect in the licence, for example, would be appropriate if the licence itself does not exclude use in the UK.

DIGITISED GOODS AND ELECTRONICALLY SUPPLIED SERVICES: LICENCES OF INTELLECTUAL PROPERTY TO CONSUMERS

15.56   Supplies of intellectual property to consumers generally relate to the licensing of software, e-books, music, video, games and other entertainment-related intellectual property. These can be referred to as digitised goods—electronic versions of things which can be supplied in physical form as well (eg books, CDs, games on disk, DVDs)—but the treatment of the electronic supply of this intellectual property is separate to that which would apply to the physical version. For example, physical books are subject to VAT at 0% but e-books are subject to VAT at 20% in the UK.

These rules also cover other relevant electronically supplied services which are licenses of intellectual property (see para **15.52**).

EU suppliers

15.57 Where digitised goods are supplied to consumers (ie individuals receiving the supply in their personal capacity, not for the purposes of a business) belonging in the EU, the supply is treated as made where the supplier belongs (VATA 1994, s 7A(2)(b)). All supplies of intellectual property by a UK taxable person to EU consumers will, therefore, be subject to UK VAT.

15.58 Similarly, supplies of electronically supplied intellectual property made to UK consumers by EU businesses will be charged at the supplier country rate of VAT. This is why many businesses supplying music, software etc over the internet are based in Luxembourg, which has the lowest EU VAT rate of 15%.

From 2015

15.59 However, from 1 January 2015, the rules on supplies of electronically supplied services to EU consumers by EU businesses will change: EU businesses will have to charge VAT on such supplies at the *consumer* country's rate of VAT. Businesses will have to be able to identify where the consumer belongs (the credit card address supplied is likely to be treated as sufficient evidence) and apply the relevant VAT rate. It is expected that a similar scheme to that which applies for non-EU businesses (see below) will be put in place so that the business will have to account to its own tax authority (ie HMRC, for UK businesses) for the VAT charged to consumers with details of which countries VAT has been collected for, and each EU tax authority will pass on VAT to the consumers' tax authorities.

Non-EU suppliers

15.60 Non-EU businesses supplying digitised goods and electronically supplied services to consumers already have to charge VAT to those consumers at the relevant (consumer) country rate. As a result, non-EU licensors of these types of intellectual property to UK consumers are required to charge and account for UK VAT at 20% on these supplies. This is intended to ensure that non-EU businesses do not have a competitive advantage in this area over EU business: without these rules, for example, purchasing from a US supplier of downloadable software would cost a UK consumer almost 17% less than the same purchase from a UK supplier of the same software (software that costs £10 from a US supplier would cost £12 from a UK supplier, if VAT is the only difference).

15.61 Under the normal VAT rules, these businesses would be required to register for VAT in each country in which they license such intellectual property to consumers and account for VAT each quarter for supplies in that country to that country's tax authority. Where such a business makes supplies to consumers in 10 EU Member States, for example, it would have to make 10 separate quarterly returns and payments of VAT.

15.62 As this would be administratively rather demanding, a special scheme has been put in place for non-EU businesses supplying digitised goods and other electronically supplied services; a similar scheme will operate for EU businesses from 2015 (see above). Under the special scheme, a non-EU business can choose to register in just one EU Member State. The business will account for all EU VAT collected on a single quarterly return and payment to the tax authority in that Member State, detailing the amount due in respect of each Member State. The local tax authority will account to the other relevant authorities for the VAT collected on their behalf.

Example 15.8

Chaucer Inc, a software business in the US, sells (ie licenses) music tracks online to consumers in France, Italy, Spain, the UK and Portugal. Chaucer has to collect VAT for each of these countries, at the local VAT rate, on these sales.

Chaucer decides not to register for VAT in each country but, instead, registers with HMRC in the UK. Each quarter it submits a VAT return in the UK which lists the countries for which VAT has been collected and the total amount collected for each country (it does not need to give details of individual consumers, or individual transactions, although it will need to keep appropriate records of these for compliance purposes as usual). It also makes a single payment of the total VAT collected to HMRC. HMRC, in turn, will keep the UK VAT collected but will pass on to France, Italy, Spain and Portugal the amounts of VAT charged by Chaucer to consumers in each of these countries.

15.63 Registration under this special scheme does *not* enable the non-EU business to recover or off-set VAT that it may incur on purchases in the EU against the VAT that it has to charge.

Compliance issues

15.64 These rules for supplies by non-EU businesses are not universally complied with: it may be difficult, for example, to persuade a US business established in Nevada that it needs to collect and account for VAT in Europe when it may not be required to collect sales tax on the same supplies from Californian consumers just over the state border. The EU has acknowledged that there are difficulties with enforcement, although increasing use of third-party payment processors who also deal with VAT compliance (Paypal, Kagi etc) has improved the position.

15.65   At one point, the European Commission did indicate that it might withdraw protection for intellectual property from businesses that did not comply with these VAT rules. Given that digitised goods in particular are easy to copy, this would not necessarily be an idle threat; in practice, the logistical issues (eg establishing whether the business was in fact the ultimate owner of the intellectual property etc; the supremacy of international agreements) mean that the Commission has not, to date, made any moves to make this more than a suggestion.

Alternative structure for larger non-EU businesses

15.66   At present, larger non-EU business (ie those with sufficient EU business to make this commercially viable) may choose to set up a subsidiary in an EU Member State—usually Luxembourg, as it has a low rate of VAT— and make supplies to EU consumers from this subsidiary so that it only has to charge a single rate of VAT: the rate applicable in the country in which the subsidiary is established. This will allow the subsidiary to also recover VAT incurred on purchases in the EU, and can give the subsidiary a competitive advantage.

15.67   For example, supplies by a Luxembourg subsidiary to a Swedish consumer will be charged at the Luxembourg rate of VAT, which is currently 15%. The same supply by the non-EU parent to a Swedish consumer would be charged at the Swedish rate of VAT, currently 25%.

15.68   This advantage is, however, time-limited: EU businesses will need to charge consumer country rates of VAT from 2015 (see above).

RESEARCH AND DEVELOPMENT

15.69   Businesses may carry out research and development on their own account, in which case their primary concern will be with recovery of VAT on purchases of goods and services for the purposes of that research and development. The extent to which VAT can be recovered will depend on the supplies made by the business; if any of these are exempt from VAT then the recovery of VAT on purchases for research and development associated with the exempt supplies will be restricted (see para **15.12**).

15.70   The VAT rules on general purchases are outside the scope of this book, but there are some specific matters relating to intellectual property that are considered below.

Pre-registration expenditure on research and development by others

15.71   Businesses that are not registered for VAT cannot reclaim the cost of VAT on supplies made to that business, so that such VAT is an absolute cost to unregistered businesses (see para **15.5**).

15.72   When a business registers for VAT, however, it can reclaim in its first VAT return VAT charged on certain supplies received before registration (VAT Regulations, SI 1995/2518, reg 111). In the case of purchases of goods, VAT incurred in previous four years can be reclaimed but, in the case of purchases of services, only VAT incurred in the six months before registration can be reclaimed.

15.73   The distinction between goods and services is usually straightforward but, in the case of research and development outsourced by a business, it is important to be clear what is being delivered by the research and development.

15.74   Certain types of outsourced research and development—such as testing—will clearly be services. On the other hand, where the object of the outsourced research and development is to produce a working prototype, this may be a supply of goods and the business can claim VAT incurred up to four years before registration instead of being limited to six months.

15.75   The contract is critical: if the outsourced research and development is, instead, to provide research and development studies (a feasibility study for an invention, for example, with outline design and costings and a report of findings), then this will generally be treated as a supply of research and development services even if a model of the proposed invention is produced (*Aegis Technology Ltd v C & E Comrs* [1995] VAT Decision 13588).

Grants

Central government: general research

15.76   Grants from central government for general research—ie not for research specifically commissioned by government for a particular purpose—are regarded as paid in order to fulfil statutory and public duties to fund research and not to provide a specific benefit for one or more particular entities (the 'common good' is not regarded as a specific benefit).

15.77   In this case, the grant is not consideration for a supply for VAT purposes (even though any resulting intellectual property may vest in the grant-making government body) and so it is outside the scope of VAT (HMRC Information Sheet 4/08).

Private funding

15.78   Grants from private bodies, whether made alone or in conjunction with government bodies, are more likely to be regarded as resulting in a supply of research and development services for VAT purposes where the private funders receive from benefit from any intellectual property resulting from the funded research (see HMRC Information Sheet 4/08). This will still depend on the nature of the contract and the nature of the entity funding the research. Where it is a commercial entity, it is much more likely that there will be a supply for VAT purposes than if the entity is a charity, for example.

Implications for the research and development provider

15.79   Where the supply of research and development is not regarded as a supply for VAT purposes, then the research and development provider may find that it is restricted in the amount of input VAT that it can reclaim: input VAT can only be reclaimed on supplies purchased for the purposes of the research and development provider's business. Where part of the research and development work carried out is not a supply for VAT purposes then the VAT costs incurred in doing that research may not be recoverable if they cannot also be related to other, VATable, supplies made by the research and development provider (*University of Southampton v Commissioners for Revenue and Customs* [2006] EWHC 528 (Ch), [2006] All ER (D) 273).

Imports for research and development

15.80   Goods imported in the UK are generally subject to UK VAT on import; where the goods are imported by a UK VAT registered business, the business can recover this VAT in the same way as any other input VAT (VATA 1994, s 24(1)(c)).

15.81   Certain specific goods may be exempt from VAT on import where the import is for the purposes of scientific research (amongst other categories of exemption).

European Research Infrastructure Consortium: special VAT relief rules

15.82   A European Research Infrastructure Consortium (ERIC) is an entity created by the EU to facilitate joint research work across Europe; to be recognised as such, the body must be specifically set up by a decision under EC Council Regulation 723/2009, art 6(1)(a).

15.83   EU regulations establishing the concept of ERICs also provide for VAT exemption for these bodies: at the time of writing, the UK is still working on providing this exemption. A consultation on the exemption closed in June 2012, but the proposal is that a Treasury Order will exempt from VAT imports by and supplies to an ERIC.

Research and development services: place of supply

15.84   A business may also carry out research and development on behalf of others: if it a taxable person, it may be required to charge VAT on the value of those services. The business will also be concerned with recovering VAT on its own purchases relating to the research and development, as above.

15.85   The VAT charge for the supply of research and development services will depend on where the service is considered to be supplied (see para **15.25** onwards). The general rule for services supplied to business customers is that they are supplied where the customer is located (see para **15.25**).

15.86   Some EU Member States (*not* the UK) may apply 'use and enjoyment' provisions (see para **15.53**) to the supply of scientific services, including research and development: in this case, it is important to be clear where the use and enjoyment of the services actually takes place, to minimise the risk of an incorrect charge to VAT.

CHECKLIST: PLACE OF SUPPLY AND VAT CHARGE

15.87

In summary, the VAT treatment of intellectual property is (in broad outline) as follows, assuming that the supply of intellectual property is not an exempt supply:

UK supplier of intellectual property:

- To UK business: 20% VAT unless services are used outside the EU and the 'use and enjoyment' provisions apply.

- To EU business: no UK VAT charged, recipient applies reverse charge if registered for VAT.

- To EU consumer: 20% VAT.

- To non-EU business: outside the scope of VAT (unless 'use and enjoyment' is in the UK).

- To non-EU consumer: outside the scope of VAT.

UK recipient of intellectual property:

- Business recipient from a UK business: 20% VAT unless services are used outside the EU and the 'use and enjoyment' provisions apply.

- Business recipient from non-UK entity: recipient accounts for 20% VAT through reverse charge.

- Consumer recipient from UK business: 20% VAT.

- Consumer recipient from EU business: supplier country rate of VAT.

- Consumer recipient from non-EU business: 20% VAT charged by supplier on relevant intellectual property.

The VAT issues relating to specific transactions are addressed in Chapter 17.

Chapter 16

International intellectual property tax issues and planning

Summary: The highly mobile nature of intellectual property increases the opportunities for companies, but also increases the anxiety of tax officials who are concerned with the possible loss of tax. Cross-border tax law is also, generally, not designed for intangible assets which poses its own set of problems.

This chapter provides an overview to the issues, and detail on such areas as deal specifically with intellectual property. The wider discussion on international taxation generally is outside the scope of this book.

- UK tax residence (para **16.9**)

- Importing intellectual property into the UK (para **16.35**)

- Exporting intellectual property from the UK (para **16.79**)

- Transfer pricing (para **16.94**)

- Controlled foreign companies (para **16.139**)

- UK tax treaties (para **16.173**)

- UK tax relief for foreign taxes (para **16.182**)

- EU Interest and Royalties Directive (para **16.189**)

- Comparison of jurisdictions (**16.194**)

INTRODUCTION

16.1   Intellectual property is one of the key concerns in international taxation. Surveys (such as those described in *The Failure of IFRS3* by Thayne Forbes, Intellectual Asset Management, January 2007) have consistently indicated that around 80% of the value of the FTSE 100 companies, for example, is represented by intangible assets (intellectual property and goodwill, which is likely to include some unregistered intellectual property assets), and those companies consistently trade globally, using that intellectual property in many countries outside their home jurisdiction.

16.2   The lack of any physical barrier to the movement or exploitation of intellectual property has meant that tax authorities have become increasingly concerned about the potential for tax manipulation and avoidance. The last few years have seen a substantial rise in legislation in respect of, and general scrutiny of, intellectual property transactions across borders.

16.3   At the same time, increased ease of communications has meant that companies may not necessarily recognise that intellectual property has been used cross-border: for example, where an employee moves from the parent company to an overseas subsidiary and introduces know-how and similar unregistered intellectual property of the parent company to that subsidiary without any formal acknowledgement. If customer databases and similar intellectual property are shared on a global network of the group, the entire group has access to the value of that information and intellectual property. It is unlikely that any thought has been given to more than sharing the costs of information technology in setting up the network: the value of the information shared on that network is often overlooked by companies.

Intellectual property law approach and tax law approach

16.4   The issues with international tax can be exacerbated by a mismatch in approach between intellectual property law and tax law. Intellectual property lawyers are generally most concerned with establishing who has the legal title to a particular intellectual property asset, as that generally determines who can enforce the rights attaching to the intellectual property and can protect that intellectual property.

16.5   Tax is most concerned with who has the economic benefit of the intellectual property: who uses that intellectual property and what is charged for that use by whom, and who develops the intellectual property used by a group. Cross-border transactions can make identification of assets and the associated economic benefits more difficult.

16.6   Accordingly, key areas of review and concern in minimising the costs of taxation of cross-border intellectual property transactions are those within groups and between other connected parties: transfer pricing and controlled foreign companies rules.

16.7   More generally, the question of withholding taxes (see para **16.48**) and the availability of tax reliefs will need to be considered in many cross-border intellectual property transactions.

16.8   In general terms, the UK will only tax income and gains that:

- are earned by a person who is UK resident in the tax year in which the income or gains arise; or

● have their source in the UK.

UK TAX RESIDENCE

16.9 The following is an outline of UK tax residence. The topic is a specialist area with many complexities, and the detail is outside the scope of this book.

16.10 Broadly, a UK tax resident (corporate or individual) will be subject to UK tax on their worldwide income and gains, with relief available for tax paid or withheld overseas (CTA 2009, s 2; ITTOIA 2005, s 6). There are exceptions, such as for non-domiciled individuals, but these are not specific to intellectual property and so are outside the scope of this book.

Companies

16.11 A company will be resident in the UK under UK law if either:

● it is incorporated in the UK (CTA 2009, s 14); or

● its place of central management and control is the UK (per case law, eg *Wood v Holden* [2006] STC 443).

Note that the provisions of UK tax treaties may override these provisions, particularly the tie-breaker clause on residence (see, for example, Article 4(5) of the UK/US tax treaty).

16.12 The incorporation rule now in CTA 2009, s 14, was introduced in March 1988. All companies incorporated in the UK since that date will be resident in the UK for tax purposes unless they can successfully claim to be resident in another country under the tie-breaker clause in a tax treaty between the UK and that other country: most UK tax treaties have such a tie-breaker clause (see para **16.16** for more details).

16.13 Companies incorporated in the UK before March 1988 will generally also be UK resident unless they migrated by Treasury consent before that date.

16.14 The incorporation rule means that the central management and control test in case law is now only relevant for companies incorporated outside the UK. HMRC's view of the level of control required is derived from case law: it is the highest level of control in the company that is considered, usually the board of directors (eg *De Beers* (1906) 5 TC 213). The location of board meetings is, therefore, very important, although an individual shareholder with significant influence can also determine the location of central management and control (eg *Bullock v Unit Construction Co Ltd* (1959) 38 TC 712 and *Laerstate BV v Revenue and Customs Commissioners* [2009] UKFTT 209).

Dual residence

16.15 A company may be dual resident, if it is managed and controlled in the UK, but was incorporated in a jurisdiction that regards any company incorporated there as tax resident (eg the USA). In such cases, the company will have to rely on a tax treaty to minimise the prospect of double taxation, or rely on unilateral relief where the treaty does not apply.

16.16 Tax treaties will generally resolve the issue of dual residence through a tie-breaker clause, considering the place of effective management (see OECD Model Treaty, Article 4, para 3. Note that this is a slightly different concept to 'central management and control', which forms part of the UK domestic test of residence for a company). HMRC's view is that the two may not be in the same place, with effective management being more closely linked to the day-to-day operations of the company. Central management is usually determined by the location of board meetings, or the location of a key director (see HMRC Statement of Practice SP1/90).

Permanent establishment

16.17 Where a non-resident company has a taxable presence in the form of a UK permanent establishment, that permanent establishment is subject to UK corporation tax on its profits in the same way as a UK company. The tax treatment set out in Chapters 3–14 (depending on whether the intellectual property is pre– or post–1 April 2002) will apply to intellectual property transactions of the permanent establishment as though it were a UK company, so the permanent establishment will be subject to UK tax in the usual way on its worldwide income and gains derived from intellectual property and may also be able to claim UK tax incentives for expenditure on research and development (see Chapter 10).

16.18 A detailed explanation of the concept of 'permanent establishment' is outside the scope of this book but, in brief, a permanent establishment is a fixed place of business through which a non-UK resident company does business in the UK; it may also be referred to as a 'branch' of the non-UK company. It is not a separate legal entity from the non-UK company, unlike a subsidiary.

16.19 The requirement that there be a fixed place of business means that the company must have some physical place available for its use in the UK— usually an office, but it could be a workshop, a warehouse or similar site. Some degree of permanence is required; a company will not usually have a permanent establishment as a result of using an office in the UK for two weeks. The fixed place of business must be at the disposal of the non-UK company, so that its employees can come and go as necessary, rather than at times specifically dictated by another (for example, temporary use of an office within a customer's premises to complete a project is unlikely to create a permanent establishment).

16.20   There are certain exemptions for particular activities: purely ancillary activities (marketing etc), and storage activities, are unlikely to create a permanent establishment.

16.21   The definition of a permanent establishment may be determined by a tax treaty between the UK and the company's home jurisdiction. Where no treaty exists, UK domestic law will determine whether a non-UK company has a permanent establishment in the UK. In practice, the UK domestic rules (CTA 2010, s 1141) largely follow the OECD Model Tax Convention, which is also followed by most UK tax treaties and so the rules are broadly similar.

16.22   As the permanent establishment is not a separate legal entity from the non-UK company, it is likely that the UK taxable profits of the permanent establishment will also be taxable in the jurisdiction where the non-UK company is located (assuming that jurisdiction imposes tax on the worldwide income and gains of its taxpayers); relief will generally be given in the jurisdiction of the non-UK company. The UK will not give relief to the permanent establishment against UK tax for tax paid by the non-UK company in its home jurisdiction (subject to any provision to the contrary in a relevant tax treaty).

16.23   Establishing the profits of the permanent establishment is an art rather than a science; the profits are allocated to the permanent establishment as though it were an independent company dealing with the non-UK company at arm's length (CTA 2009, s 21).

16.24   A detailed explanation of the allocation of expenses between the permanent establishment and the non-resident company is beyond the scope of this book, but one point to note in particular is that no deduction is given in determining the profits of the permanent establishment for the payment of royalties, or similar payments, to the non-UK company for the use of the non-UK company's intellectual property and other intangible assets (CTA 2009, s 31).

16.25   Where the permanent establishment contributes to the creation of intellectual property by the non-UK company, however, that contribution can be a deductible expenses when calculating the UK taxable profits of the permanent establishment.

A company resident outside the UK may also be taxed on income and gains in the UK (including those relating to intellectual property) if it has a permanent establishment in the UK, to the extent that the permanent establishment has income or gains from intellectual property.

16.26   For UK tax purposes, a non-resident company has a UK permanent establishment if it has (CTA 2010, s 1141):

- a fixed place of business in the UK through which the business of the non-resident company is carried on; or

- a dependent agent which has and habitually exercises authority in the UK to do business on behalf of the company.

16.27   The UK statutory definition of a permanent establishment is similar to that used in tax treaties, but applies in a domestic law context. Where a tax treaty also applies, the provisions of that tax treaty will take precedence in determining whether there is a UK permanent establishment.

16.28   Where a non-resident company has a UK permanent establishment, the profits and gains (including any income, gains or deductible costs relating to intellectual property) attributable to that permanent establishment will be subject to UK tax.

Individuals

16.29   The position for individuals is derived from a mixture of statute and case law: there is no single, straightforward, test of residence and the question is largely one of fact (*IRC v Lysaght* (1928) 13 TC 511).

16.30   At the time of writing, the UK government is consulting over a statutory residence test in an effort to make it easier for individuals to be able to determine whether or not they are UK tax resident. The new statutory test is expected to come into force from 6 April 2013.

16.31   In outline, both at present and under the proposed new rules, an individual will be subject to UK tax on income from intellectual property if they are present in the UK for more than six months of the tax year (eg ITA 2007, s 831). However, an individual may also be resident in the UK if he makes regular visits to the UK (see, eg, the *Lysaght* case above) and has sufficient ties to the UK.

UK source income

16.32   In addition to taxing residents on income and gains derived from intellectual property, the UK may also tax non-residents on income or gains derived from UK sources, usually by way of withholding taxes (see paras **16.49** and **16.56** onwards).

16.33   Intellectual property royalties are generally regarded by UK tax law as being UK source income for a non-resident where they are paid from the

UK, so that UK withholding tax (see para **16.56**). may need to be deducted from the payment. The non-resident recipient may be able to claim tax treaty relief to reduce the withholding that needs to be made, and/or get credit for the UK tax withheld against local tax due in the jurisdiction in which the recipient pays tax. Note that payments to non-UK authors and other non-UK creative professionals for producing a piece of work are *not* generally taxed as royalties (see para **18.287**).

16.34   A non-UK resident may also be subject to tax on the proceeds of sale of a UK patent (ie those registered in the UK under the Patents Act 1977) (see para **16.36**).

IMPORTING INTELLECTUAL PROPERTY INTO THE UK

16.35   An 'import' of intellectual property in this context means a transaction in which a UK taxable person brings intellectual property into the UK, either by way of outright transfer or by way of licence. In addition to the basic UK tax rules on acquisitions and licences (see Chapter 5 and Chapter 11), there are some specific tax matters that need to be taken into account when dealing with a cross-border transaction.

Transfer/assignment

Non-UK resident transferor: patents

16.36   The sale of a UK patent (ie one registered in the UK under the Patents Act 1977) by a non-UK resident will be subject to tax in the UK, even if the transferor is otherwise entirely outside the scope of UK tax (CTA 2009, s 912 for corporate transferors; or ITA 2007, s 587 for non-corporate transferors; see para **7.34**). This is because income and gains from a UK patent are treated as having a UK source, regardless of where the patent is actually used.

This may be overridden by a tax treaty in some cases (see para **16.173**).

16.37   Tax is charged on the net proceeds of sale of the patent, ie after the capital cost of the patent is deducted, together with any applicable expenses (CTA 2009, s 913).

16.38   In practice, the tax will generally be withheld from the proceeds of sale by the transferee (see **16.49**), rather than accounted for directly by the transferor. This withholding is made on the *gross* proceeds of sale and so, if the transferor has a capital cost or expenses to deduct which will reduce the UK tax due, the transferor will have to submit a tax return to HMRC claiming a repayment of part of the tax withheld.

Example 16.1

Radcliffe Inc sells a UK patent to a company in the UK for £100,000. It originally acquired the patent for £20,000 and incurred costs of £5,000 in the sale. The UK transferee will have to deduct £20,000 as withholding tax from the payment, but Radcliffe Inc's actual tax charge will be (assuming that the tax rate has reduced to 22%, and ignoring any tax treaty):

(£100,000 – £20,000 – £5,000) × 22% = £16,500

As a result of the withholding tax, Radcliffe Inc has effectively overpaid UK tax by £3,500. It will need to file a UK tax return in order to obtain a repayment of that excess tax payment.

16.39   These rules apply only to non-UK transferors with no presence in the UK. Where the proceeds of sale are taxed in the UK as trading income (eg where the transferor has a permanent establishment in the UK which will be taxed on the proceeds of sale), then these rules do not apply.

Spreading the tax charge

16.40   UK recipients of payments on the sale of patents can elect to spread the tax charge over a period of time, to reflect the fact that such amounts are generally not part of the normal pattern of income of the business (see para **7.41**). Similar arrangements are available to non-residents who are subject to tax in the UK on the profit on sale (ie where no tax treaty relief is available).

16.41   Where the patent is sold for a lump sum paid in a single payment, a non-UK resident transferor company can elect to be taxed as if it had received the payment in six equal instalments over six accounting periods, beginning with the accounting period in which the payment is actually received (CTA 2009, s 916).

16.42   Where the payment is actually made in instalments, then the non-UK resident company will usually be subject to tax in each accounting period in which an instalment is made (ITA 2007, s 917). The company can elect to be taxed in respect of each such instalment amount in six equal instalments over the six accounting periods starting with the accounting period of the payment.

16.43   Where the transferee has withheld tax from the payment (see para **16.49**), the transferor will need to complete a UK tax return to make an elect to spread the payments and to obtain a repayment of the tax originally withheld.

Example 16.2

Cross Ltd (a non-UK company) sells a UK patent to a UK company. The terms of the sale are such that Cross Ltd receives £60,000 on sale and then will receive £240,000 at each of three milestones in development of the patent. In the third year after the sale, the first milestone is reached.

If Cross Ltd elects to spread the tax charge, its UK tax position will be:

On the initial payment: £10,000 charged each of in years 1–6

On the first milestone payment: £40,000 charged in each of years 3–9

ie for years 3, 4, 5, and 6, Cross Ltd will pay UK income tax on £50,000.

The UK transferee will have withheld tax on the full payments on sale, and on the milestone, so Cross Ltd will have to file a UK tax return in order to get a repayment of the excess tax withheld. It will also have to file UK tax returns each year to pay the UK tax due on the instalments.

Other intellectual property

16.44   These rules above apply only to UK patents sold by non-UK resident transferors. There is no equivalent UK tax charge on sales by non-UK residents of other types of intellectual property, including non-UK patents.

UK resident transferee

16.45   For the UK-resident transferee receiving intellectual property from overseas, the tax implications and issues are the same as for any other acquisition.

Transfer pricing

16.46   If the transferee is a company, the transfer pricing position needs to be considered if the acquisition is from a group company, as this will determine the acquisition price for tax purposes (see para **16.94** onwards). Otherwise, consider whether the related party rules apply to deem the acquisition price to have been market value (see para **18.69**).

Tax deduction for costs of acquisition

16.47   Amortisation (see para **11.25**) will be available to give a tax deduction over time for the acquisition cost of the intellectual property (assuming that the acquisition is within the corporate intangibles tax rules: see Chapter 8).

16.48   If the acquisition is not within the corporate intangibles tax rules, capital allowances may give a tax deduction over time for the costs of acquisition if the intellectual property transferred is a patent or industrial know-how (see Chapter 5).

Withholding tax on payment to non-resident patent transferor

16.49   As the UK imposes tax on non-UK resident vendors of *patents*, the UK resident transferee will generally need to withhold tax on the payment to the transferor (ITA 2007, s 910). The tax withheld is 20% (the basic rate of income tax) of the gross payment; there is no deduction for any expenses that the transferor might have in relation to the payment (see para **16.38**), nor does the transferee take account of any election that the transferor might make to spread the payment (see para **16.40**).

16.50   This is subject to any tax treaty reliefs available to the transferor. Where the transferor is in a country with which the UK has a tax treaty, and that tax treaty gives primary taxing rights in respect of gains on sale to the country of residence, then the transferee will not have to withhold tax on the payment if it receives the appropriate treaty claim from the transferee.

16.51   The amount withheld is not accounted for through self-assessment. Instead, a non-corporate payer is required to notify HMRC 'without delay' (ITA 2007, s 963(2)). An assessment will be raised for income tax equal to the amount deducted from the payment (ITA 2007, s 963(3)). A corporate payer is required to send a return to HMRC for each quarter in which it makes such payments, and to account for the tax withheld with the return (ITA 2007, s 945).

Other intellectual property

16.52   There is no requirement to withhold tax on payments in respect of transfers of intellectual property other than UK patents. This is in contrast with a wide requirement to withhold tax on payments of royalties (see para **16.56** onwards).

Licensing

Non-UK licensor

16.53   A non-UK licensor is not specifically subject to tax in the UK on the royalties received under the licence but, in effect, a non-UK licensor may be subject to tax in the UK through withholding tax on the royalties (see para **16.56** onwards) unless a tax treaty applies to eliminate that withholding tax (see para **16.173**).

UK licensee

16.54 A UK licensee will want to obtain a tax deduction for licence payments; the fact that the payments are being made to an overseas licensor does not change their eligibility for deduction from profits for UK tax purposes (see Chapter 5 and Chapter 11).

16.55 Note that, where the licensee and licensor are connected, the transfer pricing rules may amend the royalties or other payments made under the licence where necessary (see para **16.194**).

Withholding tax

16.56
- any royalties which are 'qualifying annual payments' (see below) where paid by an individual (ITA 2007, s 900) or a non-individual (ITA 2007, s 901) (see para **16.58**);

- royalties in respect of patents (ITA 2007, s 903; see para **16.63**);

- royalties in respect of copyright, design rights (registered or unregistered) or public lending rights in respect of a book, in all cases where the usual abode of the owner of the royalties is outside the UK (ITA 2007, s 906, see para **16.64**); and

- sales of UK patents by a non-UK owner (ITA 2007, s 910 and see para **16.49**).

This requirement, and the rate of withholding tax applied, may be overridden if there is a tax treaty between the UK and the recipient's country of residence. Where there is a treaty, and the recipient has the benefit of that treaty, the provisions of the treaty will take precedence over UK domestic law (see para **16.173**).

16.57 Any agreement for paying a patent royalty without deduction of tax will not override the licensee's obligation to deduct tax; the licensee will still be required to account to HMRC for the tax that should have been deducted.

16.58 Where the payment is made through an agent in the UK, it is the agent that is required to withhold tax from the post-commission amount (ITA 2007, s 908).

16.59 An individual who acquires a licence over intellectual property for commercial purposes relating to the individual's trade, profession or vocation, is required to deduct income tax from payments of royalties which are qualifying annual payments (ITA 2007, s 900). A similar requirement applies to other entities (ITA 2007, s 901) although there is no requirement that the payment be for commercial purposes.

16.60   In practice, almost all royalties will be paid for commercial purposes and so the additional requirement in s 900, compared with s 901, is unlikely to have much impact.

16.61

A 'qualifying annual payment' is an annual payment (see below) which meets the requirements of ITA 2007, s 899. This requires that the payment:

- arises in the United Kingdom (this will be met where the payer is within the scope of UK tax); and

- (inter alia) is subject to income tax under ITTOIA 2005, s 579 (ie as miscellaneous income from intellectual property—see para **6.16** and para **6.51**); or

There are other circumstances under which an annual payment may be 'qualifying', but this is the only circumstance which applies specifically to intellectual property. There is no geographical limitation: if the requirement to withhold applies, it applies to UK recipients as well as to those overseas.

16.62   Given that the royalty must be taxed as miscellaneous income under ITTOIA 2005, s 579—that is, not as trading income or income from a profession or vocation—it is clear that the requirement to withhold tax on payments of intellectual property royalties under s 900 or s 901 is limited. It is intended to ensure that tax is captured on payments which may otherwise be less visible to the tax authorities—one-off payments to amateur writers, for example.

16.63   An 'annual payment' is one which is 'pure income profit' in the hands of the recipient, which has a 'quality of recurrence' (*Asher v London Film Productions Ltd* [1944] KB 133, CA). Most royalties will meet this definition, unless the royalty includes an element of payment for services (such as technical services, in the case of a patent or know-how) in which case it cannot be pure income profit because there will be some cost element to the provision of the services.

16.64   There is a specific requirement to withhold tax on patent royalties (ITA 2007, s 903) which applies where the recipient is within the scope of UK tax (ie is a UK tax resident individual or company, or is the UK permanent establishment of an overseas business). Section 903 specifically does not apply to any patent royalties that are qualifying annual payments, as these will be subject to withholding tax under s 900 or s 901 (see para **16.58**).

16.65   There is also a specific requirement to withhold tax on royalties or other periodic payments paid where the usual abode of the owner (or vendor) of the intellectual property is outside the UK (ITA 2007, s 906). This applies only to royalties in respect of copyright, design rights and public lending rights in respect of books. Accordingly, there is no requirement to withhold tax on payments of royalties in respect of trademarks, for example, unless the royalty is a qualifying annual payment (see para **16.58**). The royalty (or other periodic payment) must be charged to income tax or corporation tax, so the recipient must be within the scope of UK tax.

16.66 Where tax is withheld under s 900 or s 903 by an individual with sufficient income, the amount withheld must be accounted for through that individual's self-assessment tax return (ITA 2007, s 900(3); s 903(5)). There is, accordingly, a cashflow advantage for the individual as tax paid under self-assessment does not have to be accounted for until 31 January following the end of the tax year in which the tax is withheld.

16.67 Tax withheld by an individual under s 906 must be notified to HMRC 'without delay' (ITA 2007, s 963). An assessment for the tax withheld will be raised by HMRC.

16.68 Tax withheld by a company is not accounted for through self-assessment or by notification 'without delay'. Instead, a corporate payer is required to notify HMRC by making a return in each quarter in which it makes payments on which it has to withhold tax (ITA 2007, s 945), and accounting to HMRC with the return for the tax withheld.

Exceptions from withholding tax

16.69 No tax needs to be withheld where the payer is a company which has reasonable belief (ITA 2007, s 930) that:

- the person beneficially entitled to the royalty is either:

  — a UK resident company (ITA 2007, s 933); or

  — a partnership, each member of which is a UK resident company or a local authority (ITA 2007; s 932); or

- the person beneficially entitled to the income in respect of which the payment is made is a non-resident company which (ITA 2007, s 934):

  — carries on a trade in the UK through a permanent establishment; and

  — takes the royalty into account in computing its UK chargeable profits.

This exemption is not available where a company makes a payment as trustee or agent for another person (ITA 2007, s 930(4)).

16.70 Payments of royalties to associated companies in EU Member States can also be made without deduction of tax (ITTOIA 2005, ss 757–767), as a result of the EU Interest and Royalties Directive (see para **16.189**).

16.71   Where the licensee is a company, it may not have to withhold tax at the full 20%. Where the company reasonably believes that the licensor (or whoever is beneficially entitled the royalty payment) is entitled to tax treaty relief, the licensee company can withhold tax at the applicable treaty rate rather than at 20% (ITA 2007, s 911).

16.72   The company does not need to obtain advance approval from HMRC, but if HMRC are not satisfied that treaty relief is due in respect of one or more royalty payments, they may direct that such payments must be made under deduction of tax. The direction may later be varied or revoked.

16.73   If the beneficial owner of the income believed, before a payment of royalty was made, that relief was available but subsequently becomes aware that it was not available, it must immediately notify HMRC and the paying company.

Example 16.3

Row Ltd is a UK licensor of a copyright, paying royalties to a licensor in the USA. Ordinarily, Row Ltd would have to withhold tax from the payment at 20% unless it had received a treaty claim form and had confirmed that no withholding was required.

However, Row Ltd has a long history of trading with this company and reasonably believes that it has the benefit of the UK/US tax treaty. As the treaty rate on royalties withholding between the UK and the USA is 0%, Row Ltd will not have to deduct withholding tax from the royalty payments.

16.74   If the licensor is *not* in fact entitled to the treaty belief, the licensee will be liable for the tax which should have been withheld and will be liable for penalties (an initial penalty of up to £3,000 and potential daily penalties of up to £600 per day). Licensees should be careful to ensure that they are confident that the tax treaty will apply before agreeing not to withhold tax.

VAT

Import by UK business

16.75   Where intellectual property is transferred or licensed by a person outside the UK to a UK business, the supply is deemed to be in the UK but the supplier—if not a UK taxable person—is not required to charge VAT on the supply (see para **15.19**). Instead, where the intellectual property is supplied to a UK taxable person for the purposes of their business, the supply is subject to a 'reverse charge'.

16.76   The 'reverse charge' rules treat the recipient as if it had supplied the services in the UK in the course or furtherance of his business and the supply were a taxable supply. If the recipient is a taxable person, he is both liable to account for output tax and eligible for input tax credit (to the extent that the services which are the subject matter of the reverse supply are attributable to taxable supplies). The reverse charge is therefore effectively neutral for businesses that do not make exempt supplies (see para **15.45**).

Import by UK consumer

16.77   Supplies to UK consumers by EU businesses will be subject to VAT at the supplier country rate of VAT until 31 December 2014. From 1 January 2015, EU businesses will be required to identify whether their consumer customers belong and apply the consumer country rate of VAT.

16.78   Supplies to UK consumers by non-EU businesses are generally outside the scope of VAT. However, where a non-EU business supplies an EU consumer with digitised goods (e-books, downloaded music, software etc), that non-EU business is required to charge VAT at the consumer country rate of VAT and account for that VAT to the relevant country (see para **15.60**).

EXPORTING INTELLECTUAL PROPERTY FROM THE UK

Transfer/assignment

UK-resident transferor

16.79   The transfer of intellectual property overseas by a UK resident transferor is treated in the same way as any other disposal of intellectual property (see Chapter 7 and Chapter 14), with the net proceeds of transfer being subject to UK tax, although there are a couple of points that need to be considered.

Transfer pricing

16.80   If the transfer is to a connected company, the transfer pricing position needs to be considered as this will determine the disposal price for tax purposes (see para **16.94**). Otherwise, consider whether the connected or related party rules apply to deem the disposal price to have been market value (see para **18.66** onwards).

Exit taxes

16.81   The transfer will be a disposal, subject to UK tax, even where the intellectual property is transferred to another group company if that company is outside the UK. The no-gain, no-loss provisions (see para **18.162**) between group companies do not apply to transfers to non-UK resident group companies unless the transfer is to a UK permanent establishment of the non-resident company, so that the intellectual property does not leave the UK tax net (TCGA 1992, s 171). Where the intellectual property is transferred at an early stage, this taxable gain may be fairly small.

16.82   As a result, where the UK entity and the non-UK entity are connected (under TCGA 1992, s 286), the transfer will give rise to a tax charge on any latent gain in that intellectual property for the UK transferor. This is because the transfer will be treated as taking place at market value, where the parties are connected (see para **18.66** onwards).

Withholding taxes

16.83   On export, the payment is received by a UK business (individual or corporate) and so UK withholding tax will not apply. However, other jurisdictions may impose withholding taxes on payments for the transfer of intellectual property, as the UK does for transfers of UK patents (see para **16.49**). Where the UK transferor has the benefit of a tax treaty with the jurisdiction from which the payment is to be made, a claim should be made for treaty benefits (the precise form varies with the treaty; HMRC's International Manual has details of the various forms and processes for treaty claims) to minimise the amount of tax withheld.

16.84   Where no treaty is available, or the treaty does not reduce the withholding tax to nil, the transferor can elect to set the balance of tax withheld against UK tax due on the disposal (see para **16.184**).

Anti-avoidance

16.85   On transfers of UK intellectual property overseas, companies should consider the controlled foreign companies rules in particular (see para **16.139**) and individuals need to consider the specific anti-avoidance rules relating to income and gains of overseas companies (see para **16.157**).

Licensing

16.86   Royalties and other income from licensing intellectual property are subject to tax in the UK in the usual way, even when received from overseas (see para **6.30** and para **12.46**).

16.87   As with outright transfers of intellectual property, the transfer pricing rules may require an adjustment to the licensing income when the licence is with a connected party (see para **16.102** onwards).

Withholding taxes

16.88   The UK is not the only jurisdiction which imposes withholding taxes on royalties (see para **16.56** onwards) and so any royalties and other licence income received from overseas may have had tax deducted at source before payment.

16.89   Withholding taxes on royalties are more common than withholding taxes on disposals of intellectual property; as noted above, the UK licensor should claim tax treaty benefits wherever possible to minimise tax withheld (see para **16.83**), and should be able to claim unilateral relief in the UK against tax due in the UK on the royalties and other income from the licence (see para **16.184**).

VAT

To EU business

16.90   A supply of intellectual property—whether a transfer, assignment or licence etc—by a UK taxable person to a business in another EU Member State is therefore supplied outside the UK (as the supply is treated as made where the customer is based). As a result, that UK supplier will not be required to charge UK VAT on that supply of intellectual property, as the supply is not in the UK unless the 'use and enjoyment' provisions (see para **15.53**) override this.

To non-EU business

16.91   Supplies to non-EU business purchasers are also considered to be supplied outside the UK and so are outside the scope of UK VAT unless the 'use and enjoyment' provisions (see para **15.53**) override this.

To consumers

16.92   Where intellectual property is licensed or transferred to consumers (ie individuals receiving the supply in their personal capacity, not for the purposes of a business) the supply is treated as made where the supplier belongs (see para **15.28**).

16.93   All supplies of intellectual property by a UK taxable person to EU consumers will, therefore, be subject to UK VAT. Consumer supplies of intellectual property are most likely to be electronic services such as downloaded software, music and e-books, as these 'digitised goods' are limited licences of copyright. Note that this rule, as to where the place of supply is located, will change from 2015 (see para **15.62**).

TRANSFER PRICING

16.94   International groups of companies trade within their groups: they exchange technology, intellectual property, physical assets, management skills and other know-how. Without some restraint, these transactions could easily be used to move profit around the group to the most tax-advantageous location. Tax authorities are, understandably, not inclined to encourage such actions.

16.95   Transfer pricing is a mechanism which tries to ensure that profits are not skewed between the countries within which a group operates. Instead, companies are required to account (for tax purposes) for intra-group transactions as though they were made at arm's length: in effect, treat them as though they were made between independent companies. The value of the transaction should generally reflect a reasonable—not excessively large or small—profit.

16.96   The UK requires companies to record international group transactions on an arm's length basis for tax, and report accordingly on the company's self-assessment tax return. HMRC can, and will, query whether the transfer pricing is appropriate, to check whether it does in fact reflect arm's length pricing and terms. Companies are required to keep documentation to show how they arrived at their transfer pricing policy.

What is transfer pricing?

16.97   Businesses seek profits. In a transaction between unconnected parties, both buyer and seller are looking for profit, so the buyer is looking for the lowest price and the seller for the highest price; between them, they negotiate to an arm's length price that reflects the negotiating powers of the parties and the value of the goods or services that are the subject of the transaction.

16.98   Where the parties are connected, however, that drive towards profit can take a different form because the buyer and the seller can work together to maximise the profit for the group as a whole. And where the buyer and seller are in different countries, that can mean setting the price to minimise taxes by ensuring that the profit is earned in the country with the lowest taxation rates.

Example 16.4

Company A is an intellectual property holding company for the group; company B is a manufacturing business that produces some of the products that are made by the group with the intellectual property belonging to the group. Company A grants company B a licence to use the IP. Company B is tax resident in a country with a 30% corporate tax rate; company A is tax resident in a country with a 20% corporate tax rate.

The market rate for the licence which company A grants to company B is, say, £1,000,000 per annum. However, to maximise profit by minimising tax, the companies decide between themselves that company B will in fact pay a licence fee of £2,000,000; this means that it just about breaks even overall on operations. The effect is to save £100,000 of tax in the group, since company A pays only £200,000 on the extra £1,000,000 of profit; company B would have paid £300,000 on that profit.

16.99   Unsurprisingly, most tax authorities are not particularly impressed with the potential for flight of revenue to lower tax jurisdictions. The response is transfer pricing: these are rules which tax authorities put in place to enable them to require companies to set group transaction prices on an arm's length basis, taking into account the terms and conditions of the transaction. This is intended to eliminate the possibility of companies manipulating tax profits.

16.100   Transfer pricing rules only affect taxable profits. The rules do not adjust the accounts, but instead, if the intra-group prices of transactions are not at arm's length (taking into account the terms and conditions of the transaction), they require an adjustment in the tax return to make up the difference. The rules affect not only direct group members but can extend to joint ventures and similar situations where there is the potential for profit manipulation to reduce overall tax within the transaction.

16.101   Not all countries require intra-group transactions to be at arm's length: Malta, for example, does not have transfer pricing regulations: this is, at least in part, because their effective tax rates are low enough that multinational groups are unlikely to be substantially engaged in attempting to remove profits from those countries.

UK transfer pricing rules

16.102   The UK transfer pricing rules are in TIOPA 2010, Part 4, and are based on the OECD Transfer Pricing Guidelines for Multinational Enterprises and Tax Administrations (the OECD Guidelines). The following is a broad outline of the UK transfer pricing rules, as these are not specific to intellectual property and so a closer examination is outside the scope of this book.

16.103   The UK rules apply to transactions between two persons (broadly) under common control (TIOPA 2010, s 148) that contain provisions that are not at arm's length and as a result of such provisions a potential tax advantage is created. In such circumstances, the transaction is recomputed for tax purposes as though it was on an arm's length basis (TIOPA 2010, s 147).

Transactions

16.104 A transaction, under UK transfer pricing rules, includes any agreement, understanding or practice between the companies, and includes a series or chain of related transactions, not all of which may include both companies (TIOPA 2010, s 150). It includes unenforceable transactions, and transactions which an independent party would not have entered into. Any transaction relating to intellectual property (licensing, assignment, research and development, cost-sharing etc) will be potentially within the scope of transfer pricing where the parties are connected.

Person

16.105 The definition of 'person' is wider than simply a company; it can include transactions with an individual that controls the company. It is also not restricted to cross-border transactions; the UK rules apply to intra-UK transactions, in an attempt to ensure that the transfer pricing rules do not contravene the European Treaty, so that intra-Europe transactions are not at a disadvantage compared to intra-UK transactions (as a result of Case C-324–00 *Lankhorst-Hohorst GmbH v Finanzmt Steinfurt*). There is an argument that the UK over-reacted to this case in bringing UK–UK transactions within the scope of transfer pricing, particularly following the ECJ case of C-311/08 *SGI v Belgium*, but in practice HMRC seem not to be focusing on UK–UK transactions in any case.

Provision

16.106 The term 'provision' is not defined in the UK rules on transfer pricing, but HMRC guidance indicates that it is intended to be the same as 'condition' in the OECD Guidelines (HMRC Manual INTM420010). All the provisions or conditions of a transaction must be taken into account, not just the price. For example, in an intra-group licence of copyright, would a third party have licensed copyright for the same period of time at the same royalty rate, or would the term of the licence generally require a higher royalty rate on an arm's length basis?

Participation in management

16.107 A person will directly participate in the management of a company if that person controls the company; control in this context means owning at least a 50% interest in the company (TIOPA 2010, s 157).

16.108 Indirect participation in the management of a company will arise where a person has control when the rights and powers which that person is entitled to acquire are taken in account, and/or where rights and powers of persons connected with that person are taken into account, which would together give the first person control of the company (TIOPA 2010, s 158).

UK tax advantage

16.109 A UK tax advantage is obtained where, as a result of the provisions of the transaction, the UK profits are lower than, or UK losses are higher than, they would have been if the provisions had been on an arm's length basis (TIOPA 2010, s 155).

Compliance

16.110 UK large companies are required to self-assess for transfer pricing, making the necessary adjustments to profits (TIOPA 2010, s 147).

16.111 Small and medium-sized companies are excluded from the transfer-pricing regime if their cross-border transactions are with countries with which the UK has a tax treaty with a non-discrimination article (TIOPA 2010, s 167). However, such companies may be required to implement transfer pricing on receipt of notice from HMRC even where the transaction is with an appropriate treaty company (TIOPA 2010, s 167A and s 168; note that s 167A was introduced in Finance Act 2012 with effect from 1 April 2013). In practice, this means that both small and medium-sized companies should consider carefully the implications of entering into exports and imports of intellectual property with any companies in non-treaty companies, where there is a control connection between the UK and non-UK companies.

Summary

16.112 Transfer pricing adjustments to profits are required in the UK when:

- there is a transaction
- between two companies
- where one company participates directly or indirectly in the management of the other, or another person (or persons jointly) participates directly or indirectly in the management of both companies,

and the terms of the transaction are not those that would have been agreed between two independent parties (ie not on an arm's length basis), as a result of which a UK tax advantage is obtained by one or both companies.

OECD Guidelines

16.113 The OECD Guidelines are the basis for the UK rules on transfer pricing (TIOPA 2010, s 164). These require any profits which would have accrued on an arm's length basis to be included in taxable profits (whereas the UK rules require adjustment if there is any UK tax advantage).

16.114 The OECD has recognised that the guidelines relating to transfer pricing of intellectual property and other intangible assets are not as precise as they could be, and has begun a project looking at the transfer pricing aspects of intangibles. At the time of writing, this project has not yet made any specific recommendations as to changes to the transfer pricing guidelines for intellectual property.

Arm's length principle

16.115 The OECD Guidelines contain detailed guidance on how to establish an arm's length principle in transactions; the main methods used are set out in the following paragraphs. As these are not specific to intellectual property, this is a broad overview rather than a detailed description.

Comparable uncontrolled price

16.116 This is the most straightforward comparator and was previously the most preferred under OECD Guidelines. A recent update to the OECD Guidelines has removed the supremacy of this method, and businesses are required to use the most appropriate transfer pricing method. Nevertheless, where a comparable uncontrolled price can be found, tax authorities may still prefer this method

16.117 A comparable uncontrolled price can be difficult to establish: it is the price that is charged for the same transaction between one of the parties and an independent party, or between two independent parties. The most usual scenario where such a price can be established is where one party licenses its intellectual property externally to third parties and also licences it within the group on the same terms. In this case, the transactions with independent parties are likely to set the basis for the intra-group licences for transfer pricing purposes.

16.118 In general, however, it is difficult to find a reliable comparable uncontrolled price because companies do not readily disclose such market sensitive information; there are databases that gather information but it is almost always necessary to make adjustments to take into account differences between the reported transaction and the actual intra-group transaction.

Resale price

16.119 This method looks at the price used for resale of the goods or services to an independent party by the group purchaser. This price is then reduced by a realistic profit margin for the group purchaser to establish the price at which it is sold to the group purchaser. The margin is the amount that a party would be expected to require to cover expenses and make an appropriate profit.

16.120 The profit margin should be established by reference to the margin made by the group purchaser on general sales to third parties or, if necessary, by considering the gross profits of third parties in similar sales. As above, the difficulty with this is determining the comparable third parties and comparable transactions to establish an appropriate gross profit.

Cost plus

16.121 This method is most often used for intra-group services, establishing an arm's length price by applying a mark-up to the costs of the supplier. The mark-up represents the profit of the supplier and is determined by comparison with similar transactions. Again, the difficulty lies in establishing appropriate comparisons.

Profit split

16.122 This method looks at the overall profit earned from the transaction and allocates that profit between the parties involved, according to their function in the transaction and the risk that they have within the transaction. Again, third party comparables for analysis should be obtained to establish the allocation where possible.

Transactional net margin

16.123 This method establishes the operating profit margin as a percentage of a particular base—for example, return on capital employed or operating profits compared to sales—and is generally the method of last resort. It is useful where there are no comparators that can be found for other methods, for example, where the transaction involves something unique. This method may be used more for intellectual property transactions than in other areas, although it is not a preferred method.

Importance for intellectual property transactions

16.124 Intellectual property is considered to be a material risk area for transfer pricing purposes, as it can be difficult for tax authorities to be able to identify where intellectual property transactions have taken place. In some cases, the companies themselves may not consider that a transaction has taken place, and not all tax authorities will agree between themselves on the contributions of provisions in transactions to profits.

16.125   Multi-national groups with significant intellectual property will often also have significant cross-border activity: research and development, marketing, intellectual property holdings, and regulatory compliance management, as well as centralised service functions such as finance and operations. All of these functions contribute towards profits of the group entities and appropriate pricing structures need to be in place to ensure that each group company pays for the services and goods it receives from other group companies, and to ensure that it is in turn paid for the services and goods that it supplies to other group companies.

16.126   The UK transfer pricing rules cover all intra-group intellectual property transactions, including licensing, cost-sharing, services agreements and transfers of IP. There are penalties for non-compliance with the rules, as a tax return that is completed without regard to transfer pricing by a large company, or a medium-sized company that has received a notice from HMRC, is regarded as fraudulently given at worst, and negligently given at best: either is subject to penalties and interest on any adjustments required to implement the transfer pricing rules.

16.127   In addition, transfer pricing rules require companies to maintain documentation showing why the particular method used to calculate it was chosen, how the arm's length principle used in intra-group transactions, or to adjust taxable profits for such transactions, was arrived at. There are penalties for not maintaining such documentation. Generally, adequate documentation is not quick and easy to produce and so cannot be created when the tax authority requests it, particularly not in Poland, for example, where the tax authority provide only seven days' notice when requesting sight of transfer pricing support documentation.

Unanticipated assets

16.128   For example, in 2006, GlaxoSmithKline settled one of the largest transfer-pricing disputes to date, at $3.4bn, with the US tax authorities (per IRS press release). The dispute was over the contribution of marketing intangibles to profits of GSK's US subsidiary in respect of a drug manufactured by the UK parent and supplied to the US subsidiary.

16.129   The IRS contended that the marketing of intangible assets, arising in GSK US as a result of its work, contributed more to the profits earned by the group overall than had been provided for in the transaction between the UK and the US.

16.130   The particular difficulty was disagreement between the US and UK tax authorities. Many transfer pricing disputes are with one country, and an appropriate adjustment in the other country can often be made when the dispute is resolved in the first country. In this case, however, the UK tax authority held that the UK intellectual property in the drug was responsible for more of the profits, that an arm's length transaction would result in more profit for the UK company compared to the US subsidiary: essentially agreeing with GSK's analysis of the intra-group transaction.

16.131 The UK/US tax treaty contains dispute resolution procedures which, in this case, proved unhelpful and resulted in a stalemate with the US insisting that the US marketing intangibles generated more profit in the US and the UK continuing to insist that the UK intellectual property required profit to be recognised in the UK. The dispute took 14 years to reach the settlement of $3.4bn; the US tax authority's original assessment had been for $5bn.

16.132 This was a reasonably extreme case, but does reflect the problems with companies and tax authorities not always being aware of, or agreeing on, the precise nature of the transactions arising between group members.

Barriers to entry

16.133 Intellectual property assets can create a substantial barrier to entry into the market for competitors, given the monopoly nature of many intellectual property rights.

16.134 Even where the intellectual property is not specifically a barrier to entry, such assets can enable a company to earn more profits than a competitor because of the value inherent in, for example, brand names. Where a group wants to enter a new territory, the value perceived by customers in the brand will often precede entry—given the speed and globalisation of communication—and can give any subsidiary established in that new territory an advantage over existing competitors.

16.135 The value to the subsidiary of unfettered access to the group intellectual property assets can be substantial; not only the core intellectual property underlying the goods or services sold and the brand assets but, for example, customer databases showing who in the territory has perhaps already imported the goods or services produced by the group, and marketing intangibles created in other territories.

16.136 The tax authority in the parent company's jurisdiction will want to see appropriate payment by the subsidiary for the use of those intellectual property assets, assuming that the parent company owns those assets, that they have not been transferred to an intellectual property holding company in a more sympathetic jurisdiction. In general terms, the tax authority will expect to see arm's length licences between the parent and the subsidiary.

16.137 In the first year or so, such transfer pricing will not be challenged. However, if the subsidiary is successful, over time it may be argued that the subsidiary itself is contributing to the value of some of the group intellectual property. Without some research and development function it is unlikely that the subsidiary will be regarded as contributing to core IP, but it may be contributing to the value of other unregistered intellectual property such as marketing intangibles, customer databases and group know-how. At this point, the tax authority in the subsidiary's jurisdiction may challenge the transfer pricing used on the grounds that the subsidiary is now paying for an asset that it is developing: the licences may no longer be on arm's length terms, and perhaps the pricing should be adjusted to reflect the non-monetary value being contributed by the subsidiary. Without such adjustment, the subsidiary could, arguably, be regarded as paying at least in part for value that it has created itself.

Group assets

16.138 Tax authorities are particularly interested in determining whether a group licensee has had some involvement in the development of the intellectual property that is the subject of the licence—in particular, has it added value to the intellectual property? For example, where a company pays a royalty for the use of a trademark, its use of that trademark may add value to the trademark in the local jurisdiction. In that case, the licensee's tax authority is likely to expect to see that the arm's length price takes this into effect: that is, that the value added by the licensee is reflected in the price being paid by the licensee for the use of the trademark.

CONTROLLED FOREIGN COMPANIES

16.139 In order to reduce the risk of companies diverting profits overseas without good commercial reason, UK companies are subject to tax on the profits of their 'controlled foreign companies'. Many other countries have similar rules (eg the Subpart F rules for US persons with shareholdings in overseas companies). A controlled foreign company (CFC) is one which is resident outside the UK, controlled by persons resident in the UK. The reform of the rules removes the requirement that the company be in a lower tax jurisdiction than the UK, although there is an exemption for CFCs in countries with effective tax rates similar to the UK.

Control

16.140 'Control' is determined by considering the rights of the UK residents with an interest in the company, together with any rights held by persons connected with the UK resident. Broadly, a person will have control if they have power to secure that the affairs of the company are conducted in accordance with their wishes, where that power arises through shareholdings, voting power, or by the documents governing the non-UK company (TIOPA 2010, s 371RB).

New CFC rules

16.141 The CFC rules have been substantially re-written, with the new rules (in TIOPA 2010, Pt 9A) applying to accounting periods beginning on or after 1 January 2013. The old rules on CFCs are outside the scope of this book but were, broadly, much more difficult to escape for intellectual property holding companies, as HMRC tended to take the view that the main reason for having an intellectual property holding company outside the UK was for tax avoidance purposes. The following focuses on the intellectual property aspects of the controlled foreign company rules—there are many other provisions that can apply to trading companies and to finance operations in particular.

When do the new CFC rules apply to intellectual property profits?

Let-out 1: the gateway

16.142 Where an entity is capable of being a CFC, the profits have to pass a gateway test in order to be capable of being caught by the rules. For an intellectual property holding company, the relevant part of the test is Chapter 4, covering profits attributable to UK activities. The other parts of the gateway test relate to finance profits and captive insurance businesses, and so will be less relevant to intellectual property businesses.

16.143 Chapter 4 will apply, so that the test is met and the profits are within the scope of the CFC charge for the UK shareholder *unless* one of the following four conditions is met:

- the first condition is that the assets and risks of the CFC must not be held under an arrangement which has as its main purposes, or one of its main purposes, the reduction or elimination of liability to tax in the UK of another person, and the CFC expects its business to be more profitable than it otherwise would be;

- the second condition is that the CFC does not have any UK managed risks or assets;

- the third condition is that, if it does have UK managed assets and risks, then the CFC would be commercially effective even if it did manage the assets and risks directly;

- the fourth condition cannot be met by a company whose business is the exploitation of intellectual property, so it is not considered further here.

It should be possible for a non-UK company holding intellectual property to meet one of these conditions so that the profits are outside the UK tax charge.

16.144 In particular, a CFC with appropriate substance should be able to have no UK managed assets and risks. One of the points of the new CFC rules is that they should not catch companies with appropriate substance and management in their local jurisdiction, even if that company pays little local tax. The key is to ensure that profits are not *artificially* diverted from the UK. HMRC are finally beginning to accept that businesses are not required to operate solely from the UK and that it is open to a business to move some or all of its operations outside the UK.

Let-out 2: taxable profits

16.145 Where the gateway test cannot be met, so that the profits of the cell could fall within the CFC charge for a UK shareholder, the profits within the UK tax charge are calculated. Excluded from those profits are profits from 'trading income', which will include intellectual property profits *unless* the profits come from intellectual property that was transferred to the UK within the previous seven years or so. There is no bona fide commercial exclusion, so it is questionable whether this meets EU law requirements post-*National Grid Indus* (C 371/10) but, in practice, it means that profits from non-UK connected intellectual property will be outside the CFC tax charge.

Let-out 3: entity-level exemptions

16.146 If the CFC fails the gateway test, and cannot exclude the intellectual property profits, there are still a number of exemptions available.

Low-profits exemption

16.147 The principal exemption likely to apply to an intellectual property business in this case would be the general exemption for CFCs with low profits; in particular, the profits of a CFC with accounting profits (or assumed UK-equivalent taxable profits) of less than £500,000 and non-trading profits of less than £50,000 will be exempt from the charge (TIOPA 2010, s 371LB).

16.148 There are other exemptions which could apply but the main ones have a requirement that the intellectual property not be UK connected, so companies that fail the second let-out above will probably fail to qualify for these as well.

Intellectual property holding company exemption

16.149 There is an intellectual property holding company exemption (ICTA 1988, Sch 25A, Pt 2B, inserted by Finance Act 2011): this exemption applies, however, only for profits of a CFC whose sole business is foreign-to-foreign licensing of intellectual property with a minimal UK connection.

16.150 The intellectual property itself must have a minimal UK connection, which is to say that it cannot have been transferred from someone (related or otherwise) in the UK in the accounting period or the previous six years before the accounting period started.

16.151 Where the CFC itself creates (or subcontracts someone else to create) the intellectual property, then the intellectual property will not have a substantial UK connection, provided that the R&D was not done in the UK by a connected person or paid for by a UK connected person. The intellectual property must also not be maintained or enhanced in the intellectual property by a connected person.

16.152 In addition, the CFC itself cannot have substantial income from the UK (substantial is not yet defined), hence the focus on foreign-to-foreign licensing.

Excluded territories exemption

16.153 There is an exemption for CFCs in particular named territories, but this is subject to the same test for intellectual property income as the taxable profits exclusion: it must not be derived from intellectual property transferred by related parties from the UK in the accounting period or the six years before that (TIOPA 2010, s 371KB). It is questionable whether this meets EU law requirements, given that it is an absolute test with no motive element. Even if the intellectual property is transferred for full market value as part of a commercial transaction, an EU CFC could still be caught and its UK corporate shareholder subject to tax on profits.

16.154 This condition is relaxed for a number of favoured trading partners: the USA, Canada, Germany, France, Japan and Australia. CFCs in these countries can still come within the excluded territories exemption where it has intellectual property income from intellectual property transferred from the UK within the previous six years. For this to operate, the CFC must actually carry on business in the jurisdiction of residence (ie it cannot have a permanent establishment elsewhere, through which the business is actually carried on). In practice, few companies are likely to set up intellectual property holding companies in these jurisdictions for tax reasons, but it does simplify matters for groups that want to restructure their intellectual property holdings.

Tax exemption

16.155 An exemption is also available for CFCs in higher-tax jurisdictions, ie those in which the local tax charge (ignoring designer tax rates) is at least 75% of the corresponding UK tax charge (TIOPA 2010, s 371NB).

Summary

16.156 The revised CFC rules provide a reasonable territorial exclusion for intellectual property income from the UK tax charge on CFCs, with the principal issue being with intellectual property that has had some connection with the UK in the last seven years or so. It is questionable whether the rules properly comply with EU law but, in general, it is a substantial improvement on the old CFC rules (which rather seemed based on the view that any non-UK intellectual property ownership was tax avoidance).

INDIVIDUALS: OVERSEAS INCOME AND GAINS

16.157 The UK has two sets of rules designed to prevent individuals from avoiding UK tax by transferring assets and/or sources of income overseas. These rules are not specifically aimed at intellectual property, but can apply where intellectual property is transferred overseas or held overseas and there is a connection to a UK individual.

16.158 These rules have been challenged by the EU and, at the time of writing, HMRC had launched an initial consultation aimed at considering how to change these rules to comply with EU requirements. The following is, therefore, likely to have changed from April 2013.

Overseas income

16.159 Broadly, where a UK individual transfers an asset to a non-UK company in exchange for shares in that company, the income of that company will be taxed on the UK individual (ITA 2007, s 720) unless a motive defence (ITA 2007, ss 736–742) can be established. For example, where an individual transfers a UK patent to a non-UK company in exchange for shares, there is the possibility of that individual being subject to UK tax on the income which the company derives from that patent.

16.160 The motive defence requires that the taxpayer demonstrate that the avoidance of tax is not the main purpose, or one of the main purposes, for which the structure is set up.

16.161 The distinction between tax avoidance and tax mitigation is still in the process of being worked out by the UK Tax Tribunals; HMRC's record in challenging ordinary tax planning in the Tribunals has not been particularly good and the cases appear to depend on what the taxpayer's intentions were (see, for example, *Carvill v IRC* [2000] STC (SCD) 143).

16.162 The motive defence is strongest when the non-UK company has a genuine economic activity and has substance appropriate to that activity, with those running it having the necessary skills to do so. Accordingly, a transfer of UK intellectual property to a passive intellectual property holding company is likely to be challenged in these circumstances. If, instead, the intellectual property is actively managed by the company and there is active licensing of the intellectual property to other jurisdictions with the company appropriately managed in the local jurisdiction where it is resident, then the motive defence is more likely to be available.

16.163 Note that this charge applies only to individuals; companies need to consider the effect of the controlled foreign company rules instead.

Overseas gains

16.164 Gains made by overseas companies can be subject to UK tax if they are attributed to individual shareholders (or other participators such as option holders and loan creditors) (TCGA 1992, s 13). This clause can apply to both corporate and non-corporate shareholders.

16.165 A UK tax charge on the shareholder can arise where:

● a non-UK resident company

● which would be a close company if it were UK resident

● makes a chargeable gain.

16.166 There are a number of exemptions which apply and, in particular, there is no attribution of gains arising on assets used for the purposes of a trade carried on by the overseas company outside the UK. Intellectual property used by the close company for the purposes of its trade would therefore be outside the scope of the charge. However, if the intellectual property was held as an investment by the company then the UK shareholders could be subject to UK tax on gains arising in the company.

16.167 Where there is a tax treaty between the UK and the company jurisdiction, it may provide that the company's country should have primary taxing rights in respect of any gain. This would override the UK tax rules so that no UK tax charge would be imposed.

Close company

16.168 A close company is one controlled by five or fewer participators or controlled by any number of participators who are also directors (CTA 2009, s 439).

Attribution of gain

16.169 Where the provisions apply, any gains made by the non-UK resident company are attributed to all the participators in the company and taxed in the UK on UK resident participators as capital gains of those participators (TCGA 1992, s 13(2)). There is no requirement that a participator actually have any entitlement to share in the specific profits which result from the gain (TCGA 1992, s 454).

16.170 The amount attributed will depend on the 'interest of the participator in the company' (TCGA 1992, s 13(3)). This is generally calculated by reference to that participator's shareholding in the non-UK company. However, HMRC take the view that a full review of the circumstances is required to ensure that the apportionment is 'just and reasonable', considering the participators' economic interests in the company (HMRC Manual CG57283). It should be noted that this test is not contained in the legislation, which simply refers to the participator's 'interest in the company'.

16.171 However, no attribution—and hence no tax charge—is made for participators with an interest of 10% or less in the non-UK company (TCGA 1992, s 13(4)).

Reliefs

16.172 Where the company is later sold, or the proceeds of sale of the intellectual property are distributed to shareholders, the UK shareholders may be able to claim tax relief on any UK tax on the proceeds of sale or the distribution, to the extent that these reflect the gains already taxed in the UK.

UK TAX TREATIES

16.173 The UK has a wide network of tax treaties, intended to reduce or eliminate double taxation between the UK and other countries; in general, the UK does not have substantive tax treaties with low-tax jurisdictions (its tax treaties with the Channel Islands etc are rather limited in scope).

16.174 From the point of view of intellectual property, tax treaties are most significant for their ability to reduce or eliminate withholding tax on royalties relating to intellectual property.

Treaty withholding tax: royalties

16.175 Royalties on intellectual property—and withholding tax—fall within Article 12 of the OECD Model Treaty. The OECD takes the view, rarely followed by tax treaties in practice, that royalties should only be taxed in the country where the beneficial owner is resident. That is, that the licensor's country should have taxing rights, not the licensee country. Note that fees paid to non-UK authors and other non-UK creative professionals may not, however, be regarded as royalties for treaty purposes (see para **18.287**).

16.176 In practice, most of the UK's tax treaties start from the premise that the UK has taxing rights over royalties paid by UK residents, by way of withholding taxes. Some of the treaties provide for a reduced rate of withholding tax, including a nil rate of royalty in some cases, but this is not the starting point for the tax treatment of cross-border royalties.

Anti-avoidance

16.177 Article 12 of the OECD Model Treaty also contains an anti-avoidance clause that denies the benefit of the treaty to any excessive royalties, and this is echoed in the UK treaties. The UK provisions tend to be rather wider than the OECD provision. The clause applies where the amount of the royalties exceeds the amount that would have been agreed on an arm's length basis: in this case, the anti-avoidance provisions mean that tax must be withheld at the full rate (ie 20% at the time of writing) on the amount in excess of the arm's length royalty.

Interaction with transfer pricing

16.178 This could, in effect, mean double tax recovery for the UK. The paying company (the licensee) will have a reduced deductible royalty if an adjustment is required when calculating taxable profits in accordance with transfer pricing requirements (see para **16.112**), so that it pays higher corporate taxes overall, but will also be required to withhold tax on part of the payment actually made.

Example 16.5

Lee Ltd pays a royalty of £10,000 to its overseas parent company. It is later established that the appropriate arm's length price for the royalty would have been £5,000.

Lee Ltd therefore can only deduct £5,000 from taxable profits in respect of the royalty, so that it pays tax on £5,000 more (£10,000) than it had expected. At the same time, it is required to withhold tax on £5,000 of the royalty under the anti-avoidance provisions in the applicable tax treaty.

Claiming treaty benefits

16.179   A UK taxpayer is not automatically entitled to the benefits of UK tax treaties; the taxpayer must be resident in the UK and some tax treaties also require the taxpayer to be a qualified person. Note that it is tax residence that determines entitlement to treaty benefits—the domicile and/or citizenship status of individuals is not relevant.

16.180   The UK tax treaties have not, historically, required that taxpayers be anything other than resident in the UK. However, some tax treaties— particularly those with the USA, and those modelled on the USA agreements— have a clause that limits the benefits of the treaty to companies and individuals which meet specific conditions. This is to ensure that the UK is not being used simply to get the benefit of the tax treaty. Newer UK tax treaties are beginning to impose similar limitations of benefit and so the relevant treaty should always be checked to ensure that the requirements (if any) for eligibility for treaty benefits are met.

16.181   An individual must be UK resident to have the benefit of the treaty. For a company, there are various possible routes to qualification, including being listed on a recognised stock exchange. For private companies, the most usual route to qualification is that at least 50% of the shareholders are UK resident individuals. Other conditions limit the benefit of the treaty even if an intermediary company (for example) was placed between non-resident individuals and the UK company.

DOMESTIC RELIEF

16.182   The UK has a system of unilateral credit relief for tax withheld on overseas income of the UK company. This provides a credit against UK taxes on the same income where:

- there is no tax treaty with the country that is the source of income; or

- the UK taxpayer cannot claim the benefit of an existing tax treaty to reduce taxes; or

- where a treaty claim does not reduce the withholding tax to nil.

Treaty claims required

16.183   Note, however, that HMRC will require the UK taxpayer to have made all appropriate treaty claims before allowing relief for withholding tax.

Where the taxpayer is loss-making, or where the UK tax rate is lower than the overseas withholding tax rate, the taxpayer will not be able to claim full unilateral relief for the tax withheld and it may be more appropriate to claim relief by expensing the tax.

Unilateral relief

16.184 Where a UK taxpayer receives a royalty that is subject to tax in the UK and has also suffered withholding tax in the country of source, the UK taxpayer will be entitled to unilateral relief from UK tax in respect of that withholding tax (TIOPA 2010, ss 17–18).

16.185 The credit is only given against the UK tax which is charged on the same income, which must be calculated as for UK tax purposes. Where the UK tax charged is less than the overseas tax withheld, the balance of overseas tax unused cannot be set against UK tax charged on other income. If the UK company is loss-making, no UK credit relief is available for foreign taxes.

Example 16.6

AH receives a royalty of £1,000 from an overseas licensee. The licensee has deducted 30% withholding tax, as required by local law, so that AH receives a net royalty of £700.

In calculating his UK tax due, AH will treat the receipt as follows:

Royalty received	£1,000
UK tax thereon at 40%	£400
Less tax withheld	(£300)
Net UK tax due	£100

Example 16.7

Gibson Ltd receives a royalty of £1,000 from an overseas licensee. The licensee has deducted 30% withholding tax, as required by local law, so that Gibson receives a net royalty of £700. Gibson is a small company for UK tax purposes.

In calculating its UK tax due, Gibson will treat the receipt as follows:

Royalty received	£1,000
UK corporation tax thereon at 20%	£200
Less tax withheld	(£300)
Net UK tax due	£0

Gibson Ltd will have £100 of unrelieved foreign tax credits; these may be carried forward or expensed (see below).

Expensed relief

16.186   A taxpayer can also elect to treat any unrelieved tax as an expense of the business (TIOPA 2010, s 112); this is not as generous a relief, as UK tax relief will only be a percentage of the withheld tax, but it does provide some relief for loss-making businesses, or where the tax withheld is more than the UK tax on the same income.

Concessionary relief

16.187   UK tax credit is usually only available for tax withheld on overseas income; where the intellectual property is registered in the UK, the income will usually be regarded as UK source (HMRC Manual INTM345230). As a result, under the general rules, no credit for overseas tax (whether under a treaty or through unilateral relief) would be available.

However, this rule is mitigated in some circumstances by a concession relating to copyrights, patents, designs, secret processes or formulae, trademarks 'or other like property' (ESC B8).

16.188   Where payments are:

- received from a non-resident by a person carrying on a trade in the UK; and

- those payments are consideration for the use of the intellectual property in the overseas country;

the payments are treated as income arising outside the UK even where the intellectual property is registered in the UK, so that double tax relief can be claimed on any overseas tax withheld. Where the payments include an element of consideration for services also supplied, where that element is more than incidental, the concession will not apply to that element.

EU INTEREST AND ROYALTIES DIRECTIVE

16.189   In addition to tax treaties between the UK and EU Member States, the Interest and Royalties Directive should eliminate any withholding tax on royalties paid between associated companies in Europe.

16.190   The Directive is implemented into UK law (ITTOIA 2005, ss 757–767) so that a company making a qualifying payment is not required to deduct tax and the company receiving the payment has no liability to income tax in respect of that payment.

16.191   The conditions (ITTOIA 2005, s 758) for a payment to qualify are as follows:

- the company making the payment must be a UK company or a UK permanent establishment of an EU company;

- the person beneficially entitled to the income is an EU company (but not a UK permanent establishment or a non-EU permanent establishment of such a company); and

- the company making the payment and the company beneficially entitled to the income must be 25% associates.

25% associates

16.192   Two companies will be 25% associates if one owns at least 25% of the share capital or voting rights of the other, or if a third company owns at least 25% of the share capital or voting rights of each of them (ITTOIA 2005, s 761).

Exceptions

16.193   There are a couple of exceptions, where a withholding tax can still be imposed (subject to any tax treaties):

- where the royalty payment exceeds an arm's length price, in which case the exception from withholding taxes only applies to the arm's length amount (ITTOIA 2005, s 763); or

- the main purpose in paying the royalty was to obtain the exemption (ITTOIA 2005, s 765).

INTERNATIONAL COMPARISONS

16.194   The following is a brief summary of intellectual property tax incentives and rates in various countries. Note that tax is only part of the overall picture when considering any jurisdiction. Other matters, such as infrastructure, customer location, staff location, etc, also need to be considered (see para **18.71** for more information on considering holding companies):

	Main corporate tax rate	Intellectual property tax rate	Headline research and development incentives[1]	Transfer pricing rules?	CFC rules?	Domestic royalty withholding rate
Australia	30%	N/A	40%/45% refundable credit	Y	Y	30%
Brazil	34%	N/A	up to 200% deduction	Y	Y	25%
Cayman Islands	0%	N/A	N/A	N	N	0%
China	25%	15%	150% deduction	Y	Y	10%
Cyprus	10%	2%	N/A		N	10%
France	33.33%	N/A	30% credit	Y	Y	33.33%
Germany	approx. 30%[2]	N/A	N/A	Y	Y	15%
Hong Kong	16.5%	N/A	N/A	Y	N	4.95%
India	30%	N/A	up to 200% deduction	Y	Y	10%
Ireland	12.5%[3]	N/A	125% tax credit[4]	Y	N	20%
Japan	25.5%	N/A	112% deduction	Y	Y	20%
Jersey	0%	N/A	N/A	N	N	20%
Luxembourg	21%	5.76% on innovation income	N/A	Y	N	0%
Malta	35%[5]	0%	Y[6]	Y[7]	N	0%
Netherlands	25%	5% on 'innovation income'	50% reduction on wages taxes	Y	N	0%
Russia	20%	N/A	150% deduction	Y	N	20%
South Africa	28%	N/A	150% deduction	Y	Y	12%
Switzerland	8.5%[8]	N/A[9]	N/A	Y[10]	N	0%
UK	24%[11]	10% on patent income[12]	225% deduction (SME)/130% (large)	Y	Y	20%
USA	35%[13]	N/A	120% incremental credit	Y	Y[14]	30%

1 Local incentives may be available in sub-jurisdictions; these are not covered here.
2 Including municipal taxes.
3 For trading income only.
4 Changed from Finance Act 2012 onwards.
5 Part-recoverable by shareholders on payment of dividend, to an effective rate of 5%.
6 Tax credit for R&D expenditure depends on size of enterprise.
7 No formal rules but general anti-avoidance provisions can have similar effect.
8 May be higher in some cantons: between 12% and 22%.
9 Note some of the cantons have reduced canton tax rates for intellectual property income.
10 No specific transfer pricing legislation but tax authorities can adjust unjustified expenses.
11 Reducing to 22% from April 2014.
12 From April 2013.
13 Plus state taxes.
14 Subpart F rules.

Chapter 17

Intellectual property transactions

Summary: This chapter considers a number of (generic) types of intellectual property-related transactions that a business may undertake and briefly *outlines* the general tax issues that should be considered in each case; more detailed information on these tax issues is cross-referenced in the tax. Where there are specific tax matters that apply a particular transaction type, these are discussed in more detail.

- Licensing (para **17.1**)

- Transfer/assignment (para **17.34**)

- Litigation (para **17.52**)

- Business reconstructions (para **17.71**)

- Mergers and acquisitions (para **17.83**)

- Software (para **17.91**)

- Websites (para **17.120**)

LICENSING

(See also Chapter 6, Chapter 12 and Chapter 13 for more general information on the tax treatment of exploitation of intellectual property.)

Introduction

17.1   Licensing intellectual property ensures that the owner retains the rights to that property and can continue to receive income from third parties in respect of the property and, depending on the licences granted, may be able to exploit the property again, either later in time or in another territory, directly, or indirectly.

The types of licence that may be granted are generally as follows.

Exclusive licence

17.2 An exclusive licence gives the licensee the right to exploit the intellectual property licensed without challenge from the owner and without competition, even from the licensor. It may be restricted as to territory, in which case the rights will only apply to that territory: the licensor will be free to grant licences in respect of the same intellectual property in other territories, or can exploit the intellectual property directly in those other territories.

17.3 A company which has an exclusive licence to a patent may be able to claim patent box relief (see Chapter 13) on income derived from the use of that licence, but the licence must meet the specific requirements of the patent box legislation (see para **13.16**). Patent box relief is not available to holders of licences that do not meet these criteria.

Sole licence

17.4 This is similar to an exclusive licence, except that the licensor may compete with the licensee by directly exploiting the intellectual property, although the licensor cannot grant additional licences to third parties within the same territory (if the licence is not global).

Non-exclusive licence

17.5 This licence only gives the licensee the right to exploit the intellectual property without being challenged by the owner. There is generally no restriction on the licensor granting licences to others, either in the same territory or elsewhere, or on the licensor directly exploiting the intellectual property. Some consumer-related transactions are non-exclusive licences of intellectual property, such as downloads of software, music or e-books (see para **15.56** for the VAT implications of these in particular).

Taxation of licensors

UK companies

17.6 Companies that grant licences over intellectual property will generally be within the corporate intangibles tax rules and the income will be subject to tax as and when it is recognised in the profit and loss account of the company (see para **12.47**). As a result, the accounting policy as to revenue recognition of royalties (see para **12.8**) is likely to be the most important issue when considering tax on the income. Where the licensee is overseas, withholding tax may also be a consideration (see para **16.88**), together with transfer pricing (see para **16.94**).

Revenue recognition: specific issues

Access fees and advance royalties

17.7   Businesses such as those in the biotech sector often receive payments during the development phase of projects. These vary in contractual nature but, where fees are for access to review intellectual property and milestone payments on the achievement of certain goals, the current practice of recognising the revenue on receipt of the fees appears appropriate.

17.8   One of the main reasons for this is the level of risk involved in development. The nature of long-term development projects such as those in the biotech area is such that any real surety of success is only gained at the very last stage. Hence, it is sensible and prudent only to recognise the milestone payments at the earliest when they have been agreed to be due by the development partner (in this case the big pharmaceutical company) if not when the cash is safely in the bank.

17.9   An important point to address as a result of this is the setting of milestones. In order for the revenue to be clearly earned and the cash clearly due and payable the milestones must be easily measurable. Performance against these milestones will therefore always relate to a historical event at the time of payment.

17.10   For advance royalties, it is harder to determine a single standard treatment, as the contract is key to understanding the benefits delivered at the time of the payment and those that are to be delivered after the payment has been made. However, assuming advance royalty payments are really that—in that they are non-refundable but do result in a real reduction of future, potential royalties—then an element of the payment received will need to be deferred until such time as that future performance is either achieved or reasonably certain to be avoided, through failure of the project, for example.

Software licences

17.11   In some cases fees for software licences may be recognised immediately, rather than being spread over the life of the licence. This appears contrary to the usual treatment of licence fees but, where there are no ongoing support requirements as part of the licence, the seller has no future obligation to the customer and there may be no need to show any liability in the balance sheet in the form of deferred revenue.

The tax treatment will follow the accounting treatment so that the full fee will be taxed.

UK unincorporated businesses

17.12   For individuals and other unincorporated businesses, the principal issue for tax purposes is whether the receipts from licences are to be regarded as capital or income (see para **6.23**). Income will be subject to income tax (at up to 50%, although this rate is expected to reduce to 45% from 2013–14), whereas capital receipts will usually be subject to capital gains tax at up to 28%.

17.13   In practice, the exploitation of intellectual property by a business in granting licences will usually be regarded as a business activity and the licence fees will be income of the trade, profession or vocation regardless of the form which they take (see para **6.24**). The tax treatment of the licensee does not necessarily reflect in the tax treatment of the licensor.

17.14   A lump sum payment may still be treated as capital (see para **6.33**) where the licensor's trade, profession or vocation does not usually involve the licensing of intellectual property. Recurring licence fees, however, are more likely to be treated as income.

Copyright

17.15   Payments to authors and similar creators of copyright for licences of copyright will always be taxed as income, although post-cessation rules ma modify this where the profession has ceased (see para **18.253**).

Licensing intellectual property developed by others: wider tax implications

17.16   Where a company's trade relies to a significant extent on exploiting intellectual property developed by others, various tax incentives otherwise available may be restricted. This is a policy decision by the Treasury to restrict tax incentives to trades which are perceived to be less risk-oriented than most, to ensure that the incentive is targeted appropriately and to encourage innovation in the UK.

17.17   In outline (as the detail is outside the scope of this book), the tax incentives that may be affected are:

- Enterprise Investment Scheme (EIS): this scheme provides income tax and capital gains tax relief for individuals investing in qualifying companies. The trade of the company must not include, as a substantial element, one or more of a number of non-qualifying activities, including receiving royalties or other licence fees in respect of intellectual property not developed by that company;

- Corporate Venturing Scheme (CVS): this is a corporate form of the above relief, providing tax relief for companies investing in another qualifying company. As with EIS, a qualifying company for CVS purposes cannot include, as a substantial element, one or more of a number of non-qualifying activities, including receiving royalties or other licence fees in respect of intellectual property not developed by that company;

- Enterprise Management Incentives (EMI): this scheme provides income tax and National Insurance tax relief for employees granted share options in qualifying companies. As with EID and CVS, the trading activity of the company whose shares are subject to option cannot include, as a substantial element, receiving royalties or other licence fees in respect of intellectual property not developed by that company (amongst other non-qualifying activities).

Tax deductions for licensees

17.18   A licensee is principally interested in when it will be able to claim a tax deduction for the licence fees paid.

Companies

17.19   For companies, the tax deductions for the costs of acquiring a licence will depend on the treatment of payments in the accounts (see para **11.9**). Where the cost of the licence is amortised over the useful economic life of the licence, then the tax deductions will be similarly amortised (see para **11.25**). Note that the royalties in respect of licenses from related parties (see para **18.69**) cannot be left on inter-company loan accounts; the tax deduction for the payer is only available if the royalty is actually paid within a reasonable time (CTA 2009, s 851).

Unincorporated businesses

17.20   Non-exclusive licences do not prohibit the licensor from exploiting the intellectual property, either personally or by licensing others. Payments for non-exclusive licences will generally be regarded as revenue (immediately deductible) rather than capital (deductible only on disposal or expiry of the licence), regardless of whether the payment is a lump sum or royalties: the licensee is not gaining an asset of enduring benefit to the business. This is particularly the case where non-exclusive licence payments are related to the actual use of the intellectual property, for example where the payments are dependant on the number of products made using the intellectual property, or are related to the turnover of the licensee business. As with exclusive licences, special rules apply to patent licences.

Exclusive licences: non-patent

17.21 Where an exclusive licence is granted, a lump sum payment for the licence is likely to be considered a capital payment, since the licensor has effectively disposed of a part of a capital asset: under an exclusive licence, only the licensee can exploit the intellectual property under the terms of the licence. An exclusive licence ensures that even the licensor cannot exploit the intellectual property for the duration and scope of the licence. Royalty payments will usually also be considered to be capital in nature, where the licence terms are such that the licensee has effectively gained an enduring asset.

Patent licences

17.22 Capital allowances may be available for licences of patents or industrial know-how where the transaction is treated as capital; these allow a tax deduction for the licensee over a period of time, rather than only on the disposal or expiry of the licence (see paras **5.60** and **5.104**).

Licence fees: taxable/deductible amount

17.23 Note that transfer pricing rules (see para **16.94**) or connected or related party rules (see para **18.66** onwards) may require a business to recognise a different amount to that agreed, whether as licensee or licensor.

VAT on licences

UK licensor

17.24 A licensor who is a taxable person (see para **15.19**) is required to charge UK VAT (generally at 20%) on the grant of a licence over intellectual property where:

- the licensee is a business and belongs (see para **15.26**) in the UK; or

- the licensor belongs in the UK and the licensee is a consumer belonging within the EU (see para **15.28**).

17.25 The exception is where the intellectual property supply is exempt for the purposes of VAT; no VAT is charged, and the licensor is likely to be limited as to the amount of VAT that they can recover on purchases related to the supply. As noted before, a supply of intellectual property is unlikely to be exempt in its own right (see para **15.11**).

EC Sales List

17.26   No UK VAT is charged on supplies of intellectual property to EU businesses, as these businesses are expected to account for VAT in their own country under the reverse charge procedures (see para **15.33**).

UK licensee

Licence from a UK licensor

17.27   A licensee who is a taxable person and is charged UK VAT by a licensor will usually be able to recover that VAT (by offset against output VAT charged, or by recovery from HMRC) where the licence is entered into in the course of the licensee's business and the licensee does not use the intellectual property to make exempt supplies.

Licence from a non-UK licensor

17.28   A licensee who is a taxable person who obtains a licence of intellectual property from a non-UK licensor is required to operate the reverse charge in respect of the licence fees.

17.29   The licensee effectively self-charges VAT on the licence fee as if it were the licensor, and then takes a deduction for that VAT in calculating its liability to account to HMRC for VAT in that quarter (assuming that the intellectual property is not used to make exempt supplies).

Example 17.1

Coleridge Limited licenses project management software from a US business that its staff use to keep track of the progress of client projects. The licence fee paid by Coleridge to use the software is £1,500 per VAT quarter.

If Coleridge Limited does not make any exempt supplies then, in preparing its VAT return, Coleridge treats the licence fee as a supply that it *makes* and so has to account for £300 in output VAT. At the same time, it also treats the licence fee as a supply that it *receives* and so has £300 in input VAT. The effect on the VAT return is neutral (the output VAT and the input VAT match) so that Coleridge does not, in practice, have any VAT payment to make.

If 50% of Coleridge's business was made up of exempt supplies (eg it provided services related to land, which are generally exempt under VATA 1994, Sch 9, Group 1) then, as the software is used across all of Coleridge's projects, 50% of the input VAT would not be recoverable. Coleridge would, therefore, treat the licence fee as a taxable supply that it makes, accounting for £300 of output VAT, and would still be required to treat the fee as a supply received, with associated input VAT. In this case, however, only 50% of the VAT charge could be treated as input VAT as half of Coleridge's supplies are exempt. Coleridge would have to account for £300 of output VAT under the reverse charge but could only offset £150 of input VAT against that. There would be a balance of £150 that would be an absolute cost to the Coleridge, accounted for to HMRC.

17.30   The reason for the reverse charge is to ensure that there is no substantial VAT advantage in acquiring intellectual property (or other services) from outside the UK. In the example above, if there were no requirement to account for VAT through the reverse charge, Coleridge Limited would be better off licensing software from a non-UK licensor as there would be no VAT liability. If the software was licensed from a UK licensor, that UK licensor would be required to charge output VAT of £300 which Coleridge could not fully recover.

Consumer licensee

17.31   Where the licensee of the intellectual property is a consumer (ie usually where the transaction is a non-exclusive licence of music, e-books, software etc downloaded via the internet), UK VAT must be charged and accounted for by non-EU businesses (see para **15.60**).

Ongoing royalties

17.32   Where there is a single payment, such as a lump sum fee, the VAT treatment is straightforward: VAT is due when the intellectual property is supplied (usually the date from which the licence or transfer/assignment is effective) unless the date of payment, or the date of invoice (if applicable), is earlier (VATA 1994, s 1(2) and s 6). The time of supply is important to determine in which VAT quarter the VAT should be accounted for.

17.33   Where, however, there are ongoing royalties under a licence, the time of supply is not the date from which the licence is effective. In these circumstances, a separate supply is treated as taking place each time a payment is made for the use of the licence or, if earlier, a VAT invoice is issued in respect of the royalty payment (Value Added Tax Regulations 1995, SI 1995/2518, reg 90). VAT is therefore accounted for in each VAT quarter in which a royalty payment is received (or invoice issued, if different).

TRANSFER OR ASSIGNMENT OF INTELLECTUAL PROPERTY

17.34   See also Chapter 7 and Chapter 14 for more information on the tax treatment of the disposal of intellectual property and see Chapter 5 and Chapter 11 for the tax treatment of the acquirer/assignee.

The transfer or assignment of intellectual property generally involves the outright disposal of an intellectual property asset to another person (for transfers in the course of business acquisitions, see para **17.81**).

Tax treatment of transferor/assignor

Companies

17.35   Companies that transfer intellectual property will generally be within the corporate intangibles tax rules and the gain (credit) will be subject to tax as and when it is recognised in the profit and loss account of the company (see para **14.2**). In some cases, where the payment for the transfer is received over a period of time (milestones etc), the timing of the recognition of that income in the accounts (see para **12.9**) is likely to be the most important issue when considering tax on the income. The amount recognised will depend on whether or not the transferee and transferor are related (see **18.69**) and whether transfer pricing (see para **16.94**) applies.

Unincorporated businesses

17.36   For individuals and other unincorporated businesses, the principal issue for tax purposes is whether the gain on the transfer is to be regarded as capital or income (see para **7.16**). Income will be subject to income tax (at up to 50%, although this rate is expected to reduce to 45% from 2013–14) whereas capital receipts will usually be subject to capital gains tax at up to 28%. Where the transfer is to a related company, such as on incorporation, the tax treatment may be beneficial (see para **7.23**) for the transferee company but may still give rise to a tax charge for the unincorporated transferor.

Trading in intellectual property

17.37   For businesses that actively deal in intellectual property, buying and selling rights (eg a broadcasting rights re-seller), the transfer of intellectual property will be part of the business activity and the profit on disposal will be income of the trade, profession or vocation regardless of the form of payment. The tax treatment of the transferee does not necessarily reflect in the tax treatment of the transferor.

Copyright

17.38   Payments to authors and similar creators of copyright for transfers of copyright will always be taxed as income unless it can be demonstrated to HMRC that the profession has been completely discontinued (see para **18.253**).

Patents

17.39 Payments for transfers of patents will also be taxed as income, regardless of the nature of the transaction (see para **7.33**). This can have adverse tax implications for individuals who own patents; where the patent is transferred as part of the sale of a business and its assets, the gain on the patent will still be subject to income tax and the transferor will not be able to claim entrepreneur's relief (see para **7.37**) on that gain, as that relief is only available against capital gains tax.

Tax treatment of transferee/assignee

Companies

17.40 As with licensing, for companies, the tax deductions for the costs of acquiring intellectual property will depend on the treatment of payments in the accounts (see para **11.9**). Where the cost of acquisition is amortised over the useful economic life of the licence, then the tax deductions will be similarly amortised (see para **11.25**).

Unincorporated businesses

Patents and know-how

17.41 Capital allowances will generally be available on the acquisition of patents or industrial know-how by an unincorporated business; these allowances give a tax deduction for the licensee over a period of time, rather than only on disposal or expiry of the licence (see para **5.60** and **5.104**).

Other intellectual property

17.42 Unincorporated businesses will not, generally, receive a deduction for the costs of acquiring any other form intellectual property until that intellectual property is disposed of or otherwise expires (the costs will be deductible at that point from any proceeds of disposal).

VAT on transfer or assignment of intellectual property

UK transferor

17.43 The VAT issues on transfer or assignment are broadly the same as those for licensing. transferor who is a taxable person (see para **15.19**) is required to charge UK VAT (generally at 20%) on the transfer of intellectual property where:

- the transferee is a business and belongs (see para **15.25**) in the UK; or

- the transferor belongs in the UK and the transferee is a consumer, regardless of where the consumer belongs for VAT purposes (see para **15.28**).

17.44 The exception is where the intellectual property supply is exempt for the purposes of VAT; no VAT is charged, and the transferee is likely to be limited as to the amount of VAT that they can recover on purchases related to the supply. As noted before, a supply of intellectual property is unlikely to be exempt in its own right (see para **15.11**).

EC Sales List

17.45 Transfers or assignments of intellectual property to EU VAT-registered businesses must be reported to HMRC on the quarterly EC Sales List (see para **15.33**).

UK transferee

Transfer from a UK transferor

17.46 A transferee who is a taxable person and is charged UK VAT by a transferor will usually be able to recover that VAT (by offset against output VAT charged, or by recovery from HMRC) where the intellectual property is acquired in the course of the transferee's business and the transferee does not use the intellectual property to make exempt supplies.

Transfer from a non-UK transferee

17.47 A transferee who is a taxable person who obtains intellectual property from a non-UK transferor is required to operate the reverse charge (see para **15.45**) in respect of the value of the transfer.

17.48 The transferee effectively self-charges VAT on the value of the transfer as if it were the transferor, and then takes a deduction for that VAT in calculating its liability to account to HMRC for VAT in that quarter (assuming that the intellectual property is not used to make exempt supplies).

Milestone payments and similar consideration

17.49 Where future payments to be made in respect of a transfer of intellectual property, which cannot be ascertained at the time of the transfer— such as milestone payments on achievement of specific criteria—there are various points at which VAT needs to be considered.

Initial payment

17.50 First, VAT will be charged (directly or by reverse charge) on any initial payments (including deferred, but ascertainable, payments) at the time of the transfer.

Milestone payments

17.51 Second, VAT will also be charged on later events occurring (whether milestone events, or by reference to use of the intellectual property), a separate supply is treated as taking place each a payment is made under the transfer agreement or, if earlier, a VAT invoice is issued in respect of the payment (Value Added Tax Regulations 1995, SI 1995/2518, reg 90). VAT is therefore accounted for in each VAT quarter in which such a payment for the transfer is received (or invoice issued, if different).

LITIGATION

17.52 Owning intellectual property often requires the enforcement of the monopoly rights associated with the intellectual property against infringers. Taken to an extreme, this enforcement can be a business in its own right.

17.53 If enforcement is successful, the owner of the intellectual property will generally receive compensation in respect of:

- damage caused to the value of the intellectual property by the infringement; and/or

- payment for use of the intellectual property in the past by the infringer (often calculated by reference to the additional profits earned by the infringer); and/or

- payment for future use of the intellectual property where the owner agrees to allow the infringer to continue to use the intellectual property by way of licence.

17.54 A court award will generally be clear as to what elements are covered; in settlement, it may be less clear cut, particularly in settlements where the defendant does not acknowledge liability. In such a case, the parties need to decide for themselves what the proper construction of the settlement agreement is for tax purposes. It may be necessary to obtain specialist advice (eg from intellectual property or tax specialist counsel) in order to be able to complete the self-assessment return for the trade, profession or vocation involved.

Payments for past and future use

17.55   The tax treatment of the last two of these elements of the awards (payments for past use and payments for future use) are usually treated for tax purposes as any other licensing payments in general (see para **17.6**).

17.56   Any interest added to a payment for past use is also likely to be subject to tax as income of the trade, profession or vocation for the owner, as it represents (in effect) the interest that could have been earned by the owner if the payment had been made at the time of use. Such interest would be taxable income of the trade.

Compensation for damage caused

17.57   Compensation received for a reduction in value of the intellectual property as a result of the activities of the infringer is, generally, regarded for tax purposes as a part-disposal of the intellectual property asset (see paras **6.10** and **12.53**) because what is received is a capital sum derived from an asset (the intellectual property). For companies, the tax treatment will generally depend on the accounting treatment of the compensation receipt where the intellectual property is a post-1 April 2002 asset (see para **8.33**).

17.58   From the infringer's point of view, the payment is unlikely to be deductible for tax purposes as the infringer does not obtain any asset in exchange for the payment and it is not a payment in the normal course of business (in practice, HMRC are generally reluctant to permit tax deductions for payments of compensation for unlawful activity).

Costs of undertaking litigation

17.59   The costs of undertaking litigation are generally deductible for tax purposes. Where the owner succeeds in their claim and the defendant pays some or all of their legal costs (either in settlement or as part of a court award), that payment will reduce the amount that can be deducted for tax purposes as the owner will be regarded as having incurred less expenses as a result of payment; this is regardless of whether the infringer settles the legal fees directly, or makes a payment to the owner in respect of legal fees incurred.

VAT on settlements and court awards

17.60   The VAT treatment of settlements and court awards will depend on exactly what the payment under the settlement or award is for: no distinction is, in practice, made between court awards and out-of-court settlements of intellectual property disputes (Customs & Excise Press Notice PN/82/87. This applies only to settlements after litigation has commenced, but the Tribunal has held that the same principles should apply to pre-litigation settlements: *Holiday Inns (UK) Ltd* [1993] VAT Decision 10609).

17.61   In practice, settlement agreement or court awards should clearly state that any amount(s) to be paid are exclusive of VAT and reserve the right for the supplier (generally the claimant) to charge VAT as appropriate, to ensure that there is no later dispute as to whether the settlement is inclusive or exclusive of applicable VAT.

17.62   Where the settlement or award does not mention VAT then the owner of the intellectual property is still required to account to HMRC for VAT on the consideration but the owner's ability to charge VAT to the infringer will depend on whether it is normal custom and practice in the particular business sector concerned to charge VAT where the contract is silent on the point. Where the owner cannot charge VAT then the total consideration received is treated as being VAT-inclusive (ie 120% of the VATable amount) so that the owner accounts for VAT out of the consideration actually received.

Elements of the settlement/award

17.63   Where a settlement or award encompasses more than one element, with differing tax treatments —for example, payment for damage to the value of intellectual property and a payment for future, licensed, use of that intellectual property—then an apportionment of the value of the settlement or award will be needed; if possible, the apportionment should be in the settlement or award itself.

Payment for past use of intellectual property

17.64   Where the settlement/award contains an element of payment for past use of the intellectual property, that is a taxable supply subject to UK VAT (assuming that the general requirements for VAT to be charged are met: see para **15.8**) as the payment will be regarded as consideration for that use of the intellectual property. The payment is, in effect, treated as if it had been consideration for a licence of the intellectual property.

Payment for future use of intellectual property

17.65   In the same way, where an element of the settlement/award is payment for a future use of the intellectual property, that will also be a taxable supply for VAT purposes, subject to UK VAT if appropriate (see para **15.8** and *Cooper Chasney Ltd v C & E Comrs* [1990] 3 CMLR 509).

Payment for infringement: damage to the value of intellectual property

17.66   Where an element of the award is compensation, rather than a payment for use (past or future) of the intellectual property, then the payment is outside the scope of VAT as it is not consideration for a supply of that intellectual property (Customs & Excise Press Notice PN/82/87 and *Holiday Inns (UK) Ltd* [1993] VAT Decision 10609: this case did not specifically deal with intellectual property, but the same principles apply). This applies even where the compensation is paid as consideration for the claimant agreeing to cease the litigation.

Interest

17.67   VAT is not charged on any interest element in a settlement or award in respect of intellectual property as it is not considered to have any connection with a supply and is not value received in return for a commercial transaction: it is, in effect, compensation for loss of the use of income during the period of infringement (see *B A Z Bausystem AG v Finanzamt München für Körpershaften* [1982] 3 CMLR 688).

Compromise payments without admission of liability

17.68   Where a compromise agreement is reached, and a payment is made without admission of liability by the defendant, then (depending on the exact terms of the compromise agreement) it may be that no taxable supply can be regarded as having taken place and the payment may be regarded as being outside the scope of VAT (*Reich v C & E Comrs* (1992) VAT Decision 9548). HMRC may agree to treat the payment as compensation, rather than consideration for a supply of intellectual property.

VAT and costs of litigation

17.69   Legal fees are generally subject to UK VAT unless the client is a non-UK business and receives the services for the purposes of a business carried on outside the UK; in some cases, intellectual property owners may prefer to have disputes dealt with in the UK courts, where the court has experience in such matters. Such VAT is generally input VAT of the business, recoverable to the extent that the business makes fully VATable supplies (see para **15.2**).

17.70   Where the infringer pays some or all of the legal costs of the owner, the VAT position remains unchanged as it is the owner that is the lawyer's client. Where (and to the extent that) the owner can recover the VAT paid, it is usual for the infringer to make a payment that is VAT-exclusive, as the UK VAT is not an absolute cost of the owner (see para **15.5**). Where the owner is not UK

VAT registered, or makes exempt supplies and so cannot recover the VAT, then it would be appropriate for the infringer to pay the VAT-inclusive fees.

RECONSTRUCTIONS: TRANSFER OF TRADE

17.71   Where intellectual property assets are acquired as part of the transfer of the trade of a company, the transfer of those assets will be treated as a tax-neutral transfer (as defined above) where the transfer is part of a scheme of reconstruction, or meets other specific criteria.

Scheme of reconstruction

17.72   Where intellectual property assets are transferred as part of a scheme of reconstruction (TCGA 1992, s 136) the transfer of those assets is treated as tax-neutral (CTA 2009, s 818) provided certain conditions are fulfilled:

- the assets must be chargeable assets of the transferor immediately before transfer and of the transferee immediately after transfer; and

- the scheme of reconstruction must be for bona fide commercial reasons, and not part of a scheme whose purpose—or main purpose—is the avoidance of tax. The transferee can apply (FA 2002, Sch 29, para 88) to HMRC for clearance as to these two conditions.

17.73   A scheme of reconstruction has the same definition as for capital gains purposes (CTA 2009, s 818(6)) and most often covers an arrangement whereby the business of one company is transferred to another company in exchange for the issue of shares in the new company to the shareholders of the old company; the shareholdings and shareholders in the old and new company must be substantially the same (see *Fallon (exors of Morgan deceased) v Fellows* [2001] STC 1409, where the High Court held that a partition of the company was not a scheme of reconstruction (despite notification by HMRC that it qualified) because the shareholders of the old company were divided into two, each group exchanging their shares in the old company for those of one of the new companies).

17.74   The transfer needs to be done for bona fide commercial purposes, and not be part of a scheme or arrangement whose main purpose is the avoidance of corporation tax, income tax or CGT.

17.75   There is a clearance procedure (CTA 2009, s 832) that gives some comfort that the transfer will be tax-neutral; it is basically the same procedure as that available under the existing capital gains regime. Application needs to be made to HMRC in writing, setting out the details of the scheme. HMRC must request any additional information within 30 days of receiving the application. Such information needs to be provided within 30 days (or longer, if HMRC allow). HMRC must notify the applicant of their decision within 30 days of either receiving the application or receiving the additional information requested.

Transfer of UK trade between EU companies

17.76 A transfer of a UK trade including intellectual property from one EU company to another will be treated as tax-neutral in respect of the intellectual property assets where the trade is transferred in exchange for shares (CTA 2009, s 820); similar conditions to those for a scheme of reconstruction (above) apply, and clearance can be obtained from HMRC on application by the transferor and transferee.

Transfer of UK trade on EU merger

17.77 A transfer of a UK trade including intellectual property assets which occurs when two EU companies merge to form a Societas Europea (SE) can be treated as tax-neutral in respect of the intellectual property assets (CTA 2009, s 822); similar conditions to those for a scheme of reconstruction (above) apply, and clearance can be obtained from HMRC on application by the transferor and transferee.

Transfer to non-resident company

17.78 Where a UK company transfers a non-UK trade, including intellectual property assets, to a non-UK company, the gain on the assets may be deferred if certain conditions are fulfilled (CTA 2009, s 827):

- the trade must be exchanged for shares (or shares and loan stock) issued by the transferee to the transferor, representing at least 25% of the ordinary share capital of the transferee (either alone, or together with shares in the transferee already owned by the transferor); and

- where the proceeds of realisation of an intellectual property asset transferred as part of the trade are more than the cost of that asset for tax purposes, the proceeds of realisation for tax purposes are reduced by:

  — the excess over the cost, where the consideration consists entirely of shares or shares and loan stock; or

  — the appropriate proportion of the excess over the cost, where the consideration is not entirely shares or shares and loan stock.

Example 17.2

PatentCo transfers its French trade, including a French patent originally acquired for £70,000, to a French purchaser. The proceeds of realisation attributed to the patent are £100,000, and the consideration for the transfer is satisfied entirely in shares.

The proceeds of realisation (£100,000) are reduced for tax purposes by £30,000 (£100,000 – £70,000), so that the gain is deferred. As the proceeds of realisation are reduced to the original cost of the patent, no taxable gain arises.

17.79   The 'appropriate proportion' is the proportion of the consideration that is represented by the shares (or shares and loan stock).

Example 17.3

If, in Example 17.2, the consideration for the transfer was satisfied 50% in shares and 50% in cash, then the proceeds of realisation would be reduced for tax purposes by £15,000 (50% of (£100,000 – £70,000)), so that the half of the gain is deferred; the remaining half of the gain would be brought into account as a credit for tax purposes.

17.80   If the transferor later realises disposes of the shares (or shares and loan stock), a credit equal to the relief needs to be brought into account for tax purposes; if only a proportion of the shares or loan stock is disposed of, an appropriate portion of the relief must be brought into account (CTA 2009, s 829).

17.81   If, within six years of the transfer of the trade, the transferee realises any of the intellectual property assets transferred, the transferor must bring into account the deferred proceeds (or an appropriate proportion, where not all the assets are realised) for tax purposes.

17.82   As above, the transfer of the trade must be for bona fide commercial purposes and not for the avoidance of tax; clearance can be obtained from HMRC on application.

MERGERS AND ACQUISITIONS

17.83   Mergers and acquisitions are, in general, share-based transactions in which a target company is acquired. As such, there is little direct impact in terms of intellectual property: any intellectual property of the target continues to be owned by the target immediately after the transaction, and so there is no change in (for example) amortisation deductions (see para **11.25**) for the intellectual property held by the target purely as a result of the change in ownership of the target.

17.84 In particular, the change in ownership does *not* bring pre-1 April 2002 intellectual property owned by the target company into the corporate intangibles tax regime, as there is no change in ownership of the intellectual property.

There are a few matters which can arise in mergers and acquisitions of companies that should be considered, however.

Roll-over relief

17.85 On acquisition of the shares of a target company, the purchasing company may be able to treat the intellectual property of the target as acquired intellectual property to roll-over the gain on intellectual property which has been disposed of (see para **14.32**). An election for this treatment is required by both the target and the acquiring company, as the target company will see the tax cost of its intellectual property (and so any amortisation deductions) diminished by as a result of the roll-over claim.

Degrouping charges

17.86 Where the target is acquired from a group, due diligence is required by the acquirer to determine whether any intellectual property has been acquired by the target from another group company in the preceding six years. If it has, there is the possibility that a degrouping charge (see para **18.172**) may arise on the acquisition. This should either be taken into account in determining the price for the acquisition or, where feasible, the target's former group should be asked to absorb the charge within the group (see para **18.190**).

Acquisition of a business and its assets (ie not company shares)

17.87 Where the acquisition is of a business and its assets, that *is* a change of ownership of the intellectual property assets for tax purposes. The acquiring company will usually be able to amortise the cost of acquiring the intellectual property over its remaining useful economic life (see para **11.25**) and so the acquisition documentation should attribute some value (as appropriate) to the intellectual property assets specifically (see also para **17.34** on transfers/ assignments of intellectual property and Chapter 11 on acquisitions of intellectual property.)

Acquisitions from connected parties

17.88 Where the business and assets are transferred from a connected party, note that the change of ownership does not necessarily mean that the assets will be post-1 April 2002 assets of the acquirer: the assets will only be post-1 April 2002 assets for the acquirer where they were acquired from an unconnected party or created on or after 1 April 2002 (see para **8.33**).

17.89   Where the business and assets are transferred from another connected company, or similar third party, transfer pricing rules may apply (see para **16.94**).

17.90   Note that, where the business and assets are acquired from a connected individual (eg on incorporation of a sole trader's business, see para **7.23**) then the intellectual property is treated as having been acquired at market value (see para **18.66**) and amortisation deductions (see para **11.25**) will be based on this amount where the assets are post-1 April 2002 assets.

SOFTWARE

17.91   Almost all businesses will now use computer software; businesses with a particular emphasis on intellectual property creation may use software more than most. Ordinarily, the costs of a computer services department will be deductible as revenue expenditure.

17.92   The rules in respect of tax recognition and deductions for software will normally follow the same rules as for other intellectual property, but there are some specific rules that may apply to software creation or acquisition in certain cases.

Developing software

Companies

17.93   The development costs of software will generally follow the same rules as to deductibility of expenditure as expenditure on creation of other types of intellectual property (see Chapter 3, Chapter 9 and Chapter 10).

Unincorporated businesses

17.94   Where a business develops its own software, whether the expenditure (such as the salaries and associated costs of the staff who developed the software) is revenue or capital will largely depend on the economic function of the software within the business (see para **3.26**).

17.95   Where the expenditure is on improvements to an existing system, a distinction needs to be drawn between expenditure on the piecemeal improvement of an existing system—which will be revenue, rather than capital—and expenditure on significant improvements, which may be capital.

17.96 In deciding whether in-house software development is revenue or capital, HMRC will take into account (HMRC Manual BIM35820 onwards):

- the business function or effect of the software or improvement, rather than the nature of the software/improvement itself (for example, expenditure on software that keeps track of the progress of a development project may be more likely to be revenue expenditure than that spent on software that is the project under development);

- the scope, power and longevity of the software as a business tool;

- a short-term software project can have a significant impact on the business, but in general, expenditure on creating any software that has an expected life of less than two years will be treated as revenue expenditure;

- the centrality of the software to the functions of the business (for example, expenditure on creating software that handles a peripheral function— tracking costs, for example—is more likely to be revenue expenditure); and

- the costs of the project, both to develop and implement. The greater the cost, the more likely it is that the expenditure will be capital.

Other factors will also be taken into consideration; for example, where new hardware is necessary to develop and run the software, expenditure on the project is more likely to be considered capital.

17.97 The accounting treatment will also be considered: if the expenditure has been capitalised under SSAP13, it is less likely that HMRC will agree that it can be added back to the profit/loss in the accounts and deducted as revenue expenditure (HMRC Manual BIM35822).

17.98 In general, expenditure will be deductible as revenue where the software development project is not one that significantly impacts the business (either alone or as part of a larger series of projects) (HMRC Manual BIM35830).

17.99 Expenditure may also be deductible as revenue even where the software development project as a whole is considered to be capital: see the section on capital allowances below.

Acquiring software

Companies: electing for capital allowances

17.100 As with creating software, the tax deduction for the costs of acquiring software will depend on the accounting rules, in general (see paras **11.9** and **11.5**).

17.101 However, in the case of software, companies can elect to opt out of the corporate intangibles tax rules in respect of computer software acquisitions (CTA 2009, s 815); the effect of the election is to preserve the capital allowances rules on that expenditure, which can be advantageous, particularly to companies which can use the annual investment allowance for that expenditure (see para **3.75**).

17.102 The election is available where the company has incurred capital expenditure on software that qualifies as a fixed asset of the company. Where the software does not qualify as a fixed asset under FRS10, the cost will be written off as incurred and no election is available (or necessary, since a full deduction for the cost will have generally been given in the profit and loss account).

17.103 The effect of the election is to exclude the sections of CTA 2009, Part 8 that would otherwise block the application of the capital allowances legislation. Certain provisions may still apply if credits have been taken into account for tax purposes before the election is made.

17.104 The election must be made in writing to HMRC within two years of the end of the accounting period in which the expenditure was incurred, and is irrevocable.

Unincorporated businesses

Capital or revenue expense

17.105 Expenditure on acquiring computer software (either licensed or acquired outright) to be used in a business is generally regarded as capital expenditure on plant, qualifying for normal capital allowances rather than a deduction in calculating taxable profits (see para **5.9**); this is particularly likely to be the case where the software is acquired as part of a package with hardware (and see para **17.119**).

17.106 Certain purchases are treated as payments of revenue expenditure regardless of whether the payment is made in a lump sum or as recurring payments, and the expenditure will be deductible as a trading expense in calculating profits for tax purposes when paid by a business, particularly software that is not expected to have a useful life of more than two years. The fact that upgrades to the software are expected to be available within two years of purchase does not automatically mean that the useful life expectancy is less than two years (HMRC Manual BIM35815).

17.107 Recurring payments for software will normally indicate that these are revenue expenditure (HMRC Manual BIM35815) although the acquisition agreement will still be of relevance; recurring payments are most likely to be revenue expenditure if they are equivalent to rental payments for the software. If the recurring payments are instead considered to be instalments of a lump sum payment, they may be deemed to be capital payments.

17.108   Revenue expenditure on software is deductible in accordance with accounting practice which normally requires the payments to be spread across the useful life of the software in accordance with the accruals concept in SSAP2 (*Gallagher v Jones* (1993) 66 TC 77).

17.109   For companies, the accounting treatment will generally set the tax treatment (see para **11.9**). For unincorporated business, a lump sum payment for a licence or to acquire software outright will generally be capital expenditure if the licence is such that it will have a sufficiently enduring benefit in the business (see para **5.6** for more details on what constitutes such a benefit). The terms of the agreement, the effect on the business of the acquirer and the life expectancy of the software will generally determine the treatment. In particular, HMRC will consider:

- the business function or effect of the software, rather than the nature of the software itself;

- the scope, power and longevity of the software as a business tool;

- the centrality of the software to the functions of the business; and

- the costs of the project, both to acquire and implement. The greater the cost, the more likely it is that the expenditure will be capital.

17.110   Software that is purchased outright (rather than used under a non-exclusive licence) is specifically stated (CAA 2001, s 71) to be plant for the purposes of giving allowances for capital expenditure on it.

17.111   Capital allowances are also available for expenditure on software that is not acquired outright where 'a right to use or otherwise deal with' computer software for the purposes of a trade is acquired, provided that the expenditure is not deductible as a revenue expense (CAA 2001, s 71). These capital allowances are available on qualifying expenditure even where no physical asset is acquired: for example, where software is acquired by download over the internet.

Annual investment allowance

17.112   Purchased software qualifying for capital allowances will, in the first instance, qualify for the annual investment allowance. The first £25,000 of expenditure on plant and machinery in an accounting period will qualify for this allowance (CAA 2001, s 51A ff, inserted by FA 2008, Sch 24) which provides an immediate full write-off of that first £25,000 against profits for tax purposes.

Example 17.4

Alfred purchases software, qualifying for capital allowances, for £15,000. If Alfred makes no other plant and machinery acquisitions in the same accounting period, then the entire acquisition cost will be covered by the annual investment allowance and Alfred will be able to deduct the full acquisition cost of £15,000 from profits when calculating taxable profits for that period.

If the software had cost £50,000, then only the first £25,000 qualifies for the annual investment allowance deduction. The balance of £25,000 would be carried forward in the plant and machinery pool, and capital allowances of 18% per annum on the brought forward unrelieved expenditure would be available.

Short life asset elections

17.113 Where the annual investment allowance has been used on other acquisitions, and the software acquired is expected to have a relatively short useful life (the short life period: a maximum eight years for purchases made on/after 6 April 2012) an election can be made for it to be treated as a short life asset (CAA 2001, s 83) so that the cost of the software can be written off over its useful life. Remember that where the life expectancy is less than two years, the expenditure will be treated as revenue and can be written off as an expense immediately.

17.114 Where a short life asset election is made, the software is not included in the general pool for capital allowances but is, instead, put into a separate pool of its own. The deduction for each period is 20% (20% before April 2012) on a reducing balance basis but, if the software is sold or scrapped within the short-life period following the end of the accounting period, a balancing adjustment is given so that the cost is written off.

Example 17.5

Leo purchases software for £50,000. Leo chooses to use its annual investment allowance on other assets which cannot be the subject of a short life asset election, and so makes an election in respect of the software acquisition costs.

The software is subject to plant and machinery allowances in its own pool, rather than the main pool, and is sold in the third year after acquisitions.

In the first year, Leo can claim capital allowances of £9,000 (18% of £50,000). The unrelieved expenditure carried forwards is £41,000.

In the second year, Leo can claim capital allowances of £7,380 (18% of £41,000). The unrelieved expenditure carried forwards is £33,620.

In the third year, Leo sells the software for £20,000. The balancing allowance in respect of the software is £13,620 (£33,620 unrelieved expenditure less £20,000 disposal proceeds), which is deductible as an expense in calculating Leo's taxable profits for this accounting period.

17.115 If the software had remained in the general pool for capital allowances, no balancing adjustment would have been available and the cost of the software would have been spread over a much longer period than its useful life—around 20 years.

Example 17.6

In Example 17.5, if Leo had not made the election, the software costs would have been added to the general plant and machinery pool. On disposal of the software, the disposal proceeds would have been brought into the pool but would be unlikely to be more than the unrelieved expenditure in the entire general pool and so no balancing allowance would be available. Leo would continue to deduct declining amounts of capital allowances in respect of the software for more than 20 years after disposal of the software.

17.116 If, after making an election, the software is neither sold nor scrapped within the short life period, it is taken back into the general pool for capital allowances purposes at the end of the short life period. There is no balancing allowance or charge on the transfer to the general pool and so it is good practice for a business to make an election on any qualifying asset that may have only a short useful life for the business. There is no risk to the company of a balancing charge on transfer to the general pool if the asset is not sold but, if the asset is sold at less than the unrelieved expenditure in the software pool within a short time, the company gets the benefit of a balancing allowance much earlier than would have been available though the general pool.

Example 17.7

If, in Example 17.5, Leo had not disposed of the software in the third year, Leo would claim capital allowances on the special software pool in the third year. At the end of the fourth year, if the software was still not disposed of, the unrelieved expenditure on the software would be transferred to the general pool. There is no additional cost to Leo of making the election but, if the software had been sold in time, Leo would have benefited from the allowance shown in Example 17.5.

17.117 The election must be made on or before the normal time limit for amending a tax return for the period in which the expenditure is incurred, for income tax purposes, and no later than two years after the end of the accounting period in which the expenditure is incurred for corporation tax purposes.

17.118 Where the expenditure is incurred in instalments, the cut-off date for making the election is calculated by reference to the first period in which a payment is made.

Software acquired with related hardware

17.119 Where expenditure on software is treated for accounting purposes as part of related computer hardware, the profits (other than royalties) and losses relating to that software are excluded from the intangible fixed assets regime. FRS10 defines expenditure on such software as 'software development costs that are directly attributable to bringing a computer system or other computer operated machinery into working condition for its intended use within the business' (CTA 2009, s 813; ¶2 FRS10).

WEBSITES

Website development costs

17.120 Websites are principally copyright assets (with copyright in the content and in the software), created by many businesses, and the accounting treatment of the costs of development are not always straightforward to identify.

17.121 The accounting treatment of website development costs is covered into two interpretations of the accounting standards: UITF 29 (for UK GAAP) and SIC 32 (for IAS).

17.122 Both interpretations test whether expenditure will create 'an enduring asset' that will give rise to future economic benefits that, in total, would exceed in value the cost of developing the website. Both conclude that 'this would be the case only if the website was capable of generating revenues directly, for example by enabling orders to be placed' (UITF 29, ¶6; SIC 32 ¶(a) makes a similar point).

17.123 If the website can generate such revenue then at least some of the expenditure on the website will be capitalised as creating an enduring asset, with deductions taken over the useful economic life through amortisation, rather than written off as an expense as incurred.

17.124 If the company cannot demonstrate how a website developed solely or primarily for promoting and advertising its own products and services will generate probable future economic benefits, the expenditure on developing such

369

a website should be recognised as an expense when incurred. In effect, such a website is a form of advertising. Under accounting standards, advertising and marketing costs will be written off as an expense through the profit and loss account when they are incurred as it is not possible to associate the expenditure with an identifiable future benefit.

Tangible or intangible

17.125 Where the website will be an enduring asset, the two interpretations take slightly different routes as to how to categorise that asset. SIC 32 considers that a website is capable of being an intangible fixed asset (within IAS 38), whereas UITF 29 takes the view that websites should be treated as software development cost that should be treated as part of the cost of the related hardware and so should be considered tangible fixed assets (within FRS10, ¶2). The UITF approach rather overlooks the fact that many businesses will not own the hardware on which the website is hosted: in this case, where there is no associated hardware owned the company, it would seem more appropriate to treat the website as an intangible fixed asset, in line with the SIC 32 interpretation for international accounting standards.

Planning costs

17.126 These include the costs of undertaking feasibility studies, determining the objectives and functionalities of the website, exploring ways of achieving the desired functionalities, identifying appropriate hardware and web applications and selecting suppliers and consultants.

17.127 The planning costs do not directly generate future economic benefits for the company and so should be written off as they are incurred.

Application and infrastructure development costs

17.128 These include the costs of obtaining and registering a domain name, and developing hardware and operating software that relate to the functionality of the site (for example, updateable content management systems and e-commerce systems, including encryption software, and interfaces with other IT systems used by the entity).

17.129 Where the website generates revenue, and so has an enduring benefit to the company, these costs will generally be capitalised and so the deduction for the expenditure will be given through amortisation, over the useful economic life of the website; this should be a relatively short period, as websites continued to be substantially redeveloped on a regular basis, as web technology improves.

17.130 Some of these costs may, however, qualify as research and development costs under SSAP13 or IAS 38: where this is the case, the costs will be excluded from the corporate intangibles tax regime (CTA 2009, s 814; see above) and will, instead, generally be deductible as an expense of the company (CTA 2009, s 87), provided that they are not capital expenditure. These costs may also qualify for research and development tax reliefs (see Chapter 10). Capital expenditure on qualifying research and development should be eligible for the research and development capital allowance (see Chapter 4).

Design costs

17.131 This is expenditure to develop the design and appearance of individual website pages, including the creation of graphics.

17.132 Design costs will also generally be capitalised where the website is recognised as an asset, as part of the cost of the asset. As such, the deduction for this expenditure will be given through amortisation, over the useful economic life of the website as above.

Content costs

17.133 This is expenditure incurred on preparing, accumulating and posting the website content; the accounting treatment will depend on the nature of the content: most content is effectively advertising and promoting the company's products and services and will be an expense, written off as it is incurred. If, on the other hand, the content is a core part of the revenue-generating activities of the website then it will be capitalised and written off over the useful economic life of the website, through amortisation.

Maintenance and operational costs

17.134 Once the website has been developed, ongoing maintenance costs will be written off as an expense of the company as they are incurred (under FRS 15). The maintenance costs should be distinguished from redevelopment costs, which may be treated as expenditure on a new website where the redevelopment is substantial.

Chapter 18

Structures and businesses

Summary: This chapter considers the tax issues relating to:

- typical structures used by businesses, and
- particular types of intellectual property businesses.

In general, the following provides an overview of the tax issues, with references to the appropriate sections of the detailed tax chapters. Where, however, there are tax issues specific to the structure or the type of business, these are considered in more detail in the text of this chapter.

- Structures

  Joint ventures (para **18.1**)

  Cost-sharing arrangements (para **18.24**)

  Transactions between connected/related parties (para **18.66**)

  IP holding companies (para **18.81**)

  Group companies (para **18.137**)

- Intellectual property businesses

  Creative professionals (para **18.231**)

  Hobbyist inventors (para **18.292**)

  Performers (para **18.299**)

  Film production companies (para **18.337**)

  Research companies (para **18.408**)

- Businesses using intellectual property

  Franchises (para **18.417**)

  Manufacturing and services companies (para **18.444**)

  Trading in intellectual property (para **18.448**)

  Intellectual property investment (para **18.449**)

JOINT VENTURES

18.1 The term 'joint venture' is not specifically defined in English law: it denotes simply a structure whereby two entities work together to a specific aim. For example, a joint venture may cross-market intellectual property such as trademarks and copyright protected material, either as an aim in itself, or as part of a wider project. The 'oneworld' alliance set up by various airlines (including British Airways) is a form of joint venture, cross-marketing the brands of the airlines but also reducing costs through bulk buying, sharing best practice and similar activities. This joint venture is managed by the oneworld Management Company, but the overall structure itself is contractual (not least because the airline industry is heavily regulated).

18.2 A joint venture may be established through the parties setting up a specific entity to carry on the intended joint activities, or it may simply be a contractual arrangement (see, for example para **18.24** for details of cost-sharing arrangements, which can be a very specific and limited form of joint venture). The following considers joint ventures as a structure through which two entities are working together to exploit intellectual property jointly; this may also involve developing the intellectual property but is not limited to that.

18.3 There are substantial corporate and intellectual property law issues that will flow into the choice of structure for a joint venture; the following considers the tax issues that may arise, particularly with regard to the intellectual property involved.

Contractual joint ventures

18.4 The tax issues relating to contractual joint ventures will be similar to those arising in a cost-sharing arrangement: para **18.24** has details of the tax treatment of expenditure and receipts in such arrangements, and these will accordingly also apply generally to contractual joint ventures.

18.5 The principal difference will be in the exploitation of the intellectual property: in a cost-sharing arrangement, each party is exploiting the intellectual property on their own account once it has been developed, and the arrangement effectively ends once the development is complete. Joint ventures are usually longer-term and more open ended.

18.6 In practice, contractual joint ventures are more likely to involve cross-marketing and sharing of intellectual property such as know-how, together with other joint activities designed to reduce costs. This type of joint venture is not intended to produce receipts specifically derived from the joint venture activity but, instead, is intended to enhance and develop each participant's own business and assets through the costs reductions, improved processes and greater marketing exposure. The financial rewards of the joint venture come from this enhancement; as such, the resulting receipts are the income of the trade (and taxed accordingly).

18.7   The joint venture contractual arrangements may require payment between the parties, if there is an imbalance (for example, where one party provides training to the staff of others: if this is not matched by other services between the parties, it may be appropriate for the training provider to be compensated) then there will be taxable income for the recipient. Again, this will be treated as income of the trade and taxed accordingly.

18.8   A contractual joint venture is less likely to be suitable for projects which are intended to create and deliver products or services jointly. This would require customers to contract with both parties together: this is not impossible, but is more complex than dealing with a single joint venture entity (see below) and carries a number of risks, particularly that of creating a partnership (see below). Where no partnership is created then, as each party enters into the contracts on their own account, receipts arising will belong to the participants in their own right and will be treated as income of the trade.

UK partnership

18.9   There is a risk that the participants will be treated as carrying on a trade in partnership, particularly in jurisdiction such as the UK where a partnership may be created without formalities where two or more persons carry on business together with a view to profit (Partnership Act 1890, s 1). This may have unwelcome consequences, both in terms of compliance risk and particularly for non-resident partners. The partnership is required to file a tax return, even though the partnership itself is not subject to tax; instead, the partners are taxed on their share of the profits.

18.10   Where a partnership arises by operation of law, the terms of the partnership are set by law and may not be quite what the parties had intended. The following is an outline of the UK partnership tax issues that should be considered (further details of partnership law, and fuller details of the partnership tax rules, are outside the scope of this book).

18.11   Non-UK partners in a UK partnership will be taxed in the UK on their share of the partnership income arising in the UK (ITTOIA 2005, s 849 (for individuals); CTA 2009, s 1259 (for companies)); a tax treaty is unlikely to be helpful (although it may reduce double taxation in the home jurisdiction) as the non-UK partner will be treated as carrying on a trade in the UK through the partnership's activities here.

18.12   UK partnerships are treated as transparent for UK tax purposes: the income and expenditure of the partnership is attributed to the partners in their relevant profit share (fixed by law where there is no formal agreement). To the extent that this income and expenditure relates to intellectual property, the provisions in Chapters 3–14 will apply to the participants directly to determine how the income is taxed and any associated expenditure relieved. For example, research and development relief may be restricted (it is only available to companies, and the intended result of the research and development must be relevant to the trade of the company).

18.13   Where a partner contributes assets to a partnership—including intellectual property assets—they are treated as disposing of part of the asset (as the other partners are deemed to acquire a share in the asset); this may have unintended tax consequences where the partnership has not been formally set up and such costs anticipated (see paras **6.10** and **12.53** for details of the tax consequences of part-disposal of intellectual property assets).

Entity joint ventures

18.14   Where the joint venture is intended to be a business venture producing goods or services for sale to third parties, rather than enhancing the existing businesses of the participants, then it would be more usual for the joint venture to be set up as a separate entity, in which the participants are the owners.

18.15   It is this entity which carries on the joint venture business; the entity may be a partnership (ordinary or limited: see above for a brief description of the tax consequences of being a member of a UK partnership. A limited liability partnership is treated as tax transparent for UK tax purposes where it is carried on with a view to profit), or a company.

Intellectual property tax issues

18.16   Where the joint venture entity is a company, then it is the company that will be earn the income and incur expenditure: the provisions of Chapters 3–14 will apply to the extent that such income and expenditure relates to intellectual property (the relevant chapters depending on whether the intellectual property is pre- or post-1 April 2002 intellectual property).

18.17   Contributions of assets, including intellectual property assets and exclusive licences to intellectual property assets, to the joint venture company by the participants will be treated as a disposal of each asset by the relevant participant. Where the asset is intellectual property, see Chapter 7 (pre-1 April 2002 intellectual property) or Chapter 14 (post-1 April 2002 intellectual property) for details of the tax treatment although note that the participant (as a shareholder) and the joint venture company will usually be regarded as related (see para **18.69**) and so the contribution will take place at market value for tax purposes, regardless of the actual consideration paid, if any. A participant company may be able to reinvest the gain on an intellectual property contribution into acquisition of other intellectual property assets (see para **14.32**), but will not be able to reinvest the gain into any shares acquired in exchange for the contribution (as there is no roll-over relief between acquisitions and disposals of intellectual property assets and shares). The transaction is unlikely to be an intra-group tax-neutral transfer from a participant company unless the joint venture has an unusual share structure; most joint venture companies do not qualify as a subsidiary for group tax relief purposes (see para **18.141**).

18.18   Where the participant is an individual, there is more scope for relief: holdover relief may be available, although this will require the co-operation of the other joint venture participants, as a claim for relief must be made jointly by the participant and the joint venture company. Holdover relief effectively defers and transfers the capital gain: it becomes chargeable when the company eventually disposes of the intellectual property asset, and it is the company which is taxable on the gain (TCGA 1992, s 165).

18.19   Roll-over relief for capital gains of an individual is unlikely to be available, even if there are suitable acquisitions and even though the relief is available for disposals of goodwill and certain type of intellectual property asset (unregistered trademarks etc) will be regarded as part of the goodwill. In practice, HMRC take the view that such intellectual property is inseparable from the overall goodwill of the individual's business (HMRC Manual CG68210) and will challenge any attempt to claim roll-over relief on the transfer of intellectual property alone: the individual would need to transfer the entire business to the joint venture in order to be able to claim such relief (see para **7.23** for more details on incorporation tax issues).

Other tax issues

18.20   The following is a very brief outline of the UK tax issues relating to share ownership: further details are outside the scope of this book, as the focus is on taxation of intellectual property.

18.21   The participants will be shareholders in the joint venture and, as such, will usually participate through dividend receipts and growth in value of the share capital. A UK corporate participant should be able to receive both dividends and realised capital gains on the shares without tax, provided that the joint venture is structured to ensure these: the UK exempts most dividends from tax when received by a UK company and similarly exempts capital gains on the sale of most shareholdings by UK companies through the substantial shareholdings exemption.

18.22   A UK individual participant in a joint venture company is not so fortunate. UK individuals are taxed on the receipt of dividends, although a tax credit applied to the dividends will reduce the tax payable (to nil, where the participant is not a higher-rate taxpayer, although that is likely to be of little practical help if the joint venture is successful). UK individuals are also subject to capital gains on the sale of shares although, where the company qualifies, entrepreneur's relief may be available to reduce the rate from 28% to 10% on some or all of the gain.

Transfer pricing

18.23   Regardless of the form of the joint venture, transfer pricing may need to be considered if the participants are sufficiently connected with each other and/or with the joint venture entity (see para **16.94** for more details of the connected required). Where transfer pricing does need to be considered, the transactions between the affected parties must be treated, for tax purposes, as taking place at arm's length.

STRUCTURES: COST-SHARING ARRANGEMENTS

18.24   The following is a general overview of contractual cost-sharing arrangements and the principal UK tax issues to be considered when contemplating entering into such an arrangement.

What is a cost-sharing arrangement?

18.25   A cost-sharing arrangement is 'a framework agreed amongst business enterprises to share the costs and risks of developing, producing or obtaining [intellectual property] assets … and to determine the nature and extent of the interests of each participant in those assets … [a cost-sharing arrangement] is a contractual arrangement rather than necessarily distinct juridical entity or permanent establishment of all the participants' (OECD Transfer Pricing Guidelines, para 8.3, where such arrangements are described as 'cost contribution arrangements').

18.26   This definition comes from the OECD Transfer Pricing Guidelines, as a cost-sharing arrangement will generally raise transfer pricing issues where the arrangement is agreed between group companies, or entities which are in some way associated (see para **16.94** for more details on associated entities for transfer pricing purposes).

18.27   Cost-sharing arrangements can apply to other areas of business (such as cost-sharing arrangements in respect of administration, or outsourced services); these are outside the scope of this book.

What is not a cost-sharing arrangement?

18.28   A cost-sharing arrangement must be distinguished from various apparently similar structures, including sub-contracted research and development. A cost-sharing arrangement involves joint development *and ownership/use* of intellectual property. An arrangement to sub-contract research and development is generally a provision of services by a research and development company to the principal (see para **18.408** for more information on research companies). Only the principal will be entitled to the ownership, risks and rewards associated with the resulting intellectual property. The research and development company is compensated for its services only and does not have any share in the developed intellectual property.

18.29   A cost-sharing arrangement is also not the same as most joint venture agreements (see para **18.1**), although it could be considered as a limited joint venture; arrangements under a joint venture agreement are, usually, much wider than those under a cost-sharing arrangement. A cost-sharing arrangement is usually for the joint development of specific intellectual property (and so, in that sense, is a limited joint venture) but not for joint exploitation of the intellectual property later.

18.30   Finally, a cost-sharing arrangement should be distinguished from an advance sale or licence of the developed intellectual property asset. An advance sale or licence arrangement usually requires one party to develop and own the intellectual property, but obliges that party to grant a licence over some or all of the rights in the intellectual property asset once the project is complete. This is not joint development of the intellectual property asset, even where the future licensee makes an advance payment to the developer which is used by the developer to fund part of the research and development, as the advance payment is not specifically a contribution to the research and development: instead, it is usually treated as an advance royalty for the anticipated intellectual property.

Cost-sharing: intellectual property assets involved

18.31   A cost-sharing agreement will usually make reference to two or three different categories of intellectual property.

Foreground intellectual property

18.32   This is the intellectual property which is expected to result from the arrangement, and will be shared by the participants in the arrangement either through joint ownership or by royalty-free licence from the owner of the developed intellectual property. Each participant has an undivided share in the resulting intellectual property so that it effectively can exploit all the rights in that intellectual property (albeit usually limited to exploitation in a particular jurisdiction) even though it has only contributed a proportion of the development costs.

18.33　An outright sale of the intellectual property would, however, usually require the consent of all the participants and the proceeds of sale would be shared between the participants. The division of the proceeds would depend upon the contractual arrangements and, in the case of associated participants, transfer pricing principles.

Background intellectual property

18.34　This is existing intellectual property, belonging to a participant, which is used in the research and development work on the foreground intellectual property, or is to which the participants all require access to enable the foreground intellectual property to be viable. The background intellectual property is licensed by the owner participants to the others; the other participants will generally need to pay for access to that background intellectual property, to reflect its value to the arrangements.

Example 18.1

A Ltd and B Ltd, who are unconnected, enter into a cost-sharing agreement to develop a particular pharmaceutical drug and share in the resulting intellectual property. For the drug to be effective, it must be taken in the form of a particular capsule package. The material of the required capsule package is background intellectual property belonging to A Ltd. B Ltd will have to pay for access to A Ltd's background intellectual property in order to be able to exploit the foreground intellectual property in the drug that results from the cost sharing arrangements.

18.35　Where the other participants do not have background intellectual property of equivalent value to contribute to the project, the licence for the background intellectual property will (usually) be drafted so that the owner of the background intellectual property receives some consideration for the licence from the other participants.

18.36　This may be in the form of a royalty paid to the owner of the background intellectual property (in which the royalty receipts are treated as any other licence receipts: see Chapter 6 and Chapter 12), paid throughout the course of the arrangements. Alternatively, the consideration is in the form of a royalty paid once the resulting foreground intellectual property is exploited. Finally, the contribution of the background intellectual property may be recognised through a reduction in the owner's contribution to the cost-sharing arrangements.

18.37 The licence will not generally be treated as a part-realisation of the background intellectual property as the licensor will usually not be excluded from using the background intellectual property.

Sideground intellectual property

18.38 Some contracts may also refer to 'sideground intellectual property'. This is usually defined as intellectual property developed independently by the participants during the course of the cost-sharing agreement, but outside the scope of the agreement. Such intellectual property is referred to in the cost-sharing arrangement contracts to ensure that there is no argument later as to whether the intellectual property should be shared: it is generally agreed that such intellectual property belongs to the party which created it and is not covered by the arrangements to share ownership of the foreground intellectual property resulting from the cost-sharing arrangements.

Developing qualifying intellectual property assets

18.39 As the intention is that new intellectual property will be developed as a result of the cost-sharing arrangements, the intellectual property developed should be qualifying intellectual property for the purposes of the corporate intangibles tax rules for UK taxpayer companies, provided that one of the exclusions from the corporate intangibles tax rules does not apply (eg where the participant is a dual-resident investment company: see para **8.29** onwards for more details of the exclusions).

Tax issues: connected participants

18.40 Cost-sharing agreements are most common between associated entities, for example, group companies working together to produce intellectual property which they will own jointly but exploit separately. In particular, cost-sharing arrangements often take place between group companies in different jurisdictions to ensure that the resulting intellectual property is owned jointly and so can be exploited independently by each company involved in the arrangements. Such arrangements can be useful in minimising—or at least containing—tax concerns, particularly:

- the impact of transfer pricing provisions (see para **16.94** for more details on transfer pricing and the association or connection required for the provisions to apply); and

- withholding taxes between the group companies, as each company owns an undivided share in the intellectual property and so does not need to pay royalties to another group company which may attract withholding tax (see para **16.56** for more information on withholding taxes).

18.41 Cost-sharing arrangements are not necessarily a once-and-for-all solution to these concerns: for example, where a group expands to a new territory after intellectual property has been developed in a cost-sharing arrangement, the subsidiary will not have a share in the intellectual property. The group will need to consider how it deals with the exploitation of the intellectual property in the new jurisdiction: the tax authorities in each of the jurisdictions where the intellectual property is owned will usually expect to see some benefit accruing to the group company in that jurisdiction, unless the contractual arrangements were drafted to exclude that possibility.

Transfer pricing of cost-sharing arrangements

18.42 Cost-sharing arrangements are useful from a transfer pricing perspective because, as each company involved in the arrangements usually owns an undivided share in the resulting intellectual property, the intellectual property asset developed can be used by each company without them having to make further payments to other group companies. The impact of transfer pricing is, in effect, corralled to the cost-sharing arrangements. This is particularly useful where the tax authorities in the relevant jurisdictions do not agree on the transfer pricing adjustments for payments in respect of intellectual property; either because they do not agree on the value of the intellectual property, or they do not recognise the intellectual property as existing (for example, the Chinese tax authorities have historically been disinclined to allow tax deductions for payments to a foreign company for the right to use unregisterable intellectual property).

18.43 The use of cost-sharing arrangements means that transfer pricing issues between the participants are largely confined to the question of whether the elements of the cost-sharing arrangement itself are dealt with on an arm's length basis: these costs can be considerably lower than the costs of licensing fully developed proven intellectual property. The costs involved in cost-sharing arrangements may also largely be the types of costs for which comparables can be readily established, making it (relatively speaking) easier to come to an agreement with the tax authorities on the appropriate transfer price. In contrast, establishing an appropriate royalty rate for the licence of intellectual property by one group company to another can be very difficult.

18.44 The arm's length principle that applies for transfer pricing purposes means that, where the participants in a cost-sharing arrangement are connected, the value of each participant's contribution to the arrangements should be consistent with the contribution that an independent third party would make (see para **16.94** for more details). As a result, it is necessary not just to consider the transfer pricing treatment of the discrete elements of expenditure incurred in the arrangements but also whether, overall, the contribution reflects the benefits expected from the resulting intellectual property.

Which costs?

18.45 The various elements of the contribution also need to be considered to determine where to draw the boundary between expenditure which is included in the arrangements and which is excluded from the arrangements. Some proportion of overhead costs may be expected to be included (eg payroll costs related to research and development staff). Certain countries will have specific regulations which will determine whether they will accept, or require, sharing of particular costs. For example, the US cost-sharing regulations explicitly require the sharing of stock option costs where the US company grants stock options to staff involved in the research and development.

Expected benefit, not comparative cost burden

18.46 There is an expectation that, for transfer pricing purposes in cost-sharing, the participants will share costs according to the extent to which they expect to benefit from the resulting intellectual property and not that they will share the intellectual property in accordance with the costs contributed.

18.47 This approach can raise some issues for transfer pricing, particularly the question of whether it is possible to determine at the outset the relative benefit that will accrue to each participant, for example, where they use their share of the intellectual property to manufacture different products. The long-term nature of many cost-sharing arrangements also means that the relative benefits can be difficult to determine at the outset.

18.48 Where the anticipated benefit is cost savings (or, for the same reasons, an increase in profits), it can also be difficult to reliably determine the relative benefit; unanticipated factors can have a disproportionate effect in one market but not another.

Background intellectual property licences

18.49 Where transfer pricing has to be taken into account, the arm's length value of any background intellectual property contributed to the cost-sharing arrangements must be established so that the appropriate offsetting payment can be established and taken into account (either directly, by payment of royalties, or indirectly by offset of royalties expected against royalties due for the background intellectual property of another participant). Establishing an appropriate value for the background intellectual property is difficult (as is the case for most intellectual property: see para **16.124**); some countries, particularly the USA, have specific rules to establish the appropriate royalty for background intellectual property. In the case of the US rules, these vary somewhat from their normal transfer pricing rules.

Tax issues: unconnected participants

18.50   Cost-sharing arrangements can also be agreed between otherwise unconnected companies, most often in respect of joint research with universities or government bodies. The existence of these arrangements is one of the reasons why cost-sharing arrangements between associated companies are accepted by many tax authorities.

18.51   Where the parties are not connected or associated in any way, transfer pricing should not be an issue: contractual arrangements between unconnected parties will usually be treated as taking place on an arm's length basis (as the arm's length price is taken to be that freely negotiated between unconnected parties). As a result, establishing the appropriate deductions and receipts for tax purposes is considerably more straightforward.

Expenditure

18.52   Contributions to expenditure on research and development will generally be deductible as an expense of the trade for each of the participants (see para **9.14**) when recognised in the profit and loss account of the participant (see para **9.21** for further details on recognition of expenditure).

18.53   The principal contributions to the cost-sharing arrangement expenditure are not generally treated as royalties and so should not be subject to withholding taxes, even where part of the contribution reflects compensation to the owner of background intellectual property (but see below for specific royalty payments).

18.54   Research and development tax reliefs will potentially be available to the extent that the nature of the research and development meets the criteria, and to the extent that the expenditure qualifies for the relief (see Chapter 10). This will, at least in part, depend on the contractual arrangements between the participants and the way in which contributions are calculated and accounted for.

18.55   To get research and development relief, a UK participant must be directly incurring qualifying expenditure on the research and development or (if an SME) sub-contracting the research and development to another participant. Merely contributing to the overall costs of the arrangement, or to the specific costs of another participant, will not entitle the first participant to research and development relief; in these cases, a UK participant actually carrying on the research and development and with a net receipt from the arrangement may be treated as having received a subsidy for its research and development expenditure and so will only be able to claim the large company research and development relief (assuming it is within the scope of UK corporation tax) even if it is an SME (see para **10.67**).

18.56   Where one or more of the participants has to pay a specific royalty for use of the background intellectual property of another participant or intellectual property of a third party, that royalty will usually be deductible as a trading expense when calculating taxable profits (see para **9.6**) following the accounts treatment. The royalty expenditure is unlikely to be capitalised in the accounts: see para **9.14** for more details of the accounts treatment of research and development costs. The royalty payment will not be qualifying expenditure for research and development relief (see para **10.82** for details of what does qualify). The payer may be required to deduct withholding tax before making the payment, particularly if the recipient is overseas (see para **16.56** onwards).

Background intellectual property licence

18.57   Where background intellectual property is contributed to a cost-sharing arrangement, the owner of the background intellectual property may receive a royalty payment from the other participants once the foreground intellectual property has been developed, to reflect the value of the background intellectual property to those other participants in exploiting the foreground intellectual property. Such royalty receipts will generally be taxable as income of the trade when recognised in the accounts (see para **12.46**).

18.58   If the contribution of the background intellectual property has, instead, been recognised by a reduction in the contribution to expenditure required from the owner of the background intellectual property, then this reduction will not be treated as a receipt related to the background intellectual property: instead, the reduced contribution will mean a reduced deduction in calculating the taxable profits of the trade.

Receipts from exploitation of intellectual property

18.59   If the research and development undertaken through cost-sharing arrangements results in viable intellectual property (usually described as 'foreground intellectual property'), the participants will share that intellectual property but will exploit it separately (for joint exploitation, see para **18.1**). This may be through:

- joint ownership, with each participant owning the intellectual property (usually in proportion to each participant's contribution under the cost-sharing arrangements); or

- licensing from the intellectual property asset owner, where a single participant owns the resulting intellectual property. The cost-sharing contracts will generally require the owner to licence the intellectual property asset to the other participants at no additional cost beyond their contribution to the development

18.60   These are not all the possible ways of sharing in the intellectual property, but will be the most common. The decision as to which sharing model to use will depend in part on the choice of the participants and partly on local law: not all jurisdictions recognise joint ownership of certain types of intellectual property and those that do may impose requirements on the joint owners which are not considered commercially appropriate (for example, the USA requires that joint owners of a patent must act together to enforce a patent: if one of the joint owners does not join in with enforcement action, the action is deemed to have been terminated). UK patent law generally requires a joint owner of a patent to obtain the other's consent to assign its share of the patent, or grant a licence over it. These domestic law provisions may be capable of being overridden by contract, but they must be taken into account when considering the form in which the intellectual property is shared.

18.61   The receipts from exploitation of the foreground intellectual property will be taxed as trading income of each participant, when recognised in the profit and loss account of the participant (see Chapter 12). If the new foreground intellectual property is sold to a third party, or an exclusive licence granted, such that the intellectual property is considered to have been realised, each participant will be treated as having realised an intellectual property asset (see Chapter 14 and Chapter 13 where the intellectual property is a patent).

Buying-in to a cost-sharing arrangement

18.62   Most cost-sharing arrangements are established before research and development work begins, so that the parties share all of the risks involved. In some cases, a participant may join in established research and development activity. In this case, the new participant will generally have to buy in to the arrangements to reflect the benefit that it receives from the research and development that took place before it joined the arrangements. Where the participants are associated companies, transfer pricing will require that this buy-in takes place at on an arm's length basis: this will reflect the benefit to the new participant, rather than a mechanical calculation of a share of the costs already incurred by the other participants.

TRANSACTIONS BETWEEN CONNECTED OR RELATED PARTIES

18.63   A group relationship is not the only link between entities which can have tax consequences: in a number of instances, tax law imposes particular provisions in respect of transactions between entities which are linked but not part of a group for tax purposes. These provisions are largely a form of anti-avoidance, to ensure that the link is not exploited to reduce tax that would otherwise be due (eg by selling at below market value from a high tax jurisdiction to a low tax jurisdiction).

18.64   In most cases, the linked entities are described as *connected* persons; however, the corporate intangibles tax rules use another term, *related*, to describe the link. These terms are described below.

18.65   Note that the transfer pricing rules (see para **16.94**) will have priority over the connected party rules and related party rules where transfer pricing is also applicable to a transaction.

Connected persons: general rules

18.66   The 'connected persons' rules apply, generally, to intellectual property transactions involving non-corporate entities or pre-1 April 2002 intellectual property. In outline, entities can be connected:

- through family relationships: an individual is connected with:

  — their spouse or civil partner (connection is not severed by separation, only by decree absolute for a marriage or by dissolution order for a civil partnership);

  — any relative: sibling, ancestor (parent, grandparent etc) or lineal descendant (child, grandchild) of the individual or their spouse or civil partner;

  — the spouse or civil partner of any relative;

- as trustee of a settlement: a trustee is connected with:

  — an individual settlor;

  — any person connected with an individual settlor (as above);

  — any close company (or one which would be close if UK-resident) where the trustee is a participator, and any companies controlled by such a close company;

  — the trustees of any sub-funds or superior funds within the same settlement;

- through partnership: individual partners are connected with:

  — each other and each other's spouses or civil partners and relatives, although there is an exception for bona fide commercial transactions;

- through control or a major interest in a company: an individual is connected with:

  — any company which the individual controls (either alone or with connected persons);

— any other person with whom the individual acts to secure or exercise control of a company;

● through control: a company is connected with:

— any individual who (alone or with connected persons) controls the company;

— a partnership which is under the same control as the company;

— another company where:

(i) both are controlled by the same person;

(ii) a person has control of one company and persons who are connected with the first control the other;

(iii) a person controls one company and that person together with connected persons controls the other;

(iv) the same group of persons controls both companies;

ITTOIA 2005, s 620; CTA 2010, s 1122 (see para **5.113** for more details of what constitutes 'control').

Effect of being connected

18.67 Where two persons are connected, any transactions between them are deemed to take place at market value, regardless of the actual consideration (if any) that passes between them. This will, accordingly, set the value in respect of intellectual property for:

● receipts, when calculating income tax or capital gains tax, if any, arising from a transaction; and

● expenditure, when calculating:

— expense deductions on acquisitions (see Chapter 5); or

— capital gains on disposal (see Chapter 7); or

— capital allowances: patent capital allowances will be restricted (see para **5.60**). Know-how allowances are not available when the two parties to a know-how transaction are related by control (see para **5.112** for more details).

18.68 The purpose of the connected persons rules is, in effect, to ensure that tax cannot be avoided through manipulation (eg by transferring an asset before sale to a company which has losses so that, on sale of the asset, the overall tax is reduced: this is a very simplified example, but serves to illustrate the point).

Related parties: corporate intangibles tax rules

18.69 The rules on related parties serve a similar purpose within the corporate intangibles tax rules to the connected persons rules above.

Effect of the related parties rules

18.70 Related parties are regarded by HMRC as those entities which effectively share economic interests with a UK corporate taxpayer company. It is considered that this creates opportunities for tax advantages to be obtained and so transactions in intellectual property between related parties are subject to specific rules (CTA 2009, Pt 8, Ch 12).

Note that these provisions do not cover transactions between group companies which are so closely related that they form, or are within, a group for tax purposes: see para **18.137** for information on groups, transactions and other matters involving group companies.

Definition of a related party

18.71 The definition of a 'related party' is not the same as the definition of a 'connected person', a term which is also used elsewhere in tax legislation. This is deliberate, because the corporate intangibles rules relate to corporation tax only and so it was felt that the generally broader definition of 'connected person' was not entirely appropriate (HMRC Manual CIRD45120).

18.72 There are four circumstances in which a person is a related party of a company (CTA 2009, s 835(2)–(6)):

- where both are companies and one controls or has a 'major interest' in the other;

- where both are companies and both are under the 'control' of the same person (unless that person is a public body);

- where the company is a close company and the person is, or is an associate of, a participator in the company that controls or holds a major interest in the company (note: this is the only circumstance in which an individual can be a related party);

- where both are companies and are members of the same group (although, as noted above, the group transfer rules would generally apply in this case).

18.73 A company does not cease to be a related party of another company simply because it is subject to insolvency arrangements, either in the UK or under similar rules elsewhere, so that the appointment of a liquidator does not break the relationship between the parties and they continue to be related despite the liquidation (CTA 2009, s 835(7)–(9)).

What is a major interest

18.74   A person has a major interest in a company if (CTA 2009, s 837):

- that person and one other person together have control (as above) of the company; and

- the rights and powers by which they have control represent, for each of them, at least 40% of the total such rights and powers in the company.

This will principally cover joint ventures where neither party has control of the joint venture company.

Definition of control

18.75   A person has 'control' of a company if that person has the power to ensure that the company's affairs are conducted in accordance with their wishes through either (CTA 2009, s 836):

- shareholdings or voting power in the company, or through another company (such as a holding company); or

- powers conferred by the articles of association, or any other document (such as a shareholder agreement) which governs the way the company (or another company) is run.

This is a wide test, concerned with whether the ongoing activities of the company can be controlled as a matter of fact, rather than considering only the ability to receive profits or assets on a winding up.

Rights and powers

18.76   To determine whether a person has control of, or a major interest in, a company it is necessary to consider the rights and powers (CTA 2009, ss 838–839):

- that a person has directly, or exercisable jointly with another person;

- that the person is entitled to acquire in future or will, in future, become entitled to acquire;

- held by others but exercisable on behalf of that person, or under their direction, or for the benefit of that person (but note that rights and powers under security arrangements for a loan are not included);

- of any 'connected' person;

- of any person connected to a 'connected' person

18.77   The rights and powers which a person has as a partner in a partnership are ignored unless the person controls or has a major interest in the partnership. This was specifically introduced to ensure that partners in an investment partnership are not automatically connected with other partners with whom they have no other connection (CTA 2009, ss 839, 840).

Connected

18.78   A person is connected with another person through close family relationships, as a trustee of a settlement, or by virtue of control or a major interest where the second person is a company (CTA 2009, ss 842, 843), as noted in para **18.66**.

Who is a participator or associate

18.79   An 'associate' and a 'participator' in a close company are defined in the same way as for the general close company rules (CTA 2010, s 448 and s 454) except that, for the corporate intangibles tax rules, a person cannot be a participator in a close company solely by reason of being a loan creditor (CTA 2009, s 841).

Effect of the related parties rules

18.80   These rules will affect:

- whether or not a pre-1 April 2002 asset is within the corporate intangibles tax regime: a transfer of a pre-1 April 2002 between connected parties will not bring it into the regime (see Chapter 8);

- the value at which a transfer of intellectual property takes place: between related parties, it will be market value (CTA 2009, s 845);

- whether roll-over relief is available on part-realisation of an asset: no relief is available on a part-disposal to a related party (see para **12.62**);

- the deductibility of a royalty paid to or for the benefit of a related party: these can only be deducted when actually paid in certain circumstances (see para **17.19** for more details).

INTELLECTUAL PROPERTY HOLDING COMPANIES

18.81   To maximise value, groups are increasingly looking to the effective management and utilisation of intellectual property and, in particular, the ownership of that intellectual property. One area of focus has been the concept of an intellectual property holding company: a single repository in the group for intellectual property rights, so that these can be actively managed and protected, and also leveraged to encourage growth and development of the business.

Business considerations

18.82   Before establishing any centralised intellectual property holding and/ or management structure, the group should consider a range of key business matters. These should ultimately be more important to the group than the tax rate as any decisions on centralisation of intellectual property need to ensure that the business as a whole is more effective, not simply the group tax rate. Points to consider in detail include:

- ownership of the intellectual property: before any active steps are taken, the group should ensure that it understands which entities in the group currently own the intellectual property, and consider the tax issues relating to any potential transfer of that intellectual property (see para **17.34**) to a centralised holding structure. The intra-group licensing arrangements should be considered as well, both current and future;

- future intellectual property: the current research and development activities of the group should be reviewed. Any plan to centralise intellectual property management should include consideration of the best location(s) to carry on future research and development, looking at the commercial perspectives (where are people currently based, where are the necessary skills) as well as tax incentives (see para Chapter 10 and Chapter 13 for the principal UK intellectual property tax incentives). There should also be a review of the interaction between that research and development and the holding of the intellectual property: is a centralised holding structure the most appropriate, or would some form of cost-sharing arrangement and joint ownership (see para **18.1**) be more effective?

- how will the intellectual property be exploited by the group as a whole: the most appropriate location and holding structure for intellectual property may depend on the business needs of the group, whether manufacturing (are there any particular quirks of the manufacturing locations that could affect the holding structure) or the provision of services (again, are there local issues in any of the jurisdictions in which the group operates).

Decentralised holding of intellectual property

18.83   For some groups of companies, a centralised holding of intellectual property makes commercial and tax sense. It focuses attention on the intellectual property and can assist in ensuring that it is properly managed. It should not be automatically assumed, however, that a specific intellectual property holding company to centralise the intellectual property is the best solution: for some groups, a decentralised holding structure may make more sense, particularly where the various elements of group carry on different businesses and there is little exchange of intellectual property (including know-how, in particular) between the companies within the group and little requirement to licence the intellectual property outside the group. In a decentralised model, each entity within the group owns the intellectual property needed for its operations and maintains that intellectual property as necessary.

18.84   From a tax perspective, a true decentralised model means that each company effectively approaches its intellectual property on a stand-alone basis: in a multinational group there may be some transfer pricing issues (see para **16.94**) where there is some licensing of intellectual property within the group but these should be minimised (perhaps limited to the overall company brand) where each company owns and develops its intellectual property as necessary. Each company then creates and/or acquires and exploits its intellectual property as if it were a stand-alone company so that the tax treatment generally follows that set out in Chapters 8–14.

Centralised management of intellectual property

18.85   This is a form of halfway house; in this business model, the intellectual property of the group is owned in a variety of location but managed by one centralised team. This type of centralised structure reduces costs and provides substantial benefits, assisting with a coherent intellectual property strategy and minimising duplication of effort and intellectual property across the group.

18.86   Where the intellectual property is centrally managed in a multinational group, the key tax issues will be similar to those for a decentralised model, albeit from a slightly different perspective: transfer pricing rules will need to be considered for licences of intellectual property between group companies, which are likely to be more widespread as the central management should consolidate intellectual property and avoid duplication, and also for the services provided by the central intellectual property management team to the group companies.

Centralised intellectual property holding: intellectual property holding companies

18.87   In contrast, a centralised intellectual property holding structure owns and manages the intellectual property for the group in (usually) a single location. For some groups, with geographical splits, it may be appropriate to have two or more intellectual property holding companies, each for a specific geographical area where the companies within that area have similar requirements and considerations with regard to intellectual property.

18.88 For groups where the companies have similar businesses, the centralised administration and holding of intellectual property should assist the management strategy of the group as a whole, making it more likely that intellectual property assets will be recognised, maintained and enforced in a consistent manner across the group. The background work of identifying and maintaining the assets can make it easier for the group to spot opportunities in their existing intellectual property assets that can be exploited, and perhaps to also spot gaps in those assets which should be filled.

18.89 A holding company may also develop new intellectual property for the group, although in most cases the relevant research and development will be carried out by another group company on behalf of the holding company, to maximise any available research and development incentives.

18.90 The intellectual property holding company will principally hold the intellectual property assets of the group: the intellectual property that forms the basis of group products and services will then be licensed to group companies, with licence fees being paid by those companies back to the intellectual property holding company and so relocating part of the profits relating to the intellectual property to a lower tax jurisdiction. Intellectual property that is not being used directly by the group can either by licensed to third parties for income, or held for capital growth and later sale: centralising the holding of the intellectual property can generally make it easier to identify the appropriate opportunities and develop appropriate packages for external exploitation. Whether licensed internally or externally, the intellectual property holding company activities should include some measure of oversight to ensure that the licensee's performance is kept under review, to ensure that the value of the intellectual property is maintained.

18.91 The following considers the principal tax issues that are likely to affect a centralised intellectual property holding structure, looking at UK intellectual property holding companies and overseas intellectual property holding companies for a UK group.

UK intellectual property holding company

18.92 When considering intellectual property holding companies, the usual reaction is to assume that such companies are set up offshore, in low tax jurisdictions. However, for a UK group with no current or planned overseas operations, it will be difficult to establish an overseas holding company to obtain tax benefits. To resolve the tax issues that arise, particularly with regard to controlled foreign companies (see para **16.139**), it is generally necessary that there be a good commercial reason for the intellectual property of the group to be held overseas. Without reasonable overseas operations, it would be difficult to sustain a commercial argument for the overseas holding company.

18.93   Where there are nevertheless commercial benefits for centralised holding of intellectual property, however, the group could consider establishing a UK intellectual property holding company to obtain those benefits.

18.94   For a UK group, setting up a UK intellectual property holding company within the group is (generally) relatively straightforward in tax terms, as the UK has a range of tax reliefs for group company transactions:

- transfer of intellectual property to the holding company would be tax-neutral (see para **18.162**);

- transfer pricing rules (see para **16.94**) do apply to UK–UK transactions such as intra-group licences, but compensating adjustments can be made to minimise the impact of such rules (and, in practice, HMRC are not generally pursuing UK–UK transactions under these rules at the time of writing);

- where the group as a whole qualifies as an SME, any research and development subcontracted from the holding company to another group company may still qualify for SME research and development relief (see para **10.64**).

Overseas intellectual property holding companies

18.95   Intellectual property assets increasingly carry an expectation that they will be held offshore, in a low tax jurisdiction, so that the group as a whole can minimise the tax costs of exploiting that intellectual property as there are no physical barriers to the exploitation of intellectual property. This has been fuelled in part by press coverage of low tax rates achieved by various high profile companies, often US businesses using structures in Ireland and Switzerland (the 'Double Irish' sandwich structure, by the way, relies on a particular quirk of US tax law; it is not something that can be replicated by a UK-headquartered group).

Intellectual property protection

18.96   The first, and key, consideration has to be the protection available for intellectual property in the jurisdictions under consideration. Intellectual property assets, unlike physical assets, require a regulatory infrastructure to protect much of their value. Selecting a jurisdiction that does not charge corporate tax on profits or gains may be initially attractive but if it also does not offer any protection for intellectual property owned in that jurisdiction, its attractions will be limited.

18.97   Besides the existence of a regulatory framework of protection, various ancillary points should be considered:

- the costs of protection: particularly registration fees and the administration costs of maintaining registrations;

- the efficiency of local protection: how quickly can registrations be obtained, and a priority date established when appropriate;

- corporate legislation: a robust corporate and associated legal framework will make set-up and administration smoother; and

- location: given the need for substance (see below), it is important that the jurisdiction be accessible. A group of companies operating in Europe would probably not choose to locate an intellectual property holding company in New Zealand (to pick an extreme example).

Location: tax considerations

18.98   The most attractive tax jurisdictions are, at first glance, those that offer tax rates of 0% or thereabouts. Very low (and non-existent) tax rates do, however, come at a cost that needs to be balanced against the benefits.

Withholding taxes

18.99   Where the intellectual property is to be exploited by licensing it to other jurisdictions, the holding company jurisdiction should be one that will minimise the possibility of withholding taxes in the countries from which royalties are paid (see para **16.56** for more information on withholding taxes).

18.100   There is no particular point in having an intellectual property holding company in Guernsey, for example, if the intellectual property is to be exploited by licence to the US. The withholding taxes deducted by the US payer will be sufficient to make the structure redundant: it would be more tax effective to maintain the intellectual property in the UK, so that no withholding tax is deducted from the royalty, as the UK corporate tax rate on the net royalty (after expenses) will be less than the US withholding tax on the gross royalty. In general, there are few countries that impose any withholding tax on capital gains and so assets held for capital gains are generally less subject to such concerns.

18.101   Even where the intention is to hold intellectual property for investment purposes, with a view to development and sale onward to a third party in future, the withholding tax position should still be considered: plans do not always unfold as intended, and it may be necessary to license the intellectual property (for example, in settlement of infringement proceedings) rather than sell it outright.

Transfer pricing rules

18.102   The ideal intellectual property holding location would have no transfer pricing rules (see para **16.94**): this does not mean that such rules can be ignored, as the holding company would be likely to be licensing out the intellectual property to other group companies which may well be in locations which have transfer pricing rules. These rules will limit the scope to move profits from higher tax jurisdictions to a lower tax jurisdiction as a consequence, as any royalty rate on licences would need to be within the arm's length price.

18.103   Transfer pricing rules may be less of an issue where the holding company holds non-core intellectual property as a investment for eventual sale or licensing to a third party as these transactions will be at market value, given the independent status of the purchaser or licensor.

Extracting profits

18.104   Properly established, the intellectual property holding company could accumulate significant funds which could be used by other parts of the group.

18.105   Part of the planning for the holding company should be some consideration as to how these funds could be taken out of the holding company. One option is for the holding company to provide loans to group members, but note that (for example) the UK controlled foreign companies exemption for intellectual property holding companies (see para **16.149**) requires that the holding company have very little finance income. This would substantially restrict the ability of the intellectual property holding company to also make loans.

18.106   For a UK headquartered group, there is usually the possibility of a straightforward repatriation of profits by way of dividend. Provided that the group as a whole is not regarded as 'small', it should be possible to ensure that the dividends fall within the UK exemptions from corporate tax on dividends (CTA 2009, Pt 9A).

18.107   UK companies in small groups can only get an exemption from tax on dividends where the dividend payer is in a jurisdiction which has a tax treaty with the UK which contains a non-discrimination article. The UK has very few such treaties with very low tax jurisdictions. 'Small' in this context follows the EU definition: fewer than 50 employees, annual turnover and/or balance sheet assets of not more than €10m (EC Recommendation 2003/361/EC, also contained in HMRC Manual CIRD92800).

Substance

18.108   An intellectual property holding company will usually be a subsidiary (directly or indirectly) of the group parent company. This allows the group to dispose of intellectual property without directly impacting the parent company. In some cases, intellectual property may be held in several special purpose companies to enable the entire company to be sold, rather than just the intellectual property: this will depend on the tax regime in the jurisdiction chosen.

18.109   It is no longer sufficient for a group to simply establish an intellectual property holding company to get tax advantages; many jurisdictions will simply look through the structure and attribute (and tax) the profits and gains of that company to its parent unless there is some substance to the company in its jurisdiction of residence. The company cannot simply be a name on the register; it will need to have some management and decision-making activity, at least, in the jurisdiction.

18.110   What amounts to sufficient substance will depend on a case-by-case basis but, in general, the company will need to have genuine economic activity in the jurisdiction to minimise the risks of the parent being taxed on the profits of the intellectual property holding company. For example, there should be appropriate staff in the location, with the necessary skills to manage the intellectual property on a day-to-day basis.

UK tax implications of an overseas holding company

18.111   Any restructuring to maximise value of intellectual property is likely to involve the transfer of ownership of some or all of the intellectual property assets of the group. Putting a holding company in place, for example, will involve the transfer of ownership assets from the various group companies that own the assets to the new holding company.

18.112   Unsurprisingly, it is not always straightforward to transfer intellectual property to an overseas intellectual property holding company: most higher tax jurisdictions such as the UK tend to have a range of anti-avoidance rules that will come into effect to discourage businesses from relocating assets to lower tax jurisdictions overseas. Any structuring to create an intellectual property holding company in such a jurisdiction will require careful planning and genuine economic activity and substance in the jurisdiction of choice to enable the holding company structure to be tax effective.

18.113   Transfers from either UK companies and UK individuals to a new intellectual property holding company overseas will have to consider various measures in particular.

Transfers from a UK company

Capital gains tax on transfer

18.114 Any transfer of existing intellectual property assets to a new offshore holding company is likely to result in a capital gain for a UK group company transferring the asset. Even if the intellectual property is transferred for book value, transfers between group members are deemed to take place at market value for tax purposes where one of the parties is overseas (within the UK, group transfers take place on a no-gain, no-loss basis: the latent gain is not taxed until the asset is disposed of outside the group: see para **18.162**).

18.115 It is unlikely that the tax on gains arising on such transfers to European group companies is valid within the terms of the European Treaty, given that there is no tax on latent gains on transfers between group companies within the UK. The EU has formally challenged the UK corporate exit tax on the basis that it infringes the freedom of establishment in the Treaty (EU Press Release, 22 March 2012). Recent cases at the ECJ on similar matters have generally gone in favour of the EU (see, for example, *Commission v Portugal C-38/11*).

Attribution of income: controlled foreign companies rules

18.116 Where the intellectual property is transferred to a wholly-owned subsidiary in a low-tax jurisdiction, the UK parent company may be subject to corporation tax on the profits of the subsidiary if the controlled foreign companies rules apply (see para **16.139** for more details of these rules).

Transfers from a UK individual

Capital gains tax on transfer

18.117 The transferor and the overseas holding company are likely to be regarded as connected (as, presumably, the transferring individual will be a shareholder with control of the company), and so there will be a tax charge for the transferor on any latent gain in the intellectual property transferred, as transfers between connected persons will be deemed to have been transferred at market value (TCGA 1992, s 18).

Attribution of gains and income

18.118 The European Commission is currently formally challenging the UK's attribution of gains and attribution of income rules as contrary to the freedom of establishment under the EU, and has requested that the UK amend its legislation to remedy this. At the time of writing, consultation is underway in the UK to amend the rules, although there is some concern that the proposed amendments do not fully address the problems underlying the rules.

Attribution of gains: individual and corporate

18.119 Gains made by overseas companies can be subject to UK tax if they are attributed to individual shareholders (or other participators such as option holders and loan creditors) (TCGA 1992, s 13). This taxing clause can apply to both corporate and non-corporate shareholders, although corporate shareholders are more likely to be taxed under the controlled foreign companies rules.

18.120 Full details are outside the scope of this book but, broadly, TCGA 1992, s 13 applies where:

● a non-UK resident company

● which would be a close company if it were UK resident

● makes a chargeable gain.

18.121 There are a number of exemptions which apply and, in particular, there is no attribution of gains arising on assets used for the purposes of a trade carried on by the overseas company outside the UK.

18.122 In some cases, older UK tax treaties give primary taxing rights in respect of any gain to the jurisdiction in which the gain arises; this will potentially override the attribution of gains rules in TCGA 1992, s 13. More recent tax treaties are written to eliminate this override.

18.123 A close company is a company controlled by five or fewer participators or controlled by any number of participators who are also directors (CTA 2010, s 439).

18.124 Where the provisions apply, any gains made by the non-UK resident company are attributed to all the participators in the company and taxed in the UK on UK resident participators as capital gains of those participators (TCGA 1992, s 13(2)). There is no requirement that a participator actually have any entitlement to share in the specific profits which result from the gain (TCGA 1992, s 454).

18.125 The amount attributed will depend on the 'interest of the participator in the company' (TCGA 1992, s 13(3)); this is generally calculated by reference to that participator's shareholding in the non-UK company. However, HMRC take the view that a full review of the circumstances is required to ensure that the apportionment is 'just and reasonable', considering the participators' economic interests in the company (HMRC Manual CG57283). It should be noted that this test is not contained in the legislation, which simply refers to the participator's 'interest in the company'.

18.126   However, no attribution—and hence no tax charge—is made for participators with an interest of 10% or less in the non-UK company (TCGA 1992, s 13(4)).

Attribution of income: individuals

18.127   In addition to the potential attribution of gains, there is also a potential income tax charge for individuals who transfer assets overseas. Where the asset is transferred to an overseas company in exchange for shares, income earned outside the UK by that non-resident company may be treated as taxable income of the individual (ITA 2007, ss 720–730). The charge applies only to individuals; companies need to consider the effect of the controlled foreign company rules instead (see para **16.139**).

18.128   Broadly, where a UK individual transfers an asset to a non-UK company in exchange for shares in that company, the income of that company will be taxed on the UK individual unless the motive defence (ITA 2007, ss 736–742) can be established. The motive defence requires that the taxpayer demonstrate that the avoidance of tax is not the main purpose, or one of the main purposes, for which the structure is set up.

18.129   The distinction between tax avoidance and tax mitigation is still in the process of being worked out by the UK Tax Tribunals; HMRC's record in challenging ordinary tax planning in the Tribunals has not been particularly good and the cases appear to depend on what the taxpayer's intentions were (see, for example, *Carvill v IRC* [2000] STC (SCD) 143).

18.130   The motive defence is strongest when the non-UK company has a genuine economic activity and has substance appropriate to that activity, with those running it having the necessary skills to do so.

Other points to consider

New intellectual property

18.131   There is a longer-term alternative to transferring the existing assets of the group, which is to effectively draw a line under the current portfolio and accept that the economic benefits of those assets will continue to be taxed in the same way. New assets developed or acquired will be developed or acquired by the new holding company; no transfer of assets from group members will be required in these circumstances.

18.132 This approach, letting the existing intellectual property burn out in its current ownership, is most suitable for groups with fast-developing, short-lived intellectual property assets—consumer games software, for example—where the current line of products will be in remainder bins within a couple of years. Even here, though, there will still be associated intellectual property (trademarks, marketing intangibles, etc) which the group will probably want to centralise.

18.133 The potential UK tax implications can be minimised where the overseas holding company is set up to create intellectual property, rather than to receive transferred existing intellectual property. The intellectual property activities of the group would be taken over by the intellectual property holding company over a period of time as the new intellectual property is created, established and brought into use. New intellectual property is less likely to cause UK tax issues, as the structure can be set up to have fewer links to the UK in funding, research and development, or management.

18.134 New intellectual property can be particularly helpful where the overseas holding company is to act primarily in foreign-to-foreign licensing, with little UK involvement. In such a case, subject to the other requirements being met, a UK corporate shareholder would be likely to be able to claim the intellectual property holding company exemption from the controlled foreign companies profits tax charge (see para **16.139**) and a UK individual shareholder would be less likely to be caught by the attribution of income rules (see para **18.127**).

UK research and development tax relief implications

18.135 The holding company can outsource the creation and development of the intellectual property; it is not required to undertake these activities directly. It should be noted that, if the intellectual property development is qualifying research and development, it could be sub-contracted to a UK company in order to claim the research and development reliefs (see Chapter 10).

18.136 However, that UK company would only to be able to claim the large company relief (see Chapter 10), even if the group as a whole qualifies as an SME, as it would be acting as subcontractor to the overseas company. Where the overseas holding company and the UK research and development company are connected for tax purposes (see para **18.78**), the controlled foreign company exemptions (see para **16.139**) may not be available to eliminate a UK tax charge on profits for the UK parent if the intellectual property was originally transferred from the UK.

UK GROUP COMPANIES

18.137 There are various tax advantages and disadvantages to being in a group: for example, UK group companies can transfer assets between themselves without an immediate tax charge; on the other hand, a company's tax rate may be increased as a result of being in a group. Many of the tax implications of being in a group arise automatically, rather than by election, so it is important to be able to determine whether or not a company is in a group.

When is a company in a group?

18.138   There are a number definitions of a group in company law, for accounting purposes, and for tax purposes. The following looks at the tax definitions that apply in the context of intellectual property tax. Unfortunately there is no single definition that applies for all group tax purposes.

Corporate intangibles tax rules definition of a group

18.139   There are various reliefs and charge, in particular, in the corporate intangibles tax rules that depend upon a company being in a group: for example, a disposal of intellectual property from one group company to another is tax-neutral. If the recipient company leaves the group within a specific period of time, there is a tax charge that is applied (see below for more details of this relief and charge).

18.140   Accordingly, it is important to establish whether a company is part of a group for the purposes of the corporate intangibles tax rules. These follow the general principles of the tax law rewrite program and so are reasonably self-contained and, in particular, have their own definition of a group. This definition does, in practice, follow the definition for capital gains tax purposes.

General rule

18.141   The general rule is that a group is formed of a principal company and its 75% subsidiaries, together with the 75% subsidiaries of these subsidiaries (and so), provided that those subsidiaries are effective 51% subsidiaries of the parent company (CTA 2009, ss 765–766).

Principal company

18.142   A principal company is, generally, the top company in the group and is defined in the negative. A company will be a principal company unless it is a 75% subsidiary of another company except where (CTA 2009, s 767):

● that subsidiary is not part of another group of companies because it is not an effective 51% subsidiary of the principal company of that other group; and

- a further company is not thereby enabled to be the principal company of a group of which the subsidiary would be a member.

18.143 A group of companies continues to be the same group as long as the same company is the principal company of the group; changes in the subsidiaries do not affect the group as a whole. If the principal company is taken over and becomes a member of another group (because there is a new principal company) then the first group and the post-acquisition group are treated together as being the same group so that the takeover will not, for example, create any de-grouping charges (see below). The question of whether a company ceases to be a member of the group is determined according to whether and when it leaves the second group (CTA 2009, s 769(2)).

75% subsidiary

18.144 A company is a 75% subsidiary of its parent company if the parent company owns at least 75% of the ordinary share capital, directly or indirectly (CTA 2010, s 1154). 'Indirect' ownership means that there are intermediary companies between the parent company and the subsidiary. This is a shareholding test only; there is no requirement that the parent company have any beneficial entitlement to profits or assets on a winding up.

Effective 51% subsidiary

18.145 A company is an 'effective 51% subsidiary' of its parent company if the parent company (CTA 2009, s 771):

- is beneficially entitled to more than 50% of the profits available for distribution to equity holders of the subsidiary; and

- would be beneficially entitled to more than 50% of the assets of the subsidiary available for distribution to equity holders on a winding up.

18.146 An 'equity holder' in this context is (CTA 2009, s 772; CTA 2010, s 158):

- a person who holds ordinary shares in the company; or

- a loan creditor of the company in connection with a non-commercial loan, except loan creditors who carry on a banking business and who have lent money to the company in the ordinary course of their banking business.

Example 18.2

These categories are best illustrated by a diagram:

A Ltd

has a 100% shareholding in

B Ltd

has a 80% shareholding in

C Ltd

has a 76% shareholding, with pro-rata entitlement of profits and assets, in

D Ltd

has a 80% shareholding, with pro-rata entitlement of profits and assets, in

E Ltd

A Ltd and B Ltd are members of the same group; A owns more than 75% of B Ltd so that B Ltd is a 75% subsidiary of A Ltd.

A Ltd and C Ltd are members of the same group; A indirectly owns 80% of the shareholding in C Ltd through B Ltd, so C Ltd is a 75% subsidiary of A Ltd.

A Ltd and D Ltd are members of the same group; D Ltd is not a 75% subsidiary of A Ltd (as 80% of 76% is 60.4%) but A Ltd will (through B Ltd and C Ltd) be beneficially entitled to more than 50% of the profits of D Ltd available for distribution and more than 50% of the assets on a winding up.

A Ltd and E Ltd are not members of the same group. Tracing the ownership through B Ltd, C Ltd and D Ltd, A Ltd indirectly owns less than 75% of the shares in E Ltd (80% x 76% x 80% is 48.64%). Similarly, A Ltd will not have more than 51% beneficial entitlement to profits and assets of E Ltd.

Therefore, the group of which A Ltd is the principal company consists of A Ltd, B Ltd, C Ltd and D Ltd, but not E Ltd (even though E Ltd is a 75% subsidiary of D Ltd).

E Ltd may, however, be the principal company of another group (if it has subsidiaries), even though it is the 75% subsidiary of D Ltd. This is because E Ltd is not an effective 51% subsidiary of A Ltd and D Ltd cannot be a principal company because it is an effective 51% subsidiary of A Ltd.

Dealing with potential multiple groups

18.147 A company cannot be a member of more than one group for tax purposes. If circumstances arise through which a company could be a member of two groups (usually this will be where the company is owned by two or more companies which themselves have a common ultimate parent) then the legislation sets out a series of tests which have to be considered in turn. Once one of the tests is satisfied, this determines which group the company belongs to.

18.148 The tests operate by setting out terms which are to be ignored (CTA 2009, s 768) in applying the effective 51% subsidiary requirement unless a parent company is established:

- any interest which a head of group has in the profits available for distribution to equity holders of a head of another group; or

- any interest which a head of a group would have in any assets of the head of another group available for distribution to its equity holders on a winding up;

- the company is a member of the group whose head has the greatest percentage of beneficial entitlement to profits available for distribution to equity holders of the company;

- the company is a member of the group whose head has the greatest percentage of beneficial entitlement to assets available for distribution on a winding up to equity holders of the company;

- the company is a member of the group the head of which owns directly or indirectly a percentage of the company's ordinary share capital that is greater than the percentage of that capital owned directly or indirectly by any other head of a group.

Example 18.3

```
                    A Ltd
          /                      \
          B Ltd (76%)      C Ltd (100%)
          D Ltd (76%)        |
          E Ltd (76%)        |
          \                  /
```

F Ltd (80% owned by E, 20% owned by C)

(Assume that all entitlements to profits for distribution and assets on a winding up follow the shareholdings pro rata).

A Ltd, B Ltd, C Ltd and D Ltd are all members of the same group, as B Ltd and C Ltd are 75% subsidiaries of A Ltd and D Ltd is a 75% subsidiary of B Ltd and an effective 51% subsidiary of A Ltd (76% × 76% is 57.76%).

E Ltd is not a 75% subsidiary of A Ltd, and is not a 75% subsidiary of B Ltd either. It can, therefore, be a principal company of a group.

F Ltd is a 75% subsidiary of E Ltd and so E Ltd and F Ltd form a group.

However, F Ltd is also an effective 51% subsidiary of A Ltd: A Ltd owns 20% through C Ltd and also owns 35.11% through B Ltd and its subsidiaries so that A Ltd has a 55.11% beneficial entitlement (albeit indirect) to the profits and assets of F Ltd. F Ltd could also therefore be a member of A Ltd's group.

To determine whether F Ltd is in a group with E Ltd or in a group with A Ltd, the terms in the test in CTA 2009, s 768 have to be considered in turn until a resolution is found.

Ignoring E Ltd's interests in the profits available for distribution has no effect. F Ltd is in a group with E Ltd because it is a 75% subsidiary of E Ltd and not because it is an effective 51% subsidiary of E Ltd. Ignoring A Ltd's interest in the profits available for distribution breaks the group relationship with A Ltd because an entitlement to both profits *and* assets is required for F Ltd to be an effective 51% subsidiary of A Ltd.

There is no need to consider the further tests: F Ltd will be within E Ltd group and not A Ltd's group.

Leaving the group

18.149   A company will not cease to be a member of a group simply because another company in the group is wound up; the company will also not cease to be a member of the group for tax purposes simply because a resolution for winding up of the company has been passed (CTA 2009, s 769(3)).

Example 18.4

A Ltd owns 100% of B Ltd which, in turn, owns 100% of C Ltd. All three companies therefore form a group, of which A Ltd is the principal member.

If B Ltd is wound up, A Ltd and C Ltd will continue to form a group (the assets of B Ltd, including the shares in C Ltd, will be distributed to A Ltd) and there will be no de-grouping charge on any assets which had previously been transferred between group members in the relevant time period (see below).

Research and development relief definition

18.150   Where research and development is carried out by one group company on behalf of another, the research and development will be qualifying research and development (for the large company research and development relief) for the company doing the research and development if the qualifying activities of the two companies together would be qualifying research and development for the company making the payment (see para **10.5**).

Definition of group

18.151 The definition of group (CTA 2009, s 1082(4)) used for the research and development tax relief is the same as that used to determine whether two companies are in the same group for corporation tax group relief purposes.

18.152 This definition is a simpler definition than that for the corporate intangibles tax relief rules: two companies will be members of the same group if one is the 75% subsidiary of the other, or both are 75% subsidiaries of the same third company.

75% subsidiary

18.153 This is a more involved definition than that for the corporate intangibles tax rules. A company is a 75% subsidiary of a second company where:

- the second company directly or indirectly owns at least 75% of the ordinary share capital of the first (CTA 2010, s 1154(3)); and

- the second company does not hold those share as trading stock (CTA 2010, s 151(3)); and

the second company is also beneficially entitled (CTA 2010, s 151(4)) to:

- at least 75% of the profits available for distribution to equity holders of the first company; and

- at least 75% of the assets available for distribution to equity holders on a winding up of the first company.

Patent box definition

18.154 The rules for the patent box regime (see Chapter 13) have a number of provisions which apply to group members (for example, for determining whether various conditions are met—the active ownership condition, the development condition—whether the requirements for an exclusive licence are met, the amount of routine expenses to bring into the calculation, and the use of set-off amounts, and anti-avoidance provisions).

18.155 The legislation contains a definition of group for the purposes of the patent box regime which is substantially wider than most tax definitions of group: a company is a member of a group at any time if any other company is at that time associated with it (CTA 2010, s 357GD).

18.156 This definition is extremely wide, and has no geographical restriction. It will bring into the definition joint ventures and smaller groups that would not normally be caught by group arrangements. This clearly has an advantage for some measures, making it easier to meet the active ownership condition (see para **13.29**) or the development condition (see para **13.35**), for example, as there is a wider pool of companies to draw on for support.

18.157 However, the definition may create considerable difficulty in determining the amount of routine expenses which must be brought into account (see para **13.115**), or establishing the use of patent box losses (see para **13.175**), particularly for smaller companies which may find it easy to obtain the relevant information from other companies which would not necessarily consider themselves to be part of the same group.

Detailed definition

18.158 A company (A) will be associated with another company (B) at a particular time (the 'relevant time') if *any* of the following applies (CTA 2010, s 357GD(3)):

- in the accounting period in which the relevant time occurs, the financial results of the two companies are, or are required to be, consolidated in group accounts or would be required to be consolidated if an exemption did not apply (CTA 2010, s 357GD(4),(9)); or

- for company A's accounting period which includes the relevant time, the companies are connected (see para **18.66**) (CTA 2010, s 357GD(5)); or

- at the relevant time, one of the companies has a major interest in the other (CTA 2010, s 357GD(6) and see below); or

- in the accounting period which includes the relevant time, the financial results of company A are consolidated in group accounts with the results of a third company, and at the relevant time that third company has a major interest in B (CTA 2010, s 357GD(7) and see below); or

- for an accounting period which includes the relevant time, there is a connection (as defined in CTA 2009, ss 466–471) between A and a third company, and at the relevant time that third company has a major interest in B (CTA 2010, s 357GD(8) and see below).

Accounts may be consolidated under either Companies Act 2006, s 399 or any corresponding foreign law (CTA 2010, s 357GD(10)).

18.159 A company (C) has a 'major interest' in another company (B) if:

- C and another person (D) together control B, and

- C and D each have interests, rights and powers representing at least 40% of the holdings, rights and powers as a result of which they have control of B (CTA 2009, ss 473–474).

Generally, this means that C and D will each normally own 40% of the shareholding in company B for a combined shareholding of more than 80%.

18.160 The test can still be met where C and D have smaller shareholdings but also have powers that override those of the other shareholders (CTA 2009, s 473). Any holdings, rights and powers over company B which are held by companies controlled by C or D are taken into account when assessing the holdings, rights and powers of C and D (CTA 2009, s 474).

Example 18.5

Raban Limited owns 100% of Cross Limited, so Raban and Cross will be in a group for the purposes of the patent box.

Raban Limited has a 42% interest in Christie Limited, and the other 58% is owned by an unconnected company, Bosch Limited.

As a result, Christie Limited and Cross Limited will be in a group for the patent box purposes, even though they will not be generally considered to be in a group for other tax purposes.

GROUP TRANSACTIONS

18.161 Given the economic links between group companies (as defined for general tax purposes, see para **18.139**), the corporate intangibles tax rules or other tax provisions will act to determine the tax consequences of group transactions. The rules are generally intended either to ensure that a group is not disadvantaged by internal transactions, or to ensure that the group does not take advantage of tax rules to gain an unintended advantage. The transfer pricing rules in particular (see para **16.94**) need to be considered when looking at transactions between group members, to establish the value at which the transaction is treated as taking place.

Transfers of intangible assets

18.162 In a group transfer, as the intellectual property asset has not left the group, the group overall has not received any actual benefit (or suffered any actual loss) which should be reflected for tax purposes and so the tax treatment is arranged to ensure that there should be no tax consequences at the time of the intra-group transfer. There may be a tax charge if the recipient company later leaves the group (see para **18.172**), to make sure that the rules are not abused. The same treatment applies for intra-group transfers of assets under the normal capital gains rules.

18.163   The rules apply when there is a realisation or part-realisation of a qualifying (post-April 2002) intellectual property asset when it is transferred from one group member to another. The transfer will be treated as tax-neutral (CTA 2009, s 775) unless one of the exceptions (see below) applies. Broadly, such transfers will either be an assignment of the intellectual property from one group company to another, or the grant of an exclusive licence from one group company to another (see Chapter 14 for more details of what constitutes a realisation or part-realisation of an intellectual property asset).

18.164   A tax-neutral transfer ensures that (CTA 2009, s 776):

- the transfer is regarded, for the purposes of the corporate intellectual property tax rules, as not involving any realisation of the asset by the transferor or any acquisition of the asset by the transferee; and

- the transferee is treated, for the purposes of the corporate intellectual property tax rules, as having held the asset since the date of acquisition by the transferor, and as though the transferee had done to the asset anything that was done by the transferor (eg incurred expenditure on further development, granted licences, etc).

Effect of the tax-neutral transfer

18.165   The transferee effectively acquires the tax history of the asset: the original cost of the asset is treated as though it was the transferee's original cost, and all amortisation and other costs and receipts which have been brought into account for tax purposes as debits and credits are treated as though the transferee had incurred them. Note that this does not mean that the transferor and transferee's tax returns need to be restated; the transfer of the history only applies to post-transfer tax matters. As a result, the transferee's amortisation deductions continue the deductions previously taken, and on a realisation the amounts brought into account are the same as they would have been if the transferee had always owned the asset.

Example 18.6

BrandCo acquires a trademark in 2008 for £100,000 and amortises that trademark over 10 years. In 2010, it transfers that trademark to a subsidiary. No tax debit or credit is brought into account by BrandCo on the transfer.

The subsidiary is treated as though it had acquired the trademark in 2008 at £100,000 and so the tax written down value of the asset for the subsidiary immediately after acquisition is £80,000 (£100,000 less two years amortisation) and continues to amortise it over the next eight years.

(See para **11.25** for details of amortisation of intellectual property.)

When is a group transfer not tax-neutral?

18.166   There are some circumstances in which the tax-neutral treatment does not apply.

Type of company

18.167   First, if one of the companies is either:

- an incorporated friendly society; or

- a dual resident investing company,

the tax-neutral treatment does not apply.

Where these types of company are involved, the market value provisions on transfers between related persons (see para **18.69**) will apply (CTA 2009, s 775(4)). These types of company are excluded because an incorporated friendly society is generally exempt from tax, and a dual resident investing company could be used to obtain double tax reliefs and so is excluded from most group relief provisions.

Branch tax exemption

18.168   Second, the tax-neutral treatment does not apply on transfers of intellectual property which have been held overseas in a permanent establishment (fixed place of business: see para **16.19**) of the transferor company, where the transferor has elected to exempt the profits of the permanent establishment under the foreign branches exemption rules introduced in Finance Act 2011 (CTA 2009, s 775(4)(c)).

18.169   If the asset has been used only by the exempted permanent establishment, the transfer is treated as taking place at market value (under the related parties rules: see para **18.69**). This ensures that any gain in value during the ownership of the permanent establishment remains exempt: if the transfer was tax-neutral, the transferee would be subject to tax on the entire gain, including the gain relating to the period of ownership of the permanent establishment, when it eventually realised the asset. Using market value means that the transferee will only be taxed on a realisation on the gain (if any) that arises during the time that it owns the asset.

Example 18.7

IPCo has a permanent establishment (PE) in France and a subsidiary (SubCo) in the UK. IPCo has elected to exempt the profits of the PE from tax in the UK under the foreign branches exemption. The PE decides to transfer a patent with a current market value of £50,000 to SubCo: the patent was acquired by PE for £10,000 and has only been used by PE. SubCo sells the patent three years later for £60,000.

If the transfer was tax-neutral, SubCo would be taxed on the later sale on a gain of £50,000 (ignoring amortisation etc for simplicity) because it would be deemed to have acquired the asset for £10,000: but £40,000 of the gain relates to the PE's ownership and would have been exempt if the PE had sold the patent to a third party instead of SubCo.

To maintain the exemption, the transfer from the PE to SubCo takes places at market value. The exemption means that the PE is not taxed on the transfer, and SubCo acquires the patent with a base cost of £50,000 so that, on the later sale, SubCo is only taxed on a gain of £10,000 (again, ignoring amortisation etc). The PE's exemption from UK tax on gains is effectively preserved by the use of the market value rule.

18.170 If the asset has been only partly used by the PE, then the transfer value is calculated to be between the tax-neutral value and the market value using the formula:

WDV + FPEA

where WDV is the tax written down value of the asset and FPEA is the 'foreign permanent establishments amount' attributable to the transfer (ie the amount which would be considered to be the profit or gain for the permanent establishment) for the accounting period in which it took place if the transfer had been made at market value (CTA 2009, s 848A).

Example 18.8

In the same group as the example above, the PE decides to transfer to SubCo a registered design which was transferred to the PE by IPCo five years ago, after it had been used by IPCo for three years. The transfer to the PE was tax-neutral (it is only transfers from a PE which are not tax-neutral). The written down value of the registered design is £5,000 (the WDV) at the date of transfer by the PE to SubCo; assume that the market value of the intellectual property asset is £20,000 at the date of transfer and the gain for the PE on that transfer would be £5,000 (the FPEA). SubCo later sells the design for £20,000.

Now, the transfer value is calculated as WDV+FPEA: £5,000+£5,000 = £10,000.

The PE is exempt on its gain, so there is no tax payable as a result of the transfer. SubCo acquires the registered design for a base cost of £10,000 and so, when it later sells the design for £20,000, it is taxed on a gain of £10,000 (ignoring amortisation etc for simplicity). This reflects the gain in value during IPCo's earlier ownership as the asset has not, in fact, gained in value during

SubCo's ownership (as the market value on transfer is the same as the sale price) and the PE's gain is exempted by being taken into account in calculated the transfer value (SubCo's base cost).

Excluded assets

18.171   Where the intellectual property asset is excluded from the corporate intangibles tax rules, the general tax rules on the taxation of capital gains of companies will apply: these provide a similar relief for certain types of intangible asset, particularly goodwill. As a result, unregistered intellectual property which is treated as part of the goodwill of the company may be capable for being transferred intra-group on a no-gain–loss basis (TCGA 1992, s 171). Other forms of intellectual property will not be within the scope of the capital gains relief and so transfers between group members will give rise to a taxable capital gain or a capital loss, with the consideration for the transfer being the market value of the asset at the date of transfer under the connected persons rule (see para **18.66**).

LEAVING THE GROUP FOLLOWING AN INTRA-GROUP TRANSFER

18.172   The treatment of intra-group transfers as tax-neutral could, without safeguards, be open to abuse. For example, transfer an intellectual property asset intra-group on a tax-neutral basis and then sell the shares in the subsidiary to which the asset was transferred to a third party (ie using the company as a 'wrapper' for the intellectual property asset). Provided that the subsidiary has been owned for at least one year, the tax relief for companies selling shares (the substantial shareholdings exemption) would mean that the group as a whole would pay no tax on what is effectively a transfer of the intellectual property asset to a third party, whereas corporation tax would have been due if the intellectual property asset had been sold directly to the third party.

18.173   To stop transactions of this sort, and ensure that some tax is due when an intellectual property asset leaves the group as a result of the sale of a group company, a de-grouping charge is applied when a company leaves a group within six years of acquiring an intellectual property asset from another group company, if it still owns that intellectual property asset at the date it leaves the group (CTA 2009, s 780 for qualifying intellectual property assets; TCGA 1992, s 179A for excluded intellectual property assets).

18.174   This raises some practical implications for companies, particularly with regard to record-keeping. It should not be assumed that, simply because a transfer is tax-neutral, it should not be properly documented and appropriate records kept. Six years is a relatively long time and, even if there is no intention at the time of the group transfer for the transferee to leave the group, circumstances and businesses can change substantially in that time. Without adequate records to be able to make proper disclosure, a vendor group may find itself at a negotiating disadvantage if the purchaser finds a substantial de-grouping issue when doing due diligence on a target company.

Comparison with de-grouping provisions for excluded intellectual property assets and non-intellectual property assets

18.175   Following the Finance Act 2011 substantial revision of the treatment of non-intellectual property de-grouping charges (TCGA 1992, s 179(3A), as inserted by Finance Act 2011), the de-grouping provisions for intellectual property assets are now very different to the non-intellectual property de-grouping charges (which will also apply to excluded intellectual property assets (see para **8.29** for excluded intellectual property assets). The reason given by HM Treasury for not including intellectual property assets in the revision was that the qualifying intellectual property asset de-grouping provisions within the corporate intangibles tax rules are separate to the provisions for other assets in the capital gains tax rules for companies. This was a slightly surprising answer given that the intellectual property asset de-grouping provisions had, up until Finance Act 2011, been largely identical to those for other assets, albeit in separate parts of the legislation.

18.176   In particular, the de-grouping charge on qualifying intellectual property assets on a sale of shares is *not* attributed to the vendor and is not added onto the gain for the disposing company. As a result, a de-grouping charge relating to a qualifying intellectual property asset cannot be relieved through the substantial shareholdings exemption. On a sale of a subsidiary's shares, any de-grouping charges relating to qualifying intellectual property assets will have to be considered and treated separately to those relating to other assets.

18.177   The following considers the relief available under the corporate intangibles tax rules for qualifying (generally post-April 2002) intellectual property assets; a brief description of the de-grouping provisions for excluded intellectual property assets follows at the end of this section (see para **18.194**).

Deemed disposal and re-acquisition for company leaving group

18.178   The de-grouping charge is created by a deemed disposal and reacquisition of a qualifying intellectual property asset: the company leaving the group is taxed as though it had sold that intellectual property asset and immediately re-acquired it at the same price (CTA 2009, s 780(2)). The deemed disposal and reacquisition is treated as having taken place immediately after the original transfer to the company leaving the group, and treated as having taken place at market value on the date of that transfer.

18.179 If the deemed disposal at market value results in a gain, that de-grouping gain is brought into account for tax purposes in the accounting period in which the company leaves the group, not the accounting period in which the transfer took place.

Example 18.9

IPCo acquires a patent in 2006 for £40,000. It transfers the patent to its subsidiary, SubCo, on 1 January 2008. The market value of the asset at the date of transfer is £50,000; this transfer is tax-neutral (see para **18.163**), and SubCo is treated as having acquired the asset in 2006 for £40,000.

At the end of 2012, SubCo is sold to BuyCo. It still owns the patent at the date of sale and so the de-grouping provisions apply. SubCo is deemed to have sold the patent on 1 January 2008 for £50,000 and immediately re-acquired it. SubCo will have realised a gain of £10,000 on that deemed disposal, and will suffer a de-grouping charge in respect of that gain in the 2012 accounting period.

Asset transferred to associated company

18.180 The charge cannot be avoided by further intra-group transfers: If the asset has been transferred to another company, associated with the company which is leaving the group, which also leaves the group at the same time then the de-grouping charge will still arise in the first company (CTA 2009, s 780(1)(f)). Two companies are considered to be 'associated' for these purposes where one is the 75% subsidiary (see para **18.144**) of the other or both are 75% subsidiaries of a third company (CTA 2009, s 788(3)); note that this is a different definition to that of 'associate' in the patent box rules (see para **18.158**).

Example 18.10

Assume, in the example above, SubCo had transferred the patent to a subsidiary of its own (SubCo2, which is not also a subsidiary of IPCo, as the shareholdings are not 100%, although SubCo 2 is a 75% subsidiary of SubCo) before leaving the IPCo group. As the shares in SubCo are sold to the purchaser, SubCo2 is also transferred to the purchaser's group as a subsidiary of SubCo, still owning the patent. SubCo will still be subject to the same de-grouping charge, even though the asset is now held by SubCo2.

Pre-group membership transfers

18.181   There is no requirement that the original transfer to the company leaving the group has to have taken place as an intra-group transfer: the deemed disposal and reacquisition on leaving the group will still apply even if the company originally acquired the asset before it entered the group (CTA 2009, s 780(1)(d)(ii)). However, in this case, the intellectual property asset will usually have been acquired for market value (as a transaction between third parties, or between related parties: see para **18.69**) and so a deemed disposal at market value immediately after acquisition should not result in a gain (nor will it give rise to any amortisation adjustments).

Example 18.11

IPCo sells a patent for £50,000 to IPCo2 in 2009; at the time, the companies are not connected and so the market value of the patent at the date of transfer is £50,000. In 2010, IPCo2 is acquired by IPCo's parent company so that IPCo and IPCo2 are now members of the same group. In 2012, IPCo2 still owns the patent and is sold to another, unconnected, company and leaves the group. On leaving the group, the de-grouping provisions will operate because there has been a transfer of an intellectual property asset to IPCo2 by another company in the group in the previous six years, even though there was no group relationship between them at the time.

As a result, IPCo2 is deemed to have disposed of the patent immediately after it acquired it from IPCo. That deemed disposal is treated as being for market value at that date (£50,000). As this is the same as IPCo's acquisition cost there is no gain and so no de-grouping charge actually arises.

Effect of amortisation on de-grouping

18.182   As the company leaving the group is taxed on the gain arising from the deemed disposal at market value, the deemed market value reacquisition immediately following the original transfer will give rise to an amortisation adjustment for the company. Until the company leaves the group and triggers the de-grouping charge, it will (generally) receive amortisation deductions which reflect the value and date at which the intellectual property asset was originally acquired by the transferor. As it is now being taxed as though it had acquired the asset at market value on the date of the transfer, these amortisation deductions are adjusted to reflect that market value and the deemed shorter period of ownership. The de-grouping gain is then altered by these amortisation adjustments to establish the amount that is brought into account for tax purposes on de-grouping.

Example 18.12

In the first example above, IPCo acquires the patent in 2006 for £40,000. Assuming that the patent has a useful economic life of 10 years, the amortisation deduction will generally be £4,000 per year (ignoring any impairment reviews). When SubCo acquires the asset on the intra-group transfer in 2008 it inherits this tax history and continues to receive tax deductions for amortisation of £4,000 per year.

SubCo leaves the group on 31 December 2011 and triggers a de-grouping charge: it is now deemed to have acquired the patent in 2008 for £50,000 (market value at the date of transfer). At that date the remaining useful economic life has been reduced by two years and so is now eight years. SubCo is, therefore, entitled to amortisation deductions of £6,250 per year from the date of transfer. Assuming that the date of transfer is the first day of an accounting period, SubCo is entitled to an additional £2,250 (the revised amortisation deduction of £6,250, less the amortisation deduction already given) for each of the three accounting periods between the date of transfer and the date on which SubCo leaves the group (total adjustment: £18,750). SubCo will continue to be entitled to amortisation deductions of £6,250 for accounting periods after it leaves the group.

The amortisation adjustment is given by deduction from the deemed gain on de-grouping so that it, in effect, reduces the de-grouping charge.

In the example above, SubCo has a de-grouping gain of £10,000. This will be reduced by the amortisation adjustment of £6,750 so that the de-grouping charge in the 2011 accounting period is in fact based on an adjusted gain of £3,250 (£10,000–£6,750).

Exceptions to the de-grouping charge

18.183   There are some circumstances in which the de-grouping charge will not apply; some of these were re-written in July 2011 as part of the Finance Act 2011 changes, even though the intellectual property asset de-grouping provisions generally were not amended in the same way as the de-grouping provisions for non-intellectual property assets (see above).

18.184   The principal exemption is where an intellectual property asset has been transferred and the transferor and the transferee leave the group together; there is no de-grouping charge in respect of that transfer because the overall effect is neutral.

Transferor and transferee leave group together

On or after 19 July 2011

18.185   In order for the exemption to apply, the transferor and transferee must (CTA 2009, s 783, as amended by FA 2011) either be grouped under the same parent company so that:

- both be 75% subsidiaries and effective 51% subsidiaries of the same third company on the date of the transfer of the intellectual property asset; and

- continue to both be 75% subsidiaries and effective 51% subsidiaries of that third company until immediately after they cease to be members of the group,

or one of the two companies must be the parent company of the other so that one company:

- is a 75% subsidiary and an effective 51% subsidiary of the other on the date of the transfer of the intellectual property asset; and

- remains a 75% subsidiary and an effective 51% subsidiary of the other company until immediately after they cease to be members of the group.

Before 19 July 2011

18.186   The pre-Finance Act 2011 exemption was slightly different, in that it carried a further specific requirement that the intellectual property asset transferred between the transferor and the transferee must not previously have been transferred to the transferor by a company which does not leave the group (CTA 2009, s 783 before amendment by FA 2011).

18.187   In practice, this will make little difference: the post-Finance Act 2011 exemption does not contain any reference to the asset not having previously been transferred intra-group but, if the intellectual property asset was transferred intra-group to the transferor within the six years before the companies leave the group, the de-grouping provisions will still apply to that first transfer as the asset has been transferred to an associated company. It is only the second transfer, between the companies leaving the group, which is exempted by CTA 2009, s 783.

Anti-avoidance

18.188   Anti-avoidance provisions (CTA 2009, s 783(2)) apply to ensure that the definition of a group cannot be used to avoid a de-grouping charge when a transferee company leaves a group which is treated as a different group to that which the transferee company belonged to when the transfer occurred, if there is a relevant connection between the two groups. There will be a relevant connection (CTA 2009, s 784) if, at the time when the transferee company ceases to be a member of the second group, the company which is the principal company of that second group is under the control of one of the following:

- the company that is the principal company of the first group or, if that group no longer exists, was the principal company of the first group when the transferee company ceased to be a member of it; or

- any person or persons who controls the parent company of the first group or who has done at any time since the transferee company ceased to be a member of the first group; or

- if a person who controls the parent company of the first group is a company that has ceased to exist, any person or persons who has controlled that controlling company; or

- if any person under the above categories is a company, then any person or persons who controls that company.

Example 18.13

IPCo acquired an trademark from TMCo in an intra-group transfer while they were both members of Group A. IPCo and TMCo both leave Group A at the same time, and so no de-grouping charge arises.

Having left the group, IPCo and TMCo together make up Group B. If TMCo later leaves Group B, there would be no de-grouping charge without the anti-avoidance provisions, because the transfer took place in Group A but TMCo leaves Group B. However, if there is a relevant connection between Group A and Group B (broadly, where IPCo is controlled by the parent company of Group A or by a person who controls that parent company), then there will be a de-grouping charge when TMCo leaves Group B within six years of the date of the transfer.

Other exemptions

18.189   There is no de-grouping charge where:

- the parent company of a group becomes a member of another group, so that the first group is absorbed into the second (CTA 2009, s 785: note that this does not stop a de-grouping charge where a company then leaves the second group within six years of having had an intellectual property asset transferred to it by another group member before the parent company became a member of the second group); or

- a company ceases to be a member of a group because another member of the group has ceased to exist (eg where the parent company is wound up) (CTA 2009, s 788(1)); or

- a company ceases to be a member of a group as a result of an exempt distribution under CTA 2010, s 1076 or 1077 (exemption from tax on distribution to its members by a parent company of the shares in one or more 75% subsidiaries) subject to clawback provisions if there is a chargeable payment (CTA 2010, s 1088) made for those shares within five years of the distribution (CTA 2009, s 787); or

- a company ceases to be a member of a group as a result of a merger carried out for genuine commercial reasons (CTA 2009, s 789; as the UK does not generally recognise mergers of companies other than to form a Socieatas Europea, s 789 contains the conditions which must apply for a transaction to qualify as a merger).

Reallocation of a de-grouping charge between group companies

18.190   Where a company triggers a de-grouping charge on leaving a group, it can jointly elect with a continuing group member to transfer the de-grouping charge to that group member (CTA 2009, s 792).

18.191   The re-allocated de-grouping charge is treated as a non-trading credit (see para **14.19** for more information on non-trading credits). This election is useful principally where the continuing group member has non-trading debits which can be used to effectively minimise or eliminate the de-grouping change; a purchaser might also insist on the election as a condition of purchase so that it is not subject to the de-grouping charge.

18.192   The continuing group should, however, be aware that any amortisation adjustment that arises as a result of the de-grouping provisions cannot be transferred with the de-grouping charge. Where possible, this should be taken into account in any consideration for the disposal of the shares of the company leaving the group.

Example 18.14

IPCo is sold to another company, leaving the IP Group. At the time it leaves the group, it holds a design right that was transferred to it by another group company four years ago. A de-grouping gain arises of £150,000, and IPCo is entitled to an amortisation adjustment of an additional £50,000 as a result of the deemed reacquisition at the date of transfer.

Only the de-grouping gain can be reallocated to a continuing member of the IP Group (assuming that a joint election is made). IPCo continues to have the benefit of the additional £50,000 amortisation adjustment. This will reduce UK corporation tax by £11,500, if the corporation tax rate in the accounting period in which IPCo leaves the group is 23%.

18.193   The continuing group member must meet certain criteria, but these are not particularly onerous. It must:

- be a member of the group immediately before the intellectual property asset-holding company leaves the group; and

- be within the scope of UK corporation tax, either directly or through a corporation tax charge (unsurprisingly, otherwise the gain would not be taxable in the UK); and

- not be a qualifying friendly society or a dual-resident investing company (as these are outside the scope of the corporate intangibles tax regime).

Excluded assets: de-grouping charges

18.194   Where intellectual property assets are excluded from the corporate intangibles tax rules (either because the asset is not qualifying—eg it is a pre-1 April 2002 asset—or because the owner is a non-qualifying entity), a de-grouping charge may still apply under the corporate capital gains tax rules. The detailed scope of the corporate capital gains tax rules is outside the scope of this book, but the following is an overview of the provisions.

On or after 19 July 2011

18.195   Where a company's shares are sold to a third party so that it leaves a group owning an excluded intellectual property asset that has been transferred to it by another group member within the previous six years, a de-grouping gain or loss in respect of the excluded intellectual property asset arises in the company which has sold the shares, and is added to (or deducted from) the gain or loss arising on the sale of the shares (TCGA 1992, s 179, as amended by FA 2011). The de-grouping gain or loss is still calculated on the basis of a deemed disposal and reacquisition of the excluded intellectual property asset at the time of the original transfer. There is no amortisation adjustment as no amortisation deductions are available in respect of excluded assets.

18.196   The original transfer must have taken place at a time when both companies were members of the same group (TCGA 1992, s 179(1)), unlike the corporate intangibles rules where a de-grouping charge can apply to a transfer which took place before the transferee joined the group.

18.197   An adjusted gain on the sale of the shares may be eligible for substantial shareholdings relief so that the de-grouping gain is effectively exempt from corporation tax.

18.198   Where the transferee leaves the group as a result of something other than the sale of shares (eg where new shares are issued, diluting the parent company's holding) then the pre-FA 2011 rules continue to apply and the de-grouping charge arises in the transferee in the same way as for qualifying intangible assets. The charge may be reallocated to a continuing group member by joint election.

ROLL-OVER RELIEF IN GROUPS

18.199 Roll-over relief (see para **14.32** for full details) can be claimed on a realisation (including a part-realisation) where the new asset is acquired by another member of the same group, rather than the company making the realisation or part-realisation (CTA 2009, s 777(1)).

Example 18.15

BrandCo sells a design right at a gain of £100,000 on 1 August 2011. IPCo incurs £250,000 expenditure on 30 September 2010. If BrandCo and IPCo are each members of the IP Group at the time of their respective transactions, BrandCo will be able to defer the gain on that realisation of the design right against the qualifying expenditure on the intangible assets acquired by IPCo.

18.200 The conditions for the roll-over relief claim against a group company's acquisition to be made are (CTA 2009, s 777(3)) that:

- the company making the part-realisation must be a member of a group at the time of that part-realisation; and

- the company acquiring the new asset:

    — must be a member of the same group mentioned when the expenditure is incurred (though there is no requirement that the two companies need to be members of the same group simultaneously); and

    — must not be a dual resident investing company, and

- the new assets:

    — must be chargeable intangible assets (eg not held for non-commercial purposes) of the company acquiring them immediately after the expenditure on them is incurred; and

    — must not be acquired by a tax-neutral transfer (see para **18.162**) from another group company.

The relief must be claimed by both companies, not just the company making the part-realisation, as the relief will reduce the acquisition cost for tax purposes of the company acquiring the asset.

18.201 There is no requirement that the company which makes the gain and the company which incurs the expenditure on a new asset against which the gain is reinvested are members of the same group at the same time. They each simply have to be a member of that group at the relevant times: for the company making the gain, that is the time at which the intellectual property asset leading to the gain is realised. For the company incurring expenditure on a new asset, it is the time at which the new asset is acquired. As there can be up to four years between the acquisition of the new asset and the gain on the realisation of the old asset, it could be that the two companies are never in a group together at the same time.

Example 18.16

Considering the example above, assume that IPCo out of the IP Group is sold in December 2010 and BrandCo joins the IP Group in March 2011. BrandCo can still claim roll-over relief against IPCo's acquisition (assuming, of course, that IPCo consents to the joint election: this is something that could be required by any contract for the sale of IPCo's shares, for example) even though the two companies were never members of the IP Group at the same time.

Roll-over relief on acquisition of a new group company

18.202 Roll-over relief is principally focused on the acquisition of intellectual property assets; where a company has incurred a gain on the sale of an intellectual property asset, that gain can be deferred by the use of roll-over relief on the acquisition of new intellectual property assets.

18.203 However, where new intellectual property assets are brought into the group through the acquisition of shares in a company, the relief would not normally be available: the subject of the acquisition is the shares in the company, not the intellectual property itself.

18.204 A claim can be made to treat a company acquisition as an acquisition of the underlying intellectual property assets for the purposes of the corporate intellectual property tax rules, so that roll-over relief can be claimed in respect of an earlier disposal (CTA 2009, s 778).

18.205 A company is 'acquired' when it is brought into the group; that is, when company A acquires enough shares in company B to make the company a subsidiary of company A: the group test here being the 75% subsidiary test (see para **18.144**).

Example 18.17

Company A has disposed of a patent at a gain. Company A also owns 65% of company B; if it acquires another 10% of company B's share capital then company B will be brought into company A's group. Company A can claim roll-over relief on the patent gain against any relevant intellectual property held by company B.

There is no restriction on relief if the holding in company B is not 100%.

Subsidiaries

18.206   If company B has any subsidiaries that also become subsidiaries of company A as a result of the acquisition of shares in company B (ie they become effective 51% subsidiaries of company A: see para **18.145**) then the relevant intellectual property assets of those subsidiaries can also be treated as acquired, and utilised for roll-over relief (CTA 2009, s 778(2)).

Relevant intellectual property assets

18.207   The intellectual property assets held by company B (or the subsidiaries) must be 'chargeable intangible assets'; ie they must be within the corporate intangibles tax rules (CTA 2009, s 756 and s 779(3), (4)).

Deemed expenditure for relief

18.208   When a claim is made, company A is deemed to have incurred expenditure on acquiring the eligible underlying intellectual property assets of company B. It is this deemed expenditure which enables company A to claim roll-over relief on the gain on disposals (CTA 2009, s 779(1)).

18.209   The amount of the deemed expenditure is the lower of (CTA 2009, s 779(2)):

- the cost of acquiring the shares in company B which bring it into the group (in the example above, that would be the 10% holding acquired); or

- the tax written down value of the relevant intellectual property assets held by company B and/or its subsidiaries.

Claim and effect of claim

18.210   The claim for relief needs to be made jointly by the acquiring company and the company being acquired (CTA 2009, s 778(4)), and the effect of the claim is that:

- the tax written down value of the underlying assets are reduced by the amount available for relief; and

- where the expenditure on acquiring the company exceeds the amount of the gain for which relief is sought and there is more than one asset on which relief is based, the company owning the underlying assets can decide how to allocate the reduction;

- where the assets on which relief is based are held by more than one company then the companies holding those asset can decide how to allocate the reduction amongst them.

Roll-over relief and de-grouping

18.211 Where a company leaves the group and there is a de-grouping charge (see para **18.172**), the company incurring the charge can treat this as a disposal of an intellectual property asset for roll-over relief purposes (CTA 2009, s 791), and defer the gain against the acquisition of another intellectual property asset. This is an exception to the general rule that roll-over relief cannot reduce a gain on the deemed realisation of an intellectual property asset (see para **14.40**).

18.212 Various adaptations to the roll-over rules are made for this to apply:

- the asset which gives rise to the de-grouping charge must have been a relevant intellectual property asset for the group company from which the de-grouping company acquired the asset (CTA 2009, s 791(2); see para **14.34**);

- the time limits for reinvestment run from the date of the event that triggers the de-grouping charge, not the date of the intra-group transfer (CTA 2009, s 791(3); see para **14.45**); and

- the proceeds of realisation are the market value of the asset on the deemed realisation on de-grouping (CTA 2009, s 791(4)).

The reacquisition cost of the asset for the company leaving the group after the deemed realisation is not reduced by any de-grouping charge (CTA 2009, s 791(5)).

Reallocation of de-grouping charge

18.213 Where the de-grouping charged is reallocated to a continuing group company (see para **18.173**), the company taking on the charge is deemed to have realised the relevant asset so that it can claim roll-over relief on the deemed disposal (CTA 2009, s 794). The de-grouping company must have initially satisfied the requirements above for the deemed disposal to be capable of being relieved by roll-over relief. If only part of the de-grouping charge is reallocated, then roll-over relief can be applied to the corresponding part of the deemed disposal.

INTELLECTUAL PROPERTY TAX INCENTIVES: EFFECT OF BEING IN A GROUP

18.214   See above for definition of 'group' for the purposes of the research and development tax reliefs (see para **18.154**) and the patent box (see para **18.150**): the following is an outline of the impact of being part of a group on the incentives.

Research and development

SME subsidiaries can still qualify for relief

18.215   One of the more common misconceptions about the SME research and development relief is that it is not available for companies which are subsidiaries within a group. The 'independence' test (see para **10.70**) might seem a barrier, suggesting that the company cannot be a subsidiary of another company but, in practice, the definition of 'independent' is wide enough to allow certain subsidiaries to qualify.

18.216   An SME is independent if less than 25% of its capital or voting rights can be owned by one or more companies *that are not SMEs* (see para **10.67** for details). That means that, provided that the group as a whole meets the criteria for being an SME for research and development tax relief purposes, the parent company will be regarded as an SME and so subsidiaries within the group will still qualify as independent for the purposes of the definition. There is no geographical requirement, so the parent company (and/or any intermediary companies) can be outside the UK. Only the claimant company needs to be within the scope of UK corporation tax.

18.217   Note that ownership of 25% of more by venture capital companies, institutional investors and public investment corporations will not disqualify a company from being an SME, provided that they do not have actual control of the SME (HMRC Manual CIRD91300)).

Group research and development companies: relevance to trade

18.218   Where the trade of the company is the carrying out of research and development (for example, where a single group company provides all research and development functions for the group, creating new intellectual property for the group to exploit) then the research and development carried out is still considered to be relevant to that trade (see para **10.4** for more details of the requirement that the research and development be relevant to the trade of the company).

Subcontracting: large company relief

18.219 Where research and development is carried out by one group company on behalf of another, the research and development will be qualifying research and development (for the large company research and development relief) for the company doing the research and development if the qualifying activities of the two companies together would be qualifying research and development for the company making the payment (see para **10.5**).

Subcontracting: SME relief

18.220 Where research and development activities are subcontracted by an SME, and the subcontractor is connected to the SME, then the costs that can be claimed by the SME as qualifying research and development expenditure may be restricted (see para **10.112**). Similar restrictions apply where staff are provided by a connected company (see para **10.126**). Two companies will be 'connected' for reasons other than group membership (see para **18.66**) but two companies in the same group will always be connected, so that where work is subcontracted between group companies, the potential restriction on qualifying research and development expenditure must be considered.

Patent box

18.221 Various provisions of the draft patent box proposals contain amendments, or additional requirements, where a company is part of a group. Note that the definition of a 'group' for patent box purposes is very wide (see para **18.154**).

The development condition

18.222 The development condition (see para **13.35** for more details) for the patent box can be met by a company through one of a number of criteria. These all relate, directly or indirectly, to group membership, requiring that:

- the company has carried out the qualifying development activity at any time and has not joined or left a group in the meantime; or

- the company has carried out qualifying development activity, and has continued to carry out development activity of the same description for at least 12 months after leaving or joining a group; or

- the company is a member of a group and the qualifying development activity was carried out by another company which was a member of the same group at the time it carried out the development (eg where the group includes a research and development company which is separate to the intellectual property holding entities); or

- the company is a member of a group and the qualifying development activity was carried out by another company which at some point in time was a member of the same group and that other company has carried out development activities for at least 12 months after joining the group and did not leave the group during that time.

The active ownership condition

18.223 The active ownership condition (see para **13.29** for more details) applies *only* to companies that are within a group, and requires the company to have either:

- carried out the development activity itself; or

- be actively involved in the ongoing management of the qualifying intellectual property rights (note: active management of other intellectual property rights is irrelevant, it must be the patents and associated rights that are managed).

18.224 To meet this condition, almost all (or all) of the qualifying intellectual property rights (see para **13.12**) held by the company in an accounting period must be intellectual property rights in respect of which the company either:

- performs a significant amount of management activity; or

- meets the development condition by carrying out the development itself (ie not by attribution of another group company's activity).

This requirement is intended to make sure that a passive intellectual property holding company cannot qualify for the patent box relief.

Exclusive licence requirements

18.225 To be exclusive for the purposes of the patent box relief, a licence must give various rights (see para **13.17**) including:

- the right to bring proceedings for infringement of the rights without consent of the grantor or any other person; and

- the right to receive the whole (or greater part) of any damages awarded in respect of any infringement.

18.226 A group may have an intellectual property holding company which licenses intellectual property to other group members but maintains sufficient rights to continue to manage the intellectual property within the portfolio; this licence would not meet the strict criteria for an exclusive licence. Nevertheless, a group company with the benefit of a licence over qualifying intellectual property rights from the intellectual property holding company will be able to elect into the patent box regime as if it had an exclusive licence, provided that it has all rights other than those required to enforce, assign or licence the intellectual property right and the intellectual property holding company has those other rights (see para **13.20** for more details).

The amount of routine expenses

18.227 A company claiming patent box relief is required, as part of the patent box calculation, to deduct a 'routine return' (see para **13.112**). This is calculated as 10% of certain specific expenses incurred by the company or, where the company is a member of a group, incurred by another group company on behalf of the patent box claimant company (see para **13.115**). This does not prevent the patent box claimant from buying services from other group companies: the provision of services under a specific agreement is not treated as payment of expenses on behalf of the claimant. That said, the expenditure on the services by the claimant is likely to be treated as a routine expense in any case.

Loss set-offs

18.228 A patent box claimant with relevant intellectual property losses is required to set these losses off against relevant intellectual property profits (see para **13.177**). The legislation provides a series of required set-offs, including a requirement that any remaining losses must be set-off against any relevant intellectual property profits of group companies for the relevant accounting period. The 'relevant accounting period' is any accounting period which ends at the same time as the group company's accounting period or during which the group company's accounting period ends, if they do not end on the same date.

18.229 Where losses are carried forward to a subsequent accounting period, the set-off of any carried forward amount remaining after set-off against the company's own relevant intellectual property profits must against be set-off against any group companies' relevant intellectual property profits.

18.230 In effect, a company in a group cannot carry forward relevant intellectual property losses unless and until all relevant intellectual property profits in the group have been reduced to nil.

TYPES OF INTELLECTUAL PROPERTY BUSINESS

CREATIVE PROFESSIONALS: AUTHORS, ARTISTS, COMPOSERS ETC

18.231 Creative professionals are generally regarded as carrying on a profession (that of author, artist, composer etc) creating copyright works. The receipts are, accordingly, generally taxed as income of a profession under ITTOIA 2005, Pt 2 (see para **6.52**).

18.232 However, receipts from a creative work can also arise on an occasional basis, where the activities are not sufficient to amount to a profession; will usually be taxed as miscellaneous income (see para **6.51**). Where there is an outright disposal of a creative work by a non-professional the receipt may instead be taxed as a capital gain (see para **7.22**).

18.233 Where copyright royalties are received from the UK by a non-UK resident, the royalties are generally subject to withholding tax at the basic rate of income tax (20% at the time of writing; see para **16.65**).

Creative professional or occasional author/artist etc?

18.234 A detailed review of the distinction between someone carrying on a creative profession and someone who does not do so is beyond the scope of this book (although see para **3.12** for a brief overview). In most cases it is fairly obvious that someone is carrying on a profession, such as authors, composers, artists etc who systematically exploit their creative activities on a commercial basis. There is more difficulty with occasional authors who may only produce one or two works.

18.235 Case law has not set out hard and fast rules. In *Billam v Griffiths* (1941) 23 TC 757 the individual had written a handful of plays in his spare time; only one was commercially successful, but he was held to be carrying on a profession as an author in respect of the income from the play and the sale of the film rights. The High Court appears to have attached some importance to the fact that the taxpayer was described as 'professionally known as George Billam' in an agreement relating to the successful play.

18.236 On the other hand, in *Nethersole v Withers* (1946) 28 TC 501, an actress who had dramatised one novel was held not to be carrying on the profession of author when she sold the film rights to the play. The reasoning in this case appears to be the passage of time: almost 20 years passed between the dramatisation and the sale of the film rights, and the Commissioners held that Miss Nethersole had ceased to carry on the profession of author many years before the film rights were sold (although see para **18.253** below for the current position on cessation of a trade, profession or vocation).

Services

18.237 In the case of *Hobbs v Hussey* (1942) 24 TC 153, the taxpayer (a clerk) agreed to write his memoir, and sell the copyright, for a flat fee; the court held that the transaction was one of services. The key point was the order of events: the decision might have been substantially different if the taxpayer had already written his memoirs. The receipt was taxed as what is now miscellaneous income (see para **6.51**) as the taxpayer was not considered to be carrying on a profession as an author. A similar conclusion was reached in *Housden v Marshall* (1958) 38 TC 233, in which a jockey was paid for the first British serial rights over reminiscences of his racing career, which were written up by a ghost writer.

18.238 Accordingly, where the payment to an occasional author is, in effect, for services—such as assisting a ghost writer—the payment will be taxed as income under the general sweep-up provisions in ITTOIA 2005, s 687 if that income cannot otherwise be taxed as income of a trade, profession or vocation under the provisions of ITTOIA 2005, Pt 2.

Receipts of a creative professional: income or capital?

18.239 Ongoing royalties received by a creative professional will be taxed as income (see para **18.231**); there is unlikely to be any particular dispute about that treatment. Other transactions may be appear more complicated: the sale of film rights, for example, or a one-off payment for a creative work.

18.240 In practice, case law has generally determined that receipts of creative professionals in respect of their works will almost always be taxed as income rather than capital. The majority of such case law pre-dates the introduction of capital gains tax and addresses a number of attempts to have such receipts taxed as capital, to escape tax altogether. The introduction of capital gains tax has reduced the benefit of capital treatment, although the difference between capital gains tax (28% at the time of writing) and income tax (up to 50% at the time of writing, together with Class 4 National Insurance Contributions) may still create some interest in the status of a particular receipt.

Income receipts

18.241 The courts have established that any receipts on the sale of copyright by a creative professional will be considered to be part of the income of the profession for tax purposes, as the professional is considered to create and dispose of copyright material as part of the profession.

18.242 Any receipts on the disposal of copyright by a creative professional will therefore be taxed as trading income, under ITTOIA 2005, Pt 2 (see para **7.59**). The best-known case on the point is *Glasson v Rougier* (1944) 26 TC 86: the taxpayer in this case being better known by her pen name, Georgette Heyer. Heyer had entered into contracts with her publisher to transfer the publishing rights in three of her books to the publisher in exchange for a lump sum payment. The court held that the lump sum should be taxed in the same way as the royalties that it, in effect, replaced.

18.243 The case of *Howson v Monsell* (1950) 31 TC 529 developed the point further: the taxpayer was an author (under the name Margaret Irwin), who had sold the film rights to two of her books for fixed amounts. The judge held that, as authors carry on a trade of creating copyright, the receipt from the disposal of rights is considered to be the result of professional activity, rather than a capital receipt.

Grants and prizes

18.244 Professional creators of copyright may enter competitions for prizes (particularly authors, artists and architects). HMRC consider that an award, grant, bursary or prize from such a competition is normally taxable as a professional receipt if it comes to the recipient as a result of the exercise of a profession or vocation as a copyright creator (HMRC Manual BIM50710). This applies regardless of whether the entry is made by the creator or on the creator's behalf by an agent, such as a publisher.

18.245 However, a prize which is unsolicited and which is awarded as a matter of honour, distinction or public esteem for the work of a creative professional is not taxable (eg the Nobel Prize for Literature: nominations for this prize are only accepted from a very limited group of people).

18.246 Where the award is received by someone who is not a professional author or artist, the receipt will generally be taxed as miscellaneous income (see para **6.51**). Where, exceptionally, the award is received by an employee in the course of their employment, it will be taxed as income from the employment.

18.247 A number of Arts Council awards are not taxable. As the awards vary from time to time, it is recommended that the documentation for each award is checked on application, as this will generally indicate whether the award is taxable.

Public lending right payments and copying payments

18.248 Public lending right is the right of authors to receive payment for the loans of their books by public libraries, established by the Public Lending Right Act 1979. Payment for UK lending is made to registered authors through the Public Lending Right office, funded by the Department for Culture, Media and Sports. A number of other countries have similar schemes; payment to UK authors for these is administered by the Authors' Licensing and Collecting Society (ALCS). ALCS also administers payment to authors from licences for photocopying and scanning copyright material, and other small literary rights.

18.249 Such payments are treated as intellectual property payments for tax purposes (ITA 2007, s 907(1)(c)) and therefore part of the income from the profession as an author.

Capital receipts

18.250 In general, as is clear from the cases already discussed, a creative professional will be subject to income tax rather than capital gains tax on the disposal of any copyrights: the comment made by HMRC (following the courts) is that such a professional's capital asset is their brain, not the copyrights produced by the brain (HMRC Manual BIM35725).

18.251 An individual who does not, and has not, carried on a creative profession may be subject to capital gains tax on the disposal of a copyright. In general, this will be where the copyright has been held as an investment (see, for example, *Shiner v Lindblom* (1960) 39 TC 367).

Receipts after the cessation of the profession

18.252 Normally, income receipts are subject to tax on an accruals basis (ie as it is earned, even if not yet paid: ITTOIA 2005, s 27) and so income which is received after the profession has ceased (eg after retirement) has usually already been taxed in an earlier accounting period.

18.253 However, where receipts do arise after cessation of the profession which have not already been taxed—for example, where the income has not been accrued for because it is not considered prudent to do so—it will now generally be caught by the post-cessation rules (the case of *Nethersole* discussed above would have a rather different outcome today). These rules apply to receipts by the creative professional and third parties (eg personal representatives, where the creative professional has died). The receipt will be subject to income tax (ITTOIA 2005, ss 241–247).

Overseas receipts: withholding taxes

18.254 It is not only the UK that imposes withholding taxes on copyright royalties; many other countries will also require that the local payer of the royalty deducts withholding tax before making the payment to the creative professional. Withholding taxes are deducted from the gross royalty (see para **16.83**) and take no account of any expenses that may have been incurred in creating the copyright work; as a result, they can be disproportionately large compared to the UK tax which is charged on the profits (ie the royalties less expenses).

Treaty relief

18.255 Where there is a tax treaty between the UK and the country where the payer is located, it is usually possible to claim a reduction on the withholding tax, sometimes to nil. To the claim the reduction, the creative professional will generally have to complete a form claiming the benefit of the treaty. The forms vary from country to country but most will require some form of confirmation from HMRC that the recipient is entitled to the benefit of the treaty. If the form does not have a specific wording for HMRC to confirm, the creative professional can request a letter from HMRC with the confirmation (the UK does not issue specific certificates of tax residence).

Unilateral relief

18.256 Where there is no tax treaty, or the treaty does not reduce the withholding tax to nil, the foreign tax withheld can be used to reduce the UK tax due on the same income (TIOPA 2010, s 9), provided that the creative professional is tax resident in the UK. This unilateral relief is limited to the amount of withholding tax that would be deducted after all relevant claims and elections have been made: for example, where there is a relevant tax treaty that reduces the withholding tax, the relief is calculated on the basis that a treaty claim has been made: HMRC will not give relief where the taxpayer cannot be bothered to deal with the treaty claim paperwork.

Example 18.18

Fred is a composer, a session musician and is also employed as a music teacher at a local school. As a result, he receives employment income (from teaching), self-employment income (as a session musician), and self-employment income as a composer. He receives royalty payments from his publisher, an overseas company, who deal with licensing his music. The overseas publisher deals with the withholding tax issues on this licensing, but they are required to withhold tax at 10% from the royalty that they pay to Fred. Assuming that all appropriate treaty claims and elections have been made, Fred's tax position in 2011/12 is:

Employment income £15,000

Self-employment profits (sessions) £25,000

Overseas royalty payment £10,000 (assume no associated UK expenses to deduct)

Total £50,000

Less personal allowance (£7,475)

Taxable income £42,525

Tax on £35,000 at 20% = £7,000

Tax on £7,525 at 40% = £3,010

Total tax due = £10,010

To calculate Fred's tax relief for the withholding tax suffered, the tax attributable to the royalty payment must be established. This is calculated (TIOPA 2010, s 36(2)) by comparing the UK tax due on overall income with the UK tax due on income excluding the overseas royalty payment.

Excluding the royalty, taxable income is £32,525

Tax on £32,525 at 20% = £6,507

So the UK income tax attributable to the royalty payment is (£10,010–£6,507) = £3,503

As this is higher than the tax withheld of £1,000 (£10,000 at 10%), the full withholding tax suffered can be deducted in calculating Fred's UK income tax, so that his final UK tax due will be £9,010.

Multiple sources of income

18.257   Where the creative professional has more than one source of overseas income from which tax has been withheld, it must repeat this comparison for each source of income, starting with the income with the highest rate withholding tax, to establish the relief that can be deducted.

Example 18.19

If Fred in Example 18.17 had had total overseas royalties of £10,000 made up of two payments of £5,000, one from a country which withholds tax at 20% and one which withholds tax at 10%, the comparison would be as follows:

Taking the 20% withholding rate payment first:

Excluding the first royalty, taxable income is £37,525

Tax on £35,000 at 20% = £7,000

Tax on £2,525 at 40% = £1,010

Total tax due is £8,010

So the UK income tax attributable to the first royalty payment is £2,000 (£10,010-8,010); the tax withheld on this payment is £1,000, so the relief on the withholding tax is available in full as it is less than the UK income tax attributable to the royalty.

Then taking the 10% withholding rate payment:

Excluding both royalty payments, taxable income is £32,525

Tax thereon at 20% = £6,507

UK income tax attributable to the second payment is £1,503 (£10,010–£2,000 (already attributed) –£6,507). The tax withheld on this payment is £500, so relief is available in full as it is less than the UK income tax attributable to the royalty.

(Note: although this comes to the same result as if the overall £1,500 withholding tax was deducted from the total royalties when calculating the relief, it is necessary to consider the payments separately as relief is given against each overseas income element separately, not as a whole).

18.258 Where the creative professional makes a loss, or otherwise does not have enough UK tax liability to offset the withholding tax, or any part of the withholding tax is disallowed (eg because an appropriate treaty claim has not been made) the withholding tax can be treated as an expense instead (TIOPA 2010, ss 35–36). This is not as valuable a relief as the offset, but it is better than nothing.

Example 18.20

Considering Fred in Example 18.17, if he had not bothered to make a treaty claim and tax had been withheld at 30% instead, the total withholding tax suffered would have been £3,000. As a treaty claim would have reduced this to £1,000, only that £1,000 can be offset against UK tax due. The balancing £2,000 can be deducted as an expense.

This would reduce the UK taxable royalty payment to £8,000, and Fred's tax position for 2011/12 would be:

Employment income = £15,000

Self-employment income (sessions) = £25,000

Overseas royalty payment (after deduction) = £8,000

Total = £48,000

Less personal allowance (£7,475)

Taxable income = £40,525

Tax on £35,000 at 20% = £7,000

Tax on £5,525 at 40% = £2,210

Total tax due = £9,210

To calculate Fred's tax relief for the withholding tax suffered, as above:

Excluding the royalty, taxable income is £32,525

Tax on £32,525 at 20% = £6,507

So the UK income tax attributable to the royalty payment is (£9,210–£6,507) = £2,703

As this is higher than the allowable tax withheld of £1,000, the full withholding tax suffered can be deducted in calculating Fred's UK income tax, so that his final UK tax due will be £8,210, whereas, if the full £3,000 withholding had been allowed as set-off, his UK tax due would be £7,010 (ie a further £2,000 deducted from the calculation in the first example, as full relief would be available as the UK tax attributable to the £10,000 royalty is more than £3,000).

18.259   Note that the withholding tax can only be offset against UK tax on the same income; there is no offset against general income. Similarly, the tax withheld must correspond to UK income tax as the UK will not provide relief for taxes which do not correspond to UK taxes. In practice, it is unlikely that tax withheld on a copyright royalty will not correspond to UK income tax.

18.260   The residence requirement means that any creative professionals living outside the UK who are, nevertheless, subject to UK income tax on their royalties cannot set-off withholding taxes against the UK taxes due on the royalty. However, they can claim the withholding tax as expense in calculating UK tax due on the royalty (TIOPA 2012, s 112). As above, this is not as generous as a set-off but is better than nothing.

Gifts by a creative professional

18.261   A gift of copyright by an author does not create a market value receipt of that copyright for the author (*Mason v Innes* (1967) 44 TC 326) as authors are not considered to create copyright as trading stock. The rules which apply income tax at market value on the personal consumption of trading stock (*Sharkey v Wernher* (1955) 36 TC 275) will not, therefore, apply. *Mason v Innes* concerned an author in particular, but the principle should apply to all creative professionals producing copyright works.

18.262   The taxpayer in *Mason v Innes* was an author and had given his father the rights in a novel which the taxpayer had written; the taxpayer had been allowed a deduction for tax purposes for expenses involved in writing the work. The court held that, although the writing of the novel and the disposal of the rights took place in the course of the taxpayer's profession, the rights given away were not his stock-in-trade and so the decision in *Sharkey v Wernher* did not apply.

18.263   The court may have been influenced by the indignation of Lord Denning, one of the judges in the case, at the idea that a painter might be taxed on the gift of a portrait to his mother. On a less emotional basis, the fact that spreading relief (see below) would not apply to any deemed market value receipt also indicated to the court that a gift could not create a taxable deemed receipt.

18.264 ITTOIA 2005, Pt 2, Ch 11A is a statutory enactment of the principle in *Sharkey v Wernher* but it refers specifically to trades and is not more widely applied to professions and vocations. Although the profits from professions and vocations are now taxed in the same way as trading profits (ITTOIA 2005, s 5), it is not the case that a profession is equated with a trade for all tax purposes. It is necessary to expressly extend provisions relating to trades to cover professions as well, and no such extension has been made in respect of ITTOIA 2005, Pt 2, Ch 11A.

18.265 However, HMRC accept that the decision in *Sharkey v Wernher* still does not apply to gifts (or disposals at below market value) of works produced in the exercise of a profession (HMRC Manual BIM50745).

18.266 The gift may still be subject to capital gains tax, however: a gift of an asset is treated as a disposal for capital gains tax purposes, with the consideration deemed to be market value as the parties are connected (see para **18.66**). Without a claim for holdover relief (deferring the taxation of the capital gain until the recipient disposes of the gift), the donor would be subject to capital gains tax on the market value of the copyright. Whilst this might seem to conflict with the principle that the disposal of copyright is not a capital transaction (see above), a gift of copyright is more likely to be made in a personal capacity than a professional capacity: the copyright is, in effect, transferred from the profession to the person immediately before the gift.

Spreading relief: income tax

18.267 A receipt by a creative professional for the exploitation of copyright could represent income for several years work. This could lead to unfair treatment if the receipt were taxed entirely when received: the total tax due could be higher than it would have been had the payment been received over the period in which the work was created, because taxation in a single year could lose the benefit of personal allowances and the basic and lower rate tax bands in each year.

Example 18.21

AJ is an author and has spent a number of years writing without selling new work; in the meantime, she has received small amounts for previous works. She now receives a substantial advance in respect of a new book, so that her income is:

2009/10	£17,000
2010/11	£15,000
2011/12	£16,000

2012/13   £200,000

2013/14   £16,000

Without any spreading relief, AJ would be subject to 50% income tax on some of the advance, although she has barely paid any tax over the previous few years.

18.268 To deal with this potentially unfair treatment, a relief is available for receipts by the creator of a creative work (a literary, dramatic, musical or artistic work, or a design) where the creator carries on a profession or vocation whose profits are derived wholly or mainly from those creative works (ITTOIA 2005, s 221).

18.269 The relief takes the form of an averaging of profits (ITTOIA 2005, ss 221–225) that can be claimed in respect of profits relating to an entire year, rather than on the disposal of a particular piece of work.

18.270 The relief is available to partnerships as well as individuals, but is still not available to corporate creators of copyright (these will be covered by the corporate intangibles tax rules: see Chapter 9).

18.271 The creative works must be created by the taxpayer personally (or, in the case of a partnership, created by one of the partners personally) (ITTOIA 2005, s 221(3)).

Claim

18.272 A claim for the averaging relief can be made for two consecutive years if (ITTOIA 2005, s 222) the profession, or vocation is more than two years old but not in its final year, as no claims can be made for the opening and closing years of a trade; and

- relevant profits for one year are less than 75% of the relevant profits for the other year (regardless of whether that year is immediately before or immediately after); or

- profits for one—not both—years are nil.

18.273 'Profits' are the profits of the trade, profession or vocation for the year of assessment before deduction of any losses. Where there is a loss in the trade, profession or vocation for the year of assessment, the profits are deemed to be nil for averaging purposes (ITTOIA 2005, s 221(5)).

18.274 Claims need to be made chronologically (ITTOIA 2005, s 222(3)), so a claim cannot be made if there has already been a claim made in a later year. For example:

- a claim can be made to average years 2 and 3 where a claim has already been made to average for years 1 and 2; but

- where a claim has been made to average years 2 and 3, a claim cannot then be made to average years 1 and 2.

Example 18.22

In the example above, AJ can claim to average 2012/13 and 2013/14, but could not then subsequently claim to average 2011/12 and 2012/13: she would have to make a claim to average 2011/12 and 2012/13 before she claimed to average 2012/13 and 2013/14.

18.275   The claim must be made on or before the first anniversary of the normal self-assessment filing date for the second year in respect of which a claim is made (ITTOIA 2005, s 222(5)).

Adjustments

18.276   If the profits of either year averaged are adjusted after a claim has been made (for any reason other than an averaging claim) the averaging claim ceases to have effect: a new claim can be made for the same years, and needs to be on or before the first anniversary of the normal self-assessment filing date for the tax year in which the adjustment is made (ITTOIA 2005, s 225).

Effect of relief

18.277   The relief is given by (ITTOIA 2005, s 223):

- averaging the profits for the two years if the profits of one year are less than 70% of the profits of the other (including where the profits for one year are nil); or

- where profits of one year are more than 70% (and less than 75%) of the other year then a formula is applied:

$(D \times 3) - (P \times 0.75)$

D is the difference between the relevant profits for the two years and P is the profit of the higher year.

The result is deducted from the profits of the higher year and added to the profits of the lower year.

18.278   Relief is given in the second year of assessment (TMA 1970, Sch 1B, para 3) so:

- the profits assessed for the second year are the averaged profits; and
- a calculation is made of the tax that would have been charged in the first year if the profits had been the averaged profits:
  - where this amount is greater than the tax actually charged in that year, the additional amount is added to the tax payable for the second year;
  - where this amount is less than the tax actually charged in that year, the extra payment is treated as a payment on account for the second year, reducing the tax payable in the second year.

The tax liability of the first year is not amended.

18.279   Where a claim is made to average the profits of two years and a subsequent claim is made to average the profits of the second year with the third, that subsequent claim is made without taking any account of the effects of the first claim on the profits of the second year (ITTOIA 2005, s 223(2)).

Example 18.23

FL, an artist, has been producing work for over a decade on an erratic schedule, depending on when he feels that his 'muse' is guiding him; his income is, as a result, similarly erratic.

In 2008/9, he sells a number of pieces and his profit for the year is £32,000; in 2009/10, his profits drop slightly as the flow of work dries up to £27,000; in 2010/11, as he feels that his muse has deserted him, his profit is only £15,000. Things improve in 2011/12, with profits increasing again to £29,000.

His accountant points out that the tax treatment does not need to be as volatile as FL's income, and a claim is made for averaging as follows.

2008/9 and 2009/10: the profits of the lower year, 2009/10, are more than 75% of the profits of the higher year (75% of 32,000 is £24,000), so no claim can be made to average these years.

2009/10 and 2010/11: the profits of the lower year, 2010/11, are less than 70% of the profits of the higher year (70% of £27,000 is £18,900). A claim can be made for averaging, and the profits will be adjusted by averaging the profits for the two years. The profits for each year will be, therefore:

(£27,000 + £15,000) × 50% = £21,000

The tax liability for 2009/10 would be reduced by £1,200 (at 20% on a reduction in profits of £6,000) but, as effect to the tax relief is given only in the second year, no adjustment is made to 2009/10. Instead, the £1,200 is taken to be a notional payment on account for 2010/11.

2010/11 and 2011/12: The profits for 2010/11 are now taken to be £21,000. As the profits of the lower year are, therefore, less than 75% of the profits of the higher year (75% of £29,000 is £21,750), a claim can be made. As the profits of the lower year are between 70% and 75%, the profits are calculated using the formula given above as follows:

D = (£29,000 – £21,000) = £8,000

P = £29,000

Adjustment: (£8,000 × 3) – (£29,000 × 0.75) = £2,250

The profits are adjusted by adding this to the profits of the lower year and deducting it from the profits of the higher year.

The tax liability for 2010/11 would be increased by £450 (at 20% on the increase of £2,250) as a result (ignoring the deduction given by the earlier adjustment for averaging in 2009/10); as effect to the claim is given in the second year of the claim, this £450 would be added to the tax payable for 2011/12.

The result is that the profits for the various years, and the associated tax adjustments, are altered as follows:

Year	Adjusted profits £	Prior year tax adjustment £
2008/9	32,000	0
2009/10	21,000	0
2010/11	23,250	(1,200)
2011/12	26,750	450

Inheritance tax: creative professionals

18.280 There is a specific inheritance tax business relief for 'a business carried on in the exercise of a profession' (IHTA 1984, s 103(3)). HMRC previously refused to accept that authors and similar creative professionals were entitled to business relief (on the ground that the business ceased on death) but have recently accepted that, as inheritance tax applies to the estate immediately before death, business relief will be available on death in respect of a creative professional's copyrights, and in respect of a majority shareholding in a company owning copyrights (see below).

Incorporation

18.281 Although many creative professionals carry on business in their own name, some prefer to operate through the medium of a company. In practical terms, there is no particular reason why a company should not be used: it will have the advantage of limited liability and (potentially) the deferral of tax liabilities (as a company pays tax at a lower rate than an individual, generally, until the profits are made available to the individual, the amount of tax paid on income is reduced).

Anti-avoidance

18.282 However, a degree of care needs to be taken in considering the incorporation of a creative profession. In particular, the anti-avoidance provisions relating to the sale of income from a personal occupation will need to be considered (ITA 2007, Pt 13, Ch 4).

18.283 These rules will apply an income tax charge on capital received which reflects a reward from the activities of the individual, for example, on the sale of the shares in the company at a later date, where the company has increased in value as a result of the reward earned by the company from the activities of the individual. If the individual has, throughout, received an appropriate reward (either by way of employment income from the company or through the extraction of dividends) then it is unlikely that the rules will apply (in such circumstances, the shares may have no particular value to them in any case).

18.284 The rules only apply where the main purposes, or one of the main purposes of the arrangements is the avoidance or reduction of income tax. Where the incorporation is genuinely for commercial reasons, the rules should not apply.

18.285 There is a specific exemption from a income tax charge under these anti-avoidance provisions in respect of transfers as a going concern (ITA 2007, s 784), but this is subject to the requirement that the going concern value of the business does not, to a material extent, represent prospective income derived from the author's activities (ITA 2007, s 785), unless the author receives full value for that prospective income when it arises (eg it is paid to him as an employee).

Non-resident creative professionals

18.286 Payments of royalties in respect of copyright to non-UK residents are subject to withholding tax at the basic rate of income tax (at the time of writing, 20%: see para **16.65** for more details).

18.287 However, payments to a creative professional—that is, the creator of a literary, dramatic, musical or artistic work that has been created in the ordinary course of that person's profession—are regarded as the payment of fees for professional services and not as copyright royalties (HMRC Manual INTM342590, following the decisions in *Carson v Cheyney's Executor* (1959) 38 TC 240 and *Hume v Asquith* (1968) 45 TC 251). Payments that are made to a non-UK resident creative professional for the use of their creative work are therefore not subject to deduction of UK income tax at source.

18.288 The person receiving the payment must be the creator of the work for which payment is made; this treatment does not apply where the recipient of the payment has acquired the rights from the creator. Note that a profession can only be carried on by an individual: where the copyright in the work vests in a company, the company cannot be a creative professional and has, instead, acquired the rights to the copyright from the person who created it (even where these rights vest automatically, for example, under a contract of employment).

18.289 This exemption from withholding tax also applies to payments of Public Lending Right amounts to non-UK residents (HMRC Manual INTM342610).

18.290 Despite HMRC treating payments to creative professionals as fees for professional services, which are not subject to withholding tax, they still require that a claim for relief on payments to non-UK creative professionals be made either:

- under an applicable double tax treaty; or (where there is no treaty in place)

- by letter from the claimant, agent or publisher, stating the full name of the author; residential address of the author; the full title of the work and the name and address of the payer of the royalties.

18.291 Quite what relief is being claimed, if the payment is not subject to withholding tax in the first place, is a good question. Nevertheless, it is easier to make the claim than to dispute later whether it should have been required in the first place.

HOBBYIST INVENTORS

18.292 A hobbyist inventor is generally someone who develops intellectual property without a specific profit motive; usually, the intellectual property developed is a patent.

Expenses

18.293 Specific relief is available for the expenses of registering a patent which are wholly and exclusively incurred by an inventor in devising an invention otherwise than in the course of a trade (ITTOIA 2005, s 601).

18.294 Relief can be claimed for the costs of applying for and maintaining a patent, obtaining an extension of a patent term, and for the costs of a failed application. This relief is only available where no other reliefs are available under the Tax Acts, hence its primary application to hobbyist inventors. Someone creating an invention in the course of carrying on a trade, profession or vocation will generally be able to deduct such expenses under the general rules in respect of expenses of a trade, profession or vocation.

18.295   The relief is rather limited, as it is given by deduction or set-off against the inventor's income from patents for the tax year in which the expenditure is incurred. Where expenditure exceeds income, the excess is carried forward for set-off against future patent income.

18.296   A hobbyist inventor will not, generally, be able to claim relief for any other expenses unless the invention is sold. In particular, no capital allowances are available for equipment purchased by the inventor, as such allowances are only available to those carrying on a trade, profession or vocation (see para **4.1**).

Receipts

18.297   Even though the sale of a patent is the disposal of a capital asset (except where sold by a dealer in patent rights), there is a charge to income tax on the profit from the sale of all or part of any patent rights for a capital sum where the seller is a UK resident individual (ITTOIA 2005, s 587). This applies regardless of the capacity in which the seller has held the patent (whether for the purposes of a trade, as an investment, or as a hobbyist inventor). A spreading relief may be available (see para **7.41**).

18.298   Where the profit is received by a hobbyist inventor, it is treated as relevant UK earnings for pension purposes (FA 2004, s 189(2)(c), (2A)).

PERFORMERS: ACTORS, MUSICIANS ETC, AND SPORTSMEN

18.299   Performers are not, generally, carrying on an intellectual property-based business (but see performer's rights, below); however, they will be involved in the performance of other people's intellectual property (particularly copyright) and so a brief outline of specific tax issues relating to their work follows here.

18.300   Sportsmen are also not engaged directly in intellectual property businesses, and so a detailed consideration of the wider tax issues involved in sports is outside the scope of this book. However, recent trends around the exploitation of image rights in sports are discussed below, as these are (arguably) a form of intellectual property.

Non-UK resident performers and sportsmen

18.301   Non-UK resident performers and sportsmen are treated for UK tax purposes as carrying on a UK profession or vocation when they carry out activities in the UK (ITTOIA 2005, s 13): these activities include any professional activities and may be performances, sports events, or sponsorship appearances.

18.302   Payments made by UK residents in respect of such UK activities must have UK basic rate income tax (at the time of writing, 20%) deducted from the payment unless the payment is already subject to PAYE, regardless of whether the payment is made directly to the non-resident performer/sportsman or indirectly to an agent or personal service company (ITA 2007, s 966). This requirement has a de minimis, so that no tax needs to be withheld where the total payments to an individual or group will be £1,000 or less during the tax year – the difficulty with this is establishing for certain that the payments from all sources during the year will be below the de minimis. The payer must account to HMRC quarterly for any tax withheld. The performer/sportsman will need to complete a UK tax return to claim the benefit of any double tax treaty and so reclaim the tax deducted.

18.303   Payments can include appearance fees, interview payments, box office percentages, television rights, tour income, event winnings, prize money, advertising income, merchandising income, endorsement fees for using a sponsor's equipment in a UK event, film fees etc: broadly, any payment connected with UK activity. The payment need not be in direct monetary form: providing an airline ticket to the entertainer (for example) will be considered to be a payment. A loan will also be considered to be a payment.

18.304   Either the payer or the non-resident performer/sportsman can apply to HMRC for a reduced withholding tax rate to apply (under the Income Tax (Entertainers and Sportsmen) Regulations 1987 (SI 1987/530)) to take into account expenses which are incurred in the UK out of the fees paid. A detailed budget of the expenses will need to be provided and negotiation is needed with HMRC to achieve a compromise so that the level of withholding tax reflects the tax liability of the entertainer or sportsman on the income after allowable expenses, rather than the liability on the gross income. The application must be made at least 30 days before the first payment is due to be made (see HMRC Guide *FEU50—A Guide to paying Foreign Entertainers* for more information).

2012 Olympics and Paralympics

18.305   A temporary exemption from UK income tax was declared for non-UK resident individuals who were in the UK temporarily to perform an official function at the 2012 Olympics and Paralympics Games (including competitors); the individual had to be accredited. The exemption applied to income earned from activities as a non-UK resident Olympic competitor (or other official category) carried out in the UK between 30 March 2012 and 8 November 2012. The individual must have remained UK non-resident for the 2012/13 tax year: note that the period from 6 April 2012 to 8 November 2012 is long enough to make someone tax resident in the UK under domestic rules, as it is more than six months, so an individual must not have in fact been in the UK for this entire period.

UK resident performers and sportsmen

18.306 Entertainers and sportsmen generally trade as individuals and so will not be within the corporate intangible tax rules; their income is, in fact, usually taxed as either employment income under ITEPA 2003 or (where self-employed) as income from a profession or vocation, taxed under the general rules for such income in ITTOIA 2005, Pt 2.

Performers: employment status

18.307 Performers may be employed or self-employed, depending on the nature of their role and the engagement generally. A detailed review of whether an individual is employed or self-employed in general terms is beyond the scope of this book; however, there are various points that arise specifically with regard to performers and so need to be considered by anyone engaging them. The National Insurance Contribution treatment of performers rather different (see para **18.318**). Note that a performer may be within Class 1 National Insurance Contributions even where the engagement is self-employment.

Employed?

18.308 In 1969, in *Fall v Hitchen* (1969) 49 TC 433, a dancer with a standard contract was held to be an employee; the contract engaged him for a minimum period of time to 'rehearse, understudy, play and dance as and where required by the Manager'. The dancer had no other engagements during the run of the contract.

Self-employed?

18.309 In contrast, in 1993, two actors (Alex McCowen and Sam West) succeeded in an unreported case before the Special Commissioners that their standard Equity theatre contracts were not contracts of employment. These contracts were for a specific role in a specific play, for the run of the play (or a shorter minimum period). Both actors also had other engagements in film, radio etc during the run of the play, with other engagers.

18.310 HMRC now generally accept that Mr McCowen and Mr West's position is more usual for actors and performers (HMRC Manual ESM4121) and that, accordingly, theatre performers are more likely to be self-employed with income tax applied to their profits as from a profession or vocation.

18.311 It is still possible for a performer to be engaged as an employee, but that will generally be where the performer is engaged for a regular income to perform in various productions over a period of time, with the roles to be determined by the engager (eg the permanent members of a ballet company).

Musicians

18.312 In general, musicians will be regarded as self-employed by HMRC unless a contract for an engagement is specifically one of employment (similar to that in *Fall v Hitchen*, for example, for permanent members of an orchestra; HMRC Manual ESM4121).

18.313 Session musicians in particular, who are engaged for specific recording or performance sessions rather than for a run of performances, will generally be self-employed and will not be subject to Class 1 National Insurance Contributions (they will still be within Class 2 and 4 NICs), as the terms of their contracts are normally such that no part of the payment can be categorised as salary (HMRC Guidelines on the NIC Rules for Entertainers).

18.314 However, musicians in orchestras may have widely differing contracts; HMRC have set out their interpretation of the basic types of orchestral contract as follows (HMRC Manual ESM4140):

- musicians engaged to play at musicals, pantomimes and other theatrical performances are self-employed unless the contract gives the engager rights similar to those of an employer to determine where and what the musician will play over a period of time (cf *Fall v Hitchen*);

- musicians engaged under 'first call' or 'guarantee' contracts are self-employed for tax purposes, subject to the NIC treatment (see below). These are contracts which

  — give the orchestra the right to call on the musician's services; but

  — limit this demand so that the musician may undertake other work, and

  — pay the musician separately for each performance;

- musicians who are shareholders in the major London Orchestras (London Philharmonic, London Symphony, Philharmonia and Royal Philharmonic) are self-employed. The orchestras are self-governing: the members run these orchestras themselves;

- generally, orchestral players who are paid separately for each performance and are not guaranteed a minimum amount of work by an orchestra may be treated as self-employed;

- musicians whose contracts do not fall within one of the categories above and are permanent members of a major orchestra will generally be taxed as employees.

Grants

18.315   In general, grants made to actors and other performers will be taxable as income of the profession. However, HMRC accept that a number of awards made by the Arts Council are not taxable, including training bursaries for actors (formerly in HMRC Inspectors' Manual IM2691b; not reproduced in the current manuals but not specifically denied either).

Deduction for agents fees: employed performers

18.316   Where a performer is engaged as an employee, there is a specific deduction from employment income for tax purposes for fees paid to the performer's agent (ITEPA 2003, s 352). The fees must be paid either:

- under a contract with an employment agency to act as an agent of the performer in connection with the employment; or

- to a co-operative society which has agreed to act as the performer's agent in connect with the employment.

18.317   The deduction is available for 'entertainers' (being actors, dancers, musicians, singers or theatrical artists). For 'theatrical artists', the performance does not need to take place in a theatre specifically (*Madeley and Finnigan v HMRC* (SpC547, 2006): the performances took place in a television studio). To be deductible, the fees must be calculated as a percentage of the earnings from the employment, to a maximum of 17.5% of earnings (agents fees are usually 10–15% of earnings).

National insurance: performers

18.318   The Social Security (Categorisation of Earners) Amendment Regulations 2003 (SI 2003/736) require that a performer who receives any salary element in remuneration for an engagement will be treated as employed for National Insurance Contributions purposes for that engagement. A performer who is within the Regulations is subject to Class 1 NICs on *all* earnings from that engagement (including repeat fees and royalties for performer's rights: see below), not just the salary element. The engager will, similarly, be subject to secondary Class 1 NICs. Under the Regulations, where a performer is engaged through a third party (such as an agency) the secondary Class 1 NICs are paid by the producer of the entertainment in respect of which the payments of salary are made.

18.319 A 'salary' for the purposes of the Regulations has a very precise meaning: it is a payment which meets all of the following tests:

- paid for services rendered;

- paid under a contract for services;

- payable at a specified period or interval, where there is more than one payment; and

- calculated by reference to the amount of time for which work has been performed.

18.320 The position was considered recently with regard to actors in *ITV Services Ltd v Revenue & Customs* [2012] UKUT 47 (TCC). The Upper Tribunal confirmed the ruling of the First Tier Tribunal, which had considered various types of actor agreements and concluded that only an 'all rights agreement', which provided for payment to the actor of a single all-inclusive fee in respect of the engagement (including repeat fees etc), was held to be outside the scope of the Regulations, principally because this was the only agreement with a payment that was not calculated by reference to the amount of time for which work was performed. The other agreements, including standard contracts agreed with Equity (the actors' union) all contained payments which met the definition of salary and so primary and secondary Class 1 NICs needed to be accounted for on all earnings from these agreements.

Performer's rights

18.321 Actors, musicians and other performers may also own the performer's rights which arise in their work (under the Copyright, Designs and Patents Act 1988, s 180). Performer's rights are infringed when a third party without permission:

- records or broadcasts a live performance without permission; or

- makes a copy of a recording of a live performance; or

- broadcasts a recording in public; or

- deals with an illegal recording of a live performance.

18.322 Where the performer does own the performer's rights in their work, they will be entitled to equitable remuneration when a recording of the performance is played in public. The remuneration will usually be covered by the contract for the original performance (for example, standard Equity contracts will usually contain provision for fees for certain broadcast rights, repeat fees for further broadcasts, and additional fees for overseas broadcasts and DVD release of the performance).

18.323 Alternatively, the performer may receive performer's rights fees through a collecting society (such as the PRS or the PPL): this is more usual for musicians than other performers.

18.324 For tax purposes, the remuneration for performer's rights needs to be considered in line with the circumstance of the performance: where the performance is undertaken as part of an employment contract then the remuneration will usually be regarded as income from the employment and taxed accordingly, where it is paid by the employer or someone related to the employer.

18.325 If the performer's rights remuneration is received from a collecting society it will generally be taxed as income of the profession/vocation of the performer as the payment is not made in the context of employment but is, instead, a royalty for the use of intellectual property rights belonging to the performer. Such payments are generally taxed as income rather than capital even if the profession/vocation has permanently ceased (see para **18.253**).

Image rights in sports

18.326 Image rights are rights which an individual has to prevent unauthorised use of their name and/or image, often licensed as part of sponsorship and other endorsement contracts to allow the sponsors to use the name and image in advertising. Image rights are not specifically recognised in UK law although the European Convention on Human Rights, the Data Protection Act 1998, trademark rights (including passing off), and advertising standards in the UK all combine to (arguably) provide some form of protection for a person's name and image. In practice, image rights are contractual rights under an agreement between the individual and a third party.

18.327 Image rights contracts are increasingly used in sports—particularly football—with substantial value attributed to them in some cases: Sol Campbell won almost £1.7m from Portsmouth FC for unpaid image rights payments in 2010. In a dispute with his agents over an image rights contract in the same year (*Proactive Sports Management Ltd v Wayne Rooney* [2011] EWCA Civ 1444), Wayne Rooney disclosed that he earned £760,000 in twice-yearly payments for image rights.

18.328 Team sports players are generally treated as employees of the team, as they will generally have signed a contract with the team that meets the criteria for employment. Payments for playing will, therefore, be taxed as income from employment and subject to primary and secondary Class 1 NICs.

18.329 Payments for image rights, however, are not paid under the employment contract and (usually) substantial efforts are made to ensure that the payments are not connected with the employment. As such, the payments are made without deduction of PAYE and NICs although income tax will be due later on the payment (generally taxed as income from a trade in exploiting the image rights). Some players will also set up image rights companies to which they license the rights. It is the company which then enters into contracts, paying corporation tax on the income. These can be particularly effective when set up offshore for non-UK domiciled players.

18.330 Unsurprisingly, these payments have attracted the attention of HMRC. Manchester United's bond prospectus in January 2010 contained a note stating that the club was in dispute with HMRC over payments for image rights, with a potential tax exposure of £5.3m. HMRC have enquired into the image rights arrangements at a number of clubs, not just Manchester United, with some concern that the image rights payments are in fact disguised salary payments, where the player receives less in salary than they would otherwise, and receives the balance as a payment for image rights.

18.331 HMRC have challenged such agreements from time to time (see *Sports Club v HM Inspector of Taxes* [2000] STC (SCD) 443), usually without success where the payments for the image rights are at an appropriate level in the circumstances, considering the market value of the player's image, and where the player is paid a market salary for his employment by the team.

18.332 Essentially, the more high-profile the player, the more likely it is that substantial image rights payments can be sustained compared to those paid to other players and, potentially, compared to the payments made to the player by way of salary (for example the market value in David Beckham's image rights may these days be disproportionate to his value as a player).

18.333 Conversely, image rights payments to a substitute player in a minor league club are rather unlikely to be sustainable.

18.334 Image rights contracts may also be entered into by performers but, as they are usually regarded as self-employed (particularly those whose image rights are likely to have some specific value in promoting the performance), there is generally no difference in the tax treatment of the image rights payment and the performance payment.

Other activities

18.335 Performers may also earn income from creative works (eg a music performer may also write music), in which case they will be taxed on income from that creative profession in the same way as creative professionals (see para **18.231**) unless it is a one-off matter (eg co-operating with a biography or article) in which case any income may be taxed as miscellaneous income rather than trading income (see para **6.52**).

Incorporation

18.336 Where a performer is considering setting up a company to carry on their professional activities (see para **7.23**), the anti-avoidance rules on sale of income from a personal occupation will need to be considered (see para **18.282**).

FILM PRODUCTION COMPANIES: RULES AND RELIEFS

18.337 The tax incentive for expenditure on the creation of films was completely changed in FA 2006 (now CTA 2009, Pt 15) principally in response to the increasing use of film partnership schemes to reduce individuals' income tax. The current film tax rules apply to production companies with films whose principal photography began on or after 1 January 2007. As a result of the film tax rules, expenditure on film production is excluded from the corporate intangibles fixed assets rules (see Chapters 8–14).

Apply to all qualifying film production companies

18.338 The film tax rules below define the method for calculating the profits and losses for corporation tax purposes of film production companies regardless of the type of film being made by the company (including films not intended for cinema release). These rules apply to any qualifying film production company, whether or not the film tax reliefs can or will be claimed for a particular film. A qualifying film production company will, therefore, automatically be required to calculate its profits and losses according to the requirements of the film tax rules (see below).

Election out of film tax rules

18.339 Where the company does not want to be within these rules, it can elect to be treated as a non-qualifying film production company (CTA 2009, s 1182(7)–(9)). The election must be made in the company's tax return for an accounting period (including by amendment of a return). On election, these rules will not apply to any film which starts principal photography in the accounting period of election, or any following accounting period. Existing films will continue to be within the film tax rules.

18.340 Where the film production company elects out of the film tax rules, the production expenditure on subsequent films will generally fall within the corporate intangibles fixed assets rules, as it represents expenditure on the creation of an intangible fixed asset (the master film recording).

Electing out of the film tax rules means that the film tax reliefs (see below) cannot be claimed on any films covered by the election.

18.341   The election can only be withdrawn by amending the tax return in which the election was made (CTA 2009, s 1182(8)(b)). There is therefore a very limited window of opportunity for deciding to revert to the film tax rules status, after which time the election cannot be reversed. If a relief is required for a film in future, a new qualifying film production company will need to be set up to make that film.

Qualifying film production companies

18.342   A film production company is one that, otherwise than in partnership, is responsible for all of the following elements of making a film (CTA 2009, s 1182):

*   pre-production;

*   production planning and decision-making;

*   negotiating contracts;

*   paying for rights, goods and services;

*   principal photography;

*   post-production; and

*   delivery of the completed film.

18.343   The film production company does not have to be entirely responsible for every aspect of these elements (it is usual, for example, to sub-contract out elements of set construction and special effects to specialists), but the company must have some active involvement in each category.

18.344   A film production company can be the co-producer of a film, making an effective creative, technical and artistic contribution to the film. However, in co-production, only the company most directly engaged with the film that meets these requirements can claim the tax reliefs. If no company meets all the requirements then no tax relief is available in respect of that film (CTA 2009, s 1182(4), (5)).

18.345   As only one film production company can claim tax reliefs in respect of a particular film, any co-production agreement should make it clear which of the co-producers is intended to qualify for the reliefs. The agreement should ensure that, if relief is to be claimed by one of the co-producers, that co-producer is able to meet the requirements above.

Each film treated as single trade

18.346   Each film is regarded as a separate trade, so that a film production company with more than one film in production will be regarded as having several, separate, trades: one for each film. The trade is deemed to begin when pre-production of the film begins or when income is received in respect of the film if that is before pre-production (for example, where financing is raised by pre-sales of distribution rights) (CTA 2009, s 1188).

Calculation of profit or loss of a film

18.347   General expenditure on making a film is treated as revenue expenditure for tax purposes, even where that expenditure is capitalised in the accounts as being expenditure on the creation of an asset (the master recording) (CTA 2009, s 1191(3)).

First accounting period

18.348   In the first accounting period of the film trade, the profit or loss of a film is determined for tax purposes by:

- debiting the expenditure incurred to date; and

- crediting the estimated total income of the film deemed to have been earned at the end of the accounting period (CTA 2009, s 1189(2)).

Second accounting period

18.349   In the following accounting periods, the profit or loss of the film is determined by:

- debiting additional expenditure incurred; and

- crediting additional estimated income deemed to have been earned,

during the accounting period (CTA 2009, s 1189(3)).

18.350   Expenditure may only be a debit for tax purposes if the expenditure is represented in the state of the work-in-progress at the date of the accounts, so pre-payments may not be included until they are actually so represented (CTA 2009, s 1192).

Estimated total income earned

18.351   Income of a film will include receipts from the sale of the film, or rights in it, royalties for the use of the film or aspects of it, and receipts from merchandising rights and game rights (CTA 2009, s 1190).

18.352 Estimated total income earned is determined using the formula:

$(C/T) \times I$

where C is the total qualifying cost to date represented in the state of the work-in-progress on the film, T is the estimated total qualifying cost of the film and I is the estimated total income from the film (CTA 2009, s 1189(4)).

Example 18.24

In the first accounting period, ScaryFilmCo incurs qualifying expenditure of £100,000 (fully reflected in the work-in-progress). The estimated total income from the film is expected to be £1 million, mostly from DVD sales although the film will be released in theatres before it is released on DVD and is expected to make at least 5% of total income through cinema release.

Estimated income earned in that first accounting period is, therefore:

$(£100,000/£500,000) \times £1,000,000 = £200,000$

No actual income has been earned in this period, as the film is still being produced.

18.353 Estimates of income must be made as at the balance sheet date and must be made on a fair and reasonable basis (CTA 2009, s 1194). Given the need to raise finance before development can properly begin, film production companies should have reasonably detailed budgets from which the estimates can be taken. Total income is, necessarily, the most difficult figure to estimate but an indication can usually be obtained from any distribution deals and pre-sales to distributors.

Film tax reliefs

18.354 The film tax reliefs are available only to film production *companies* (the previous film tax reliefs were also available to individuals, partnerships and other unincorporated entities). There are three incentives, based on similar principles to the research and development tax reliefs (see Chapter 10), being:

- a relief for limited-budget films, giving an additional deduction of 100% of qualifying expenditure in addition to the standard revenue expenditure deduction;

- a relief for large-budget films, giving an additional deduction of 80% of qualifying expenditure; and

- a repayable tax credit for loss-making films (the amount depending on whether the film is limited-budget or large-budget).

Qualifying films

18.355 The incentives are available to film production companies for films that are (CTA 2009, s 1195(2)):

- British films

- intended for theatrical release

- with the appropriate level of core UK expenditure, and

- where principal photography commenced on or after 1 January 2007.

18.356 A film, for the purposes of the tax incentive, includes any means of showing a sequence of visual images as a moving picture. Each part of a series of films will be treated as a separate film unless the series as a whole is a self-contained work or is a series of documentaries with a common theme (CTA 2009, s 1181).

British film

18.357 A British film is one certified as such by the Secretary of State for Culture, Media and Sport under the Films Act 1985, Sch 1 (CTA 2009, s 1197). Certification is administered on behalf of the Secretary of State by the British Film Institute (BFI) and claims for certification should be submitted to The Certification Manager, BFI, 21 Stephen Street, London W1T 1LN.

18.358 The film needs to score at least 16 points on a points system (Films Act 1985, Sch 1, para 4 (as amended)). A film will be awarded points under the system for various elements, including:

- depicting a British story;

- being set in the UK;

- percentage of principal photography being carried out in the UK;

- involvement of EU citizens or residents: director, producer, scriptwriter and up to three lead actors; and

- percentage of visual effects, special effects and music carried out in UK.

18.359 A film will generally receive either an interim certificate or a final certificate, depending on the degree to which it has been completed on application for certification (Films Act 1985, Sch 1, para 2 (as amended)). Interim certificates may be conditional or for a limited time and all interim certificates will cease to have effect when the final certificate in respect of a film is issued.

UK expenditure

18.360 For a film to qualify for relief, at least 25% of the core expenditure on the film must be UK expenditure (CTA 2009, s 1198). Where the film is a co-production, this threshold applies to the aggregate expenditure by the co-producers, not just the claimant film company.

18.361 UK expenditure on a film means expenditure on services performed in the UK, or on goods supplied in the UK (CTA 2009, s 1185).

Core expenditure

18.362 'Core expenditure' is expenditure on pre-production, principal photography and post-production (ie not development, distribution or other activities not directly connected with production of the film itself) (CTA 2009, s 1184(1)).

18.363 Core expenditure incurred between connected persons is deemed to have been an amount equal to the amount that would have been incurred in an equivalent arm's length transaction.

Theatrical release

18.364 As that definition alone could apply to a television programme, or a film released straight to DVD or online release, the rules also require that the film must be intended for theatrical release (CTA 2009, s 1196).

18.365 This means that the film should be intended to be exhibited to the paying public at one or more commercial cinemas, and also be intended to obtain a significant proportion of its earnings from theatrical release. This requirement might seem unsustainable in the current market, where almost all films take the majority of their earnings from the DVD or online markets rather than theatrical release, but HMRC accept that 5% of total estimated income will be 'significant' in this context (HMRC Film Production Manual FPC40020).

18.366 There is no requirement that the intended theatrical release proceeds must arise in the UK to any extent.

Intention

18.367 The intention must be held at commencement of development of the film, and so the relief will still be available for films on which work is, for example, abandoned, or where theatrical release cannot be subsequently obtained. In this last case, the company need to be clear that they can show that there was an intention to release the film in cinemas, as HMRC are likely to enquire into the intention: the finance plan and contracts with actors and crew should be in line with cinema release rather than television or DVD production. Some effort to obtain cinema release should also have been made, and be documented as having been made.

18.368   The legislation does not set out who needs to have the intention to make the film for theatrical release, but it should be someone who would normally have control over that type of decision: this would usually be the directors of the film production company.

Limited-budget film relief

Limited-budget films

18.369   A limited-budget film is one that satisfies the requirements for film relief and in respect of which the core expenditure is less than £20 million (CTA 2009, s 1184(3)(a)).

Additional deduction

18.370   In the first accounting period, the film production company can claim an additional deduction of 100% of the qualifying expenditure in calculating the profit or loss for tax purposes of the trade of a limited budget film.

18.371   In subsequent accounting periods, the film production company can claim an additional deduction of 100% of qualifying expenditure to date, less the additional deductions already given in earlier periods.

Qualifying expenditure

18.372   The relevant expenditure is the core expenditure (see above) on the film which is taken into account in calculating the profit or loss to the film trade (CTA 2009, s 1199).

18.373   In practice, the expenditure on which the additional deduction is based is the lower of:

- UK expenditure to date (see above); and

- 80% of total qualifying expenditure to date (CTA 2009, s 1200).

First period of account

18.374   The additional deduction is given by E x R, where E is the total expenditure to date defined as above and R is 100%.

Subsequent periods of account

18.375   The additional deduction is given by (E × R) – P, where E is the expenditure to date as defined above, R is 100%, and P is the total amount of additional deductions given in previous accounting periods.

Example 18.25

A film production company is developing a film with a total estimated cost of £10 million. The film is certified as a British film and meets the requirements for film tax relief.

First accounting period:

In the first accounting period, the company incurs qualifying expenditure of £250,000 (fully reflected in the work-in-progress). The UK qualifying expenditure is £180,000. The estimated total income from the film is expected to be £25 million.

Estimated income earned in the first accounting period is, therefore:

$$\frac{£250,000}{£10,000,000} \times £25,000,000 = £625,000$$

The profit for the first accounting period is deemed to be:

£625,000 – £250,000 = £375,000

The film qualifies as a limited-budget film (as the estimated cost is less than £20m), and so is entitled to an additional deduction of 100% of qualifying expenditure.

The expenditure on which the additional deduction is based is the lower of:

UK qualifying expenditure: £180,000; and

80% of total qualifying expenditure: 80% of £250,000 = £200,000

The film production company can, therefore, claim an additional deduction of

£180,000 × 100%

in calculating the profits of the first accounting period, giving a taxable profit of:

£375,000 – £180,000 = £195,000

Second accounting period:

In the second accounting period, a further £7,800,000 qualifying expenditure is incurred on the film and reflected in the work-in-progress at the end of the accounting period. Of this, £6,200,000 is UK expenditure.

Estimated income earned in the second accounting period is therefore:

$$\frac{£7,800,000}{£10,000,000} \times £25,000,000 = £19,500,000$$

The profit for the second accounting period is deemed to be:

£19,500,000 – £7,800,000 = £11,700,000

The expenditure on which the additional deduction is based is the lower of:

- UK qualifying expenditure to date: £6,200,000 + £180,000 = £6,380,000

- 80% of total qualifying expenditure to date: 80% of (£7,200,000 + £250,000) = £5,960,000

The additional deduction is therefore

(£5,960,000 × 100%) – £180,000 = £5,780,000

giving taxable profits of:

£11,700,000 – £5,780,000 = £5,920,000

Large-budget film relief

18.376   A large-budget film is one that qualifies for film tax relief but has core expenditure in excess of £20 million. The relief is calculated in the same way as for the limited-budget film relief, but with a reduced additional deduction.

18.377   In the first accounting period, the film production company can claim an additional deduction of 80% of the qualifying expenditure in calculating the profit or loss of the trade of that film for tax purposes (CTA 2009, s 1200(3)(b)) (compared with the 100% additional deduction available for limited-budget films).

18.378   In subsequent accounting periods, the film production company can claim an additional deduction of 80% of qualifying expenditure to date, less the additional deductions already given in earlier periods.

18.379   Qualifying expenditure for the additional deduction is calculated as for the limited-budget film relief, taking the lower of 80% of total qualifying expenditure on the film and UK qualifying expenditure on the film.

Example 18.26

HollywoodCo is developing a film with a total estimated cost of £80 million. The film is certified as a British film and meets the requirements for film tax relief.

The profit for the first accounting period is deemed to be £2 million, after qualifying expenditure of £1,500,000.

The film does not qualify as a limited-budget film, and can only claim an additional deduction of 80% of qualifying expenditure:

80% of £1,500,000 = £1,200,000

The total additional deduction of £1,200,000 gives a total taxable profit for HollywoodCo in the first period of:

£2,000,000 – £1,200,000 = £800,000

Film tax credit repayment

18.380   A film production company can claim a film tax credit repayment for an accounting period in which it has a surrenderable loss. All or part of that surrenderable loss may be surrendered for a film tax credit repayment (CTA 2009, s 1201).

18.381   To the extent that the surrenderable loss is in fact surrendered for repayment, that amount of the surrenderable loss cannot be carried forward as a trading loss.

Surrenderable loss

18.382   The surrenderable loss is the lower of (CTA 2009, s 1201(2)):

● the available loss of the film trade for the period; and

● the available qualifying expenditure for the period.

Available loss

18.383   The available loss for an accounting period is given as:

L + RUL

Where L is the actual loss of the film trade for the accounting period and RUL is the amount of any brought forward available loss of the film trade from the previous accounting period.

Pre-December 2009 losses

18.384   Note that for accounting periods ending before 9 December 2009, only the loss arising during the accounting period was taken into account in determining the amount of the surrenderable loss; unused losses brought forward from previous accounting periods were not included. The rules were revised to ensure that films which were made over more than one accounting period were not penalised.

Available qualifying expenditure

18.385 The available qualifying expenditure is the amount on which the additional deduction is calculated (see above) less any amount surrendered in earlier periods (CTA 2009, s 1201(4)).

Example 18.27

IndieFilmCo is developing a qualifying British film. In the first accounting period, it has a trading loss of £250,000; the qualifying expenditure for the period is £220,000. It will only be able to surrender £220,000 of the trading loss.

In the second accounting period, it has a trading loss of £300,000. The available loss is £300,000 + £30,000 (the brought forward unsurrendered loss from the previous accounting period, as it has not been surrendered or set off against profits).

The accumulated qualifying expenditure is now £600,000, so the available qualifying expenditure for the period is:

£600,000 – £220,000 = £380,000

The loss which can be surrendered to obtain a repayment will be £330,000, the available loss for the period.

Limited-budget film tax credit repayment

18.386 For limited-budget films, the tax credit repayment is 25% of the loss surrendered (CTA 2009, s 1202(3)(a)). In Example 18.26, if IndieCo is making a limited-budget film, it will receive a tax credit repayment in the first accounting period of £55,000 (25% of £220,000).

Large-budget film tax credit repayment

18.387 For large-budget films, the tax credit repayment is 20% of the loss surrendered (CTA 2009, s 1202(3)(b)). In the example above, if IndieCo is making a large-budget film, it will receive a tax credit repayment in the first accounting period of £44,000 (20% of £220,000).

Deductions from repayments

18.388 HMRC may deduct from the repayment any liability of the film production company to pay corporation tax (CTA 2009, s 1203(2)). HMRC can also deduct any outstanding PAYE liabilities, amounts due under the foreign entertainers' rules (ITA 2007, s 966) or any outstanding Class 1 NIC liabilities (CTA 2009, s 1203(4)).

Tax deductions for film losses

18.389   Where the loss is not surrendered for a repayment credit, the use of the loss is restricted as follows.

Pre-completion

18.390   Any trading loss in respect of a film in an accounting period before that in which the film is completed or abandoned is restricted in availability and can only be carried forward to be deducted against profits of that film in one or more future accounting periods. As each film is regarded as a separate trade, a film production company with more than one film cannot set the losses of one film against the profits of another (CTA 2009, s 1209).

On or after completion

18.391   Any trading losses brought forward from pre-completion periods (other than terminal losses, for which see below), except for any trading losses which arise from the film tax relief (ie where no repayment of film relief has been claimed in respect of that loss, see below for details) may be set against the profits of the film production company for the same accounting period or against the profits of an earlier accounting period under the normal rules. Such trading losses can also be surrendered as group relief (CTA 2009, s 1210).

18.392   Sideways relief and group relief are therefore only available in respect of such losses of a film production company as would have arisen if no film tax relief had been claimed.

Terminal losses

18.393   Where a film production company ceases to carry on a trade in respect of a film—for example, where a film is abandoned or the rights to the film are sold—the amount that could have been carried forward in respect of that film is considered to be a terminal loss and may be set against profits of other films; this is the only circumstance in which the losses in respect of one film may be set against profits of other films.

18.394   If the film production company has another film trade in respect of a qualifying film, that terminal loss can be claimed as a loss brought forward for set-off against the profits of that second film.

18.395 Alternatively, the terminal loss can be surrendered to another film production company in the same group that is also carrying on a qualifying film trade. That second company can treat the surrendered loss as a loss brought forward for set-off against profits of the qualifying trade (CTA 2009, s 1211).

Administration

18.396 Claims for film tax relief must be made in the company's tax return (FA 2006, Sch 5, para 29 amending FA 1998, Sch 18, para 83T), as must claims for the film tax credit repayment. In effect the claim must be made in the 12 months following the end of the accounting period in which the expenditure was incurred: there is no need to tell HMRC in advance, although the certifications will need to be obtained before the claim is made. As corporation tax returns must now be submitted online, the process for claiming the reliefs will depend on the software used.

18.397 In practice, most claims for film tax relief will be dealt with by the Manchester Film Tax Credit Unit, a specialist unit within HMRC, located at Albert Bridge House, 1 Bridge Street, Manchester M60 9AF.

Interim accounting period returns

18.398 Claims must be accompanied by the following certifications as to the status of the film in respect of the relief claimed:

- an interim certificate that the film qualifies as a British film (CTA 2009, s 1213(1));

- a statement of the amount of budgeted core expenditure that is UK expenditure and confirmation that the condition in CTA 2009, s 1198 (that the UK expenditure is at least 25% of total core expenditure) will be met at completion of the film (CTA 2009, s 1214(1));

- a statement of the amount of budgeted core expenditure and confirmation that CTA 2009, s 1184(2) (that the total such expenditure will be less than £20 million) will be met at completion of the film (CTA 2009, s 1215(1)).

18.399 Until completion of the film, the film tax relief claimed is classified as interim relief and may be recovered where the film does not, on completion, meet the necessary conditions.

Completion accounting period return

18.400 The return for the accounting period in which the film is completed or abandoned must be accompanied by:

- a statement that the film has been abandoned or completed (CTA 2009, s 1212(2));

- a final certificate confirming that the film qualifies as a British film and covering all interim accounting periods (CTA 2009, s 1213(3)) or, if the film is abandoned rather than completed, an interim certificate (CTA 2009, s 1213(4));

- a statement of the amount of total core expenditure that is UK expenditure (CTA 2009, s 1214(3)); and

- for limited-budget films, a statement of the total core expenditure on the film (CTA 2009, s 1215(3)).

18.401 Where a certificate of qualification as a British film is revoked (whether an interim certificate or final certificate), the company is not entitled to film relief and must amend its tax return for any period in which relief was claimed (CTA 2009, s 1213(2), (5)).

18.402 Where the statement of total core expenditure on completion shows that the film did not meet the UK expenditure requirement, the company is not entitled to film relief for any period and must amend its tax return for any period for which relief was claimed (CTA 2009, s 1214(4)).

18.403 Where the statement of total core expenditure on completion shows that the film was not a limited-budget film then the company is not entitled to the limited-budget film relief (but will continue to be entitled to the large-budget film relief if all other conditions are met) and must amend its tax return for any period for which limited-budget relief was claimed (CTA 2009, s 1215(5).

18.404 Where tax returns need to be amended because the statement of total expenditure shows that either the UK expenditure requirement or the limited-budget film requirements were not met, the amendments can be made regardless of the fact that the time limit for amendment of the relevant return may have expired (CTA 2009, s 1216).

Anti-avoidance

General rule

18.405 No film tax relief is available in respect of arrangements the main object of which is wholly or mainly the increase in the amount of film tax relief claimed by the film production company (CTA 2009, s 1205).

Connected parties transactions

18.406 Where goods or services, the costs of which are included in the core expenditure, are provided by connected parties, the amount which is to be included in the core expenditure will be the arm's length price where limited-budget relief is claimed (CTA 2009, s 1184(3)). The normal transfer pricing rules also apply to all film production companies.

Production costs: recognition

18.407 When calculating the expenditure incurred in an accounting period, any amounts which have not actually been paid within four months of the accounting period must be ignored (CTA 2009, s 1204).

RESEARCH COMPANIES

18.408 A company which exists to carry out research for others, or to carry out research with a view to creating intellectual property for sale or licence to others, rather than using any resulting intellectual property in its own products and services, will generally be focused on whether it can obtain research and development relief in the UK on the expenditure incurred in carrying on the research.

Research for others: acting as subcontractor

18.409 The availability of research and development relief in this context will depend on the nature of the company subcontracting the research and development to the research company.

Subcontractor to a UK SME

18.410 The research company will not be able to claim any research and development relief as the SME will generally be able to claim relief instead (see para **10.109**).

Subcontractor to an entity other than a UK SME

18.411 A large company (or individual, or non-UK entity) which subcontracts out work cannot claim any research and development relief and so the subcontractor may itself be able to make a claim for the large company research and development relief. This requires that (amongst the other requirements) the research and development be qualifying research and development and relevant to the trade of the research and development company (see para **10.4**).

18.412 Where the trade of the company is the provision of research and development services to others, any research and development activities will generally be relevant to that trade (HMRC Manual CIRD81400). It may be more difficult to establish that the research and development activities undertaken by the research company are qualifying research and development. If the whole project is subcontracted to the research company then it will generally be capable of qualifying, where it meets the overall requirements of the Guidelines (see para **10.11**). Where only an element of the research and development is subcontracted to the research company, the subcontracted element on its own must meet the definition of qualifying research and development for the large company relief to be available.

18.413   For example, a research company carrying out routine testing on behalf of a large company will not be able to claim any research and development relief on the expenditure, as routine testing is not an activity seeking to resolve an uncertainty which will lead to an advance in science or technology (see para **10.22**).

18.414   During 2011 the government held consultations on the possibility of amending the subcontractor relief rules so that the subcontracted work could qualify for relief by considering it as part of the overall project (see http://hm-treasury.gov.uk/d/consult_r_d_tax_credits.pdf). The suggestions were that the subcontracting company could certify the work as being part of a qualifying project, or that there could be a joint election. Various practical difficulties were raised in responses to consultation and, as a result, any changes in this area have been postponed to allow for further consideration and consultation.

Group research company

18.415   The exception to the points above is where the research company is part of a large group and carries out research activities for other group companies, paid for by those other group companies. In these circumstances, it may be able to claim the large company relief as the research will be considered with the other research and development activities of the payer company. Where the aggregate activities are qualifying research and development, the research company will be able to claim the large company research and development relief (see para **10.177**).

Research on own account to develop intellectual property for sale or licence

18.416   A company carrying on research on its own account to exploit that intellectual property will have a trade (in intellectual property); the research and development carried out should be regarded as relevant to that trade for relief purposes so that the company will be able to claim the appropriate relief (depending on its size) where all the requirements for relief are met (see Chapter 10).

FRANCHISES

What is a franchise?

18.417 Franchising is an increasingly popular business model, both between third parties and within groups. The turnover for the franchise sector (generally related to third party franchises) was estimated at £12.4bn in 2011, an increase of 5% over 2010. There were almost 37,000 businesses based on franchise in the UK (figures from the NatWest/bfa Franchise Survey 2011).

18.418 The franchisee receives the benefit of (generally) an established and proven business model, and potentially the benefit of enhanced reputation from being associated with a larger business. The franchisee may also receive the benefit of marketing and advertising undertaken nationally by the franchisor. These should all give a competitive advantage over equivalent new non-franchised businesses.

Franchise contracts

18.419 The franchisor grants rights to the franchisee over a particular business model: the rights are generally granted over intellectual property assets such as trademarks and know-how in the business model. The franchisee may also be required to buy goods from the franchisor (for example: McDonalds franchisees are required to purchase ingredients and pre-prepared food from McDonalds). This is partly to ensure uniformity of the customer experience and also for the financial benefit of the franchisor.

18.420 The franchisee owns and runs the business, but the franchise agreements will also usually contain strict control over marketing and the way in which the franchisee's business is run, as the franchisor will want to ensure that the value of the brand is protected.

18.421 A franchise should be distinguished from potentially similar arrangements such as distributorships, agencies or more straightforward licensing. Distributorships are generally arrangements to sell products; they do not generally involve the granting of rights over know-how, or a right to use the intellectual property of the manufacturer. The distributor's business is generally more independent. An agent sells products and services on behalf of the producer; again, there are usually no intellectual property rights granted other than, possibly, a limited right to use trademarks. Licensing may involve the granting of intellectual property rights to enable the licensee to manufacture certain products, or supply certain services, but the licensee's business is usually very distinct from the licensor's business.

Franchise costs

18.422 Franchise contracts usually contain various fees which are paid by the franchisee, including:

- the initial fee, for the grant of the franchise intellectual property rights;

- training and administration fees (these may be incorporated into the initial fee);

- ongoing fees, such as management services fees: these are usually based on turnover, or may be a mark-up on required purchases. These services fees reflect the franchisor's ongoing marketing and development of the brand and business model, and may also be consideration for specific services (such as advice on developing the franchisee's business and training).

Tax considerations

18.423 First, note that references to franchise taxes in the US will often be references to state franchise taxes. These are taxes generally charged by the state to companies which are registered in the state. They have no connection with franchising as a business model.

For the franchisor

Initial fee

18.424 The franchisor is granting rights over intellectual property assets (principally trademarks and know-how, in the UK) in return for fees. As the business model relies on the exploitation of those intellectual property rights by licensing to generate income, the fees will generally be treated as trading income of the franchisor). This was supported by the case of *Jeffrey v Rolls-Royce Ltd* (1962) 40 TC 443: the House of Lords held that exploitation of know-how was a trade (in that case, an extension of the existing trade). Although this was not specifically a franchise business, it had a number of elements in common with franchising (repeated licensing, providing additional services, and no reduction in value of the underlying intellectual property assets).

18.425 Fees received by a corporate franchisor will be within the corporate intangibles tax rules see Chapters 8–14) to the extent that they relate to the grant of rights over intellectual property. This assumes that the intellectual property is not an excluded intellectual property asset (see para **8.29**); where it is excluded, then the tax treatment is likely to be the same as for an unincorporated entity). These fees will be a taxable receipt of the business when they are recognised in the profit and loss account of the franchisor; under UK GAAP, the fees will generally be recognised once the services have been provided (the grant of the intellectual property licence, and any connected services such as training). This will usually be within the same accounting period as the receipt and so the corporate franchisor will be treated in a similar way to the unincorporated franchisor: the fees will be trading income in the year in which they are received.

Training element to initial fee

18.426 Where the initial fee contains an element of payment for training, and is clearly identified as such, it taxed as trading income of a franchisor (under ITTOIA 2005, Pt 2 for unincorporated franchisors, or under CTA 2009, Pt 3 for corporate franchisors). Even if the result makes little or no difference to the franchisor's tax position, the franchisee is likely to prefer such fees to be clearly identified (see below for more details).

Goodwill

18.427 The franchisee benefits from the goodwill of the franchisor but does usually not acquire an interest in that goodwill under the franchise agreement, so there is no disposal of goodwill by the franchisor. The franchisee may create goodwill in the course of operating the franchise business which is separate from the goodwill of the franchisor, although each case needs to be considered on its facts, particularly the terms of the franchise agreement and the extent to which the franchisee has freedom to operate the business (*Balloon Promotions Ltd* [2006] STC(SCD)167 and *Mertrux* [2011] UKFTT 398).

Ongoing fees

18.428 Regardless of whether the ongoing fees are a service fee or a mark-up on products purchased, these will be trading income of the franchisor, dealt with under ITTOIA 2005, Pt 2 (for unincorporated entities) or CTA 2009, Pt 3 (for companies).

For the franchisee

Initial fee: unincorporated franchisee

18.429 The tax treatment of the initial fee for the franchisee is not necessarily a mirror of the tax treatment for the franchisor.

18.430 In particular, the initial fee is likely to be treated as capital expenditure of the franchisee as it gives rise to an enduring benefit for the franchisee, even where it is paid over a number of years (see para **5.9** for unincorporated franchisees).

18.431 Know-how capital allowances are unlikely to be available to the unincorporated franchisee; such capital allowances are given for *industrial* know-how and the know-how licensed in a franchise agreement will generally be commercial know-how (see para **5.108** for more details of know-how allowances).

18.432   Without capital allowances, the franchisee will not be able to claim a tax deduction for the expenditure on the initial fee until the franchisee agreement is disposed of (where the agreement allows the franchisee to sell to a third party), or terminates.

18.433   The rights granted under a franchise agreement are likely to be wasting assets for the franchisee as the franchise agreement will usually be for a term of less than 50 years (see para **7.11** for more information about wasting assets). Renewal clauses are usually ignored in determining the term of the franchise at the outset, because there is usually no certainty that the agreement will actually be renewed. Where the franchise is a wasting asset, and is later disposed of, there will usually be restrictions on the costs which can be deducted when calculating the franchisee's gain or loss on disposal.

Initial fee: corporate franchisee

18.434   Where the franchisee is a company, the intellectual property rights received will be within the corporate intangibles tax rules (if the franchisee and franchisor are not connected, and the franchisee is not somehow excluded from the regime) but the accounting treatment is likely to also capitalise the expenditure as it will provide an enduring benefit to the company (see para **11.25**).

Training fees

18.435   In both cases, where an element of the initial fee relates to training *staff* and other similar services, if that element of the fee is clearly identifiable then it should be deductible as a trading expense under general tax rules. However, initial training for an *individual* franchisee will still be treated as capital expenditure as the training is considered to be of enduring benefit to the franchisee (HMRC Manual BIM57610).

18.436   HMRC are likely to query trading expense deductions for the training fees element if it is not clearly identified in the franchise agreements (HMRC Manual BIM57620).

Ongoing fees

18.437   Ongoing fees will be trading expenses of the trade for the franchisor and deductible under the general rules (ITTOIA 2005, Pt 2 for unincorporated entities or CTA 2009, Pt 3 for companies); as these do not reflect any grant of intellectual property rights, the fees will not be within the corporate intangibles tax regime.

VAT

18.438 VAT is generally chargeable on the initial fee and the ongoing fees, as these will relate to the provision of services and (depending on the terms of the franchise) goods. The grant of the intellectual property rights is a supply of services for VAT purposes (see para **15.16**). The franchisee should be able to fully recover the VAT charged, assuming that it is registered for VAT purposes and is not exempt or partially exempt.

Group franchising: key points to consider

18.439 The franchising format is also occasionally used within groups of companies, with one company owning and licensing the intellectual property rights and providing services to the rest of the group. This can centre the risks and rewards of the business model in a single company, generally located somewhere with a useful tax jurisdiction. As a result, cross-border tax issues will become more important than for third-party franchising, which usually operates in a single jurisdiction (principally because of the differing demands of separate market; even international franchise operations such as McDonalds will generally have a local franchisor business for each jurisdiction).

18.440 The principal additional tax issues for groups operating an internal franchise model will be transfer pricing considerations when establishing an arm's length price for the services provided between group members (see para **16.94**).

18.441 Withholding taxes may also be a concern, as many countries impose a withholding tax on royalties paid for the grant of intellectual property rights and payments for associated technical services (see para **16.83**): this, in particular, should be considered when determining where to locate the franchisor company.

18.442 Where the group franchisees are required to purchase goods from the group franchisor, customs duties may need to be taken into consideration if the goods are transported across borders (note that customs duties do not apply to the grant of intellectual property rights).

18.443 The general tax treatment of UK franchisors and franchisees within the group will not be substantially different to the treatment of third party franchise participants, but the additional issues for cross-border group franchise agreements means that the overall arrangements should be considered carefully from the outset and properly analysed to minimise the risk that unexpected tax issues arise.

MANUFACTURING AND SERVICES

18.444 A business using intellectual property:

- for manufacturing products (either directly protected by intellectual property, or produced using processes protected by intellectual property); or

- to provide services (eg a business providing custom tuning for high performance vehicles may use processes protected by intellectual property)

will, generally, seek income from the sale of products or services. This income will be taxed under general principles relating to trading income, not as income from intellectual property. However, to the extent that the income is derived from a qualifying patent or other qualifying intellectual property, the patent box relief may be available to a company (see Chapter 13).

Production

18.445 As a result, the intellectual property tax concerns of a business directly using intellectual property will principally be:

- whether it can claim research and development relief for any qualifying research and development carried out (see Chapter 10). For manufacturing businesses, this will be particularly with regard to prototypes and production (see para **10.39**);

- where it has patents, whether to claim the patent box relief (from 2013: see Chapter 13).

Group

18.446 Where the business is part of a group, other matters may also need to be considered:

- how to hold group intellectual property (see para **18.81**);

- whether to centralise research and development or carry it on directly;

- cross-border matters where intellectual property is licensed from an overseas group company (eg trademarks, patented processes), such as withholding taxes (see paras **16.56** and **16.83**) and transfer pricing (see para **16.94**).

Licensing

18.447 Where the business has non-core intellectual property that it does not use in its business, it may license that intellectual property to others to get some income from doing so. The tax treatment of such licence receipts will depend on the type of business, whether it is corporate (see Chapter 12 and Chapter 13 where the patent box relief applies) or unincorporated (see Chapter 6).

TRADING IN INTELLECTUAL PROPERTY

18.448   A business trading in intellectual property (for example a company buying and selling media rights to sporting events) will, generally, treat the intellectual property assets which it holds as trading stock. As a result, the income from the trade will be taxed under general principles applying to trading income (outside the scope of this book) and not as income derived from exploiting intellectual property which is held as a fixed asset (note that the corporate intangibles tax rules apply only intellectual property held as a fixed asset of the company: see para **8.13**).

INTELLECTUAL PROPERTY INVESTMENT

18.449   Where a company's business includes the holding of intellectual property as an investment, licensing it out to third parties, there are various UK tax implications that need to be considered.

Tax treatment of income and expenditure

18.450   The corporate intangibles tax rules that apply to intellectual property are modified for intellectual property held as an investment: in particular, any losses which result are restricted in the way in which they can be used (see para **12.74**) and cannot be carried back to reduce taxable profits of an earlier year (CTA 2009, s 753).

Restriction on reliefs

18.451   There are a number of tax reliefs which are not available to intellectual property investment companies.

Patent box

18.452   The patent box rules do not specifically exclude investment companies from claiming the patent box but the development condition requirement (see para **13.35**), which requires that the company owning the patent has created the relevant intellectual property, or undertaken significant development activity in relation to that intellectual property, is likely to exclude many intellectual property investment companies that acquire intellectual property, rather than create or develop it, from qualifying for the relief.

Investor reliefs

18.453   The UK has a number of reliefs to encourage investment in companies, including the Enterprise Investment Scheme and the Venture Capital Trust Scheme.

18.454   The details of these schemes are outside the scope of this book, but they provide tax incentives for investors and so are aimed at encouraging investment in small, higher-risk, companies.

18.455   All of these schemes exclude companies which do not carry on a qualifying trade. The definition of a qualifying trade for these schemes specifically excludes the receiving of royalties and licence fees on intellectual property, except where a substantial part of those royalties and licence fees arise from intellectual property which the company (or one of its subsidiaries) created (ITA 2007, ss 195, 306).

Index

[All references are to paragraph number]